PLATO'S SUN:
AN INTRODUCTION TO PHILOSOPHY

Writing an introductory text for philosophy is an exceedingly difficult task. The discipline has spent a century or more in existential crisis with the attack on metaphysics dating back at least to Nietzsche and carried forward in different ways by Heidegger, Wittgenstein, and Derrida, to name a few. This constant upheaval has precipitated a climate of self-doubt that goes to the core of philosophy, the result being a strange discipline with many of its most illustrious names proudly announcing its demise.

In *Plato's Sun*, Andrew Lawless has taken on the challenge of creating an introductory text, arguing that such a work has to take into account the strangeness of the field and divulge it, rather than suppress it beneath traditional certainties and authoritative pronouncements. Lawless writes within the shadow of post-modern anti-metaphysical scepticism, introducing some of the principal areas of philosophy: metaphysics, epistemology, logic, ethics, and language.

Lawless's concern is not to resolve the issues he raises so much as to set them out in a way that lets the reader experience something of the philosopher's struggle. In so doing, Lawless holds fast to the Socratic vision of philosophy as a process of inquiry that values questions above answers, pushing the inquirer beyond his or her answers. With numerous pedagogical features including glossaries of names and key terms, suggested readings, and short chapter summaries, *Plato's Sun* will be an essential text to new students of philosophy and an important aid in teaching the subject.

ANDREW LAWLESS is a professor in the Department of Humanities at Vanier College.

PLATO'S SUN

An Introduction
to Philosophy

Andrew Lawless

UNIVERSITY OF TORONTO PRESS
Toronto Buffalo London

BD
21
·L38
2005   # 56874799

·i 12615511

© University of Toronto Press Incorporated 2005
Toronto Buffalo London
Printed in Canada

ISBN 0-8020-3873-5 (cloth)
ISBN 0-8020-3809-3 (paper)

Printed on acid-free paper

Library and Archives Canada Cataloguing in Publication

Lawless, Andrew
Plato's sun : an introduction to philosophy / Andrew Lawless.

Includes bibliographical references and index.
ISBN 0-8020-3873-5 (bound)   ISBN 0-8020-3809-3 (pbk.)

1. Philosophy – Introductions.   I. Title.

BD21.L385 2005   100   C2004-906338-3

University of Toronto Press acknowledges the financial assistance to
its publishing program of the Canada Council for the Arts and the
Ontario Arts Council.

University of Toronto Press acknowledges the financial support for
its publishing activities of the Government of Canada through the
Book Publishing Industry Development Program (BPIDP).

For my wife, Jane, and my mother, Kathleen

Contents

viii   Contents

Preface

A reader who, quite reasonably, expects this text to begin with a clear and concise definition of philosophy will be disappointed. The first chapter is instead dedicated to justifying my inability to offer such a definition. Not all philosophers will approve of such dilatory tactics, but anything else would be inconsistent with my fundamental premise, which is that there is no widespread agreement about what philosophy is or what it can achieve.

The problem is that there are, and always have been, two primal, contrasting, although symbiotically related, types of philosopher: I call them the dogmatist and the sceptic. The dogmatist pursues knowledge, builds systems, and develops what a casual reader would call 'philosophies.' The sceptic passes the day in criticism of such efforts, showing why they cannot achieve their desired ends. The former says, 'Here's what I think is true.' The latter says, 'There is no truth and I'll show you why.' Each one's sense of what philosophy is – the pursuit of knowledge or enlightenment versus the practice of showing the limits of such pursuits – contradicts the other's. What's more, it is my contention that in the past century and a half a new kind of philosopher has emerged. This philosopher turns scepticism not simply on efforts to build philosophical systems but on the very existence of philosophy itself. This anti-philosophy philosopher – I have in mind certain representatives of what is generally called 'continental philosophy' but also some American pragmatists – I call a 'new sceptic.'

I do not use the term 'continental philosophy' much in what follows – referring instead to 'new sceptics' or 'neo-Nietzscheans' or 'deconstructionists' – but it will be useful to note that it is generally contrasted with 'analytic philosophy,' which is sometimes called 'Anglo-

American philosophy.' The latter name (again, one I do not use in the text) evokes a division between philosophers to the west of the English Channel, who write in English, and those to the east of *La Manche*, who write in French or German or Italian. As some of the first analytic philosophers were Austrians and as continental philosophy has made significant inroads in the English-speaking world, this division falls far short of absolute, but never mind, these are spiritual allegiances based on one's sense of what a philosopher can do and ought to be doing. For the most part there is not much dialogue between them. Colin McGinn is an English-educated professor at Rutgers University in New Jersey. In his excellent autobiography, *The Making of a Philosopher*, he writes that his is a story about what is 'often labelled "analytical philosophy,"' an approach that 'emphasizes clarity, rigor, argument, theory, truth.' McGinn warns that readers wanting to learn about 'continental philosophy, or "post-modern" philosophy, will not be rewarded' by his book because it is about 'philosophy as it is practiced today in the university departments of the world.'[1] I have to say that I find this a tad imperialistic and dismissive of non-analytic philosophers (whose allegiance to clarity, rigour, and so on would seem to be in doubt), but I quote it only as an instance of how philosophers of all hues often inhabit cosy solitudes.

What I have tried to do in this book is bring the solitudes of analytic and continental philosophy closer together by making use of both of them. I have not written an introduction to continental or to postmodern philosophy – readers will meet many analytic philosophers in these pages – but I do use, as a springboard for discussion, the kind of doubt about the nature of philosophy that 'continentalists' often espouse and some of their techniques for expressing such doubt. Should this offend philosophers of other stripes, let me point out that I do so for the most traditional of reasons: because it reflects the spirit of philosophy's great father figure, Socrates. He will appear prominently in these pages and, as I point out, in the ancient world dogmatists and sceptics alike claimed Socrates as their ancestor. Like the dogmatists, he struggled to solve problems, answer questions, make progress, but like the sceptics, he never lost track of the *aporia* – the sense of perplexity or confusion – that surrounded philosophical issues and seldom yielded even to the most careful analysis. Socrates welded scepticism to dogmatism as the twin spirits of philosophy and I have chosen to respect that fact.

Socratic traditionalism governs the structure of the present volume.

Rather than (as is so often the case) being organized around informally stated issues – What do I know? Who am I? Good (or God) and Evil, and so on – this book consists of exegeses of the standard 'branches' of philosophy. The first chapter sets out the issues noted above, contextualizing them as a struggle between rival philosophical visions, both of which are contained (in an uneasy truce) in Plato's works and, in particular, in his portrait of Socrates. There is the 'scientific' (and dogmatic) vision of the philosopher as a discoverer of truth. There is also the 'therapeutic' (and sceptical) vision of the philosopher as a debunker of all such pretensions. From this struggle emerges an explosive third possibility: If philosophy is not science, then it is 'simply' an elevated form of literature, or storytelling – not *logos* but *mythos*. This is the fundamental tension that governs much of contemporary philosophy. Can we learn things, achieve knowledge, make progress, or, do we just invent and reinvent what McGinn calls ideologies and what Jean Baudrillard has called 'grand narratives'?

Stage set, we proceed to metaphysics, a branch of philosophy so large and ancient as almost to be the tree itself. To begin there is to begin at the beginning, for consideration of what philosophy is (and whether it is) is inextricably tied to questions about the nature and importance of metaphysics. Attention to metaphysics takes us to the heart of philosophy and to the heart of current scepticism about philosophy. Chapter 2 sets out the metaphysical terrain to Kant, and Chapter 3 considers the post-Kantian suspicion of metaphysics.

Chapter 4, on epistemology, focuses on two basic approaches to knowledge: foundationalism and naturalism. Since they and the issues surrounding them grow out of the metaphysical terrain explored in the previous two chapters, the material should be easily accessible to the reader, including the addendum on philosophy of mind. This material will also allow the reader to see more clearly the effect the debate about metaphysics has had on philosophy.

Next is logic. In Chapter 2 I point out how fundamental logic is to the development of metaphysics in particular and philosophy in general. In Chapter 5 I give logic an extended treatment in that context. This treatment involves two steps: introducing the reader to the fundamentals of deductive reasoning (and a little induction) and then considering logic in the context of the 'new scepticism' about philosophy and metaphysics. Here, the central question is whether logic is fundamental, and neutrally so, to philosophical inquiry or whether it is simply a form of rhetoric – of persuasive speech. This returns us to the rival visions of philosophy as science and as literature, but now presented as 'reason' and 'rhetoric.' Chapters 2 through 5 constitute a fairly tight package of exegesis and argument.

Chapter 6 is on ethics. I begin by expressing uncertainty over how ethics fits with the subject matter of the previous chapters. Without question, ethics is an ancient and central branch of philosophy, but one that seems to stand aside from the more organically connected metaphysics, epistemology, and logic. (More solitudes.) Having admitted my unease, I plunge in, employing a strategy similar to that of the previous chapters, which is to present ethics in terms of contrasting and tension-producing perspectives. In this case, the 'aesthetic' concern for the 'good life' is set against the 'moral' concern with right and wrong. I argue that these perspectives do not always coincide – that they do not clears the space in which Greek tragedy emerged – and this tends to be glossed over in a modern world where the larger, aesthetic vision of ancient ethics is often reduced to the narrower and un-tragic concerns of moral philosophy. I try to mute this a little by situating my discussion of ethics in the context of the ancient vision of a 'good life' subject to the winds of chance and tragedy. There is also a short section on politics.

Finally, there is language. This branch of philosophy may not be as 'traditional' as the others, but given the 'linguistic turn' of twentieth-century philosophy it has to be included. Put simply, all of contemporary philosophy deals in linguistic analysis. Having prepared the ground in the preceding chapters – metaphysical and epistemological issues also surface here – I conclude with an extended consideration of two seminal linguistic figures, Ferdinand de Saussure and Ludwig Wittgenstein. Although this is too simple, it is nonetheless useful to identify Saussure as the guru of continental or new sceptical (or neo-Nietzschean) linguistic philosophy and Wittgenstein (and before him, Gottlob Frege) as the guru of the more dogmatic analytic philosophy. That said, I hasten to add that in many ways Wittgenstein is in the end the most undogmatic of philosophers. But there you go, all divisions, being artificial, crumble before the subtlety of 'real life.'

I have tried to do two things in this text. One is to outline as directly as possible the ideas and issues that constitute the subject matter of the chapters. The other is to discuss philosophical issues in an open-ended way that will let the reader experience something of what it is to 'do' philosophy. I do not draw many conclusions – a teacher I admired once

said that questions with answers are not very interesting questions –
but I do try to get the reader to a place where she can do so if she
wishes. This circumspection I extend to the definition of philosophy
itself, which is to say, I never really manage such a definition. I hope,
though, that I do manage to set out its terrain and to communicate
something of the deep and wonderful discipline that philosophy is.

At the back of the text, readers will find a glossary of names and one
of terms, as well as a short list of Greek words. I discuss and quote
many philosophers, living and dead, in these pages and it seems reasonable to introduce them. Terms are of course explained in the text,
but it is useful to collect the most important of them in one place. I have
also included a chapter-by-chapter list of suggested readings. For the
most part, this list draws attention to works cited in each chapter but it
also includes a few not-cited texts that will be useful for undergraduates and other neophytes. From time to time, I append short comments
alerting readers to 'must-reads,' 'classics,' and suchlike or to the relative accessibility or inaccessibility of the work. (But remember, education is about stretching oneself, so difficult works are not necessarily to
be avoided.) Last, there are the notes, which include not only citations
of works but also additional commentary that is useful but which
would needlessly clog the body of the text. It is not a bad idea to use this
commentary as a way of slowing down one's reading and taking time
to consider issues in more detail. I know time is of the essence, but if I
may be allowed a little pedanticism, the word 'school' comes from the
Greek word for 'leisure'; one could, a bit perversely I admit, look at
note-reading as a kind of enforced leisure.

Acknowledgments

I would like to thank my friend and Latin scholar Charles Owen for his advice, Eric Guindon for his help with the glossaries, and my dean, Fran Davis, for her support in the preparation of the typescript. I especially wish to thank my copy-editor, Kate Baltais, for her diligent and entirely ameliorative work in the preparation of the manuscript for publication.

PLATO'S SUN

1

What Is Philosophy?

In 399 BCE, on a summer's evening in Athens, Socrates was put to death for being a philosopher. To be killed for his beliefs is a fate he has shared with countless others over the course of time, but even so, some observers of the human scene – how many we do not know – have thought that this death was particularly significant because it indicated how important and yet how dangerous philosophy is to the world. With his death Socrates gave philosophers something to live for. But what?

SUMMARY

Here, we consider the question: What is philosophy? We begin by dividing philosophers into dogmatists and sceptics – respectively, those who think it possible to achieve knowledge and those who think all one can do is expose the impossibility of doing so. This age-old debate leaves little room for agreement about what philosophy is or what it can achieve. It may, like science, produce knowledge; it may, like therapy, allow us to live with our inability to produce knowledge; or it may be, like literature, be a form of intellectual storytelling. We shall see how each of these options is contained in the character of Plato's Socrates and how they have given rise to a group of 'new sceptics' who are uncertain how, or whether, philosophy can be said to exist at all.

Dogmatists and Sceptics

Philosophy as we know it in the West was born in ancient Greece in the early sixth century BCE. It began in the island cities of Ionia, whence it spread to the western reaches of the Greek world, to what are now southern Italy and Sicily, before taking root in mainland Greece and the great city of Athens. As the German philosopher Martin Heidegger once said, 'The word *philosophia* appears, as it were, on the birth certificate of [western] history.' For over a millennium, spanning the Classical and Hellenistic eras and the rise, ascendancy, and decline of Rome, philosophy was a redoubtable force in the ancient world, and it continued to be so in the medieval and modern eras that followed. Philosophy has, however, never been one thing: it has never been a single force pointing in a single direction. Until well into the modern era, in fact, 'philosophy' was a very general term – more or less synonymous with the Latin-based 'science' – referring to the whole expanse of human knowledge.[1] There is, however, today a narrower, and for our purposes more accurate, connotation in which philosophy refers to the discipline roughly demarcated by the range of concerns or areas that constitute the chapters of this book.[2] But even within these more limited confines divergent views have always existed and thrived. Even here we find no single vector, no one sense of direction that would allow philosophy to attain the (albeit often overstated) unity of the natural sciences. It is not much of an exaggeration, probably none at all, in fact, to say that philosophy is less a body of knowledge or even a set of practices (although it is that) than a series of running debates – sometimes running battles – about metaphysics, epistemology, ethics, and the like.

On the largest scale, and at the risk of simplifying too much, the participants in these debates can be divided into *dogmatists* and *sceptics*. I must emphasize that these are ancient descriptions, which I resurrect with some caution, largely because the first of them is not a designation, any philosopher, ancient or modern, would be very likely to claim for himself. 'Dogmatist' is a slightly pejorative epithet, a mild insult that the original sceptics directed at non-sceptics who, in the sceptics' view, had the temerity to evince actual beliefs without being able to demonstrate their truth. Moreover, while 'sceptic' was often, even generally, a self-designation in the ancient world, it might in some instances cause offence in the modern. In response to any and all such concerns, I would direct readers to Immanuel Kant's treatment of the terms in the preface to the first edition of *The Critique of Pure Reason* and claim it as a kind of ironic warrant for my use of the terms.[3] Still, as this is an ancient tandem with time and tradition to recommend it – if there are no sceptics, there is always scepticism, and if there are no dogmatists, there is always dogmatism – I shall (with apologies to anyone who may be offended) employ it, for I think it captures the ebb and flow of philosophy rather nicely. This is so even with individual philosophers who often alternate between the roles of the dogmatist and the sceptic. Sometimes – Descartes' *Meditations* and Berkeley's *Three Dialogues* come immediately to mind – the alternation is consciously deployed as a means of argument.

Dogmatists are, roughly speaking, philosophers who think it possible to attain, or at least work towards, knowledge of the world as it really is. Sceptics, by contrast, deny that this can be done. To the dogmatic proposition that the world exists in a certain way, that there is an objective reality of which it is possible to know at least something, the sceptic has a couple of linked responses. The first is that we have no way of knowing if there is an objective world, an absolute reality of some sort, because we can never get beyond our own entirely subjective and untrustworthy impressions of what *seems* to be 'out there.' Hence, and second, even if we could be assured that an objective reality exists, there is no reason to believe that we can ever come close to discovering it.[4] Human reason and perception are frail and fallible faculties that maroon us far short of certainty. The dogmatist, thus, spends her energy working out philosophical positions that she takes to be true, or at least plausible. Meanwhile, the sceptic expends his energy arguing that these positions are insupportable because there is no good way of knowing if they are true or even what would make them true.[5] Both of these philosophers think that the world is a mystery but only the dogmatist thinks it is a mystery that can be solved.

When I said that dogmatism and scepticism constitute the ebb and flow of philosophy, I inserted the caveat that this was a bit of simplification. Even so, I think philosophy in the West can be usefully imagined as a series of dogmatic episodes, of attempts to construct substantial philosophical world views, harried, sometimes with more force, sometimes with less, by sceptical counter-attacks. This was certainly the case in the ancient world, where the debates were often very lively. Although the school that Plato founded – the Academy – was itself for a period of time home to sceptical thought,[6] the 'Platonism' that has come down to us falls mainly, although not exclusively, into the dogmatic camp. The same can be said of Aristotelianism and the philosophy of the other two great Athenian schools – the Epicureans and the Stoics. (Aristotle's school was called the Lyceum and its members Peripatetics.) The positive doctrines that emanated from each of these schools were always the targets of sceptical forays and were, therefore, significantly shaped and reshaped by the need to respond to them. To that extent, even the most dogmatic philosophy of the schools bore the marks of scepticism. After the third century CE, however, sceptical thought began to decline – perhaps all of philosophy did – and from the fifth to the fifteenth centuries, a long hiatus indeed, it pretty much fell silent. During that time, what philosophy there was, and until the latter third of this period there was often not much at all,[7] was essentially dogmatic, governed to a significant degree by the certainties of Christian theology. In the sixteenth century, the rediscovery of the writings of the ancient sceptics[8] stimulated a rebirth of sceptical thought that had a considerable effect on the shape of modern philosophy and in particular of empiricism.[9] If, as one knowledgeable observer has argued, that sceptical revival came to an end about two centuries ago,[10] I would nonetheless submit that its ghost has continued to haunt our thought and, indeed, constitutes the spirit of those vague phenomena that we call post-modernism and deconstruction. I shall outline this contention in the next section but let me end this one by proposing a rough-and-ready test to be applied to philosophers. If, or insofar as, philosophers speak of making 'progress' in a field of philosophy, they are almost certainly, and without insult, acting as dogmatists.[11] If, or insofar as, they deny that possibility, or simply leave it out of their considerations, they are, also without insult, taking the part of a sceptic.[12]

The New Scepticism

To turn now to the ghosts of modernity, it is the thesis of this book that the philosophy of the present age, perched on the edge of a new millennium, is beset by a persistent and unique form of sceptical doubt. It may well be, as Myles Burnyeat has suggested,[13] sufficiently different from its predecessors to merit some other name – so let's call it the 'new scepticism' – but the fact remains that scepticism is an insistent presence in contemporary philosophy. The uniqueness of this new scepticism is that it takes aim not only at philosophers' claims to knowledge – indeed it's a matter of debate whether it does that – but at the very existence of philosophy itself. We can imagine dogmatic and sceptical philosophers of an earlier era gazing at the world and debating whether they 'really' know that what they are apparently looking at is 'really' there and whether any of the ideas they hold about the world can be verified. In the modern (we could almost call it Cartesian) version of this tale these philosophers are also debating whether in a fundamental sense *they* – *qua* philosophers – are really there. The new scepticism is turned outwards to the world and also inwards to the discipline.[14] Since this is not an absolutely new phenomenon – for about a century and a half now, ever since Friedrich Nietzsche roared onto the scene, philosophy has been flirting with this existential crisis – it is one no introduction to the discipline can safely ignore. To ask the question, What is philosophy? in the current climate is to invite, among other responses, the sceptical reply that one does not know what it is or even *whether* it is. A hyperbolic form of self-doubt has been added to the older debates about the nature and accomplishments of the discipline of philosophy. In the course of this book, I shall variously argue and assume that philosophy is very much alive and, moreover, that part of its charm, resilience, and importance lies in its capacity for vigorous self-doubt. I shall, however, also insist that this sceptical challenge is a serious one with a pedigree long enough and impressive enough to preclude easy refutation. Simply put, philosophy exists today in the shadow of its own self-doubt and lives with the possibility of its own death.

Let me present some evidence in support of this view. I pick two very respectable volumes off my shelf, A.J. Ayer's *The Central Questions of Philosophy* and Roger Scruton's *Modern Philosophy*. Ayer begins as follows: 'What is philosophy? Even for a professional philosopher this question is very difficult to answer, and the fact that it is so difficult is in itself indicative. It brings home to philosophers how peculiar their subject is. For one thing, it aims at yielding knowledge ... [y]et it seems to have no special subject matter. What can a philosopher be said to study, in the way that a chemist studies the composition of bodies or a botanist the varieties of plants?'[15] Scruton opens his section 'What Is Philosophy?' with, 'There is no simple answer to this question: indeed, it is in one respect the main question of philosophy, whose history is a prolonged search for its own definition.'[16] I would classify neither of these authors as a 'new sceptic.' Neither one expresses doubt about the existence of philosophy. After their respective caveats, each proceeds to offer a definition of the discipline and to write convincingly about its nature and achievements, but not before they evoke the aura of sceptical self-doubt that I have been describing. They are, I think, well advised to do so in an age that has produced an impressive number of self-betrayers who have, from philosophical pulpits, announced the end of philosophy, the futility of philosophy, or the astounding idea that what has gone under the name philosophy not 'really' philosophy at all.

In Chapter 3 I shall trace this attitude to the nineteenth-century German philosopher Friedrich Nietzsche, but for the present let us stick to the pulpits of the twentienth century. There we can find the Austrian philosopher Ludwig Wittgenstein. In the preface to his 1921 master-piece entitled *Tractatus Logico-Philosophicus*, Wittgenstein asserts that the roughly seventy pages of that book contain all there is to say about philosophy. What those pages say is that philosophical problems are, for the most part, pseudo-problems that arise because philosophers misunderstand 'the logic of our language.'[17] To put the matter bluntly, Wittgenstein's considered opinion is that, too often, philosophers sim-ply do not know *what* they are saying. With his usual forthrightness, Wittgenstein then announces that he has achieved 'on all essential points the final solution of the problems' and that, moreover, he has shown 'how little is achieved' when this is done.[18] Having dispensed with philosophy, Wittgenstein decamped from Cambridge University in England to his native Austria, where he became, first, an elementary school teacher and then a gardener. A decade later, Wittgenstein re-scinded his judgment. Having decided that there were still some philo-sophical problems worth tackling, after all, he returned to Cambridge and the practice of philosophy. Even so, he never relinquished the belief that philosophical problems are largely the result of being 'be-witched' by language, of getting lost in its endless labyrinths.[19]

In 1936, a young A.J. Ayer breezily ventured a similar opinion in his own blockbuster debut *Language, Truth and Logic*: 'The traditional dis-putes of the philosophers are,' he wrote, 'for the most part, as unwar-ranted as they are unfruitful.'[20] Unlike the sceptical Wittgenstein, however, the dogmatic Ayer was announcing not the end of philosophy but a radically new version of it called logical positivism. Tuned to the irresistible power of science and mathematics, this new version would have little in common with what had gone on under the name philoso-phy in the preceding two and a half millennia. In 1944 the German philosopher Theodore Adorno, recognizing the power of this sort of vision, sent forth a sceptical message from his American exile: 'The conceptual shells that were to house the whole, according to philo-sophical custom, have in view of the immense expansion of society and the strides made by natural science come to seem like relics of a simple barter society in the late stage of industrial capitalism. [Philosophy's] task would seem to be to inquire whether and how there can be a philosophy at all.'[21] Four years after that Martin Heidegger announced in his typically magisterial way that the 'thinking that is to come is no longer philosophy.'[22] This was because what was to come would be liberated (first and foremost by Heidegger himself) from the great metaphysical dead end of philosophy and set on a new and fruitful path. But it would also, contra Ayer, be freed from the shackles of a technocratic science.

The attack on metaphysics, in which Heidegger played such an integral part, will be the subject of Chapter 3, but it can be noted here that Heidegger's evaluation of philosophy as a kind of wrong turn – taken, very early on, by Plato – attracted a number of adherents in the second half of the twentieth century. Perhaps the best known of them is the French deconstructionist philosopher Jacques Derrida, who has this to say about the fate of the ancient discipline: 'That philosophy died yesterday, since Hegel or Marx, Nietzsche or Heidegger ... or that it has always lived knowing itself to be dying ... these are problems put to philosophy as problems philosophy cannot resolve. It may be that these questions are not *philosophical*, are not *philosophy's* questions. Nevertheless, these should be the only questions today capable of founding the community ... of those who are still called philosophers.'[23] Derrida seems to be asking, a bit uncharitably perhaps, what philosophers have to talk about *except* the death of their discipline, or if not that, then, like Ayer, the end of the 'old' philosophy and the beginning of some new and, in Derrida's case, pretty much unimaginable version of it. If we believe Derrida, and there are many who do, the question is not whether the old philosophy is dying – that has been decided – but whether a new form of philosophy can rise from the ashes.

In summary, among many (although by no means all) philosophers working today there is a tendency to think, or *fear* as the case may be, that what has gone on under the name 'philosophy' is coming to an end. (The most radical – the most sceptical – suspect that it was in fact always something of an illusion, a kind of blind vision.) Where such philosophers may disagree is on the capacity of philosophy for renewal. A philosopher with a strong enough dogmatic (or optimistic) streak will always find scope for such renewal. A radical neo-sceptic may simply want either to draw the curtain down or to refuse any longer to make distinctions between philosophy and related disciplines such as literature and social science. Or she may want to follow the great Wittgenstein and take a *deflationary* view of many philosophical issues, arguing that they are really only pseudo-issues and that the point of philosophy is to get philosophers to see this. An outsider reading these words will be forgiven for wondering what sort of discipline philosophy is when some of its greatest practitioners apparently cannot wait to be rid of it. One filled with great and fractious egos perhaps, who, like Groucho Marx, decline to belong to the only club that will have them; or, alternatively, one filled with men and women who are honest enough to admit that they just do not know what sort of club they have joined.

What Then Is Philosophy?

If there exists a certain amount of definitional anxiety among philosophers, concern that the discipline has somehow lost whatever coherence it once seems to have had, some of its practitioners are in fact quite happy to accept this state of affairs. 'Philosophy,' the American philosopher Richard Rorty insouciantly tells us, 'is either a term defined by choosing a list of writers ... and then specifying what they all have in common, or else just the name of an academic department.'[24] We need to take Rorty's famous playfulness seriously, even if at first glance it is hard to know what to make of his assertion. The first of Rorty's options begs the fundamental question of how – on what grounds – the list is to be chosen. If it is not to be arbitrary, then the list-maker has to be guided by a prior sense of what a philosopher is – in which case he will have defined what philosophers have in common *before* he draws up the list. The alternative is simply to accept as philosophers those people who have traditionally been designated as such – which makes the list uncritical, if not arbitrary – and then to try and see what they have in common. Rorty's first option locks us into a circle: Philosophers are people who have something in common and what they have in common is that they are philosophers. So, for that matter, does his second option, which is that philosophy is what philosophy professors teach. We can safely assume that these circles are intentional and that what Rorty is pointing out is that there is a corpus of writers, texts, and 'concerns' that have long been categorized (and taught) under the name 'philosophy.' It is hard to say what they all have in common, yet it is not worth disputing the categorization – at least not if we still want to use the term 'philosophy' – for we have nothing more definite with which to replace it. Anyway, it is not terribly important what we call these people, for it does not change what they are doing.

If the blithe nominalism of this 'it's-only-a-name' approach appears, to those who prefer harder definitions, too frivolous to let stand, let me borrow a term from Wittgenstein and argue that there is at least a 'family resemblance' between those thinkers we call philosophers, even if we cannot always say with precision what the resemblance consists in. This suggests, however cautiously, that the matter is not quite as arbitrary as Rorty is making it out to be. (He seems to be saying that our ability to see a family resemblance comes from the fact that certain thinkers have always been linked under the common name 'philosophy.' In short, he says we see the resemblance because we have always been told it is there.) Now, if we were to try to draw a circle around philosophy and philosophers, the inner core of immediate family members – the philosophers and 'areas of concern' that appear in this book, for example – could be inscribed in bold letters. On their right to inclusion most philosophy departments would agree, although many would consider other thinkers and other themes to be equally important. As we approached the perimeter, however, the names and 'concerns' would grow less and less distinct, as indeed would the perimeter itself.[25] At the margins of the discipline, where the third cousins are gathered, we would discover no hard line separating philosophy from other intellectual pursuits. Instead, we would find merely a rough, uncertain, and therefore, uncircular border formed by names and topics as they faded into the nothingness of their own uncertain status. Different countries, and indeed different philosophy departments within each country, would of course produce different versions of these imperfect circles. Even the core names, the central philosophical Pantheon, would change at least a little from nation to nation, language to language, university to university, and era to era.[26]

So, the 'history of philosophy' will also differ from place to place and time to time.[27] All philosophers will have a story to tell about the history of their discipline but they will not all tell exactly the same story; both the plot and the protagonists will vary. In some cases they will even tell very different stories. The worst offenders in this regard are probably the 'great' philosophers themselves, those exalted inhabitants of the inner circle, who, when they don the historian's mantle, tend to tell wildly conflicting tales. From them we get narratives of progress towards modernity (Hegel), of decline and decadence since antiquity (Nietzsche), of metaphysical hope and overcoming (Schopenhauer), of metaphysical error and illusion (Heidegger), and so on. And those are only the Germans! Very often philosophy seems less like the decorous Great Conversation it is sometimes described as in this sort of book than a Babel of Voices – great egos with idiosyncratic opinions clamouring for attention.

But that is as it should be. Philosophy emptied of doubt, philosophy too certain of itself and its mission, philosophy too consensual is scarcely philosophy at all. To invoke Socrates as the great patron saint of the discipline, we can say that the heart of philosophy is formed by the fusion of the dogmatic and the sceptical spirits, by the desire to know certain things tempered by a sense that some of those things are, or may be, unknowable. What did Socrates so famously claim to know? Socrates claimed that (in the spirit of scepticism) he knew nothing of importance.[28] This was neither an idle nor a falsely modest claim. Socrates knew many things: he knew his name and those of his fellow citizens, he knew his way around Athens, he knew how the government of the city worked, he knew how to fight as a hoplite, given his father's craft[29] he presumably knew something about working with stone, and he certainly knew how to argue a point – but Socrates did not know what the good life was, or what justice was, or even what knowledge was. He knew nothing *of importance*. But he did not, as a full-blown sceptic would, despair of knowing. He hoped he might come to know some of these things, or that someone else, helped along by his persistent questioning, might. He dedicated his life to this effort. Socrates was, in short, something of a sceptical dogmatist, and in the ancient world both camps looked to him as the source and guarantor of their views. Both dogmatists and sceptics courted and claimed Socrates' posthumous approval. This is not surprising. Everything about Socrates remains enigmatic, difficult to pin down, and the matter of just who his spiritual descendants are is as well. Socrates, the man who inspired Plato's great philosophical attempts to ascertain the truth of the world was also the 'aporetic' philosopher who remorselessly pointed out to others the contradictions inherent in their opinions – their constant failure to attain truth. In Socrates' self-description, I am utterly *atopos* and I create only *aporia* ('I am utterly strange and I create only confusion').[30]

I must emphasize that – at least in Plato's version of him[31] – Socrates was a *philosopher* as opposed to a *sophist*:[32] he was *philosophos* not *sophos*, a *lover of wisdom* not a self-anointed *wise* person. As Diotima, Socrates' priestess-instructor in Plato's *Symposium*,[33] made clear to him, the lover loves only what he lacks. A philosopher, therefore, is one who loves wisdom precisely because he does not possess it. The problem is that, despite what the Sophists may claim, everyone lacks wisdom. (For who stands above a philosopher?) Since everyone, or every reasonable person, would equally desire to be wise, the name 'philosopher' would seem to have no resonance at all; it would seem to be nothing more than another word for 'human.' Something more must be said to give this *amicus sapientiae* a purchase on the world. It is this: a philosopher is a person who, like Socrates, lacks wisdom *and knows that she does*. The philosopher's life is guided by just this knowledge, by the capacity not to be misled into the illusion of wisdom that is sophism.[34] The rift that eventually opened between Socrates and his fellow citizens, the one that became an abyss and caused his death, was the result of this terrible self-knowledge and of his never-ending attempts to communicate it to others. He wanted to bring people over to his side where, together, urged on by his peculiar love, they might search for what they did not have.

For the most part, however, Socrates was unsuccessful. For the most part, his fellow citizens did not share his vision. They did not (or so Plato tells us) love wisdom enough to respect their lack of it. Understandably so, for who but someone in the grip of a mania can live so intensely with the image of his own folly? (We might recall that when the Greek hero Ajax saw that he had been foolish he killed himself.) In obedience to Apollo,[35] Socrates struggled to enlighten the Athenians, to hold a mirror to their distorted images of truth, to wrench them around to face the light of knowledge. But if the result was sometimes love for him and admiration for his efforts, just as often it was hostility and incomprehension. Like all philosophers before and since, Socrates died without attaining the knowledge and wisdom he sought, without – to use one of Plato's images – having gazed on the Form of the Good. It *is* a problem. A philosopher is an individual who loves and pursues what he does not, and never will, have. And from time to time – although one hopes this is not part of the job description – he is killed for his trouble.

The hostility that Socrates sometimes evoked in his listeners was almost certainly an effect of the apparent illogic of his aporetic method. No doubt it is strange to claim to love what one does not know, to cherish a wisdom one has never experienced. It is like being in love with a chimera. Even stranger is the corollary, which is the desire to go about demonstrating to people that their ideas are wrong without making the slightest claim to know what the truth is. But a philosopher – some philosophers anyway – will respond that this is one of the fundamental, sceptical characteristics of anyone who does philosophy: the capacity to set aside one's assumptions about the world and to accept certain ineradicable gaps[36] in one's knowledge.[37] A philosopher will tell you that if you can manage to sit quietly enough to quell the clickety-clack noise of our relentless logic and our non-stop 'pursuit' of knowledge, you will be able to embrace this incompleteness – the

Socratic *aporia* – as a necessary part of the human condition, along with a slightly paradoxical and dogmatic desire to overcome it. Then you will be in a position to think philosophically, to focus not only, or even primarily, on what you know, but on what you do not know, and this will allow you to cleanse your *psyche* – your soul – of its attachment to ignorance. Socrates tried to teach this lesson, this fundamental point of view, to his fellow Athenians. Socrates tried to show them that to embrace (although not to love) their ignorance was the first step on the path to wisdom. But this is a hard lesson to learn, one that requires a great deal of humility.

Philosophy as Therapy

If philosophy is currently in the midst of an era of sceptical self-doubt, there is perhaps something in the very nature of the discipline that makes this a not unexpected condition: in one way or another, philosophers live with scepticism. The spirit of philosophy, as Socrates embodied it, is driven by dogmatic visions of wisdom – by the desire to be wise – reined in by sceptical doubt as to whether such wisdom can belong to the living. The lack of closure inherent in this spirit is, no doubt, frustrating to some and reassuring to others, but in general, anyone who cannot make some peace with it is unlikely to be much of a philosopher. For philosophy is the somewhat chaotic, rather ill-defined terrain that sprawls between the certainties of the 'objective knowledge' of science and the 'vagaries' of something much less definite, to which we can give the name 'therapy.'[38]

We need to think a little about this term. In the ancient world, scepticism was a therapeutic philosophy insofar as it was considered a pathway to *ataraxia*[39] – the sense of calm (or 'unruffled' freedom from passion) that comes from letting go the anxious but unattainable 'scientific' desire to know with certainty what, finally, is true. We have seen that in the twentieth century Wittgenstein – in whom scepticism and dogmatism are very difficult to distinguish – also views philosophy as a kind of therapy made necessary by people getting into linguistic muddles. He presents the philosopher as a linguistic therapist whose job it is to un-muddle them.[40] In both the ancient sceptical and the modern Wittgensteinian versions, philosophical therapy is thus essentially a cure for an overdeveloped scientific impulse, a too-strong desire to know what is true, to make progress, to achieve something positive. (Wittgenstein famously, and aporetically, tells us that philosophy leaves everything as it is.) As such, philosophy could not exist without the dogmatic desire it soothes, just as Socrates could not begin to weave his aporetic magic until someone else professed what he took to be the truth about a given topic. Dogmatism makes scepticism (and philosophic therapy) possible[41] – it is the occasion for it – and scepticism's task is to make dogmatism restrained and responsible. But the benefits flow in the other direction as well, for if the sceptical spirit calms the dogmatic one overeager for knowledge, the dogmatic spirit pulls the sceptical one back from the abyss of nihilism – a philosophical condition in which scepticism has degenerated into an inability to value anything.[42] Thus it is that scepticism and dogmatism – the two great legacies of Socrates – stand uneasily together as the twin and restless spirits of philosophy.

Plato's Cave and Plato's Sun

Much of what I have been saying – it will lead us into a consideration of the relation between philosophy and literature – can be mapped onto what is probably the most famous of all philosophical fables: Plato's Allegory of the Cave. Given its brilliance and justifiable fame, this allegory has been the subject of countless readings, especially in the modern age. As such, it has also been, in the words of one commentator, 'the subject of almost infinite controversy.'[43] I am not certain how controversial is the reading that follows, but I must emphasize that it is *my* reading, and that it is slanted to my purposes. So, *caveat lector*.

The allegory describes a journey between two worlds, the dark, subterranean world of the cave and the one that lies outside it, which I shall call the sunworld. Each is filled with images that may either instruct or mislead those who gaze upon them. This is because some images are faithful copies of their originals and some are not. Let's call them, respectively, icons and simulacra. The allegory begins in the cave, where prisoners are sitting, chained and blinkered, staring at a wall onto which the light of a fire that is behind and above them projects shadows of objects and other (unchained) people who stroll along on raised walkways. These shadows are simulacra, images lacking the substance of their originals. They are not real. The shadow-vase the prisoners see projected on the wall of the cave will not hold water; it will not *function* as a vase. Yet, these men and women, chained with their backs to the fire, take them for real. In their circumstance they cannot see that they are 'mere' images. This seems unfair. For what is more misleading, more fundamentally unjust, than images that fail to announce themselves as such to people who are in no position to distinguish them from the 'real' thing? – but this is the way, the condition, of their lives. Thus deceived, the cave dwellers live in a world of simulacra, their ideas, their truths great and small, no more than shadows flickering on a wall.[44]

If the world of the cave is a shadow-world, there has to be a 'reality' that is the source of the shadows, or images, found there. Actually, there is a hierarchy of sources. Above the simulacrum of the shadow-vase sits the actual, shadow-casting vase, but above it, out in the sunworld, is the Idea or Form of the vase. This is the highest reality ('Reality,' if you will). The sunworld is the place where one can achieve the absolute knowledge that is illuminated by the sun.[45] The philosopher's job is to leave the cave and search out the Forms in which knowledge and wisdom reside. Of course, so long as the philosopher is in chains in the cave, her backside warmed by the fire of ignorance, that is impossible. It is even unthinkable, because she has no concept of a greater, brighter world. (And besides, the fire is so warm.)

Plato's allegory would end before it began were not one of the mysterious guards to unchain one of the prisoners and force her to turn around and face the fire. She has, one must realize, no desire to see this fire, which is at first too bright for her eyes. Left to her own devices, she would turn back towards the wall and its comforting shadows. Once she becomes accustomed to it, however, the fire illuminates her previous errors, exposes the shadow-world for what it is – a slough of ignorance. She understands that her life has hitherto been taken up with false images and she thinks, confidently,[46] that now she sees things aright. Alas, she does not. Her vision has improved, and she sees things more clearly, but she has taken only the first step towards knowledge and wisdom. What she must now come to understand is that knowledge is not to be found in the cave at all, that the vase she holds in her hand is, like its shadow on the wall, only an image of its archetype, or Form. It is a truer image than the shadow, an icon rather than a simulacrum, a more substantial copy, more faithful to its original, one than can actually hold water – but an image nonetheless. But how can the ex-prisoner grasp *that*? (How can *we* grasp that?) Chained, she could know nothing more substantial than shadows; unchained, she is better off but still has access only to the *immediate* source of those shadows. Now, the allegory would come to an end were our guard[47] not to intervene once again, laying 'rough hands' on the ex-prisoner, dragging her up the rugged ascent to the mouth of the cave, and thrusting her out into the awful glare of the sunworld.[48] To suffer this, to be cast out into the sunlight, is even worse than being forced to look at the fire. This world is so bright that the poor woman must once again avert her eyes – looking at the shadows of things or their reflections in water – opening them fully only in the starlit night. She is reduced to staring at simulacra, once again, although this time the simulacra of the Forms as opposed to the simulacra of the icons of the Forms that flickered across the wall of the cave. She is closer to Reality but not yet in direct contact with it.

As in the cave, Plato's ex-prisoner eventually becomes accustomed to her surroundings, gazes upon the sun, and sees how it illuminates the world. She sees the whole picture, attains full knowledge and, I have to assume, the wisdom that goes with it. But here is the catch: not in her lifetime. In that limited time span she might achieve some awareness of what the sun reveals, she might learn to live among its shadows and reflections, but only in another world, after death, across that unimaginable barrier, will she reach the end of her remarkable journey.[49] If wisdom is the reward for a philosophical life, it is a posthumous one.

The education of Plato's philosopher is a strange progress. She moves from seeing only the simulacrum of the icon of the Form (the shadow-vase) to gazing upon the icon of the Form (the vase) to glancing warily at the simulacrum of the Form (the shadow of the Idea 'Vase'). She is always at some remove from knowledge, never fully enlightened, never in contact with knowledge and wisdom. In fact, she seems to take a half step back upon leaving the cave. She is nearer to the sun, she can feel its energizing warmth, but since she cannot look directly at it or even at the things it illuminates, she is once more dependent on false images. The difference presumably – an important difference – is that she knows this to be so; she is, after all, averting her eyes. She now understands that she does not see things as they are.

The metaphor of the too-bright sun, of a light capable of obliterating whatever it falls upon, is a subtle one that turns on the recognition that for anyone capable of gazing upon it there is literally nothing to see. The sunworld is a world of pure abstractions, a world that cannot be seen, only understood. The simulacra of the sunworld are, Plato tells us, essentially mathematical concepts,[50] abstract ideas (the nature of vases, say, or the nature of justice) that point towards the even greater and absolute abstractions of the Forms: the Idea 'Vase' or the Idea 'Justice.' The Forms – great archetypal Ideas – are the highest reality, but ones that even a philosopher, so long as she is alive and tied to her senses, can never fully grasp. Unlike the 'visible' world of the cave, the sunworld is an 'intelligible' world of pure ideas in which a flesh-and-blood being can never be fully at home. So in a philosopher's life, a life filled up with the excruciating absence of important knowledge, the fullness of time brings only exalted shadows. This is why, on the day of his execution, Socrates repeated to his assembled friends the Pythagorean doctrine that a true philosopher practises death; he treats his body as a prison house of the soul. In life he ignores it as much as he can, concentrating on the pursuit of the great universal truths; in death he is liberated from it, freed at last to confront the Forms.[51] Secure in this belief, Socrates willingly drank the poison he was given (although this, it has to be said, is not a general trait among philosophers).

Poets and Philosophers

We can now turn to a brief consideration of how the allegory broaches the difficult relation that exists between philosophy and literature. This relation emerges from the accommodation between science and therapy, dogmatism and scepticism, as the possibility of philosophy's own demise. It is a curious fact that while Plato's works are salted with myths and allegories, beautiful and evocative stories that are simulacra of the sunworld, exalted reflections of a wisdom that even he cannot 'see' and articulate clearly, in *The Republic*,[52] his Socrates famously banishes the poets – let's say writers of myths – from his ideal city. The reason he gives for doing so is that they are producers of simulacra and, as such, enemies of truth. The reason Plato's myths do not make *him* an enemy of truth is that the poet's images belong to the cave world, while his – the philosopher's – belong to that of the sun. Moreover, the poet *wants* to produce myths, whereas the philosopher does so only because he has run out of options, because the 'reason' he possesses is too frail to get at the truth. When reason has run to its limit, the only way for the philosopher to go on is by telling an elevated story. He says to his audience, 'I don't know exactly, but I have heard that the truth is something like this.' Still, it must seem to the poets, and indeed to all of us who dwell in the shadows of the cave, that these are fine distinctions, dangerously subtle ones if they are to be the basis of exile. It is as if one form of literature leads to knowledge, while the other leads away from it.

Plato's famous account of the quarrel between philosophy and poetry,[53] his attempt to insulate reason from the stories of the poets,[54] sits uncomfortably at the heart of the philosophical tradition (as well as at the heart of Plato's work). It is, perhaps, a deeper and fundamentally more heartrending version of the less threatening – because more symbiotic – opposition between science and therapy that I outlined above.[55] That opposition is perhaps Plato's quarrel made liveable, because it is carried on between two ways of doing philosophy. Philosophy itself is not cast into doubt; the issue is the correct way to pursue it. What the harshness of Socrates' imagined expulsion of the poets indicates is just how forced, how difficult, how fundamentally unacceptable – although necessary – the strange marriage of scepticism and dogmatism really is. Plato is committed to the dogmatic idea that there is an absolute truth that the philosopher seeks to know and articulate; this is the quest that guides his life. Yet he is, apparently, sceptical enough – Socratic enough – to doubt whether such truth is available to even the most elevated human mind. I think he desperately wants to produce something like a Full and Final Discourse, to write down the Truth of the World. The language of this discourse would be reason, what the Greeks called *logos*. Yet, since not even Plato could produce this discourse, because it remains, despite his most strenuous efforts, a brilliant chimera, he is forced to fall back on *mythos*, the language of the poets. For Plato, this seems to be both a beautiful human language[56] and an immensely disappointing, even heartbreaking, one: a necessary accommodation, a movement away from 'science' (or objective knowledge) that the great philosopher would rather not make. Little wonder, then, that philosophers have, ever since, tended to fissure into one of the two camps and to fight over Socrates' legacy. Sometimes it is easier to be half a spirit.

The image of Plato's sun thus takes us back to a place I imagined earlier, where the dogmatist and the sceptic stand together contemplating their options. If, as the dogmatist insists, there is Truth in the world, a Full and Final Discourse, then even if a human being cannot speak it, everything he says will be, as we see in Plato's works, textured by a sharp awareness of both its existence and its absence. This truth will be a hidden god, a deity that, despite all of the philosopher's best efforts, remains beyond his capacity to know, but that is crucially significant to everything he does.[57] If, on the other hand, there is, as the sceptic insists, no such Truth, then the philosopher is free to tell stories without censure, so long as she does not claim they are true. The dogmatist will find himself saying, with Plato, 'This is what I think is true.' The sceptic will reply with, 'Let me tell you a story.'[58] The sceptic's option represents what Plato both risks and fears: that the distinction between the poet and the philosopher may be lost. Or worse, that the philosopher, lacking precise knowledge, will turn into a poet. If that happens, truth disappears from even the most distant of Plato's horizons.

What Plato seems to have recognized is that the twin spirits of philosophy are not easily accommodated to one another. Civil war is always an option, one that Plato does his best to avoid by effecting a great compromise between a dogmatic and scientific pursuit of truth and a sceptical and therapeutic modesty about our ability to achieve it. But the tension inherent in this accommodation, the eternal deferral of truth that it forces upon the philosopher, constantly threatens to turn philosophy into literature, to make *logos* subside back into the *mythos* from which it originally emerged. All philosophers since Plato have had to decide whether to respect or betray this compromise, to decide, in effect, whether, despite our sceptical doubts, the Allegory of the Cave is an icon of truth or nothing more than a shadow on the wall. Perhaps, as the American philosopher Stanley Cavell contends, 'Plato's sun has shown us the fact of our chains; but that sun was produced by our chains.'[59] But if the sun is a chimera, what's left?

Meta-philosophy

To return in closing to the self-doubt, or new scepticism, of contemporary philosophy, I think that it rests on the belief that this accommodation between the search for truth (or progress), on the one hand, and doing therapy, on the other, is one that many philosophers can no longer maintain with confidence. Plato's great compromise threatens to fracture under the pressure of the sceptical proposition that the belief that there is such a thing as philosophy is itself insupportably dogmatic. Furthermore, fracturing the accommodation between dogmatism and scepticism will return philosophy to the keeping of literature, for if the act of interpreting the world, of trying to get at, or get nearer to, the truth, cannot be distinguished from the aesthetic act of telling a story, then, the new sceptic tells us, there is no distinct activity called 'philosophy.' Rorty is among those who argue that we cannot have it both ways. To evoke the idea of 'truth' as a philosophical goal is, Rorty insists, necessarily to suggest that it is a 'fixed goal,' which is to say that there is a definite 'way the world is.' (That is what the Forms represent.) Otherwise, there is no good standard for deciding when an idea is true, and the term merely indicates the philosopher's desire to justify (or commend) her ideas to as many people as possible. In short, if there is no fixed standard – no 'Truth' – then 'truth' is a hopelessly relative and malleable term, ill-suited to serve as the goal of the philosophical life.[60] Since, Rorty concludes, there is no good evidence for the existence of a fixed standard, the pursuit of truth ought to be abandoned even if this seems to amount to abandoning philosophy. In a similar vein, the works of the late French philosopher Michel Foucault argue that the scientific (or dogmatic) perspective is essentially an interpretative one directed at excavating deep and hidden truths.[61] But, insists Foucault, 'there is nothing to interpret [because] when all is said and done, underneath all everything is already interpretation.'[62] Interpretation is, for Foucault, very similar to Rorty's unfixed truth – essentially a disguised desire to present one's story, one's version of the world, as science. This is necessarily deceptive. But if the honest alternative is to admit, with Rorty, that there is no truth, the philosopher will be forced to relinquish the power that the magisterial certainty of the word brings with it. What remains of 'philosophy' may seem a poor thing indeed.

To a clear-minded dogmatic philosopher who believes that truth is something more than a compliment we pay to ideas we like,[63] Rorty's and Foucault's positions can look a lot like philosophical nihilism: philosophers announcing the end of philosophy and turning their backs on serious philosophical inquiry. They may also seem nonsensical. If Rorty's definition of philosophy is a playful circle, Foucault's comment on interpretation is a paradox insofar as the very notion of interpretation relies on the idea that there is *something* to interpret. If interpretation is merely a facade for power, for the attempt to justify and impose one's point of view,[64] it is hardly worth using the word – because that *is not* interpretation. The only reason for doing so would be to expose the history of philosophy for the dishonest thing that it is. But that *would* be philosophical nihilism, a philosophy whose only purpose is to put an end to philosophy.

We shall return, with great regularity, to this issue in subsequent chapters. For now, I shall simply reiterate that for many contemporary philosophers Plato's dilemma is very much alive. The problem is that Plato's solution, his accommodation of both scepticism and dogmatism in his work, may no longer seem to them so available. Haunted by the inability to ride *logos* to its conclusion in Truth, and by the fear that if they stop short of it they may backslide to the point where they are 'merely' telling stories, contemporary philosophers find themselves looking for a place to exist between science, on the one hand, and literature, on the other. It is not a particularly comfortable existence.

It is, however, a remarkably enduring one. For a long time now, men and women have wandered across the philosophical terrain, looking for the light of Plato's sun, undeterred by their inability to find it. I will add, in a hopeful tone, that most of the time this meandering quest has seemed to be important, and periods of doubt, even self-doubt, have done surprisingly little to shake that belief. There is an age-old dictum, going back to Plato and Aristotle and repeated many, many times since, that philosophy begins with wonder, with an almost childlike intellectual amazement that something exists. That may be so. But as the great nineteenth-century Danish philosopher Sören Kierkegaard pointed out, wonder had better proceed pretty quickly to doubt, for doubt 'is a reflection category,'[65] and it is in reflection that philosophy really gets going. Doubt is a philosopher's essential companion even when he is most avidly pursuing truth. If the present age is one in which doubt has been transformed into self-doubt – self-reflection, in effect – that is not necessarily (although it may be) a reason to despair.

What this line of argument amounts to is that there is currently a lot of 'meta-philosophy' about – philosophizing about philosophy. In fairness, I must once again note that not all philosophers think this is necessary. Many philosophers, I am quite sure, think meta-philosophizing is completely unnecessary, a waste of a philosopher's precious time. But meta-philosophy is a fact of contemporary philosophical life and, for all its intensity, scarcely fatal to the discipline. Meta-philosophy may well be beneficial. I ought not to pre-empt the reader's judgment, however. These are issues for her to decide. So what I shall try to do in what follows is give the reader a basis on which to do so. I shall outline some of the principal – and very traditional – areas of philosophy and then give some consideration to the sceptical doubts that beset them. If I manage to do this effectively I will have provided the reader with a useful snapshot of philosophy. There is a caveat, however: it is *my* snapshot. It is *my* story, or perhaps *my* interpretation of the philosophical record. Too often, especially in introductions, authors let on that what they are going to tell is *the* story, as if it were obvious what it is. But if such a story exists – and I am not saying that it does not – it can only be illuminated by Plato's sun and that is a place where my vision, like everyone else's, fails. No, if we are anywhere, you and I, we are sitting around the fire in the cave. I have the floor and I am about to begin to explain to you what philosophy is. Even though I claim to have journeyed – or at least peeked – outside the cave and to have seen the reflection of the Form 'Philosophy,' honesty compels me to admit that I do not know exactly how this explanation should go. But I think, based on what I have seen and heard, that it is something like this ...

2

Metaphysics:
The Search for the God's-Eye View

SUMMARY

Like philosophy itself, uncertainty surrounds metaphysics. But before address-
ing that issue the reader needs to have some idea of what metaphysics is. Here
we define the term and explain its historically fundamental place in the
discipline of philosophy, linking it to the spirit of logos *(reason), and the*
concepts of 'realism' and 'anti-realism'. After a detour through the subcat-
egory of ontology, we turn to philosophers (ending with Kant) and to a central
metaphysical topic – God – to develop our grasp of metaphysics at work.

The Troubling Pursuit of Ultimate Reality

Depending on which authority one consults nowadays, metaphysics –
the study of the general conditions and nature of reality – is either the
best or the worst of philosophy, the life blood of the discipline or the
virus that is killing it. In either case, metaphysics is undeniably one of
the most – if not *the* most – fundamental of philosophical concerns. As
the American philosopher Hilary Putnam has argued, 'every philosophical program touches on deep metaphysical waters.'[1] Furthermore,
insofar as every philosophical program is – by definition? – dogmatic,
we can add that every sceptical philosopher looks to disperse those
waters. The result, as one might expect, is a degree of uncertainty that –
like philosophy itself – is reflected in definitions of metaphysics. Consider the following passage from the entry in *The Oxford Companion to
Philosophy*: 'Metaphysics is the most abstract and in some views the
most "high-falutin" part of philosophy, having to do with features of
ultimate reality, what really exists and what it is that distinguishes that
and makes it possible.'[2]

'High-falutin' nicely catches the unease, the whispered anxiety that this apparently fundamental branch of philosophy is in fact not quite respectable, that metaphysics is the product of philosophers putting on airs – in which case 'abstract' becomes a synonym for 'empty.' We shall see in Chapter 3 that this is more or less how the new sceptics view the matter. But their concerns are in essence only a more intense and perhaps introverted – self-doubting – version of a suspicion that has been around for as long as there have been sceptics of any sort.

One reason that some philosophers – including ones who are in other respects non-sceptical – dislike metaphysical systems is their tendency to contain 'Big Words,' words that insinuate absolutes into the discussion. Anti-metaphysical philosophers will argue that these are precisely the kind of empty words that trick us and lead us astray. Half a century ago, the Oxford philosopher J.L. Austin, who had a keen eye for the bewitching power of metaphysics, began his essay on 'Truth' by directing the discussion away from that unwieldy 'abstract noun' – 'a camel ... of logical construction which cannot get past the eye even of a grammarian' – towards the more manageable predicate, 'is true.' According to Austin there are a lot of very practical things to be said about the latter phrase. One can, for example, ask when a statement *is true* – but very little is to be said about the abstraction 'truth'[3] (except, perhaps, that it is a 'high-falutin' metaphysical word that cannot pay its way). The same scepticism can be directed at the phrase 'ultimate reality' in the above definition of metaphysics. It would seem to refer to something like 'the way the world is,' but as we have seen this is a proposition many sceptics reject. 'Ultimate reality,' they will tell you, is a verbal chimera, a reference to a 'Reality' that is, when all is said and done, only a dogmatist's high-falutin' fetish. For many non-sceptics, of course, the term 'metaphysics' is anything but a fetish. It is, rather, a marker for the deepest layer of 'what is,' the place where the innermost secrets of the cosmos are revealed. There is, quite simply, a deep division of opinion about metaphysics. As D.W. Hamlyn, the author of the above passage in the *Oxford Companion*, informs us, 'the exact nature of the subject has been constantly disputed, as indeed has its validity and usefulness.'

So, this much we know: when philosophers discuss metaphysics, uneasiness reigns. Yet, to re-emphasize what I have already said, valid or invalid, useful or useless, for better or for worse, metaphysics is an integral part of what many, perhaps most, philosophers have always done. (And if they are not doing it, they are very likely reacting to it, arguing why we should not be doing it.) Philosophy, the *Oxford Companion* tells us, 'at its very beginning with the Presocratics was metaphysical in character,' concerned 'to understand nature and the possibility of change within it.' Note the phrase *'at its very beginning'* and, we must add, 'ever since': the history of philosophy is a history entangled with metaphysics. Some commentators would go a step further and say that philosophy has *been* metaphysics, that metaphysics and all its abstraction just is the philosophical terrain.[4] In either case, as one commentator puts the matter, metaphysics is an 'awesome science ... whose importance has been expounded and ... dangers exposed recurrently in the history of thought.'[5] So, naturally, it is important to ask: What is metaphysics?

An Attempt at a Definition

I shall try to provide an answer that will build on Hamlyn's definition, but first a story. If philosophy has from the outset been metaphysical in character, it was not in its origins self-consciously so. No one *consciously* did 'metaphysics,' because the word, and I think we can say the concept, did not exist until the second half of the first century BCE. An untitled book by Aristotle had to be catalogued for an edition of his work being prepared by Andronicus of Rhodes.[6] Since in this collection it was to be placed immediately after the *Physics*, it was dubbed *Meta Ta Phusika*, the book that comes 'after the *Physics*.' Therein, Aristotle discusses a number of topics, among them the nature of *ousia*, which can be translated as 'substance' or, less misleadingly, 'being.' One of Aristotle's main concerns here is with what he called the science of 'being-*qua*-being,'[7] which is, I am sure you will agree, the basis of a pretty abstract rumination on the ultimate nature of reality. Thus it was that from that original location subsequent to the *Physics* the term 'metaphysics' spread backwards and forwards in time to encompass all the issues of 'reality' and 'being' that philosophers ever had discussed or ever would discuss, expanding in the fullness of time into a full-grown branch of philosophy – if not into the tree itself.

So – once again – what, exactly, is this branch? We already have one definition, but let me offer another, also by D.W. Hamlyn, this time from his book on metaphysics: 'One way of construing metaphysics is to say that it is concerned to set out in the most general and abstract terms what must hold good of conscious beings and the world in which they live if that world is tò constitute reality for them.'[8]

That is straightforward: metaphysics is concerned, 'in the most general and abstract terms,' with what we and the world must be like if it is to be real for us in the way that it apparently is. 'What must hold good,' what we and the world must be like: what does 'must' express here? Surely not a command, but what? I think it expresses something like the following circular inference: if we are to have knowledge of the world, then we and the world are necessarily constructed in a particular way, to be precise, in a way that allows us to have knowledge of the world.[9] It expresses, in other words – and here I quote one of the options of the Oxford English Dictionary – 'the inferred or presumed certainty of a fact' (in this case a set of facts) about us and the world we inhabit. 'Presumed certainty' is of course virtually an oxymoron, a certainty lacking unimpeachable warrant, pulling up short of necessity: a certainty to which, therefore, one 'really' has no claim because it is really only probability. Is this the certainty of metaphysics? Certainly (sorry), it is something like this, for as the philosopher moves beyond the empirically verifiable and begins to speak in 'the most general and abstract terms,' she begins to develop theories that she feels must be true – for what else could explain why things are as they are? Perhaps, then, we ought to say that metaphysics aims not at truth (although it does), but at the 'presumed certainty' of hyper-plausibility.

Let's try this: Metaphysics broaches Big Questions about the nature of Reality, ones which, by definition in the modern age, can yield no more than 'presumed certainty' insofar as they are incapable of empirical verification or falsification. To that extent, they resist proof at the deepest level. Here are some metaphysical questions. Must there be a creator of the universe? Do scientific theories represent nature as it really is? Is there necessarily any 'way' that nature 'is'? (Is there, in other words, an objective 'reality' behind the way the world 'appears' to us?) Do general things (e.g., colours) exist or only particular things (coloured objects)? What are numbers? Such questions can make the head swim, and indeed they often require a context to look sensible. But this is the terrain of metaphysics, whereupon philosophers think in very general terms about the nature and conditions of reality, about what must hold true. To help you get your feet on the ground, let me very briefly set out one well-known example of metaphysical thinking.

Early in the eighteenth century, the German philosopher Gottfried Leibniz asks himself whether the universe – space let's say – is finite or infinite. In response, he applies his Principle of Sufficient Reason, which states that for any existing condition there must be a reason that it is as it is.[10] But, argues Leibniz, if space were infinite, God could have no good reason for placing the Earth in one region of it as opposed to another. (Imagine trying to give someone instructions for furnishing an infinitely large room. Yes, I know 'an infinitely large room' is an oxymoron, but that, in a way, is Leibniz's point.) According to the principle of sufficient reason, this is impossible; hence, space must be finite. So with this principle, which he thinks is unassailable (it *is* a very powerful one), Leibniz commits himself to a belief in the fundamental rationality of the universe. All actions, even God's, take place for a reason, because if they did not they could never occur at all *because there would be no reason for them to occur.*

We can relate Leibniz's principle of sufficient reason to the wonderful medieval parable of Buridan's Ass,[11] in which a hungry donkey is placed equidistant between two bales of hay. Having no 'sufficient reason' to go to one as opposed to the other, the unfortunate beast starves to death. In short, according to Leibniz, Buridan, and many, many other philosophers, the universe has to be determinate rather than indeterminate because in an indeterminate universe nothing would ever get done. In the strongest terms, an indeterminate or contingent universe is an impossible universe.[12] Although this expresses a very powerful intuition about the nature of nature (including human nature), one that is still a topic of discussion among contemporary cosmologists, the downside to such hard-core rationality – or at least the pre-modern downside – is that even God himself appears not to be free of it. He too appears to be governed by the dictates of reason. And whether this is so – whether it can be so – is another contentious metaphysical issue.[13] Leibniz's metaphysics thus gives rise to as many questions as it answers, which is all well and good because philosophy is, as I said in the opening chapter, a bit of a running debate. What I want to emphasize here is that at the foundation of this debate there lie differing visions of reality, of what the universe that we inhabit must be like.

Realism and Anti-realism: Basic Metaphysical Outlooks

As one might expect after two and a half millennia of philosophy, there exists a wide range of metaphysical outlooks, far wider than I can hope to encompass in this book. A good way to categorize them, however, is to focus on the concept of 'reality,' for while everyone has a concept (often inarticulate) of reality, not everyone is, metaphysically speaking, a *realist* – at least not all the time and not about everything. In the largest sense, a realist is roughly someone who asserts that there is something 'out there,' an external or objective reality that exists independently of whoever happens to be observing it or thinking about it. If you are a 'direct realist' you will assume that this objective and external reality is immediately accessible to you – that how you perceive it is how it is. This is metaphysically efficient because it essentially curtails the need for metaphysics. A direct realist does not have to work out what reality *must* be like because he knows exactly what it *is* like. Philosophers who are such self-assured direct realists are, however, pretty thin on the ground, and if I point out that a common philosopher's synonym for 'direct' is 'naïve' the reader will begin to see why. We make far too many errors and we disagree among ourselves far too often to assume that the way the world appears to us is obviously the way it is. (Modern science has certainly done much to put the lie to this idea.) So most metaphysical realists assume either that they have to argue their way from appearance to reality, from their perceptions to the nature of the world that is the source of them, or that they have to make a very strong case as to why that is not necessary. Let's say, then, that among realist philosophers there are very few insouciant direct realists. They tend to accept, in the manner of Leibniz, that their versions of 'ultimate reality' require substantial rational support. Still, they are, like the insouciant direct realist, committed to the proposition that there is a 'mind-independent' reality that, if only it were fully accessible, is the yardstick by which all our theories, ideas, and statements need to be judged: it is what we are talking about.

This analogy will only stretch so far. But think of drawing a picture of something based on incomplete hints or 'appearances,' as a police sketch artist does when she draws a suspect based on a witness's fleeting impressions. Even though she cannot check the drawing against the 'real thing' it is, ultimately, a 'good' or 'bad' likeness, which will either help or hinder the attempt to apprehend the villain in question. I should point out – and this is one reason that is not possible to check metaphysical drawings and that, additionally, they cannot ever be per-fectly good – that, unlike most criminals, the objective or external reality to which a metaphysician points is often extremely remote from everyday life and indeed may not even be a physical reality. Plato's Forms – which are, for him, the 'ultimate reality' against which everything else is to be measured – are abstractions. But insofar as Plato attributes an independent existence to them, he is a realist about them, and indeed, Plato's metaphysics is referred to as 'classical realism.' (To insist that anything – numbers, say – exists independently of a thinking mind is to adopt a realist stance towards it.)

By contrast, an *anti-realist* rejects the idea of a mind-independent reality, or at least the usefulness of the idea, speaking instead in terms a 'reality-for-us' or 'human reality.' The analogy is thus somewhat different. The anti-realist does not think in terms of producing (i.e., understanding) the 'real thing' based on hints, clues, and so on, *because those hints and clues just are the real thing*, the human reality, beyond which lies nothing. There are, as one might suspect, a number of versions – some more radical than others – of anti-realism. A *phenomenalist*, for example, will argue that objects in the world are – to us anyway – collections of sensory experiences, experiences of shapes, colours, sounds, tastes, hardness, softness, and so on that we put together, as ideas, in our heads.[14] He may be, he almost certainly will be, a direct realist with respect to these ideas – he will assume that we have immediate access to *them* – but he will not assume that the ideas tell us the exact truth about the 'external world.' Indeed, if you were to ask him whether there is an objective world beyond these appearances, he would give you a very qualified answer. If it were not an out-and-out anti-realist answer, it would at least be an agnostic one. How can we know if there is anything more substantial than our ideas 'out there'?

On this matter of just what our ideas tell us, an anti-realist and a non-direct realist will unite against the direct realist: They will not commit themselves to the obvious truth, or accuracy, of our ideas. Where they will part company is at the next step. The anti-realist will point out that it is perfectly possible – although not, strictly speaking, necessary[15] – that one cannot get beyond these ideas or images to the physically substantial real world that they supposedly represent. If so, the question of the accuracy or inaccuracy of the representation cannot be broached because you cannot step back and have a second-level look, or 'meta-look' – a look at your look. To do so would entail stepping outside your mind, which is something no one can do. To return to the analogy of the sketch artist, even if the object you are drawing is right in front of you, and even if you and everyone else draw it in the same way, nonetheless, all you are doing is indicating what appears to you – or, by extension, what appears to humans.[16] Whether there is an external or mind-independent object that is 'really' like that is a question that can, theoretically, be asked, but from an anti-realist perspective it is a waste of time to do so. In an anti-realist universe there are no bad sketch artists.

Perhaps the most famous example of anti-realism – one which slips the bonds of my sketch analogy, I'm afraid – is the 'idealism' of the eighteenth-century Irish philosopher George Berkeley, who famously asserted the proposition *esse est percipi*: To be is to be perceived. His argument was essentially a phenomenalist one. If knowledge is the product of experience (as empiricists – a designation Berkeley applied to himself – claimed it was), then all that we really know exists are the ideas in our minds, because they are the only things of which we have direct experience. If the only entities we know are our (perceived) ideas, the *'esse'* of all unthinking 'things' – the essence, let's say – is that they are perceived. Nothing exists unperceived, which means that the only things in the world are minds and ideas.[17] There is no concrete world 'out there' awaiting our discovery – although there is, Berkeley assures us, the Great Mind of God that both makes possible and encompasses all human perception, but that is another story. The interesting thing is that once Berkeley has performed his anti-realist trick of making the world disappear, he can turn back into a realist because all that exists now are ideas and they come to us straight from God. In short, Berkeley is a realist about God but not about the physical world.

To sum up, a realist will contend that if we saw the 'external world' more clearly – if we had better access to ultimate reality – we would alter our 'picture' of it accordingly. An anti-realist will respond that if we alter our picture what has changed is not our understanding of reality but 'our reality.' In the first case we express our *idea* of reality; in the second our ideas express (or, in Berkeley's case, *are*) our reality. From this perspective, realist and anti-realist theories can be tentatively linked respectively to the dogmatic searcher after Truth and the sceptical storyteller of Chapter 1. Although this is a useful link, especially with regard to contemporary philosophy, we must exercise some caution about pushing it too far. Realists and anti-realists do face one another across a significant metaphysical divide, but each side is capable of building elaborate metaphysical systems. Berkeley's anti-realist idealism starts off sceptical and ends dogmatic, and even in its anti-realist aspects it has a metaphysical structure to match that of any realist.[18] This is a useful reminder that dogmatism and scepticism can be two edges of the same sword. Which is the business edge depends on whether the philosopher is building his system or attacking another's.

Of course, if you are a sceptic with a capital S, you will simply try to avoid building either realist or anti-realist towers and concentrate on knocking down whichever one is put in front of you.

Debating the Merits of Realism and Anti-realism

How might one choose between realism and anti-realism? There are a number of ways, I suppose. What the reader must bear in mind, however, is that what limits all discussion to the standard of what I have called 'presumed certainty' is that an appeal to hard empirical evidence is not one of them, because the reliability, indeed the availability, of such evidence is part of what is at issue. (Of course, this is the ground on which some schools of philosophy – such as the logical positivists who will appear in Chapter 3 – reject metaphysics: precisely because metaphyics does not appeal to empirical evidence.) Still, a realist may be willing to argue for the existence of a mind-independent world on the ground that our sensory experience pushes us towards this conclusion. After all, what the senses bring us – some philosophers call it 'sense-data' – is apparently independent of our desires. We cannot simply turn these data on and off or modify them at will. On the contrary, experience constantly impinges on our minds, modifying our concepts in ways that seem beyond our control. This argument appeals to common sense, which is not necessarily a bad thing (or, it has to be said, necessarily a good thing) for an argument to do. Based on the nature of our experience, on its consistency, its strength, its clarity, and so on, the conclusion that there is a 'real world' out there is a very solid inference for us to make.

Realism is thus a *reasonable* position, one that must seem perfectly sound, especially when we apply it to local physical entities such as the computer in front of me as I write. My understanding of this intricate little machine has been constantly modified by my experience of it, in ways that lead me to assert with confidence that it is indeed independent of my poor mind, which often fails to understand how it works or what it is doing. My computer has, I am happy to admit, its own objective and slightly perverse existence. But I must be careful, for if I elevate this very ordinary admission to the level of a principle, asserting the separation of the 'self' from the 'world' that the self observes (a separation that is often encouraged by the popular view of science), I enter swampier terrain. The anti-realist rejoinder is, as we have seen, that the 'self' cannot be conceptually separated from the 'world'; the world and the self are, so to speak, a single experiential package that is articulated in our concepts. My computer is in fact my-computer-as-*I*-experience-it. There is, the anti-realist tells us, no way to discard this conceptual veil and approach the 'real' world directly, *because either it is not a veil or the veil will not come off.* Yet, this is what one would have to do in order to check the truth of the assertion that there is a world 'out there,' independent of the concepts through which it is grasped. One would have to have access to the impossible meta-look. In other words, if we only know the world in terms of our concepts, then we cannot use (our experience of) the world to check those concepts. They will necessarily be self-verifying and indicative of nothing except the unenlightening fact that in my 'concept-world' things are as they appear to be – which amounts to accepting the perhaps equally unenlightening proposition that they are as they are. This was an important aspect of Berkeley's criticism of realism about the physical world: If we begin with experience, we can never get to anything beyond experience and experience, strictly interpreted, is all in our heads.[19] The evidence of the senses certainly *seems* to come from an external source, for it is obvious that we do not have control over it. But this gives us no absolute warrant to conclude that the 'external source' is a world of objects that corresponds to our ideas. It may rather be, as Berkeley insisted, the Great Mind of God implanting ideas in our similar but mortal minds.[20] While few contemporary anti-realists will go so far as to posit a Berkeleyan world of minds and ideas ensconced in the mind of God, they will for the most part stop short of the *representationalist* conclusion that our ideas mirror (or represent) an external world that is either exactly like, or at least very much like, those ideas. Instead, they will argue that rather than reaching out to, or picturing, 'reality,' concepts simultaneously express and create it. Intellectually, we move about within them.

Welcome to the metaphysical jungle, where no sooner does one adduce empirical 'evidence' based on good solid experience of the world than it disappears into a thicket of arguments that threaten to reduce it to empty circularity. I shall leave the issue here (I feel no obligation to try to resolve what generations of philosophers have failed to resolve), noting only that both realist and anti-realist positions – all metaphysical positions, in fact – operate *somewhat* like metaphors or, as I have said above, visions of the world. The realist evokes an image of a godlike contemplative 'self' isolated from the 'world' it surveys. The anti-realist responds with an active or engaged 'self' ensconced in the 'world.' So, we have metaphors of aloof contemplation and active engagement. Since metaphysicians, like the rest of us, often live and die by their metaphors, *one* way to approach the realist/anti-realist debate is to be a pragmatist and ask which picture works better – which provides a more plausible view of human experience? This will have the merit of focusing the reader on 'the presumed certainty of hyper-plausibility' and, interestingly enough, of allowing her, on the basis of the anti-realist contention that it is impossible to transcend our concepts, to adopt the realist position, because our strongest concept is of a mind-independent world. There is a rough justice in this, I suppose, because even the most radical Berkeleyan anti-realist, one who spends his career launching sceptical attacks on realism about the physical world, will still jump out of the way of the bus that is bearing down on him in the street. So let's put it this way: our senses and our reason do not always point us in the same direction, but with respect to much of our everyday experience we necessarily side with our senses. We jump out of the way of buses, we come in out of the rain. But in metaphysics – as in science – the decision is, quite properly, not so easily made. Indeed, the fact that we jump out of the way of buses is hardly conclusive evidence for realism, for in a Berkeleyan world the *idea* that a bus has run you down is every bit as painful as the *fact* that one has done so in a physical world. In both worlds you would be well advised to jump.

An Ontological Side Trip

Whether you are a realist or an anti-realist, a proponent of mind-independent worlds or mind-dependent ones, your metaphysical vision will inevitably lead you down the pathway that ends in ontology – the term derives from the Greek verb 'to be.' Ontology can perhaps be described as a large branch of the branch of philosophy that is metaphysics. Just what distinguishes ontology from metaphysics so that it requires its own name can sometimes seem a bit vague, but let's try this: Whereas metaphysics is concerned with the general framework of reality, ontology is concerned with what *kinds* of things exist within the framework. (We might say that ontology involves deciding just what one is going to be a realist about.) When philosophers construct an ontology they are essentially in the business of tidying up the world by paring it down to its basic or constituent properties. Generally, they stop either at two such entities or proceed right down to one, which is to say, they opt for either *dualism* or *monism*. The Atomists of ancient

Greece were, for example, monists who contended that everything in the universe – including our minds – is made up of elemental, or indivisible, physical entities.[21] They were therefore *physicalists*. But a monist could, alternatively, be an *idealist*, who posits the existence of mental events only. This may seem pretty surreal to anyone new to philosophy, but readers of this book have already made Berkeley's acquaintance. (The English philosopher G.E. Moore once noted that he was drawn to philosophy by his astonishment at the things philosophers say – such as denying the passage of time or the existence of physical reality.) Plato is, by contrast, a dualist who posits the existence of two *irreducible* kinds of things: the mental (or intelligible) and the physical (or visible). The Allegory of the Cave, with its objects and ideas, gives us a dualist vision. In the present day, in that area of the discipline known as 'philosophy of mind,' a dualist would argue that mental events – thoughts, emotions, and so on – cannot be reduced to (explained completely in terms of) the opening and closing of synapses and the movements of neurotransmitters in the brain. Whatever consciousness is, however 'supervenient' (i.e., dependent, or added on to) on the body it may be, it nonetheless cannot be reduced to, or described as, a purely physical event.[22] Nor, of course, can physical events be reduced to mental ones in the way that would lead an *idealist* to deny *their* existence and insist, to Moore's constant amazement, that everything is a form of thought and that the world of space and time is therefore an illusion.[23]

An important ontological issue that attaches, albeit somewhat obliquely, to the monist-dualist debate – and that goes back at least to Plato – is whether the cosmos contains only particular entities (things *or* ideas) or universal ones as well. This concerns the status of general terms in our languages. When we use the English word 'green,' or its equivalent in another language, what are we referring to? Are we referring to an actual and universal property 'Green' (or 'greenness') – something like a Platonic Form? If not, then in Plato's view all our individual terms are unanchored, for they lack an absolute referent that will hold them still. It's as if all green things have something in common – their greenness – and yet that greenness is nothing. So they have, therefore, 'nothing' in common. For a Platonist – or anyone who accepts this argument – this is a very unsatisfactory state of affairs. By contrast, Aristotle argues, in what is perhaps a more 'common sense' mode, that 'green' does not exist apart from 'green things.' Universals do not literally – or at least independently – exist. Rather, universals are markers for our ability to draw connections among objects: to establish categories or classes. Yet, just how we do this is an interesting question that never seems to get entirely resolved. The seventeenth-century English empiricist John Locke argues that we arrive at such terms by subtracting all the individual circumstances of time, place, and contingent qualities from particular or individual objects.[24] Hence, there are – really – only particular objects that have, to the human eye, certain common concrete qualities that general terms pick out. Still, the question persists: What are these qualities? What precisely do general words like 'human' or 'triangle' refer to once all individual qualities have been abstracted out of them? How, a sceptical Berkeley asks Locke, do we imagine a triangle that is neither right-angled nor equilateral nor isosceles? And yet, if triangles have a common essence, that essence cannot include these qualities.

This is a difficult – or at least a very tricky – question that leads us into the ontological thicket of how to delineate what *individual things* are. The basic issue is this: If there are distinct things in the universe, whether ideas or physical entities, what makes them what they are, what allows us to distinguish one thing from another? This may seem a trivial question, because we distinguish things all the time, and very successfully, too, but in fact it is a rather subtle question that gives rise to the concepts of 'essence' and 'accident' as well as to the logic of 'identity' and 'difference.' The latter pair of terms play an important role in ontology, for as the American philosopher Willard van Orman Quine has put the matter, 'we cannot know what something is unless we know how it is marked off from other things. Identity is thus of a piece with ontology.'[25] Suppose I want to identify an individual thing, by which I mean define it or explain what it is: myself, say. Setting aside the question of just what a general term refers to, I could begin – as we always do with definitions – by using a general term and saying that I am a 'man.' That is a good start. By distinguishing between classes of entities, general terms get the process of individuation started. But, while this will narrow down the field of possible 'me's,' it is hardly specific enough. As an individual, I need to be distinguished from all other men. To so distinguish, one could proceed to enumerate all the individual 'qualities' that belong to 'me' such as size, age, looks, a tendency to grumpiness, and so on. Certainly, these identifying characteristics would work pretty well as a way for others to pick me out in the universe, or at least on a street corner on a moderately busy day. They amount, or can amount, to a good description of me and serve perfectly well for ordinary individuation. But, if we are thinking in terms of the 'deeper' ontological issue of who, or what, I am – if we are trying to pick me out on a metaphysical street corner – we are forced to recognize that these identifying qualities also contain an element of 'difference.' To say, for instance, that I am such and such a height is to identify me with something (a particular height) that is, of course, *not me*. This is so for two reasons. First, I could be (I once was and, as I age, will be again) a different height and still be *me*, and second, this is a height I share with lots of other people. There is nothing uniquely *me* about it. So the qualities that are used to identify 'me' are like impersonal markers of identity *and* difference, things that, strangely, I am and am not. (The same can be said for all the events that make up my life. We shall come to this point in the concluding section on Kant.) They are not *essentially*, but only *accidentally*, 'me.' In search of my individuality I have, somewhat disturbingly, become something of a universal entity ('man') masquerading in specific accidents. So, what is the 'real,' the essential, 'me,' the bit that must be there if I am to be 'me'?

One way to deal with this question is to cut the Gordian Knot, dispense with the idea of essence (and universals) altogether and, taking a line modelled on what is called *constructionism*,[26] insist that nothing *needs* to be there. 'I' am simply a unique agglomeration of accidental qualities. This is not a bad solution. It has much to recommend it, in fact, but as I have noted, the package of accidental qualities tends to change over time. Over a long enough period it can, like a ship whose timbers are gradually replaced, change completely. The result may still be 'me,' just as the ship will still be 'that ship,'[27] but we are now in danger of navigating without an ontological rudder in the treacherous currents of change.

The problem, as the Greek philosopher Heraclitus famously said, is that you can never step twice into the same river, and I fear that 'I' am a lot like that flowing river. Every day brings another grey hair, some more unwanted flesh, and who knows how many dead brain cells. We might say that 'I' am like the continuity of the river, the being that endures through all these changes. But then we are back to asking what sort of being that is, since it apparently has no necessary, or enduring, qualities. We can say that I have the qualities of a 'man' but if we do, Berkeley will rise from his grave to point out that we have come back to the anomalous triangle of no particular type. Certainly, we have returned to the Aristotelian dilemma of how to grasp 'being' in the abstract – in isolation from the 'accidental' qualities in which it always appears to be clothed. It is, it seems, possible to know a substance or being (an *ousia*) only in terms of the particular qualities that adhere to it, and yet those qualities are, apparently by definition, not the substance to which they adhere, but something different – something accidental, things that can come and go. This is true even of the unifying force that is my memory, for if we say that I am the (remembered) continuity of these changes – or the awareness of them as a continuity – are we saying anything more than that I am the being who has undergone the change? (And, besides, 'continuity' can turn out to be a pretty subtle concept in its own right.) The abstract 'me' is still there but as a kind of pure being beyond our reach: a perfectly unidentifiable (and therefore perfectly metaphysical) entity. Strip away all my qualities, which from this perspective are like arrows pointing to this abstract 'me,' and you will not find 'me.' You will, apparently, find only emptiness, an absence of qualities, which is why, I imagine, Berkeley noted, dryly enough, that 'the general idea of being appeareth to me the most abstract and incomprehensible of all other.'[28] 'I' am, it seems, like Macbeth's dagger: both self-evident *and* ungraspable.[29]

Reason and Metaphysics I: The Milesians

These difficulties can be traced to the fact that, as I have said, our reason and our senses do not always point us in the same direction. Reason, tied to language, relies on general or universal terms to make sense of the world – try operating for a day without general terms – whereas our senses seem to be 'particular.' Hence, when one attempts to construct a metaphysics or an ontology that explains or accounts for or knits together experience, the result can sometimes be surprising indeed because, in opposition to everyday life perhaps, the thrust of the effort is very often away from the senses towards reason's general concepts. We can witness this 'rationalist' tendency among the very first people to be called 'philosophers,' a group of sixth-century BCE intellectuals who hailed from the island city of Miletus, which is situated just off the Ionian coast in what is now Turkey. The Milesian philosophers were known as *Physiologia* (or *physikoi*) – nature philosophers – and in terms of modern intellectual taxonomy they were more like scientists than philosophers insofar as they developed some of the first physical theories about the structure of the cosmos.

Milesian science, for I can call it that, began by positing the existence of four basic physical 'elements' – earth, air, water, and fire. Every

existing thing, so the argument went, was either an element or a combination of elements. Insofar as elements are elemental – that is, indivisible – that might seem to be the end of the theory, but it is in fact
possible to ask where the elements come from, for even indivisible
things can have origins. Or not. To the question, 'What are the elements
derived from?' 'nothing' and 'something' are both possible answers.
One reason to suspect that 'something' is the better answer is that
without a theory of origins it is hard to account for the interaction of the
elements. And if they do not interact, the cosmos would have to be
static, a conclusion that experience would *seem* to contradict. In other
words, to ask what the elements are derived from is to broach the
question of how they are, at source, related to one another and how,
based on this relation, they have combined to create the kind of cosmos
that we apparently inhabit. By posing this question, the Milesians set
off on the great metaphysical search for origins.

Let's briefly trace the path of one particular Milesian thinker,
Anaximander. Around 550 BCE, he argued that the elements were
derived from abstract pairs of opposites: 'hot and cold' and 'wet and
dry.' We can probably assume (Anaximander is not clear on this) the
following match-ups: cold:air, hot:fire, wet:water, dry:earth. Alternatively, we could imagine each element as a particular pair of opposites:
cold-wet for water, cold-dry for air, hot-dry for fire, and hot-wet for
earth. In either case, the point to note is that the elements are presented
as embodiments of abstractions. (If you take this as suggesting that
the abstract is somehow 'more real' than the concrete, that would
indeed seem to be the 'idealist' ontological inference.) According to
Anaximander, these abstractions combine and recombine to produce
change in the cosmos, a process that is of course observable only in the
elements. To take a simple example, when water evaporates because of
the heat of the air (the fire in it), the earth is left dry and hot. (Fiery,
therefore: when are forest fires most likely to occur?) Rain restores the
water (wetness) to the earth and reduces the heat (fire) in the air and the
ground, cooling them.

Even in this very simplified account, we can see that Anaximander
has the rudiments of a theory of change; he has both the element-
vehicles and the conceptual engine – the interaction of opposites – that
drives them. Together, they allow him to give an account of what
happens in nature. He takes another step, however, and provides all of
this with a common source, a place of origin, which he calls the *apeiron*.
The word means 'the limitless' or 'unbounded,' and it refers to some-

thing like an infinite primordial and inchoate *something* out of which the elements emerged. It is their common, eternal, and undifferentiated ancestor. With the concept of the *apeiron*, Anaximander has laid the foundation for a *developing* as well as a changing universe. (He has provided, we could say, both a cosmogony and a cosmology.) From it emerge the abstract pairs of opposites that coalesce into the elements of the cosmos that, in turn, constitute all existing things. The story is similar, in tone if not in substance or complexity, to the theory of evolution and it forms – potentially – a nice neat package of explanation.

The *Oxford Companion* refers to the *apeiron* as 'the earliest known philosophical term.'[30] If so, then, given that metaphysics is concerned with 'abstract features of ultimate reality' that are resistant to empirical testing, and, given that that succinctly describes the *apeiron*, the first philosophical concept was a metaphysical one. This, of course, is my point. Whatever else it is, philosophy is a process of reasoning, and metaphysics is a direct result of that process. Metaphysics is, we might say, a result of the *logic* of explanation. The ancient Greeks had plenty of stories, most famously the myths of Hesiod, which recounted how the world came to be, but the internal demands of coherence are generally much less in myths than in the developing philosophy. Put more neutrally, the demands of narrative, especially ones with lots of magic features, differ from those of 'logic.' The *aitias logismos*, or 'explanatory account,' of the philosophers, is animated by the desire for what we might call a seamless theoretical gaze. (The Greek word *theoria* can bear the meaning 'to contemplate' and is etymologically connected, perhaps, to the idea of 'the gaze of the gods.') A philosophical account requires, more in theory than in practice perhaps, that loose ends be tied off, theories tidied up, contradictions avoided. One commentator has referred to the 'Milesian Method' as 'the method of postulating whatever appears to be the best explanation of a phenomenon,'[31] and this is, in essence, the heart of the metaphysical impulse. We might say, then, that the appeal of the emerging philosophy is logical rather than, as in the Greek myths, aesthetic or, alternatively, that its aesthetic is logical rather than episodal. In short, what has made the philosophers philosophers has been their preference for 'reasoning' – or arguments – over telling stories.

This is evident in Anaximander's approach. We have seen how his metaphysics moves from what can be experienced – the elements – back towards abstractions whose existence can only be inferred: the pairs of opposites and the *apeiron*. This is a movement towards what

Anaximander thinks is *logically* required if a complete and rational account of the cosmos is to be developed from that experience. Anaximander takes his experience of nature and turns it into a theory about the nature of nature. This is an important point, worth repeating: from their origins, philosophy in general and metaphysics in particular were shaped by the demands of *logos* (rational discourse), and their practitioners were as a result unable to coexist easily with anything they perceived as incoherent. If necessary, a metaphysician will, somewhat dogmatically, invent coherence and that invention will inevitably be couched in general or abstract terms.

Reason and Metaphysics II: Parmenides

In the last section, I tinkered somewhat with my original metaphor, setting logic down beside metaphysics as the intertwined oaks from which all the other branches of philosophy subsequently grew, although, in both cases the names were coined later. Hence, while a detailed account of logic must be left to a later chapter, some further consideration of its relation to metaphysics is necessary here. For this limited purpose, there is no need think of logic as anything more than a means of establishing clear, *non-contradictory* lines of thought. Rules, techniques, formal procedures, and the like can be left until Chapter 5. As an example of logic in action, I propose to sketch the arguments of Parmenides, a Presocratic philosopher and leading light of the Eleatic school, whose reputation in the ancient world was very great indeed. Parmenides' work, a long poem of which only fragments survive, contains the first great integration of logic and metaphysics.

The interesting thing about Parmenides is that, unlike Anaximander, he is not concerned to explain how the cosmos changes and/or develops because he insists that it does no such thing. Change, he boldly asserts, is impossible. To understand why he thinks so – for it is a rather striking assertion, of a kind to make G.E. Moore blink – it is necessary to map out the logical terrain. Think of it as constituting three adjoining countries.[32] On the left as we face them is the land of *Necessity*, where everything that is, *is necessarily as it is*. If, for example, we consider my height in relation to yours, it is necessarily true that either we are the same height or we are not. You know that one of those two situations holds. That is Necessity. Now shift your attention to the extreme right, where the land of *Impossibility* lies. There, *nothing is*, because everything that might be there is ruled out as impossible. It is either an unpopulated country or a country full of nothing, depending on how you want to look at it. For example, although you know that you are necessarily either my height or not my height, you also recognize the impossibility of simultaneously being my height *and* not being my height. Such a state of affairs simply cannot exist – or at any rate, once we have a concept of 'simultaneity' we do not know how it can. The land of *Impossibility*, if it is anything, is a catalogue of just such 'non-states.' Between *Necessity* and *Impossibility* stretches the great land of *Possibility*, where plenty of things, conditions, and so on – let's call them all 'states of affairs' – exist. Of course, by definition none of these states of affairs exists *necessarily*. You may, for instance, be taller than I am. But if you are, you are not *necessarily* taller, by which I mean that there is no Grand Law of the Cosmos that states that you must be taller than I am. If you are, you just happen to be so; it is a *contingent* rather than a necessary fact.

We must not slide over this too quickly. To designate a state of affairs as contingent is to say that one can know only *a posteriori* (i.e., after the evidence has been checked) whether a claim about it is true. When you think about it that is pretty obvious: to know whether you are taller than I am you would have to discover my height and compare it with yours. Nothing I have so far written will give you a clue as to the answer. You need evidence. Possibly I am taller; possibly I am not. Of course, the land of *Possibility* is also the land of *Probability*, so if you happen to be 6'9" the chances are very good that you are taller than I am, but that does not alter the fact that you would nonetheless have to wait to see. The possibility that I am taller, no matter how improbable, would remain. (That's why you can bet the long end of the odds and still win.) In contrast to *Possibility*, the countries of *Necessity* and *Impossibility* are regions of *a priori* knowledge, which means that in them you know whether a given claim is true or false in advance of all evidence. (Just consider the examples above and you will see what I mean: What evidence do you need to know that the statement 'We are either the same height or we are not' is true?)

Most of us pass our lives in the land of *Possibility*. The neighbouring countries exist primarily to assure us of some states of affairs (logically necessary ones) and to rule out others (logically impossible ones). They establish the frontiers of *Possibility* within which we can happily spend our time in the ontological search for what is and what is not. For Parmenides, however, this country that most of us consider our onto-logical homeland is merely a chimera. To see why – for this is, on the face of it, another very strange assertion – we have to reconsider *Possibility's* desolate neighbour, *Impossibility*. According to Parmenides, if a state of affairs is impossible, then, by definition, it cannot exist, and if it *cannot* exist, then obviously it *does not* exist. If it does not exist, there is nothing to be said about it – for what meaningful statement can one utter about the non-existent since there is nothing to utter it about? For example, to say 'Unicorns do not exist' is, from a Parmenidean point of view, to utter nonsense because there are no unicorns to say it about. (We might usefully say that the word 'unicorn' has no concrete referent, but then we are talking not about unicorns but the word 'unicorn,' which manifestly does exist.) But, if impossible states of affairs do not exist, then neither do possible ones, for to say that something is possible is just to say, without prejudice, that either it exists or it does not exist. According to Parmenides, if it does not exist, it is effectively impossible that it could exist, because there is, in fact, no 'it' to bear the possibility. The 'does not exist' option is thus ruled out, and all that remains is the 'does exist' option, which now becomes equivalent to 'necessarily exists,' because it is now the only option. Hence, everything that exists exists necessarily, and the only logical homeland we have left – passports at the ready – is *Necessity*.

Parmenides now draws the following inference. If everything that exists exists necessarily, then it is impossible that anything should ever cease to exist – since then it would *not* exist *necessarily*. This means, in a strict sense, that *everything is precisely what it is and cannot change, since to do so would entail ceasing to exist as precisely what it is*. It is, moreover, logically impossible that what does exist could ever have come into existence (have been created), because it would then have arisen out of what does not exist, which, if you are still with me, you now know to be impossible. Think of this as *a rigid law of identity*: What exists, exists necessarily and is necessarily what it is and cannot be anything other than what it is. *But*, if everything is necessarily what it is, then it is impossible to make statements of the order 'This is not that,' because such statements entail talking about what is not, which, you will recall, according to Parmenides, we cannot do. To say, for example, that 'A truck is not a car' is like saying 'Truck/cars do not exist,' which, like the statement 'Unicorns do not exist,' amounts to speaking of nothing and nothing cannot be spoken of. (Or, if you prefer, when we say such things we are saying nothing, uttering an empty phrase. One might, however, want to ask why we have so many words for things that do not exist.) Hence, it is impossible to differentiate between existing things;

hence, there is no differentiation between existing things; hence, everything is one thing. Parmenides has now demonstrated, at least to his own satisfaction, the 'Oneness' of the cosmos. What is, is and must always be. The cosmos is eternal, motionless, and unchanging. Strictly speaking, nothing can be said about it – other than, perhaps, that it is – because to say something about it, to identify it in some way as I have apparently just done, is to differentiate it from something else that it is not, something temporal, moving, and changeable, and there is, as we have seen, no such thing. Parmenides' 'Way of Truth' thus leads to the conclusion that the ever-changing, multifaceted world that we appear to inhabit must be an illusion. This is something we can recognize but not, in the end, speak about, for if logic leads to the truth of 'Oneness,' that truth leads to silence.[33]

I do not expect this short disquisition to garner many converts to Eleaticism. It is not my concern either to defend or criticize Parmenides' argument, which has, in any case, far more complicated implications than I can deal with here. (Among other things, his argument underlines the difficulties inherent in the concepts of 'identity' and 'difference,' a topic to which we shall return in later chapters.) What I have tried to do is emphasize the role of logic – or 'reason' – in the argument.[34] If asked whether our senses or our powers of reason are more important to the pursuit of knowledge, I am pretty sure, given our instinctive faith in common sense, that a lot of people would come down on the side of the senses, or at least be very reluctant to discount them. As I have already said, we generally trust the senses in our everyday life, and this trust is underwritten both by experience (things generally work out all right when we trust the senses) and by the ways in which they have been honed and extended by the sophisticated instruments of modern science and technology (even though those instruments often contradict what the senses have apparently told us). Parmenides belongs to an earlier age that – in part because it lacked such instruments – put more faith in the power of *logos*. A reader may wish to point out that since we have access to both reason and the senses, and can blend them in various proportions, we do not have to choose between them. In most ordinary circumstances that is quite true; we accommodate one to the other in a whole variety of ways. There are, however, philosophical and scientific junctions when reason and experience seem to part ways, and it becomes necessary to decide which path to follow. Copernicus's development of a heliocentric astronomy was, for example, based almost entirely on the work of reason – and on the firm belief that when comparing two theoretical systems, the simpler and more 'rational' one *must* be the 'truer' – as opposed to any new evidence about the cosmos. The same could be said for Einstein's development of a general theory of relativity, which could not be tested until several years after he enunciated it. In these circumstances, the scientist (or the philosopher) is forced to abandon, or at least modify, his everyday trust in sensory experience and make some hard metaphysical decisions.

So, while from one perspective Parmenides is an extreme rationalist, who completely discards the evidence of the senses[35] in favour of what logic assures him has to be the truth, we must take care to not isolate him too much or dismiss him too readily. Besides Copernicus and Einstein,[36] we could set down, despite his very different view of things, the always-instructive Berkeley, who sees no need to talk about a physical world when ideas and God will do. Many others could also be added to the list.[37] Parmenides ignores the evidence of the senses to a degree that few contemporary thinkers, and probably no scientists, would find defensible, but he is nonetheless a subtle philosopher who helps one think about the disjunction that often divides experience and reason. He deploys a sceptical principle – that certain kinds of propositions that we take for granted turn out, on closer scrutiny, to be incomprehensible[38] – against the common sense belief that the world is obviously as our senses indicate it to be. Having, to his satisfaction, demolished this belief, Parmenides then constructs a strong dogmatic portrait of the universe as the Great Oneness. However one chooses to view this intellectual edifice, it has to be said that Parmenides is a brilliant metaphysician who deftly negotiates that hazardous terrain where, it seems, one can either deepen one's grasp of reality or exile oneself from it altogether. Closely and sympathetically read, Parmenides reminds us that even the most implausible of conclusions can contain provocative insights.

Sense and Nonsense: The Hazards of Metaphysics

With respect to the hazardous terrain, it should now be clear that one great source of danger lies in the capacity of metaphysics to produce 'real worlds' that look very different from the one we *apparently* inhabit. Since this is a trait that metaphysics shares with a great deal of science, it should not be too disturbing. It does, however, present us with three possibilities that we need to consider. The first (with apologies to

Parmenides) is expressed by the direct realist's contention that there is in fact no distinction between appearance and reality: The world really is as it appears to us and either requires or affords no further explanation. (In the ancient world, the Stoics and Epicureans took something like this position.)[39] The second is that there is a distinction insofar as appearances are real but not sufficient indications of what the world is like – starting points, we might say, in the quest for that elusive 'ultimate reality.' The Milesians and all other indirect realists take this view. The third, Parmenidean and Berkeleyan, possibility is that appearances are illusions of one sort or another that must be set aside if we are going to grasp reality. Despite their obvious difference, exponents of the second and third possibilities do share the contention that the world is not, or not completely, as it appears to be. They reject the direct realism of the first view and, in doing so, turn towards a more complicated (or sophisticated) metaphysics. For them, the cosmos is a Great Mystery to be unravelled, and, like all mysteries, the solution – the complete explanation of what the cosmos is like – depends on a course of careful reasoning that will transport the philosopher from the apparitional shadows of what she thinks she knows into the clear light of 'reality.' The existence of this reality will, as we know, be demonstrated not by empirical evidence – which (Parmenides again) belongs, by definition, to 'appearance' – but by the coherence, plausibility, and even the elegance of the metaphysics that announces it. The power of a metaphysical theory lies, as I have said earlier, in its capacity to ask, 'How else can one account for the world being (appearing) the way it is?' and to generate the answer, 'In no other way.' And as I have also said, the line between wisdom and folly is thin here and hard to discern. The power of metaphysics may be genuine, producing deep insights – even, perhaps, wisdom – but it may also be no more than a kind of shallow trickery or self-deception. For perhaps the direct realist is not so naive after all. Perhaps the contention that there must be a deeper, fuller metaphysical account that will take us from appearance to reality is a debatable proposition. If so, the pursuit of metaphysics must be undertaken with care and circumspection if the philosopher is to avoid talking nonsense.

These are deep concerns in the history of philosophy. As a means of thinking about them, let's return for a little while to the Allegory of the Cave. Plato has a particularly keen eye for the ambiguities of philosophy and there, as elsewhere, he describes what he has seen. In its evocation of shadow-worlds and sunworlds, of icons, simulacra, and

Forms, the allegory can be read both as metaphysics and as a metaphor for metaphysics. As the prisoner-about-to-become-philosopher ascends from the cave to the sunworld, she confronts different kinds of appearances that reveal different layers of knowledge. When at last she is ready, she stands before the Reality of the eternal and immutable Forms. Plato is an Eleatic at heart, although not always in practice, and his preferences are clear: the eternal over the ephemeral, the immutable over the mutable. The Forms are accorded the highest ontological status, which is to say, they are more real than their ephemeral copies, whose lesser and dependent status is measured in relation to them. A copy – an icon – has reality just because and insofar as it participates in its Form. A painting is beautiful because it participates in the Form Beauty. But this participation is always incomplete and imperfect. To recall my remarks on substance (*ousia*), a copy bears (I shall slip into the standard Latin here) not only *essentia* – the quality of the Form – but *accidentia* as well, qualities extraneous to the Form. There are always contingent aspects of the copy that distinguish it from the Form and, it has to be said, degrade or dilute it. To return to the slightly narcissistic question of who I am, I participate in the Form Humanity – I am human – because I have that essence in me, but my height, eye colour, age, grumpiness, et cetera, are, we have seen, 'merely' contingent facts about me and as such are not necessary to that participation. These qualities could be other than they are and I would still be *essentially* human. (Would I, though, still be essentially 'me'?) But given them, I am also a contingent, individual human being, not absolutely identical with the Form Humanity. I am, depending on how you want to view the matter, either a dilute or superfluous copy of Humanity.

Of course, if the copy participates in the Form, the Form can end that participation by withdrawing from the copy, fundamentally (we might say, *really*) changing what it is. Someone who is good can lose the form of Goodness and become evil as the Form Evil takes the place of Goodness in him. The *accidentia* – his height, age, weight, sex, and so on – may remain the same but he will be *essentially* different. In this manner, the Forms are a series of immutable Eleatic entities that govern what we are and what we are not, but in contrast to Parmenides' metaphysics, Plato's allows individual existing things to be, to not-be (in certain ways: I exist, but I do not exist, say, as a wise man), and *to become* as Forms enter and leave them (I could become a wise man, although my family harbours deep doubts about this). The Forms, therefore, allow Plato to do what Parmenides said we could not do – to speak of the many things in the world and to differentiate them from other things according to their participation in various Forms. They preserve us from the fate of amorphous Oneness by opening up a world of differentiated 'being' (there are many Forms) and an ontologically inferior and dependent one of 'becoming' as well. They thus establish a hierarchy of appearance and reality in which the appearances, even the relatively debased shadows on the wall of the cave, point towards reality. Part of the philosopher's job is to read these apparitional signs, to 'save the phenomena'[40] by explaining the appearances in terms of the reality, by opening the shadowy cave to the metaphysical sun. Unlike Parmenides, Plato refuses to break off all relations between experience and reason.

The Allegory of the Cave is a metaphor for what Plato thinks metaphysics does, which is to envelop the world of appearances like sunlight, allowing us to apprehend it as a coherent whole, to see it in both its ephemeral and its enduring aspects. In the prisoner's struggle from the shadows of the cave to the clarity of the sunworld, we can trace the development of human self-consciousness, self-understanding, self-criticism, and self-transcendence – a sublime metaphysical progress of self-creation that, when complete, melds us with the cosmos and allows us to see it aright. It is an inspiring rationalist vision: the fulfilment of *theoria*, where humans approach the divine. Yet, there is also something unsettling about this progress, for none of the self-creation it imagines is originally willed by those who undertake the journey. Rough hands are laid upon the prisoner in the cave, she is forced to turn around, she is dragged to the entrance and thrust out into the sunlight. Once this has been endured (and it has to be *endured*) she finds herself in a very different world. Education – which is, I think, what the allegory is really about – is, ideally, like this. Ideally, education transforms the individual, transports her to another place, takes her, as she certainly feels herself to have been taken, from a world of appearances, apparitions, and shadows, to something 'more real,' and her former life is accordingly devalued, or at least viewed – perhaps tolerantly, perhaps nostalgically, perhaps lovingly – from a different perspective.

Even though 'seeing' is a common metaphor for knowing, the oculocentrism of the allegory must not be taken for granted. The reader must not let it slip by unnoticed. The transformation in seeing, in the way the world looks to the former prisoner, is simultaneously a transformation in *being*. To see properly (to know how to pay attention?) is to know what one needs to know, and this knowing has, necessarily, tremendous implications for existence. (It has something to do with wisdom.) The philosopher in the sunworld – the educated being – is not the same person knowing more. Having experienced something qualitatively superior, having learned *how to see*, this is a different person from the one who so unwillingly left the cave. (Perhaps the difference is wisdom; perhaps she begins to see like a god.) This recognition that there is something fundamental to know that one does not know from the outset, that one's way of seeing and hence one's way of being, can, and ought to be, transformed into the clear gaze of wisdom, is the *telos* – the goal – of the metaphysical impulse. Plato's sun is the point of origin, the source of all that is real, and it draws the philosopher.

Yet, I have to come back to it: The *impulse* is precisely what is missing from the allegory. I have passed too quickly over the rough hands, failed to take sufficient account of how the allegory is couched in the language of compulsion. The prisoner is *forced* to turn around, *forced* to look at the fire, *dragged* to the mouth of the cave, *hauled* out into the sunlight. At each stage of her education, she is compelled to confront the evidence of her errors, to look more closely at how-things-really-are and to see that they are not as she thought they were. In fact, once her eyes have grown accustomed to the light, all she has to do is *look*. The problem all along was not looking per se but *being able to look*. What the ex-prisoner *really* has to do is train the 'inner eye,' the one attuned to abstractions, to mathematical objects. She has to learn to think, consider, ponder, pay attention to ideas. Then she will see what she needs to see in the way that she needs to see it. She will have entered the metaphysical space. But there is no getting around the fact that all of this, the whole progress of this journey towards enlightenment, is underwritten by compulsion. There is something terribly contingent, even arbitrary, about it: Someone or something *makes us see* what we really do not spontaneously want to see. This can make all the 'selfs' in the last paragraph look like illusions, for there seems to be no self-creation here, no internal compulsion, no personal, self-sustaining, and necessary reason for undertaking the journey. Plato's philosophers seem to be the arbitrary creations of the unseen presences lurking behind the fire. (Of course, maybe they are the elect, chosen by the gods. That would please the philosophical ego.)

Earlier in the chapter, I linked the metaphysical impulse to the work of logic and maybe the resolution of my difficulty lies there. Since logic is in essence a formalization of reason, it may be that 'Reason' is the reason for undertaking the journey out of the cave. What the prisoner must learn to do on her way to becoming a philosopher is not only to reason but also to value reason, not only to come to know but to value knowing. She must learn to appreciate the beauty of the mathematical objects, of abstract thought, of ideas, and to understand their intimate connection with her life. But why? The question will not go away. What reason is there to be rational, to love these things? If we *just are rational*, if that just is our nature, there is no need for compulsion, since our escape from the cave simply follows from our acting according to our nature. In speaking of coercion, Plato therefore seems to be saying that, for whatever reasons, we are not *necessarily* rational. But if this is so, if being rational is a choice we make or that is made for us, if it is a contingent fact about us (*accidentia* not *essentia*), then what is the reason for the choice? There could be many reasons (including the reason that it is good for us) but even if a particular reason is a rational one – that is, even if it is a well worked out justification of the choice – its rationality can carry no compulsion or else we are back to asserting that we just are rational. The reason for undertaking the journey imagined in the allegory would therefore be, at best, a good but not a compelling one. If so, then Plato's language of external compulsion (and his talk of the madness of the philosopher in *Phaedrus*) nicely captures this fact. But it also represents a kind of failure, an admission that there is an axiom, or better, an imperative, that sits outside philosophy and is not vouchsafed by reason.[41]

That is possible. There may be no self-sustaining reason for committing oneself to the metaphysical visions that philosophers feel compelled to produce. It may be, as Plato suggests, the product of a 'mania' that resists understanding. Alternatively, it may be that the reason for producing these visions is aesthetic. Perhaps philosophers are drawn by the beauty of the visions that are set in front of them, and perhaps, therefore, the outcome for those who are 'exposed' to philosophy is not knowledge but a certain taste for metaphysics. In other words, it may be that, given a philosophical training, a coherent world, constructed according to certain rational principles, is more pleasing than a chaotic one. Yes, the owners of the rough hands are a problem: Who are they and what truth, what principle, what mania, what aesthetic do they represent? Are they wise men and women – gods even – directing some among us towards a great metaphysical truth, or are they merely philosophers themselves, kidnapping unsuspecting prisoners and transforming them into true believers in the cult of reason? What is behind the appearance of the philosophers? Is it anything more than other philosophers with a taste for metaphysics? I have said that Plato, great metaphysician that he is, has a keen ear for the ambiguous nature of the metaphysical enterprise. The sceptical spirit, the spirit of his teacher Socrates, is always with him, and Plato forces us to listen to it even as he weaves his own magnificent and dogmatic visions of reality.

God and the Philosophers

Yet, that sceptical spirit is never so strong that it can erase the sense of order, of the fundamental rationality of the universe that emanates from Plato and indeed from so many texts, both ancient and modern. It is not misleading to call this order God-given, for it descends directly from the great myths concerning the creation of the Cosmos. Although the Presocratic philosophers quite consciously attempted to substitute '*logos*-driven' cosmogonies for mythic ones, their works nonetheless retained strong residues of creator-gods.[42] For his part, Plato – probably influenced by Parmenides in this matter – works his way towards a monotheist conception of a single Creator-God who is in many ways an embodied *logos*. Aristotle pushes this idea about as far as one can, positing a god who is really little more than the *process* of reason at work, a god who is, in other words, less of an individual than Plato's god. So, while they came in different shapes and sizes, gods were by no means immediately exiled from the philosopher's universe. Well into the modern era, they, or the shadows of them, stood surety for a cosmos in which philosophers could find a home.

I must add the caveat that not all ancient philosophers accept this picture. Not all philosophers, sceptical and contentious creatures that they are, accept any picture. In the ancient world the Atomists are thoroughgoing physicalists, who see the universe as a contingent and eternal place, uncreated and unpredictable. And while the Epicureans think there are gods, they do not imagine that these gods care very much about the fate of humans. (Nor, for that matter, does Aristotle's god.) For them, as for the Atomists who inspired them, death brings an abrupt end to a cosmically unplanned life. That said, *most* philosophers in the ancient world and beyond find God to be a useful metaphysical concept, well suited – necessary, in fact – to an account of how things must be. (In later eras, until the political domination of the Christian church began to fade somewhat, it was also a very prudent concept.) So, no account of metaphysics is possible without some consideration of the place of God as the great metaphysical anchor for the Great

Scheme of Things. As illustration of this, we shall leap forward in time to the beginning of the modern era and consider René Descartes' proof for the existence of God, as set out in his metaphysical *tour de force*: *Meditations Concerning First Philosophy*.[43]

Descartes' God of Reason

Descartes begins the *Meditations* by announcing his intention to establish a secure foundation for knowledge, one that will allow him (and us) to avoid the errors into which philosophers and scientists have historically fallen. In short, he begins by announcing his intention to overcome scepticism. If the reader recalls what I have said about the revival of scepticism in the sixteenth century, the fact of Descartes attempting to come to grips with it in the 1630s and 1640s should not be surprising. He is, by our designation, as much a scientist as a philosopher[44] and well aware of the extent to which sceptical thought had undercut the foundations of medieval (largely Aristotelian) physics.[45] It needs to be said that scepticism could seem much more fatal to a scientist of Descartes' time than to one in ours. Today, a scientist in whom the sceptical spirit was missing might seem a rather strange figure, but that is because he is, in many ways, a child of the sixteenth century. The scepticism revived then was an impetus to the development of empiricism, and empiricism in turn was fundamental to the development of modern science. Very roughly, the sceptic will raise an empiricist standard and argue that all we have to go on is our experience and that we must be very circumspect about what conclusions we draw from it. He will point out that experience, which is necessarily of the past, can be a notoriously unreliable guide to the future, leading us into error – by inducing wrong inferences – as often as to truth. Nowadays, we take this empirical attitude and its relation to science pretty much for granted: Sir Karl Popper's dictum that a scientific theory *must* be falsifiable is virtually a truism.[46] A good scientific theory will have been tested to the point where there is a very high degree of probability that it is true. If we can establish that probability we accept it, but we never forget that it *could*, conceivably, be wrong. (In probabilist terms, we are *morally certain* – i.e., 99.9999 per cent certain – but not epistemically, 100 per cent, *certain*.) The scientist never quite lets go of her scepticism, her willingness to be surprised. By contrast, as the late English philosopher Bernard Williams rightly reminds us, in Descartes' day, 'probabilistic and corrigibilist conception of the scientific enterprise, in any specifically modern sense, did not yet exist.' In the seventeenth century there was no stopping-off point between certainty and what Williams calls 'chaotic disagreement in which anything goes.'[47] Scepticism was not at that time an ally; it was a real and worthy opponent standing between the scientist and knowledge of the world.

To defeat scepticism Descartes begins by embracing it, adopting a strong sceptical position and then considering whether it can hold up in the strong light of reason.[48] This position has been variously translated into English – it has been called 'radical,' 'systematic,' and 'hyperbolic' doubt – but whatever its name it is a doubt so different in degree from the 'reasonable' or 'normal' doubt that most of us employ that it becomes, effectively, different in kind. Reasonable doubt – the scepticism of everyday life – is based principally on what experience has taught us, which is to say, on a sense of probability. It has a civilized, empirical bent to it. If, for instance, someone tells me he has just had lunch on Jupiter, I am inclined to doubt the veracity of his statement, because I know of no way it could be true. He may be an extraterrestrial or some such thing, capable of lunching on one planet, even so inhospitable a one as Jupiter, and dining on another – it is, conceivable. But experience, both mine and that of others, tells me that the chances of this are so vanishingly small that it would be unreasonable to believe him. Put differently, while it is logically possible that he had lunch on Jupiter, it is, in my view, metaphysically impossible: It just doesn't fit into my conception of how things are. On the other hand, experience leaves me with very little doubt that if I want to watch tomorrow's sunrise I had better look to the east. The point is that, empirically speaking, I usually know what to doubt and what to accept.

Note that I say, 'very little doubt' and 'usually.' In the world of experience, doubt is never absolute – if it were it wouldn't be doubt, but negative epistemic certainty! – but neither does it ever disappear. It is laid out on a probabilistic continuum that moves from the very doubtful indeed (lunch on Jupiter) to the highly probable (sunrise in the east). Along this continuum, there is necessarily a grey area where uncertainty begins to shade into conviction – where we are not sure whether something is or is not metaphysically possible. Here, confusion may occur, for here we are most likely to reject true statements and accept false ones.[49] And since we cannot always know where that grey area is, and how far it extends, it behooves the man of science and philosophy (who, almost by definition, lives in the grey areas) to treat most scientific and philosophical issues with a great deal of caution. This, in the first of his meditations, is what Descartes does – and more. Radical doubt, which in the first instance entails doubting everything it is not *logically impossible* to doubt, is Descartes' way of exercising the most extreme caution. *All* claims about the physical world are treated with a doubter's suspicion. The radical doubter will doubt that my friend had lunch on Jupiter – there we will agree – but he will also doubt that the sun will rise in the east tomorrow. Embracing the Parmenidean possibility that everything is an illusion, he will even doubt that I am speaking to him or that he is there to hear me. In essence, the radical doubter sets aside his experientially based notions of probability, of what is *likely* to be true or false, leaving in their stead only undifferentiated *possibility*. Writ large: the world may exist or it may not, to the radical sceptic one thing is as likely as another. Logical possibility has overruled metaphysical impossibility. In such a world, confusion is necessarily universal.

But what about logic? It is positively full of *necessary* truths, and one cannot, surely, doubt a necessary truth. After all, it has to be logically impossible to doubt what is logically necessary. To recall an example I used earlier, how is it possible to doubt that you are *either* my height or not my height? One of those conditions *must* hold. And if it is not possible to doubt such things, then there are certainties in the world, even if they are 'only' logical (or mathematical) certainties. Descartes' response is to hypothesize an Evil Demon, a malicious god, capable, apparently, of circumventing the laws of logic as well as those of physics: a god truly beyond our understanding. By his transcendental fiat even the paradoxical condition of being simultaneously my height and not my height becomes possible. The certainties of logic and mathematics are now open to doubt: maybe $3 + 2 = 4$. Like the hands that lay hold of Plato's prisoner, the Evil Demon enters the *Meditations* somewhat arbitrarily, as the principle of the possibility of the game of radical doubt, a shadowy and entirely negative prime mover who deceives us about, well, about everything – to the point where even the logically impossible becomes metaphysically possible. That is a very strange world, for the almost universal assumption among philosophers is that if something is logically impossible it is necessarily metaphysically impossible as well.

There would seem to be no escape from the snares of the Evil Demon, for Descartes has left us with recourse neither to experience nor to reason. Everything is open to doubt. Nothing is certain. Scepticism reigns supreme and the world is at an end. Madness descends, or at least, as Bernard Williams submits, we have to bring down the curtain on our scientific aspirations and rest content with the 'everyday standards' of (I would add) the ancient gentleman sceptic. Put differently, knowledge cannot be the basis of, or the justification for, our actions. A calm acceptance of appearances is all that we have to guide us. Yet (miraculously?), that is not the case. There is, it turns out, one tiny corner of logic, one foothold in sanity, that the Evil Demon cannot eradicate – the corner where 'I' reside. Descartes' argument, which in the *Discourse on Method* he famously renders as 'I think, therefore I am,' is that the Evil Demon could be deceiving him about everything but only on the condition that *he* (Descartes) exists *in order to be deceived*. In short, an indispensable condition of the Evil Demon's game of deception is that there are two players – a deceiver and a deceived – playing. This means that, necessarily, the game of radical doubt cannot, according to its own conditions of possibility, obliterate 'me,' the Cartesian ego, not completely, anyhow. When deception occurs, my 'mind' is deceived: my ideas are wrong; things are not as I *think* they are. The act of deception therefore entails the existence of a 'deceived' *mind*, but strictly speaking that is all it entails. As Descartes points out, the common prejudice is to assume that where there is a mind there is also a body, but in the game of radical doubt, where the evidence of the senses is never conclusive, that is *only* an assumption, a metaphysical prejudice in fact. The Evil Demon's defeat has, after all, occurred on the battlefield of logic, not physics. His ability to deceive has been eliminated only with respect to the mind's knowledge of itself. The existence of the body, like the rest of the physical (and much of the logical) world, remains vulnerable to his power.

No matter. Descartes has found in the necessary existence of his mind the 'Archimedean point' he was seeking, the fulcrum that will allow him to pry open the door to the rest of the world. But this remains to be done, and we must have patience, a lot of patience, in fact, for the rest of the world turns out to be much harder to save than 'I' am. At least we now know where to begin, which is in our minds. Since the senses have not yet been reinstalled as trustworthy routes to knowledge of the physical world,[50] the only possible path is through the mind. When Descartes takes an inventory of the mind's contents, he discovers there, along with ideas that presumably come from sense-experience (and another kind that we shall ignore here) – *innate* ideas – ones that are present at birth in all human beings. These ideas are remarkable chiefly for being 'clear and distinct,' in part, because they are in no way dependent on the fuzziness (the dubiousness) of experience. As a result, we can immediately see, or intuit, their truth, which means that it is possible to develop some trustworthy inferences from them. For example, Descartes understands clearly and distinctly that he is imperfect. This, he sees, just is true. After all, he doubts and makes mistakes, and these are exactly the sorts of things that imperfect beings do. He also understands, equally clearly and distinctly, that he has a concept of a perfect being. Clearly, Descartes further tells us, the lesser cannot be the source of the greater. An imperfect being such as he is could not, on his own, have generated an idea of a perfect being, since the idea refers to something beyond the scope of an imperfect being. Therefore, and again clearly and distinctly, the imperfect being cannot be the source of even its idea of a perfect being. Given the rule about the lesser and the greater, the only possible source of an idea of perfection is a perfect being. Hence, the very idea of a perfect being necessarily demonstrates that there is such a being. In other words, this being, called God, is the one being whose essence – his fundamental characteristic, in this case, perfection – necessarily entails his existence, for if he did not exist he would not be perfect.

This is known as the ontological argument for the existence of God. St Anselm of Bec and Canterbury first worked it out early in the twelfth century.[51] The central assertion of this argument is that it is contradictory to speak about a perfect being who does not exist, because existence is a necessary characteristic of perfection. This contains an inverted echo of Parmenides' assertion that it is impossible to speak of what is not. The Anselmian-Cartesian point is that we can, *pace* Parmenides, speak of beings that do not exist – Sherlock Holmes, for example, or Tarzan's friend Jane. But these are not perfect beings, and so there is no need for them to come furnished with all of the characteristics that designate perfection. If they do not exist, then they are imperfect, and that is all that has been claimed for them. To speak of a *perfect* being that does not exist is, however, a contradiction in terms: an imperfect perfect being. (If this still smells fishy, and I'm sure it does, hold your objections until the section on Kant.)

In any case, Descartes has demonstrated to his satisfaction the existence of a perfect being. God exists and, being perfect, is supremely good. A good God, unlike the Evil Demon who has now been vanquished by Cartesian logic, will not mislead us about either the existence or the essential nature of the physical world – nor about logic and mathematics either – for deception is a characteristic of an imperfect, not a perfect, being. If we humans make mistakes, it is not because God deceives us but because we try to understand more than limited beings are capable of understanding. That, however, is something *we* can understand (after all, Descartes has just asserted it) and control by keeping our will, our desire to know, within the limits of our understanding. (This is actually very good advice: do not try to develop a theory about anything you do not grasp clearly and distinctly, or if you do, be circumspect in the claims you make about it. In other words, learn the difference between knowledge – however you define it – and opinion.)

Some Questions about Descartes' God

Descartes' journey is a strange one, and his reasons for undertaking it may seem puzzling. Depending on one's view of these matters, it may or may not be necessary to attempt to prove that God exists. But why do so in order to prove that the world exists? Before (and even after) Descartes, proofs traditionally run in the other direction, the nature of the world being adduced as evidence for the existence of God. (They are, in other words, cosmological proofs.) From the 'fact' that nature – the cosmos – is orderly, a philosopher such as Aquinas infers the existence of a creator who does the ordering.[52] Whatever one makes of such a proof, it must at least seem to move in the right direction. Insofar as the world is, for most people, a more immediately accessible entity than God, the proof moves from the known to the unknown, from what is immediately accessible to what is not immediately accessible. Hence, Aquinas's proofs would seem to follow the original path of Milesian metaphysics. But this is precisely Descartes' point. According to Descartes, the world is even more unknown, even more in need of existential proof, than is God. God does not lie on the other side of the world so much as the world lies on the other side of God. Descartes' radical scepticism therefore knocks the ontological foundation out from under medieval cosmological proofs for the existence of God. If they are not allowed to begin with the world how can they ever get to God? How can they ever get started?

From a medieval perspective, Descartes would seem to be philosophically stranded, and from a medieval perspective, I suppose he is. Even Anselm accepts the existence of the surrounding world. But Descartes is trying to do something very different from his medieval predecessors, something that necessitates the different direction his proof takes. The point is this: His proof for the existence of God is not the end of his argument, not an end in itself as it was for his medieval philosophers, but a middle stage in a larger proof for the existence of a physical world. It is, we might say, the mid-point rather than the end point of his metaphysical journey. Once that end has been reached, and the existence of the world is established, Descartes will have laid a foundation upon which the scientific study of the world can be built. His rule of procedure is something like this: in order to accept empirical evidence as good evidence, it must be shown, *in a necessary and therefore non-empirical way*, that the world which apparently produces this evidence really exists in the way the evidence suggests that it does. It must also be shown that precise, logical, and mathematical reasoning underlies all certainty about this world. Science, as it were, requires a logical and metaphysical underpinning before it can proceed to its empirical work. To provide it, Descartes charts a course from the indubitable intuitions of his mind to the innate idea of God's existence and, from there, to the world. He begins, in other words, with the assertion (the invention?) of an autonomous, transcendent ego, a self-evident 'I' from which thought can proceed. At the end of the day that ego is shown to reside – through the grace of God, the great middle term in the argument – in the world. What is more, the logical-mathematical intuitions of that ego – the ones so important to doing science – have been shown to be trustworthy.

Descartes' argument, leading us from radical doubt to the world, can be described either as a circle (as his 'internal' proof for the existence of God very often is) or a great arc, moving from the certainty of the thinking self, through God, to the certainty of the physical self in the world. If the argument is circular, Descartes' dualism (the irreducibility of mind and body in his work) keeps it from being *viciously* circular.[53] The clear and distinct ideas that carry him along this difficult route end by placing the thinking self inside the physical self (without, however, really melding them into one self), and in doing so assure us that radical doubt about the fundamental nature of the world can be set aside. Descartes' proof for the existence of God amounts, thus, to a kind of metaphysical statement of faith that there is, as Richard Rorty has put it, an essential fit between us and the world – and, therefore, an essential wholeness to our 'selves.' It is as if Descartes is reminding us, in a deeper way than usual, of what we already know about ourselves and the world.[54] The *Meditations* deploy logic in the service of these deep godlike certainties that Descartes grasps so clearly and distinctly that the 'light of nature' (i.e., reason) confirms that he cannot be wrong. In this sense, Descartes is like a medieval thinker who proves what faith – dressed up, in this case, as intuition – has already confirmed to him. His metaphysical vision has turned out to be true.

Yet, there is an interesting sleight of hand in Descartes' metaphysics and especially in his use of God to anchor them. Descartes is a rationalist, and the rationalist position is that the rational human mind mirrors the mind of a rational Creator. God is, among other things, a logician, and we are the one among his many creations who can, albeit very imperfectly, mimic his reasoning. For his part, Descartes never suggests that the human grasp of reality is anything but limited, that the human mind, prone as it is to err, is anything more than a foggy mirror held up to the mind of God, *and yet*, when all is said and done, God and the world emerge from this mind. Both are subsumed by the logical swoop of Cartesian metaphysics. The result is a strange transcendental picture of the world as seen, in Thomas Nagel's trenchant phrase, from nowhere,[55] *and yet also from the human mind*. Descartes may be demonstrating the existence of God, but his unique way of doing so also establishes the sovereignty of the human 'subject,' a peculiarly modern being who in a fundamental way defines and creates her own world, a being who needs God – dare I say who channels God? – but who also is prior to God.[56]

To summarize, Descartes sets out in logical language what Plato sets out in mythic language in the Allegory of the Cave – a vision of how the world is and how we are in it. In order to give us this vision, Descartes has, however impossibly, set us above the world by creating a God and inserting us into the field of that being's absolute and objective vision. His argument is perhaps circular – moving from (mental) self to (physical) self, using the contents of his mind to prove that God exists in order to prove that he (Descartes) exists – but in its circularity it becomes a kind of geography, a delineation of the boundaries of 'reality.' Descartes' metaphysical circle is, in essence, a circle drawn by the Great Geometrician who is God, and it encompasses an uncharted map of the world that science can go about filling in. Nonetheless, however ingenious the argument – and it is at least that – there is something unsettling about the way it proceeds from Descartes to God and back again, leaping like a great arc of electricity between the mundane and the transcendental, between our world and God. There is perhaps too much magic in this, too much self-certainty about what is innate, and too much reliance on a transcendental God as a guarantor of 'this world.' In short, it may be that Descartes' argument exposes too much of the 'other-worldliness' of metaphysics to suit an increasingly modern mind. I think this is what unsettled the great German philosopher Immanuel Kant – enough, perhaps to cause him to alter forever the status of metaphysics as a philosophical pursuit. I shall end this chapter with a brief look at this alteration, for it is the springboard to the modern attacks on the citadel of metaphysics that are the subject of Chapter 3.

Kant and Metaphysics

Metaphysically speaking, Kant is fastidious, which is to say, he is very careful, very self-conscious, about mixing the mundane with the transcendent. Like Descartes and most others who came before him, Kant makes extensive use of metaphysical concepts – including the concept of God – but unlike them, he never tries to demonstrate that they referred to actually existing entities. With respect to an entity such as God Kant does not, in fact, think such demonstration is possible, because he does not think that empirical existence can be inferred from logical necessity. (To turn this on Parmenides, neither can 'empirical non-existence.') Existence, Kant says in a moment of tremendous philosophical economy, is not a predicate – a characteristic of something – so it cannot be a term in a proof, as it is in Descartes' ontological proof.[57] Existence is a *contingent* fact about entities; only if X can be shown empirically to exist can one discuss what predicates can, or have to, be applied to it. But first, *pace* Descartes, the empirical demonstration is required, and a transcendent entity such as God allows of no such demonstration. Kant's point, perhaps garnered from Hume, is that we cannot, with necessity, infer anything about the existence or nature of a transcendent 'other world,' from 'this world' and this, of course, has tremendous implications for the God-dependent metaphysics of Descartes' proof for the existence of the world.

Kant's anti-Cartesian message is that we cannot transcend experience. Thought will not reach beyond it to the absolute. To be sure, Kant's 'transcendental method' – his transcendental idealism – stands above experience and lays out its structure by delineating the *a priori* conditions of human knowledge. Kant's fundamental point is that a mind that experiences the world does so in determinate ways. Experience is structured by the intuitions of time and space and categorical judgments about quantity, quality, relation, and modality.[58] To explain: Time, for Kant, is the mind's subjective imposition of a flow of succession – before, now, after – on experience, while space is its subjective imposition of three dimensions on it. These are the conditions of experience, ones that give us – perhaps give any experiencing being – the shape of the world. Within time and space, the categories of judgment represent – very roughly – our ability to identify entities by number (quantity), by characteristics (quality), by connection to other things (relation), and by possibility or necessity (modality).[59] It is not too misleading to say that the categories allow us to individuate existing things and to establish relations among them.

To this extent, we can say that Kant, like all metaphysicians, deploys his transcendental method to establish the conditions that make it possible to make sense of the world, for without the intuitions and categories there is only undifferentiated chaos. But – and this is the unique aspect of Kant's metaphysics – while the intuitions and categories of his transcendent *method* make experience possible, they do not enjoy a transcendent *existence* in a world beyond experience. They are not universals or Forms or anything like that. Kant does not adopt a strict realist position about them. Time and space are aspects of our minds, or to put the matter in a more metaphysical and less psychological way, they are the fundamental conditions of any experiencing being's capacity to distinguish one thing and one event from another. Intuitions and categories are, in other words, the framework of the *phenomenal* world. This is Kant's term for the world as humans experience it, or, to take us out of the equation once again, for the experienced world. This world Kant distinguishes from the *noumenal* one, by which he means the world as it (in theory) 'really is,' or – somewhat differently, but perhaps more accurately – the world outside experience. This is an explicitly logical distinction: the two worlds could be identical (there may be nothing outside experience, in which case there would only be one world, and the *noumenal* reduces simply to the limit of the *phenomenal*), but they need not be. For example, when we watch television the pictures on the screen *appear* to be three-dimensional, but *in reality* they are only two-dimensional. Our minds, furnished with their intuitions of space, stubbornly add the third dimension. I am cheating here, of course, presenting a case where we have knowledge of both the 'phenomenal' three-dimensional reality and the 'noumenal' two-dimensional one, but nonetheless that is the point. It is possible to grasp the idea of there being a difference between the way the world appears to us and the way it is independently of us. Every non-direct realist accepts as much. Kant's genius is to make a virtue out of this necessity and, in doing so, create a new kind of realism vis-à-vis the world. The point is, if our knowledge of the world is rooted in experience, it must necessarily conform to the transcendental conditions of experience – the intuitions and categories – or else it could not be experienced. To see the picture on the screen – for it to be an object of experience – the intuitions and categories must do their work. Beyond these conditions, humans cannot go, and, in the final analysis, the *noumenal* is just that – the place beyond where we cannot go. It is not so much another, hyper-real, world as the limit of our reality. Described as such, it is an empty world. For if it were not, it would contain 'things' – entities, events, and what have you – and if it contained things it would be a *phenomenal* world. (And there goes my two-dimensional television set!)

This has, I suspect, been a bit of a mouthful; so let me summarize. What distinguishes Kant's metaphysics from that of his predecessors is his insistence that nothing can take us to a reality beyond experience. This allows Kant to be a direct realist about the *phenomenal* world. My television example posed the following question: We know that *we* package space in three dimensions, that *for us* – for any experiencing being – it has three dimensions (this is our 'intuition' of space), but do we equally know that it *really has* three dimensions? According to Kant, the only possible answer is that if space is an intuition, and as such a framer of experience, then space just is the intuition of three dimensions. We cannot go on to speculate about a *noumenal* space that would not really be space at all. The *phenomenal* world is our world, and we cannot aspire to, or even imagine, a transcendental, non-subjective, supra-experiential world where we could have access to a god's-eye view, the view from nowhere (and based on nothing) that Descartes and all previous metaphysicians had sought. The *noumenal* world, there-fore, establishes the universal point of view not as reality but as a limit to human experience – the end of the world rather than Plato's glorious sunlit paradise. Hence, scepticism – the possibility that what appears to us cannot be proven to be real – is defeated because what appears to us, phenomenally, just is reality.[60]

Yet, if what lies on the other side of the *phenomenal* is beyond know-ing, it is, strangely enough, not beyond using. This is the second part of Kant's genius. Consider the Cartesian ego, the self-knowing mind. What, precisely, is this ego? To recall the problems that we encountered ear-lier with respect to the definition of 'being,' is the Cartesian ego the sum of all its experiences, including its thoughts? If so, what, if anything, holds these experiences together? Those earlier remarks about qualities attached to substances can now be applied to experience. Is the ego just another name for a series of experiences, or is it the entity that has undergone those experiences? The first option may seem ontologically unsatisfactory (especially, as we have seen, to an Aristotelian). The experiences, we feel, had to happen to *someone*: to 'me' to be precise. But to get to the 'me' to which they happened, we would have to strip away all the experiences, the phenomena through which I know myself. What would be left? Something pretty ghostly: a naked ego to whom nothing has happened. Someone might propose a constructionist solution, according to which the ego is the sum of the experiences undergone by a distinct entity, but that does not seem to get us very far. We still need to know what – or where – this entity is. Here, we might consider the thought experiment in which one person's brain is transplanted to another's body. Where, in this case, does identity go? The general – or popular – assumption is that the brain carries identity with it. This amounts to adding a rider to the constructionist's proposal: 'I' am the experiences undergone by my mind and body that I *remember and knit together* in some coherent fashion. Since the brain does this, the brain gets to be 'me' in a way no other part of me does. But this seems a trifle absurd. In the first place, the memory gambit is hardly unobjectionable. If we accept it, we also have to accept that every time I forget something, some part of 'me' goes missing. This *may* be true – an Alzheimer's patient may gradually 'lose' himself – but when, at what precise point do 'I' leave the scene? A lot more would need to be said before we could turn this metaphor into a definition of 'self.'[61] In the second place, the idea that my brain carries 'me' around is a very strange locution. I think I am more likely to say that *I* carry my brain around. So, I seem to have stumbled into a dilemma: if there is no unifying 'being,' no consciousness or remembering mind or some such thing behind the experiences, how can they be knit together as 'mine'? But if there is a unifying being, what is it and how can it be known – in itself so to speak – apart from its experiences?

I had better drop these ruminations before they lead me too far astray from the point I want to make, which is that the self is a slippery concept that perhaps cannot be pinned down with Cartesian clarity. Maybe there is a being that underlies the qualities we perceive, and maybe there is not. Kant's great merit, the third part of his genius, is that he does not enter into the argument. He simply points out that a concept of 'self' is logically required in order to think about experience. The 'self,' Kant tells us, is a 'transcendental' idea,[62] which is to say, it does not represent any object of our experience, but, because of the work it does in unifying that experience, it is logically and metaphysically indispensable. Without the self, we would be unable to make sense of experience, since the experience would happen to no one and be necessarily linked to no other experiences (which is what Hume suggests).[63] Hence, to recall D.W. Hamlyn's definition of metaphysics, set out at the beginning of this chapter, one of the things that must hold good for conscious beings, if the world is to constitute a reality for them, is that they must also be self-conscious beings. (This is essentially what Descartes discovered.) They must experience events as happening to 'them.' The English philosopher, novelist, and playwright Iris Murdoch has written (and we could also apply this to the arc of Descartes' proof) that 'metaphysicians speak in quasi-tautologies that can be sources of illumination.'[64] With that in mind, let's try the following quasi-tautology: My experiences happen to me; hence, if I have experiences (and I do), then I exist. Even though 'I' remains undefined here – issues of essence and accident are not even broached – we begin to see the indispensability of the concept. Kant calls the self a *regulative* idea – a synthesizer of experience and discourse about experience – that we cannot do without.

Kant puts forward two more regulative ideas: the cosmos, or world in general, and God. (In other words, Kant's regulative ideas are the elements of Descartes' circle, there without the need for proof.) Like the self, these ideas are not the products of experience, so their existence cannot be empirically demonstrated, but they are *logically (and metaphysically) necessary* for the unification of experience. Obviously, if we are to make sense of our experience, we have to think in terms of a cosmos, an orderly place where this experience occurs. That the cosmos exists is not (again, *pace* Descartes) something to be proved, but is rather the ground of all empirical proofs and cannot, even for a brief Cartesian instant of doubt, be dispensed with. As for God, well, he plays roughly the unifying role vis-à-vis the cosmos that the self plays vis-à-vis its experiences.[65] In a post-Darwinian world, the assumption that the cosmos requires a creative and unifying consciousness in the way individual worlds do may seem too anthropomorphic. We need not be wedded to it, however, to grasp Kant's point, which is that the self-conscious deployment of metaphysics as a unifying set of ideas is what allows us to make sense of experience. The justification of a metaphysical idea rests, therefore, not with its truth but with its rationality and utility – which is to say, its indispensability. This veridical restraint – or perhaps ontological circumspection – sets Kant's metaphysics apart from most of its predecessors. Instead of producing transcendent knowledge (such as the 'Cartesian' knowledge that God exists or the 'Berkeleyan' knowledge that space does not), it shows how it is possible to know what in fact we do know (the phenomenal world of experience), or more accurately, *how what we know is constituted as knowledge.* Kant's metaphysics transcends experience, as all metaphysics does, but in his case only to unify it, to become not the master of experience but its good and faithful servant.

After Kant I

Good and faithful servants are not, however, universally appreciated. If Kant demystifies metaphysics (which is what I have suggested, although not all observers of the scene would agree), if he makes it possible to see metaphysics for the theoretical gambit that it is – a construction that holds our world together – part of his legacy is that philosophers now seem unable to enter the terrain of metaphysics without experiencing significant feelings of guilt and confusion. Glances in its direction are often stolen glances. Perhaps, once metaphysics is demystified, turned self-consciously into a necessary method of 'making sense' of things that stops short of claims to some sort of absolute knowledge, the grand tradition of metaphysics does begin to seem either unnecessarily 'high-falutin' or unacceptably artificial. And perhaps post-Kantian philosophers feel, therefore, that they can and should do without metaphysics, even if that means, however paradoxically, an end to philosophy. (I have also suggested that the germ of this feeling may reside in Descartes' metaphysics.) At the conclusion of the *Tractatus Logico-Philosophicus,* Ludwig Wittgenstein evokes the image of his little book as a metaphysical ladder that the reader has climbed and, having done so, and having seen the view, can now dispense with, because it is a view to which no one could really have access.[66] That is a Big Question, a Kantian question, and we can go no further until we stop to consider it. Must we – can we – kick away the metaphysical ladder?

3

Wittgenstein's Ladder:
The Modern Reaction to Metaphysics

SUMMARY

Here we consider the modern reaction to metaphysics. The 'new sceptics,' and their guru, Friedrich Nietzsche, come on stage. We see how they trace the errors of philosophy to metaphysics and the errors of metaphysics to Plato. This returns us to the question of what, if anything, philosophy is. The new sceptics view philosophy not as science but as literature. Their 'anti-Platonism' is thus also an 'anti-logos,' where myth and metaphor displace reason at the heart of philosophy. Some 'dogmatic' responses are set out briefly at the end of this chapter.

After Kant II

If Kant paved the way for a reaction to metaphysics, that was almost certainly not his intention. Kant's work is a paradigm of metaphysical subtlety in which the 'real' empirical world is framed by a transcendental method that can account for our experience of that world. But like all great philosophers, Kant also forces us to consider a sceptical response to what he has done. He raises – however implicitly – the question of whether we can really aspire to the kind of knowledge of a mind-independent world that a strict metaphysical realism demands. His work thus pulls the reader in opposite directions. Kant is, for the most part, a metaphysical realist, who argues that the world we perceive is independently, or objectively, real. However, he is also pretty circumspect about our capacity to grasp that reality. There is no god's-eye view available to us in his work. At most, there are shadowy *noumena* – the *idea* of a world 'in-itself' – that can never materialize behind the

phenomena that conscious beings erect on the transcendental framework. For some philosophers, this is a perfectly viable proposition: we
are limited beings who nonetheless seek a larger view. The American
philosopher Thomas Nagel is someone who has developed this aspect
of Kant in a thoughtful way – and without Kant's jargon.[1] By contrast,
there are others who take a different lesson and reject the whole of
metaphysics just because realism now seems impossible. Hilary Putnam
has suggested, in what seems a succinct summary of this view, that the
problem is not that 'reality is hidden or noumenal; it [is that] you can't
describe the world without describing it.' It is as if Kant's distinction
between *phenomena* and *noumena* has opened the door to the conclusion
that all perception is perspectival. For anyone who draws this conclusion, the aspiration to metaphysical realism, to finding truth in 'the
myth of the ready-made world,'[2] has come to an end. Then the god's-
eye view becomes what Wittgenstein says it is, a trick of language that
can be defeated by kicking away his ladder. When this happens, the
very concept of metaphysics comes under attack.[3]

These issues remain subject to contention, but this much is certain:
Since Kant, philosophers have taken a goodly number of kicks at the
ladder. Not all of them have been sceptical kicks either. Some have been
taken in the name of various dogmatic philosophies whose proponents
assume – not unreasonably – that it is possible to construct a non-
metaphysical account of the world. For the most part, however, this has
amounted to assuming realism rather than arguing a case for it. An
example of this assumption can be found in the work of the nineteenth-
century French 'positivist,' Auguste Comte, who turns a nascent sociology loose on metaphysics. Despite a certain enthusiasm for Descartes,
he takes the anti-Cartesian position. Compte argues that metaphysics
wrongly begins from the phenomena of human consciousness, which it
then uses to explain why the world is as it is, whereas positivism (in his
view) properly starts from the world, from the laws of nature and
society, and uses them to explain human consciousness. Should someone wish to argue that Comte's awareness of the world and its laws is in
the first place, built up from the phenomena of his consciousness, and
that he is therefore making a deep but debatable metaphysical assumption about our ability to perceive or represent that world objectively
(and directly) – an assumption that has, in one way or another, been
under attack since the Renaissance – I would have a great deal of
sympathy with that individual. But that is why the spirit of scepticism
is so integral to philosophy. Very often it is left to the sceptic to point

out that a particular position, set down dogmatically against another, comes with its own metaphysical assumptions, perhaps the very ones it claims to have left behind or, alternatively, ones that its opponents have considered and discarded and which require, therefore, some kind of intellectual support.[4] I have said above that scepticism keeps dogmatism responsible, and without it the Comtes of this world can often look a little too self-assured. By contrast, the great philosophers, even when they are at their dogmatic best, carry their scepticism, and hence their uncertainty, with them.

Having thus plugged the virtues of scepticism, what I want to do in this chapter is consider a particularly strong strain of intensely argued sceptical reaction to metaphysics: the 'new scepticism' (which I shall also refer to here as neo-Nietzscheanism) that is such a prominent part of post-Kantian philosophy. Like its ancestors, this brand of scepticism often takes no prisoners. Among many of its adherents, to say that an argument is metaphysical is to dismiss the argument; by extension, to say that philosophy is *inherently* metaphysical[5] is to dismiss philosophy. In short, new sceptics are dedicated either to the eradication of metaphysics – what they see as the great storehouse of shadowy, ungraspable things – from our thought or, if that turns out to be impossible, to making our awareness of metaphysics so excruciating that we can never take any of our ideas for granted. So, either we achieve the end of metaphysics or we arrive at a sceptical hyper-awareness of all the mischief it creates. Given that metaphysics is one of the original and foundational parts of philosophy, and given that philosophy may not be able to survive without it, this is no small matter for philosophers. The self-doubt of the new sceptics can make contemporary philosophy look like a very strange discipline. It is as if no one is quite certain what it is, what it has been, or what should become of it.

Origins are difficult things to determine in philosophy, but one of the primary sources of post-Kantian scepticism about metaphysics may be the work of a rather metaphysical and non-sceptical philosopher: G.W.F. Hegel. By historicizing thought, putting it in motion, so to speak, Hegel nudged philosophers away from the idea of static, metaphysical systems. Until that great last moment at the end of history, when the world spirit and the absolute idea reveal themselves for what they are, everything is a work in progress. The following is a too-simple distinction, but nonetheless a useful one: Kant is the great analytical philosopher, the guru, in one way or another, of all the analytic philosophers who were to follow, whereas Hegel is the model for historicist, sceptical,

post-modernist (etc., etc.) philosophy. It is common to distinguish between 'Anglo-American analytic' philosophy and 'continental' philosophy as the two great styles of the twentieth, and now the twenty-first,
centuries. Bearing in mind that this, too, is an oversimplification that
would strand many philosophers on the wrong sides of the divide,[6] we
can, on the broadest canvas, usefully treat this as a distinction between
Kantian and Hegelian streams of philosophy. (A philosopher's opinion
on the relative merits of the two great German thinkers often tells one a
lot about the philosopher.)

If this be so, Hegel is something of a silent or hidden god of my new
scepticism. In textual terms, the most fecund source of inspiration for
assaults on the citadel of metaphysics is to be found in the work of the
anti-Hegelian German philosopher Friedrich Nietzsche. Depending on
whom you read – as with all philosophical tales, there are several
different versions of this story – Nietzsche is was either the last metaphysician, and harbinger of all post-metaphysical philosophy, or the
first post-metaphysical philosopher. Martin Heidegger (hardly a sceptic, but certainly in the Hegelian camp) cuts a huge figure in this story of
the fate of metaphysics in the present age. Heidegger certainly sees
himself as a post-metaphysical thinker. For him, Nietzsche was the last
great name in a history of metaphysics stretching back to Plato,[7] but one
who foresaw, and greatly contributed to, the end of that history. In
these matters, the French philosopher Jacques Derrida's eminence ri-
vals Heidegger's. For Derrida, Heidegger was the last great metaphysician while – remember, there need not be a strict temporal sequence
here – Nietzsche was, perhaps, the first post-metaphysical philosopher.
Or if one reads Derrida another way – and anyone who has read
Derrida knows that there is always another way to read him – that
honour belongs to Derrida himself. There is a third reading of Derrida
(I alluded to it above, and it is the one I prefer), according to which we
can never really escape metaphysics, but only be aware of how ensnared
we are in it. As for Nietzsche himself, he appears to have thought that he
had indeed broken with the long tradition of metaphysics – Nietzsche
breaks with what Heidegger later calls the ontotheological tradition of
assuming that philosophy can achieve the absolute intellectual grasp of
being that theology attributes to God – and that he is therefore doing
something very different from his predecessors, if, indeed, he could be
said to have had any (possibly Hegel). These claims are, like so many
opinions, endlessly debatable. I shall simply note them, and without
further ado proceed to the beginning of the story, or at least the begin-

ning that Nietzsche or Heidegger or Derrida would likely point me towards. I hope that the ending will take care of itself.

This beginning lies with Plato. The English philosopher and mathematician Alfred North Whitehead famously remarked that all of philosophy is a series of footnotes to that great philosopher. Nietzsche, Heidegger, and to a lesser extent, Derrida, might well agree. They would, however, add the caveat that they are footnotes to a false, or at least a misleading, text because metaphysics and, therefore, most of the errors or deviations of philosophy, have their wellspring in Platonism. For them – for a whole raft of contemporary philosophers – Plato is, if not the villain of the piece, then the well-intentioned but misguided perpetrator of a metaphysical tangle much in need of resolution.[8] Whether this is true, whether Plato's sun is nothing more than a brilliant chimera is in my opinion open to debate; but it *is* a good story, and an important claim, that is well worth pursuing.

Anti-Platos

At bottom, it is a question of realism. Ontologically speaking, Plato's Forms are of the highest order: true, original patterns, transcendent archetypes that are both the source and the standard for all existing things. Chairs, horses, and good actions[9] are what they are because they participate in, or are determined by (Plato says different things at different times), the appropriate Forms. To know the Forms would be to know 'Being,' to know, in other words, what-things-are. In short, there are absolutes, and knowledge of them would constitute a god's-eye – or ontotheological – view of the cosmos. By comparison, we have seen that Kant has a concept of *transcendental* ideas that are not derived from experience. In one respect at least – as 'presences'[10] that structure reality – they do the same work as the Forms. The crucial difference lies in the nature of Kant's ontological commitment to them. He does not insist that these ideas are independently 'real'; he makes no claim that they necessarily exist anywhere except in the mind of a rational, experiencing being. So, Plato's ontological commitment to the Forms is greater than Kant's commitment to transcendental ideas. Since the Forms are the standard and *origin* of all things, Plato must adopt a strong realist stance with regard to them, which is to say he must logically assert their independent or 'objective' existence. The elements of Kant's metaphysics, his intuitions, categories, regulative ideas, and indeed his concept of a *noumenal* world, are by contrast more accurately intellectual principles of *coherence* that rational beings need if they are to experience the world. A chaotic universe is an incomprehensible universe. So, even if it – the *noumena*, which we cannot know – is chaotic, beings such as ourselves will impose order on it through the 'intuitions' of space and time, through the categories of judgments, and self-consciously, through regulative ideas.[11] These metaphysical concepts are *subjectively* necessary if rational beings are to be guaranteed *any kind of* consistent understanding of the world around them. But this necessity never requires the intense ontological commitment – the commitment to metaphysical realism – that the Platonic Forms do. Plato and Kant are alike in using metaphysics to ensure (or assert) the existence of order in the cosmos. Metaphysics is for both the *sine qua non* of setting out a knowable reality. For Plato the order necessarily exists, and to uncover it is to uncover an *objective* truth about the world. For Kant, however, the truth that we uncover may well be only a truth about ourselves (or about the conditions of experience), about how *we*, as opposed to the world, are constructed; it may tell us only about the *subjective* conditions of there being a reality *for us*.

A lot of questions can be asked of the metaphysical enterprise, especially in its strict Platonic version. The one that I have in mind here is whether, after Kant – whose lesser commitment I have read as insinuating a potentially lethal anti-realist worm of doubt into it – the Platonic tradition of metaphysics even merits our attention. It is possible that Kant's metaphysics has eaten away the foundations of Plato's metaphysics – and, like Wittgenstein's ladder, perhaps even its own foundations. In other words, it is possible that Kant has made it impossible to believe in universals and absolutes, or even to stomach talk of them. Perhaps even God could not have seen that his work was good because there is no such thing as 'good' to see. More to the point, even if such absolutes do exist, perhaps it does not matter that they do because, as Kant would have to admit, while a god can see them we cannot. Plato also thought that the Forms were too remote for direct human inspection – at least while one is alive – but this may be a more devastating admission than I have hitherto acknowledged. For with his concept of *noumena*, Kant may have shown us that transcendent worlds are not just remote but *hopelessly* remote: unattainable and unimaginable, beyond the reach of even Plato's myths. So, we need to return, yet again, to the always-fruitful Allegory of the Cave and ask whether a hopelessly remote truth – which is perhaps the most a metaphysical truth can aspire to be – is a truth at all. Put differently: even if what Plato's metaphysics tells us is true, even if there are universals and absolutes, is any of this of any use to us? At the end of Chapter 1, I suggested that the *idea* of Truth, no matter how remote, must affect how we think about the world. I am now asking whether, if this is so, the effect is beneficial or deleterious to our philosophical health. A remote 'Truth' may do more harm than good.

Let me rephrase. To a post-Kantian philosophical eye, the tradition of metaphysics, the pursuit of 'ultimate reality' that has come down to us from Plato, may seem to belong to a lost world. In the eighteenth century, first David Hume[12] and then Kant drove wedges between the empirical world grasped by the senses and the idea of a transcendent reality. Their message is blunt: You cannot get there from here. But, of course, wise old Plato knew as much all along, even if he did not say so directly. A philosopher who actually looked at his sun – gazed upon the Form of the Good – would be so thoroughly transformed that she would no longer *be* a philosopher. As we know, she would have found wisdom. Furthermore, since, as the Priestess Diotima taught Socrates, we love only what we lack, she would no longer be a lover of wisdom. Her quest would be at an end. Her connection with our cave world of the senses would have been broken. If there exists an appropriate designation for her in this condition, it is perhaps *daimon*, a 'divine being' who occupies a space between gods and humans. This is an uncomfortable space, it has to be said, where our ex-philosopher bears the mind of a god in the body of a human. (I am playing with Plato's images here, especially his Pythagorean-inspired one of the body as the prisonhouse of the soul.) With her god's-eye view, the *daimon* is dead to the cave world, utterly uninterested in the endless and tedious discussions of shadows that take place there. To the cave dwellers, on the other hand, she is no more than a ghost of ideas long forgotten or never unpacked, a shiver that goes up the spine for no discernible reason. It is a double but asymmetrical exile: although she knows about the cave dwellers, the *daimon* has no wish to live among them, and they, for their part, are simply unaware of her.

This is why when someone who has gazed upon Plato's sun returns to the cave, she has to do so neither as philosopher nor as ghostly *daimon* – for the *daimon* is a philosopher fulfilled – but as a politician. This individual has to return in a guise – or is it a disguise? – that the cave dwellers can see. Only then can she spin her 'noble fictions' to soothe them and bend them to her superior will and knowledge. (She does this for their good, of course; why else would she return?) The truth, the full treasure of her metaphysical wisdom, she keeps to herself, knowing that it is too rich for shadow people. Hence, even though the truth that is encased in the Forms has entered the cave with this individual, she makes it available to those within only indirectly, only after she has filtered it through the distorting prism of political myths, converted it to a comprehensible – a visible – simulacrum of wisdom. (In Plato's *Laws*, that is essentially the role assigned to art; today, I fear, the mass media have taken it on.) Thus, a rule of human existence is that we never have unmediated access to the truth. The natural human conditions are either ignorance – an image-laden, more or less deluded state that Plato called *eikasia* – or, at best, *doxa*, which is Plato's term for the half-truth of unchained opinion. *Doxa* is better than *eikasia*. The chains, the worst aspects of earthbound idiocy,[13] have been shed, some knowledge has been gained, there is access to icons rather than simulacra – but no one 'really' knows what the truth is, and contingency, intellectual guesswork about what is true, cannot be avoided. The *daimon* who returns from gazing upon the sun may govern the cave dwellers wisely. But to follow her, to accept her advice, is, on the part of the cave dwellers, either an act of faith or a lucky choice. As Plato admits, the chances are they will not follow her. An equally likely scenario is that, if this individual is too honest, if she reveals too much of herself, or if she unchains them too quickly, they will kill her. Ultimately, the philosopher-king from outside the cave is (although Plato does not quite say this) an impossibility: chimerical, paradoxical (because not a philosopher at all), and unimaginable – unless one suspends the laws of logic. The philosopher-king really is just a shiver up our spines, a fleeting sense of something that escapes us.

This much is certain: the Forms and the truths they contain are not directly available to human experience. Frail opinion – at best the simulacra of wisdom and knowledge – rather than certainty, is our lot. Even Plato, a far wiser person than most of us, can approach the Forms only by the indirect route of myths. Even he cannot tell us *exactly* what they are, only what he has *heard* (from whom?) they are like. Plato tells us stories about caves and lines and charioteers flying across the heavens, about Cronos and Zeus with their hands on the tiller of the cosmos, and about the work of the Demiurge who created it all in the first place.[14] Plato tells us wonderful stories, ones that approach wisdom and the Forms indirectly. The stories allow us (and Plato) to glance at them obliquely, protected by the smoke and mirrors of language from the too-strong glare of the sun. Reading these stories, we may feel compelled to admit what Plato himself might have been loathe to admit: that Plato is a brilliant artist and a great poet. *But* – and it is a big 'but' – do we really need to see what Plato wants us to see? *Is* there ultimately anything *to* see? Perhaps Plato is asking us to look at nothing, because everything, all the truth the myths supposedly reflect, is too far away. Such 'looking' might be entertaining – it is always fun to contemplate the impossible, the non-existent, and the unavailable. However, we do not *need* philosophy to entertain us. We need philosophy – don't we? isn't this its mandate? – to enlighten us. That is what *Plato* says in the Allegory of the Cave. But is it enlightenment to remain in arty half-darkness, glancing cautiously at shadows and icons? If we cannot have access to the Forms, perhaps we would do better to look elsewhere for enlightenment. Perhaps that is what Kant – reluctantly and in spite of himself – teaches us. Perhaps Kant drew the salutary lesson from Plato, who was honest enough not to exclude it from his work.

The Quarrel between Philosophy and Poetry

Still, Plato would likely disagree with what I have just said. Plato might well think I was throwing the baby out with the bath water. If so, he would tell us that there is no point in looking elsewhere, because only philosophy, imperfect as it is, can point us in the direction of wisdom. Nothing else will do. There are rumours that in his youth Plato considered becoming a poet but abandoned the idea. This is fascinating because as a mature philosopher he was, despite his own undeniable artistry, very hard on the poets. In Book X of *The Republic*, Plato tells us that there is an ancient quarrel between philosophy and poetry. According to Plato's philosophic diagnosis, philosophy has reason to be angry, because poetry is a potentially dangerous infection in the body politic. The problem lies in poetry's inherently imitative nature. Using a bed as his example, Plato argues that God makes the Form of a bed, the carpenter makes a copy of the Form, and the artist paints a bed from one point of view. (Poetry seems to cast a wide net here – which would make 'art' a better term – but Plato may be using painting as an analogy for poetry.) Thus, the poet/artist is three steps removed from the original reality of God's mind, condemned to an unenlightened perspectivism. As a result, the poet has no understanding of the bed *qua* bed, a fact which is evidenced according to Plato (a bit unfairly, I have to say) by his inability to build one.[15] If the carpenter's bed is an icon of the Form, the artist's is no more than a simulacrum, a shadow cast on the wall of the cave, and not fit for lying in. This is also the thrust of one of Plato's first dialogues, the *Ion*, in which Socrates makes gentle fun of the eponymous orator who is unable to say just what, based on his reading of Homer, he really knows. Plato's point, flung in the faces of all the great Greek poets, is that poetry teaches nothing because poets know nothing substantial – even though, as he allows Socrates to suggest in the *Apology*, they may write under divine inspiration. Plato, therefore, shoos us away from the temptation to waste our lives in the production of poetic simulacra: better to know how to make war, as a general imperfectly does, than to produce a debased image of that knowledge, as Homer does in the *Iliad*.

We have to ask whether Plato himself has avoided this danger, because avoiding it is precisely what his claim about the superiority of philosophy (and metaphysics) rests on. Does the philosopher, immersed in abstractions, manage to talk about, let alone know, something real? Is the philosopher really superior to the artist? The answer is not automatically, 'yes,' although (as I noted in Chapter 1), Plato seems to think that the philosophers' simulacra lie closer to the sun. But then Plato would, wouldn't he? Yet the closer Plato gets to the sun, the more he resorts to poetry and apparently leaves philosophy behind. Surely, this must mean that the status of Plato's metaphysics – its ability to approach Truth and thereby distinguish itself from poetry – is open to doubt.

Kant's metaphysical devices were essentially just that – devices, aids to clear seeing, theoretical conditions for an orderly world. This might make us feel that Kant deserves a more sympathetic hearing from the sceptics than does Plato. After all, Kant meets them half way, offering not Truth but intellectual order, not transcendence but the useful *idea* of transcendence. One could almost plead Kant's case on the grounds of utility: We need these ideas even if they do not point to anything real. Perhaps, but one could also go the other way. If we are suspicious of Plato's Forms, if we are unsatisfied with metaphysical presences that we can experience only as shadowy absences, that we can imagine only in the hints and nuances of poetic-looking myths, why should we even want to *think* in terms of a Great Order? If we don't want Plato's 'reality,' or if we despair of knowing it, why would we be interested in Kant's transcendental ideas? They may seem to be no more than a stand-in for the non-existent, a desperate re-invention in reduced circumstances of the Forms that Kant can no longer believe in. Transcendental idealism may be merely a kind of metaphysical stubbornness on his part. We might seriously consider the possibility that metaphysics, whether Platonic or Kantian, stems from a failure to look a mundane and often chaotic reality squarely in the face. Perhaps it not wrong, therefore, to suggest that the metaphysical philosophers have posited a non-existent 'reality,' and an empty but despotic 'Reason' which will lead us to it. Perhaps, by means of their intellectual artistry, Plato and Kant have persuaded us to accept *their* poetry as a vision of the Truth. If philosophers can never become *daimons*, then perhaps they are magicians, grand illusionists, tricksters, weavers of false visions: simulacra of *daimons*.

Nietzsche's Rehabilitation of Poetry

I said at the outset of this chapter that there are many contemporary philosophers who hold something like this view. They think, as the English philosopher Roger Scruton does of Kant's *noumena*, that metaphysics is no more than 'a shadow cast by thought' and that 'the task of philosophy is to free us from its illusory grasp.'[16] Wittgenstein's later work argues, in a similar fashion, that one of the primary purposes of philosophy is to liberate thought from the metaphysical illusions that language creates. But it is Nietzsche who calls Kant's *noumena* 'impermissible.'[17] His work is a wholesale attack on what he sees as the metaphysical commitment to the absolute rationalist principles of coherence and order in the world. As such, Nietzsche has pride of place among the objectors to metaphysics. As Richard Rorty explains, 'Nietzsche's charge [is] that the philosophical tradition that stems from Plato is an attempt to avoid facing up to contingency, to escape from time and chance.'[18] His effort to break free of that tradition, and by doing so to provide a space – a poetic space – where alternative visions could emerge, is the lifeblood of Nietzsche's work.

So, here is the *leitmotif*: From the half-poetry, half-philosophy of the Presocratics, Plato fashions 'an unresolvable quarrel between poetry and philosophy.'[19] The rejection of art contained in this act, the fierce concern to express the great truths of existence in precise 'scientific' or 'mathematical' terms, or at least to insist that this is how they should be expressed, and the fundamental commitment to *logos* that this entails, is met by Nietzsche with an equally Herculean attempt to reverse the current and turn philosophy back to the wisdom of poetry. The Greek word for poetry, *poiesis*, essentially means 'making,' and the Nietzschean individual – or at least the *Übermensch* – is self-consciously a maker of worlds. Worlds, cultures, and lives are all the products of the human subject. Nietzsche rejects the distinction, set out by Plato and maintained by Kant, between the transcendental and the human perspective – there is only the latter. In doing so, Nietzsche collapses the human into the personal.[20] Individuality now flourishes in all its multiplicity: There are many worlds, all of them human. The best of these many worlds, those that are authentically human, are like the creations of an artist.

Nietzsche's artist stands in stark contrast to Plato's 'scientific' philosopher, who sets out to discover *the* world that the Demiurge – the Great Craftsman – has created. To Plato, only this Great Artisan is truly a maker – poets and other artists are pseudo-makers. For this reason, Plato tells us, the philosopher must carefully control his poetic instincts and seek only to be a discoverer, which is a lesser kind of being, and appropriate to our place in the cosmos. In *The Twilight Of The Idols*,[21] Nietzsche heaps scorn on this argument, remarking that, as a result, philosophers hate 'the idea of becoming.' They want to 'dehistoricize' existence, to render the world *sub specie aeterni* – from the viewpoint of eternity. (They want, in short, to see the Forms.) Their Parmenidean motto is: 'What is, does not *become*; what becomes, *is* not.' Such philosophers, therefore, 'believe, even to the point of despair, in that which is.' They cling desperately to the vision of an eternal, unchanging reality. But this is precisely the remote Truth that they can never discover, and 'since they cannot get hold of it, they look for reasons why it is being withheld from them.' Only the Presocratic philosopher Heraclitus – who argues that everything is in a constant process of change – is spared Nietzsche's condemnation. To the rest, who have placed their hope in the 'not-yet-science' that is logic and mathematics, Nietzsche's warning is blunt: 'In these, reality does not appear at all.' There is only the Heraclitian world of change, or 'becoming'; '*another* kind of reality is absolutely undemonstrable,' and to talk of one is 'pointless.' Plato's metaphysics and Kant's metaphysical division of reality into *noumena* and *phenomena* are, in this view, futile attempts to insulate the sublime (but non-existent) realm of the changeless from the mobile, creative beauty of art. They are ways of turning away from life. To be an artist or a poet is to abandon all thoughts of *noumena* and to place the highest value on appearance, on living, on *becoming*: it is to revel in what *manifestly* is. (Perhaps an appropriate Nietzschean motto would be: If you want to lie in your own bed then first you must make it.) What counts, therefore, is one's relation to life, one's *interests*. In this context, the French philosopher Gilles Deleuze points out the insistence of Nietzsche's question: Who looks at beauty in a disinterested way?[22] His answer, perhaps, is: only a philosopher.

In Nietzsche's view, the Platonic philosopher comes off worse than the Kantian. Besotted by metaphysics, he longs to abandon the world of 'becoming' – the world we inhabit – for the static and illusory 'Truth' of the Forms. (In Chapter 2 I put forward the opposite view, arguing that the Forms actually preserve 'becoming.' In this respect, perhaps Nietzsche's Plato was not particularly Platonist. Or perhaps Plato could always think against himself and refrain from giving in to his worst instincts.) The Platonic philosopher is drawn, as Socrates is in the *Phaedo*, by the Pythagorean image of the body as the prison house of the soul – a dreary image, it has to be said, in which life is worse than death, and one few of Socrates' contemporaries would accept. The Kantian philosopher is better simply because he keeps his gaze fixed on the world of experience and avoids dark speculation. Yet, he is not blameless, either, for even though he knows it, he nonetheless averts his eyes from the difficult truth that there is no Truth.

Nietzsche, thus, summarizes western philosophy as the 'history of an error' – the error of pursuing a remote metaphysical reality. Its progress can be traced in six steps that take us from Plato through Kant to Nietzsche himself, the first philosopher, in his humble opinion, to liberate himself from the error and to say aloud, cathartically, that that is what it is.[23] In the first of these steps the 'real world' – the Forms or Parmenides' Truth – can be attained only by the wise and virtuous. In the second step it is 'unattainable for the moment, but promised to the wise, the virtuous.' Here we have the track of Platonism and its inability to gain access to the Forms. (Philosophers, remember, are not sages.) With the third step, Platonism begins to recede: the 'real world' cannot even be promised; it is only a consolation. In the fourth step, the consolation turns into the Kantian unknown. In the fifth – which takes us into a post-Kantian space – the 'real world,' because it is unknown, has become useless and may as well be abolished. ('Plato blushes for shame; all free spirits run riot.') Then comes the sixth step, when Nietzsche vaults onto the philosophical stage and abolishes the last trace of such a world.

With the fifth step – the abolition of metaphysics – nihilism, which for Nietzsche is both the death of one's values and an opportunity to create new values, has overtaken philosophy and European culture. There then begins, in the sixth step, the journey of the Zoroastrian poet, Zarathustra, to the mountaintops of the east, away from dead and deadening European cities.[24] In his travels, Zarathustra learns what the Platonists have yet to learn: that metaphysical worlds with their grand truths are illusions, and sometimes they are lies. Even if they were not, even if they really existed, they would be 'even more useless than knowledge of the chemical composition of water is to a sailor in danger of shipwreck.'[25] For, as we know, when the Platonic philosopher has completed his journey he is, if human, marooned in the sunworld, and if *daimonic*, no longer at home in the cave. Quite literally, at the end of his journey the philosopher has no place to be, except when he takes on the monstrous incarnation of the politician – who has nothing true to tell the rest of us, nothing to unveil, but much to conceal. Truth is an eternally hidden god, too remote to be of interest to us.

Textual Poetry

The Nietzschean theme that reality is not to be discovered but created or moulded out of the contingency of life, that reality emerges from a subjective act of *poiesis*, which is to say from an act of human will, resonates through some important branches of twentieth-century philosophy. One catches echoes of it everywhere – for example, and most famously perhaps, in the dictum of the French existentialist philosopher Jean-Paul Sartre that 'existence comes before essence.'[26] With this assertion, Sartre rejects Platonic essences; indeed, with it he rejects any essentialist doctrine, because they all posit metaphysical entities that pre-exist our lives and make them what they are. In Sartre's account, no divine plans, no teleological[27] structures shape our lives. We erupt into being out of nothingness and move through the world as egocentric poets rather than detached philosopher-kings. An essence, if it is anything, is simply the summation of a life, something present at the end rather than the beginning.

In the next generation of French philosophers, Michel Foucault also made extensive use of Nietzschean concepts in order to produce his own strain of anti-metaphysical thought. One such concept is 'genealogy,' which is essentially a way of doing history without recourse to essences or any of the other paraphernalia of metaphysics. Foucault's genealogist discovers in the past, 'not a timeless and essential secret, but the secret that [things] have no essence.'[28] He discovers a world that is discontinuous and contingent, which unfolds according to no plan and reveals no 'ultimate reality.' The genealogist thus stresses the primacy of contingency over a transcendental coherence and accordingly rejects any notion of a metaphysical 'presence' that would insert necessary meaning – necessity of any sort – into human existence. If there is a story line, it is – like evolution – accidental and available only to hindsight. Unlike Hegel, the Nietzschean genealogist does not think that the wisdom of hindsight – the spreading of the Owl of Minerva's wings at sunset – reveals the truth of necessity. It tells us only what has happened and cannot be undone.

A second important idea, one that begins in 'genealogy' but that is also linked to Nietzsche's poeticism, is Foucault's treatment of 'interpretation.' It introduces another dimension into the problem of the meaning of life, one we glanced at in Chapter 1[29] but to which we need to give more consideration here. In essence, the concept of interpretation nudges our focus away from the 'world' and towards the books that explain the world, inducing us to consider how these 'texts' in which we encase our ideas stand in relation both to us and to 'reality.' (This is not a bad thing for a group of people who spend so much of their lives reading.) In the course of this consideration, the 'world' – the reality that Plato so assiduously sought – begins to disappear across a distant horizon.

The first thing to note is a certain vagueness in the word. 'Interpretation' can suggest a fairly free, or subjective, rendering of something (as in a dramatic or musical performance: an interpretation of *Hamlet* or a Bach cantata) or a stricter, and one hopes more objective explanation – as in the interpretation of a non-literary text. In the latter case, unlike the former, an 'appearance and reality' structure is in play. When we read a text, the 'real' meaning has to be ferreted out, discovered behind or between the lines or some such thing. We seem naturally to enter the terrain of hermeneutics – the art or science of interpretation, which, for example, Heidegger invokes in his readings of the ancient texts. Those readings are, to use a Foucauldian term, virtually 'archaeological' attempts to excavate a meaning that lurked somewhere beneath the surface of the text. At one stage of his career, Foucault attempted the same sort of textual analysis, but he abandoned it in favour of the view that there is a metaphysical illusion at work in hermeneutics, because texts are not signposts pointing the way to reality. Nor are they apparitional enigmas to be solved. On the contrary, texts stand between us and any reality we might want to assume is out there, firmly barring our way; so firmly, in fact, that they don't even manage to reveal their own version of that reality. For neo-Nietzschean philosophers such as the later Foucault and Derrida, texts are like great labyrinths we can never quite find our way through. They contain no single, necessary meaning; to interpret one is at best to give a particular reading of it, as an actor might do with a part or a musician with a piece of music. But this means that interpretation is so open-ended that hermeneutics is fundamentally impossible. There is no essence left for the interpreter to get at, although – and this is sometimes ignored in commentaries on philosophers such as Derrida – there is a world (or a play or a song) that is the object of our attention. There is something there, and it is by no means amorphous. The world exists and the text exists, but they lack precise instructions about what we ought to say about them.

This is another version of Plato's quarrel between philosophy and poetry, in which one is asked to choose between discovering the world and making it. Metaphysics – the truth-discovering mode in which we pursue 'ultimate reality' – generates a hermeneutics that seeks a single, correct reading of a text. (This, by the way, would seem to be precisely the understanding students want when they ask: 'What does this mean?') The anti-metaphysical – truth-making – philosopher sets his gaze in the opposite direction, giving free rein to the poetic mode of interpretation, because the apparently oxymoronic notion of a 'correct interpretation' has been abolished. It is worth reproducing here the Foucauldian passage that I cited in Chapter 1: 'If interpretation is a never-ending task, it is simply because there is nothing to interpret. There is absolutely nothing primary to interpret because, when all is said and done, underneath it all everything is already interpretation.'[30]

Foucault is attacking the idea that there is a ghostly metaphysical presence – a 'true' meaning – in a text that the philosopher must 'get at' or bring out into the clear light of day. (It is like assuming that there is one correct way to play Hamlet.) The reason that there is nothing to get at is because the act of interpretation can never get beyond itself. To paraphrase Sartre, all interpretations are without hope because no salvation awaits them; there is no Last (and absolute) Judgment to determine their truth. Either a meaningless text is embedded in a meaningless world *or* a text with a plethora of meanings is embedded in a world with a plethora of meanings. You can take your choice, but in either case an indeterminate text stands between the reader and an equally indeterminate world. Neither gives any necessary shape to the other.

To all this, the metaphysical philosopher might respond, a little archly, by asking what except some kind of 'true' or 'settled' meaning can put an end to interpretation. What but that will allow one to choose from among an apparently endless range of 'possible' interpretations? How else than by reference to truth or to the author's intention – to *something* that stands still – can one sort out the 'good' interpretations from the 'bad'? How, otherwise, can one even get started? A practical if not overly metaphysical philosopher might well advise us to look to the author, to ask what she meant, to let her be *a*, if not *the*, standard for interpretation. This is sound advice perhaps (which is to say that I have always liked it), but for the committed anti-metaphysician there are two problems with it. First, in most cases the author is no longer with us, and even if she is it is unlikely that she is right there in the room as we read! All we have is the text, although, it must be admitted, sometimes we also have access to what the author said about the text. Second, and more important, neo-Nietzschean critics of metaphysics – this is certainly true of Foucault – accord very little status to the author anyway. Their position comes to something like this: You cannot ask the author what she meant, and even if you could we wouldn't listen to what she had to say. Her view enjoys no automatic privilege over any other view. To use some ontological language, a text is what it is and what it is, is – well, a text. Once written, a text is independent of its author and her intentions, assuming *they* could ever be fully sorted out. In some sense it always was, even in the act of creation. Texts can be read but not – or not 'really' – interrogated as to authorial meaning. Texts can be interpreted so long as we understand that interpretation depends on the interpreter (who, remember, is the only person present at the reading) as much as on the text. And, to paraphrase my mother, God knows where the interpreter has been. There is a slightly Kantian looking lesson here: reading a book is a subjective exercise, an act of creation that has nothing to do with the discovery of a noumenal 'reality.'

Richard Rorty has expressed the subjective and contingent nature of interpretation as follows: 'Reading texts is a matter of reading them in the light of other texts, people, obsessions, bits of information, or what have you, and then seeing what happens.'[31] This view, that in reading one is not so much allowing a text to be imposed upon oneself as imposing oneself on a text, is interesting and well worth thinking about. It may, for example, come to me as a great revelation, one that shapes my 'understanding' of text A, that it reminds me of certain themes in text B. But what if I had not read text B? My reading of text A would obviously have been different in this one respect at least. Would it have been wrong? Less good? Less complete? How are we to say? If we think it would be 'less good' or 'less complete,' how are we to establish the complete – the essential – list of background texts necessary to the 'correct' reading of the text in question? Maybe it is simply a case of 'the more background information the better,' but that seems odd because surely lots of stuff is just irrelevant. We need to know what is relevant and, indeed, what is essential.

When as an eighteen-year-old I first read the parts of Nietzsche's *Twilight of the Idols* I was quoting from just now, I was absolutely unaware of Kant and other philosophers he (obviously?) had in mind. We might all agree that this lack of information affected my 'interpretation' of Nietzsche, just as other bits of information I did have probably contributed – for better or worse? – to it. Some years later, I saw a performance of Tom Stoppard's *Rosencrantz and Guildenstern Are Dead*. While I was certainly aware of its origins in Shakespeare's *Hamlet* (that would have been hard to miss!), I was unaware of its debts to Samuel Beckett – a 'fact' of which someone older and better read kindly informed me. This new awareness, coupled with a quick consultation of Beckett's writings, altered my reading of the play. But was I – am I? – with each new bit of information, each new possibility, each new awareness of the echo of another voice, approaching nearer to *the* understanding of this, or any other, text? (I may well be approaching nearer to the standard philosophical or literary understanding of the text, but that does not resolve the issue.) Is there a complete picture and, therefore, perhaps a complete background that I need to have in order to read texts correctly?

Someone might stubbornly reiterate that if I knew what the author was thinking when he wrote it, and exactly who had influenced him, I would at least have a complete picture of what the author meant. This returns us to the issue of the author's intentions. However, it is surely a common enough idea that a text, especially one as old and as complex as, say, *Hamlet*, may have resonances and possibilities that extend well beyond the author's intentions. (Another way to put this is that if Shakespeare were alive today *he* would read *Hamlet* differently, especially if he had read Freud. For his part, Plato has Socrates complain in the *Apology* that poets generally have no idea *what* they mean.) The text outlasts the author, and the author cannot contain it. Nor is the idea that the only relevant influences are those that the author consciously recognizes incontestable, certainly not in a post-Freudian age where the concept of the unconscious is almost second nature to us. Most of us are quite willing to accept that writing and reading are not fully self-controlled, self-conscious activities. An author's labour, like a reader's, depends on a lot of contingent circumstances, including an apparently endless supply of 'influential' references and quotations, often only half-remembered or half-admitted. (Freud, for example, often seems to be influenced by Nietzsche, but he never admitted as much.) In a neo-Nietzschean formulation, there is, therefore, no one reading of a text – not even the author's – that transcends all others by being, in some final sense, 'true.' There are simply readings; the subjective and particular acts of the reader.

Put it this way: according to the neo-Nietzschean view, things do not have names or essences that we must discover; things are entities *that we create by naming*. This being the case, we must take care not to fall under the sway of an obsession with discovering an illusory true meaning in texts.[32] If we take such care, my neo-Nietzschean adviser would add, we may finally be able to free ourselves from the grip of Platonic and Kantian metaphysics. By relinquishing the dream of absolute meaning in a text, or by banishing it to the great and inaccessible beyond, we may be able to relinquish as well the dream of absolute meaning – of an 'ultimate reality' – in the world, which is to say, we may rid ourselves of the illusion that led to the misguided and obsessive reading in the first place.

Anti-logos

The point of the argument I have been running is this: To understand the nature of our obsession with discovering the meaning of a text is to begin to understand the spell of metaphysics itself. Jacques Derrida has frequently turned his attention to the question, linking the obsession with 'correct' reading to the 'transcendental motif' of 'philosophy as science'[33] – as something that produces 'real' knowledge. Derrida's response is not to treat texts as if they are devoid of structure or intention – he is often accused of this – but to approach them as diffuse, incomplete, and contradictory even on their own terms, marked by (a clumsy term) 'undecidability.' What Derrida argues, more strongly than Foucault, is that there are no *decisive* elements in a text. To take a limited example, in a well-known commentary on Plato's *Phaedrus*,[34] Derrida focuses his readers' attention on the term *pharmakon*, which Socrates uses to describe writing (in the course of relating yet another myth). Derrida points out that the word can equally well connote 'remedy' and 'poison' and that the text provides no way of deciding which it ought to be. Hence, Socrates can, with equal plausibility, be understood to be arguing both that writing is a remedy for the weakness of human memory – that it is, as he says, a form of *hypomnesis*, of 'deep memory' that will allow us to recollect (literally to 're-collect') what has been said and done – and that writing is something that poisons memory and thought, in which case *hypomnesis* could be translated as 'forgetfulness' or 'buried memory.' (Writing this on my computer, it is impossible not to be struck by the point: These machines preserve so much, but often at the cost of our own memory. They really are simultaneously cure and poison, memory enhanced and memory lost.) As Derrida tracks the argument, he plays these meanings off against one another, arguing that each is plausible and imbedded in the text and in the other meaning in such a way that neither can be discarded nor can either dominate one's reading. Like the paradoxes I shall discuss in Chapter 5, contradictory meanings – the scandal of metaphysics – simultaneously inhabit the word *pharmakon*.

We can dub this kind of reading 'anti-*logos*,' for it introduces a new and radical instability into the text by insisting on the co-presence of what are apparently mutually incompatible meanings. To the assertion that we cannot choose from among various readings of a text, Derrida has added the idea that we cannot even fully distinguish these readings one from the other. We can never get to the point where a choice could be made. This is a sceptical reading of reading that *thoroughly* discounts the possibility of finding a true reading of a text, a straightforward and correct one that does not offend the defenders of *logos*. No such thing awaits even the most attentive reader's discovery, because no text can be 'closed' with respect to what it says. And philosophers, like all readers, have access only to the text and its generous supply of multiple, intertwined, and contradictory readings.

The great Argentinean writer, Jorge Luis Borges, has written: 'Works of fiction contain a single plot, with all its imaginable permutations. Those of a philosophical nature invariably include both the thesis and the antithesis, the rigorous pro and con of a doctrine. A book that does not contain its counterbook is considered incomplete.'[35]

The concepts of thesis and antithesis are most often associated with Hegel, who argues that every idea contained the antithetical seeds of its own destruction. The result of this thesis-antithesis struggle is a synthesis of the warring ideas accommodated to one another. Every synthesis is, of course, a new thesis, and so the process continues until it reaches its culmination in a final Truth. In leaving the synthesis out of his account, Borges makes a philosophy book a war without end. I think Derrida has also done something like this – intertwined book and counterbook so thoroughly that they cannot be read separately or sequentially or in any way securely accommodated to one another. Nor can either of them be done away with. Derrida uses Hegel, but he will not let Hegel – the last great proponent of Enlightenment reason – rest. He will not let him proceed to the Truth that he was certain awaits us at the end of history. To look for this Truth, a single meaning or 'presence' in or behind or beyond a text, is as futile as asking what happened to Scarlett O'Hara after the American Civil War. (But of course someone – a romantic Hegelian, I imagine – did just that.) 'Logical' readings that sort out 'problems,' resolve contradictions, and choose between 'possible interpretations' of a text – and which, therefore, look beyond the text to the world – are misreadings. In ending the war of interpretations, they actually do violence to the text.

The reader is now in a position to see that the anti-metaphysical argument also rejects the primacy of the logic that underpins metaphysics. The fundamental logical law of non-contradiction limits choices (we can accept one or the other of two contradictory readings, but not both), and the ensuing logical discourse draws out the inferences of the choice. By contrast, the anti-metaphysics of the new sceptic is founded on the contention that rhetoric, the art of 'persuasive discourse,' is prior to logic. In Foucault's terms (and Plato's), rhetoric is about power before it is about truth. Because of this, rhetoric requires freedom from logic. So, rhetoric lives by rejecting the law of non-contradiction as a necessary or fundamental law of language. Rhetoric embraces, instead, the possibility of the free movement of a word – such as 'pharmakon' – between contradictory meanings, such as 'poison' and 'cure.' The result of this easy entanglement of contradictory readings is a multitude of inferences that can be made about a text based on a multitude of interpretative strategies. If he so wishes, the rhetorician can grant priority to one of these strategies, including the limiting strategy of logical discourse and its law of non-contradiction. He can, in short, insist on choosing logic as his ground, but he does not have to do so. I cannot emphasize too strongly that priority is the issue here. For the metaphysical philosopher, logic is foundational, ontologically prior to language and thought. One might as well object to the law of gravity as to the law of non-contradiction, which, by rendering certain readings incompatible with others, *forces* us to choose between them – which is to say, forces us along the path of Meaning and Truth. But, since for the anti-metaphysician rhetoric (we could call it 'poetry') is prior to logic, logic is just one among many linguistic strategies, and metaphysics poisons philosophy by seducing its practitioners into believing otherwise. The myth of the priority of *logos* is the great rhetorical victory of metaphysical philosophers. The concern I expressed over why one would ever begin the journey out of Plato's cave must once again be faced: What reason, the new sceptic asks, is there to be rational? Surely, it has something to do with somebody's power over others.

We now find ourselves, in a manner reminiscent of Plato's indictment of the artists, three sceptical steps removed from the metaphysical reality of the Forms. The first step back was taken by Nietzsche, when he insisted that there is only existence as opposed to essence, the second when, as a corollary of this, he and his followers insisted that there could be no single correct interpretation of existence. (After all, an essence is the gold standard of correctness.) The third step was taken by philosophers such as Foucault, Rorty, and Derrida, who, in their different ways, often seem to be arguing that since we cannot settle the question of what a given text is saying *we cannot even get to the point of interpretation*. In short, we can never get through a text to a world, or even a vision of a world, on the other side of it. (This gives new meaning to the lament: 'I can never get through my reading.') For one who accepts this line of thought, the choices may seem Hobson-like, for what remains to the philosopher are the options of silence, storytelling, or elegant babble. The last of these is the word play that comes either from trying to say the unsayable or from the refusal to stop speaking in the face of it. It, like the other two choices, would seem to entail the end of philosophy. So, the only choice, on this account, is, as Derrida has hinted, how philosophy will die.

Dogmatic Responses

Many philosophers will understandably balk at the extremity of these choices. They may feel constrained to raise an objection one more time. Surely, they may say, since there is reading, and since those I have described as new sceptics are hardly direct realists when it comes to reading (the meaning, whatever it is or is not, is not immediately obvious and not even obviously there), there must *at least* be interpretation, and if there is, how can there no limit to it? For the pragmatic Rorty, the answer would appear to be that philosophy is best described as telling certain kinds of stories that seem appropriate to the teller, that express his point of view. And no, he would add, there is no discernible limit to this activity. Rorty's work constitutes a fairly enthusiastic rejection of the metaphysical realist's assertion that 'inquiry is a matter of finding out the nature of something which lies outside the web of beliefs and desires.'[36] (Here, again, is the first step away from the 'objectivity' of metaphysics towards a Nietzschean concept of 'interest.') If philosophers have long deluded themselves in thinking that they are engaged in trying to get at the truth, Rorty seeks to cure this delusion by returning them, in the spirit of Nietzsche, from *logos* – the privileged space where reason reveals truth – to the *mythos* they sought by this means to escape. Philosophy is fundamentally a form of literature. Philosophy is about telling stories, spinning out metaphors for the way we find things to be, commenting on them, and from time to time, replacing those we dislike, or which seem worn out, with newer stories, newer metaphors better suited to the needs of the age. Rorty is a philosopher, but his muse is less Plato (despite *his* talent for telling stories) than Homer.[37] Rorty resolves Plato's quarrel between philosophy and poetry by surrendering – more wholeheartedly than Nietzsche – to poetry. (This is both the second and the third step, since philosophy is now interpretation, and interpretation, being contingent upon the circumstances of the interpreter, is so open-ended as to disappear.)

This may sound like a parody of a philosophical position. Thus, I must take care to point out that I do not think it is, and I do not mean to dismiss Rorty's position lightly or, indeed, at all. I find it both invigorating and vertiginous. It is founded upon what I think is a healthy respect for existence over essence, for a contingent, happenstance view of life over a large-scale rationalist perspective that has swallowed more than one philosopher whole. Iris Murdoch, who did not have anything like the neo-Nietzschean's negative view of metaphysics, nonetheless wrote, 'What makes metaphysics and coherence theories unacceptable is the way in which they in effect "disappear" what is individual and contingent by equating reality with integration in the system, and degrees of reality with degrees of integration, and by implying that "ultimately" or "really" there is only one system.'[38] This is a good and serious warning that Rorty seems to have taken to heart and then imbued with a considerable amount of hyperbole. If I am not fully convinced by his arguments, I suppose it is because of the hyperbole. This, I think, is the ground upon which a philosopher could mount a dogmatic defence of philosophy. Surely, even literature – *poiesis* – needs to be interrogated as to its limits. Surely, it is not possible to say just *anything*.

In this context, the Italian philosopher, semioticist, and novelist Umberto Eco has noted a similarity between the extremity of certain modern writers (such as Rorty and Derrida?) and that of the ancient Hermetics. He observes that for both groups a text is 'an open-ended universe where the interpreter can discover infinite interconnections.'[39] There is no end to interpretation because, as I have already pointed out, there is no end to the labyrinth of language.[40] But, says Eco, taking the role of a moderate dogmatic philosopher, one has to wonder. After all, interpretation has to interpret *something* (even the sceptics admit that!), and that something must set some kind of limits to what can be said. To shift the idea somewhat, philosophers must *talk* and *write* about something and – to paraphrase Parmenides – that something must be *something* or else we could not talk about it. Perhaps, as the German philosopher Jürgen Habermas has suggested,[41] there must be 'idealizations' of meaning derived from common sense or from some sort of Kantian regulation of ideas – interpretation guidelines that we can agree on – that anchor a text and that, if they do not effect closure of it, at least limit its openness. If so, then, as Eco suggests, we should at least be able to say which interpretations of a text are bad ones.[42] In short, the openness of Derrida's position beggars imagination.

The new sceptic will reply that if we can make even these moderate judgments, the metaphysics of 'origin' reappears, or threatens to, for there must be some ground for the guidelines that allow us to distinguish between 'good' and 'bad' interpretations. If not, then the interpretations are arbitrary with respect to truth, and so are all the interpretations that follow. We have not solved the problem of meaning; we have simply contained it. That is, I think, why philosophers such as Derrida and Rorty and to a certain extent Foucault tend to set up shop beyond interpretation and its companion, the metaphysical ghost of interpretable meaning – which is to say, beyond even the ghost of the idea of an original or absolute truth. Interpretation is a responsibility they do not seem to want to bear, that they seem to feel no one can reasonably bear, because it always dissolves into an arbitrary containment of ideas. Thus, Rorty's strategy is to mute interpretation with irony, ironists being people who realize 'that anything can be made to look good or bad by being redescribed.'[43] (They know about spin-doctors, in other words.) For his part, Derrida often seems to fit Alexander Nehamas's Kierkegaardian-inspired description of ironists as people who 'are unwilling to accept full responsibility for what they say [Derrida might add that this is because we cannot fully control what we say], but ... equally unwilling to deny it explicitly.' This, Nehamas says, is the 'essential uncertainty' of irony.[44] And, I would add, this essential uncertainty makes it a favourite weapon of the new sceptics, although one which may also turn into their greatest weakness. New sceptics are ironical because while they, like everyone else, are unable to eradicate the implication of truth from what they say and write, neither are they able to believe in it. As a redundancy theorist of truth would tell us, all of our ideas bear the implicit tag, 'This is true' – that is just part of the message when we say something. But the new sceptic appends a second tag that reads, 'this is not true.' This is the paradoxical instability that neo-Nietzschean philosophers accept as their lot. It is their contention that we all have to accept this paradox. Accepting it makes them fit companions for a humble and questioning Socrates, but it forever bars them (and us, if they are – ironically – correct) from the glory of Plato's sun.

I have no intention of trying to resolve this debate as if I were the proper arbiter of philosophical quarrels – although in Chapter 7 we shall see how Wittgenstein attempts to do so. For now, suffice it to say that the intention of the new sceptics is, at least in part, therapeutic. The new sceptics are trying to cure other philosophers of what they see as the delusional notion that there is an ultimate reality or absolute meaning against which their words can be measured. To quarantine themselves against this 'delusion,' the new sceptics have retreated a safe three steps back from the pseudo-reality that Christopher Norris has described as a philosophical space 'where meaning and truth are assumed to coincide in a self-sufficient state of original linguistic grace.'[45] The new sceptics have chosen to live within the dense forests of language – of the text-without-end – where they can, and perhaps will, speak forever without speaking the Truth or settling the question of meaning.

This seems an extreme choice – an almost complete abdication of the search for meaning and truth. Perhaps, in closing, I can moderate it a little by noting a simple but often unappreciated fact, one that will be the focus of Chapter 7: philosophers speak and write about *ideas*. In a fundamental sense, they live within language. To borrow from the linguistic theory of Ferdinand de Saussure,[46] we can refer to the terms (or words) philosophers use to designate ideas ('justice,' for example) as 'signifiers' and the ideas themselves – what the philosophers are talking about – as 'signifieds.' Plato essentially assumed that for every signifier there is a proper signified, that there is, so to speak, a linguistic marriage, between word and entity, made in heaven. If not, we are in danger of talking about nothing, or worse, about everything at once. To talk, Platonically, about *something*, to connect signifiers to their natural signifieds, is to be in precisely a 'self-sufficient state of … linguistic grace.' In essence, to talk about something is to make language reach out to the world – or in Plato's case, the world of Forms.

This is, of course, the very thing a neo-Nietzschean will deny can ever occur. For philosophers such as Derrida and Rorty, there are no absolute philosophical signifieds, no Forms or coherent sets of ideas that philosophers are talking about when they use words like 'justice.' Very simply, ideas are not things: they never get outside language. The word 'chair' is a signifier for an actual chair – something in the world – and that works quite well. If someone asks me what the word 'chair' means I can (setting aside all metaphysical concerns) respond by pointing to a chair, to the *thing* 'out there' in the world. I can give an *ostensive* definition. That is very reassuring. Plato, ever the realist, applies the same model to abstract terms. He assumes that words like 'justice' or 'goodness' are signifiers for Forms – of Justice or Goodness – and that these Forms exist independently, every bit as much as we assume chairs do. In a sense, Plato assumes that they are thing-like. I do not know whether anyone believes that any more – not when I put the matter as I just have anyway – but the idea nonetheless retains an appeal that is etched in the way we speak. What I mean is that many people still think of certain terms as necessarily linked to certain ideas: They may be quite willing, for example, to insist that the term 'justice' means *something*, that it is the *name* for something. Otherwise, how is it possible to accuse others of misunderstanding the word or of using it incorrectly? What our neo-Nietzschean wants to do is remind the reader that philosophical terms cannot be anchored in this way – that they do not *point* to something in the world. Nor, moreover, do philosophical terms necessarily point to a specific package of 'other words' within language. Signifiers bounce around in the great labyrinth of language, where there are so many possible connections to signifieds (i.e., to ideas, variously expressed) that a particular signifier-signified relation can never be securely fixed. Without the support of the world – without a chair to point to[47] – no one rendering of a term is necessarily privileged over all the others. 'Justice' is an idea. Since ideas are expressed in words, and then referred for meaning or clarification to other words, all we have are words referring to more words. Exactly which words other words ought to refer to is, without an outside or 'worldly' point of reference, ultimately 'undecidable.' A reader may want to object that language is not as unstable as *all that*, and if so I have a great deal of sympathy with that reader. Yet I would also suggest that neither is language, perhaps, as stable as Plato hopes it is (and fears is not).

In summary, the new sceptic has arrived at a twofold conclusion. First, one can never 'really' say *what* ideas the terms – the words in a text – refer to. Second, one cannot claim that the ideas, if ever we could nail them down, refer to a reality beyond themselves. In their anxiety to approach 'ultimate reality,' metaphysicians ignore these two conclusions, but they do so at their peril. Those who accept these conclusions will realize that philosophers can no longer go on believing in progress towards a final version of philosophy (Rorty calls it the Final Vocabulary; in Chapter 1, I called it the Full and Final Discourse), one that, at the end of a very long philosophical day, will describe 'ultimate reality' for us, or solve all our philosophical problems. They must kick away Wittgenstein's ladder and stop looking for what is not there. Having done so they can turn their minds to science or literature or the therapeutic activity of trying to prevent philosophers from becoming too philosophical.

In her final response, the defender of metaphysics (and logic) – in a sense, anyone who stills thinks it worthwhile to talk about 'reality' – might fall back on tradition, pointing out that to turn one's back on metaphysics and, indeed, philosophy with nothing but silence or stories or elegant babble to put in its place does not a seem particularly useful thing to do. To dissolve the boundaries between philosophy and literature is as senseless as the desire of some modern philosophers – logical positivists, Comtean positivists, and Marxists, for example – to remove the borders between philosophy and science. Both desires run counter to the normal divisions of western thought – ones that, *pace* the new sceptics, we do fundamentally understand – and to the logical thrust of our rationalist intellectual traditions. They undermine the substantial and still workable intellectual foundations of western civilisation, the ones that are responsible for so much of what we know and do. It's a kind of suicide and to what end? Isn't Kant, if not Plato, right? Do we not need some metaphysical framework for our thought? Is our belief in the power of reason no more than a centuries-old cloud of unknowing? 'No,' I can imagine Nietzsche saying, 'no more than that.' But are *we* convinced? I'm not sure I am.

Concluding Thoughts

The debate about metaphysics is a good entry into the debate about the history – or genealogy – of philosophy and of coming to understand the import of the question with which I began this book: what, if anything, is philosophy? It helps to understand the discomfort contemporary philosophers often feel as they contemplate an uncertain position between literature and science. The central theme of this chapter has been the Nietzschean return to poetry. It needs to be pointed out, however, that there are other philosophers who have favoured co-habiting with science, instead. I shall speak more of them in the next chapter and in Chapter 7, but it is worth making brief mention here of the Logical Positivists, and in particular of the Vienna Circle, which flourished in the 1920s and 1930s. One of their leaders, Rudolf Carnap, encapsulates the attitude of the circle when he pronounces metaphysical statements to be 'entirely meaningless.'[48] Such statements, he explains, have content, but not 'theoretical' content. They do not, in other words, tell us what reality must be like. On the contrary, they are only subjective statements that 'serve for the expression of the general attitude of a person toward life.' Carnap suggests that this is because metaphysics is grounded in mythology and has never outgrown it. At best, it is a 'substitute for theology,' a halfway house between religion and science. In a strange, inverted echo of Nietzsche, Carnap suggests that metaphysical issues are better left to the artists, and philosophy, cleansed of metaphysics, can become a branch of science.

I think that the good news here is that so long as philosophy can survive in the somewhat uncertain and claustrophobic space between science and literature, it can take an interest in, enrich, and be enriched by, both kinds of pursuit. There is no reason why philosophers cannot remain free to approach all the Big Questions, even if these are no longer seen as metaphysical questions, or as open to metaphysical solutions.[49] (Of course, that's open to debate!) An optimist such as myself may even feel encouraged by the very precariousness of the philosophers' position, since it indicates how much we have to consider and to debate, which means that, for a while longer anyway, philosophy will go on. Perhaps, like the tightrope walker in Nietzsche's *Thus Spoke Zarathustra*, philosophy could not survive on safer terrain, even if it has to perish to be where it is.[50]

4

Epistemology:
The Ghost in the Metaphysical
Machine?

SUMMARY

After a brief outline of the origins of epistemology in ancient Greece, we focus on a comparison of two major modern approaches: foundationalism and naturalism. We see how Kant functions as a kind of transition point from the former to the latter; how naturalism fits with the sceptical reaction to metaphysics; and how that outlook affects such issues as the problem of relativism and uncertainty over the nature of truth. We shall also see how naturalism has affected science. There are short addenda on ancient epistemology and the philosophy of mind.

Beginnings

As I prepare to move this tour of the philosophical terrain from the quicksands of metaphysics to what I hope will be the more solid ground of epistemology – the theory of knowledge – I am brought up short by the Canadian philosopher Charles Taylor's somewhat dour comment that 'epistemology, once the pride of modern philosophy, seems in a bad way these days.'[1] I think, 'Oh no, here we go again, here is yet another central concern of philosophy riven by discord.' And, indeed, it is. How could I have forgotten? Epistemology is also uncertain ground. The uncertainty concerns not just methods of procedure – ways of 'getting' knowledge – but fundamental questions about what knowledge is, in what sense it is attainable and even, at the end of the day, whether a theory of knowledge, if indeed such a thing can still be said to exist, is a very important part of philosophy at all. (A character in

American author Richard Russo's novel *Nobody's Fool* comments that it seemed to be the goal of his philosophy teacher to make the world disappear bit by bit. Of late, philosophers are apparently doing this to philosophy.) There is suspicion in some quarters that as with metaphysics, so with epistemology: What once was a source of pride is now embarrassment. Insofar as metaphysics – including ontology – and epistemology have strong links, this should not be surprising. After all, one's version of reality will bear heavily on what one can claim to know and how one can know it. Hence, any change in a philosopher's metaphysics will produce significant eddies in his epistemology. Many of the issues swirling through contemporary epistemology, therefore, have their headwaters in the metaphysical ones set out in Chapters 2 and 3. As you may have guessed, chief among them is scepticism over whether there are any 'absolutes' to be known and whether, if there are not, we can continue speak 'dogmatically' of knowledge – as I did above – as *something* we can 'get' by employing some fundamental procedure.

The close proximity between the two branches of philosophy – the fact that when a metaphysician sneezes an epistemologist catches cold – is historical as well as structural. Epistemology is one of the oldest offshoots of the metaphysical branch, born of its ancient distinction between 'appearance' and 'reality.' I am not claiming that philosophers invented the idea of 'knowledge': Concepts of knowledge obviously predate philosophy. Like all language-using beings, Homer's ancient characters certainly possess them. The men, women, and gods of the *Iliad* and *Odyssey* are well aware of the difference between believing something to be true and knowing it to be so. The gods can, for example, deceive the humans, and the humans know this all too well. What the philosophers invented was epistemology – a *theory* of knowledge.

Since the theory of knowledge grows quite naturally out of the intellectual soil of ancient Greece it is difficult to assign it an exact origin, but perhaps pride of place should go to the Presocratic philosopher, Xenophanes of Colophon. He can be credited with turning the commonplace distinction between the way things are and the way they appear to be into an epistemological one by adopting, quite self-consciously, a stance that was more *generally* sceptical than anything to be found in pre-philosophical literature.[2] Homer's characters may doubt particular claims about particular things ('How do I know he's telling the truth?'), but they are not sceptical about – they do not worry over – their grasp of the general structure of the cosmos. They accept that it is as they have been taught it is. If there are mysteries – and there are – the proper reaction is to tremble respectfully before them. In general, though, the outlines of the cosmos are clear to them, or at any rate as clear as they can be to mortals. They have, we might say, no self-consciously metaphysical point of view. By contrast, Xenophanes' incipient scepticism sweeps across the whole of the cosmos, the offspring of a deep metaphysical uncertainty about whether humans have any immediate access to 'reality.' *Knowledge* belongs, in the first instance, only to God (Xenophanes was a monotheist), whereas the lesser certainty of *belief* or *opinion* more properly describes the human condition. In other words, epistemology, like metaphysics itself, grows from a rejection of an insouciant direct realism – that is, a rejection of the conviction that appearance and reality are one. For Xenophanes, knowledge is not ready to hand but veiled, something to be ferreted, so far as it is possible to do this, out of appearances. Often this means distinguishing reality from anthropomorphic projections, ideas of gods and spirits and the like, things that are prototypes for Plato's shadows. Xenophanes' term for what I have called 'belief' or 'opinion' is *doxa*. In the last chapter I noted Plato's use of the word *doxa*, but Xenophanes is perhaps the first to employ it as an epistemological concept. *Doxa* is rooted in the verb *dokeo* _which can mean to think or to suppose or even to imagine. What those in pursuit of knowledge (note that a metaphor of hunting or discovery seems naturally to emerge here) have to do is investigate this *doxa*, examine what *seems to be*, and try to validate or falsify it in the context of experience. If they do so properly, they may arrive at the condition called knowledge.

Thus it is that, in the words of one commentator, 'after Xenophanes, the problem of human knowledge was on the agenda of philosophy.'[3] We must not slide too quickly over the word 'problem,' because that is very much the point. If attaining knowledge were not a problem, if it were not hidden and difficult – yet possible – to uncover, there would be no epistemology. As Karl Marx once put the matter, if appearance and reality coincided – if direct realism was always true – there would be no need for science: in Greek, no need for *episteme*.

It is important to emphasize that the epistemology that grew from these Xenophanean origins is *reflexive*, as well as *general*. The epistemologist seeks not particular bits of knowledge – how to build a house or remove an appendix – but knowledge of what knowledge is, of how to recognize it, and how to go about attaining it. Rooted in a profound respect for the possibility of error, which just is to say in the sceptical premise that the way the world appears to humans is not necessarily the way it 'really' is, and in the equally strong and dogmatic belief (unless we are very rigid Kantians) that we can learn to see behind at least some of these 'appearances,' epistemology reflects the indirect realism of its metaphysical parent. Not all ancient schools of thought accepted this distinction, of course. Some insisted that there was no line to be drawn between *doxa* and *episteme*, their idea being, roughly, that what you see is what you get. Nonetheless, after Xenophanes epistemology was, and has remained, a fundamental part of philosophy, a large branch on the great tree grafted off the even stouter branch of metaphysics. In fact (I have to let go of the arboreal metaphor here) modernity has perhaps reversed the order of priority between these two great philosophical concerns. In the modern philosophy we usually date from Descartes, epistemology has tended to take precedence over metaphysics and to become, as Descartes terms it, the 'first philosophy.'

Contemporary metaphysics is hardly encompassed or exhausted by the theme of appearance and reality. Therefore, I had better generalize the connection between metaphysics and epistemology by underlining something else – a piece of common sense, really – that I noted in the first paragraph above: One's metaphysical postulates (or lack of them) concerning the nature of reality are fundamental to one's epistemology, insofar as any approach to knowledge is crucially determined by the sense of what there is to know. Very roughly, the more there is to know, the higher the status of epistemology. I say 'roughly' because it is necessary to ask, as well, how *available* knowledge is – how accessible 'reality' is. The status of epistemology will grow with the 'hiddenness' of reality and contract with its 'openness' – in direct proportion, that is, to the metaphysical gap between appearance and reality. The rule of thumb is, the less obvious the world – the more metaphysically removed reality is – the more important (or necessary) epistemology is, *to a degree*. Having stated this rule, let me insert a caveat, for there usually is one in philosophy. If 'reality' is deemed too remote, too hidden ever to be uncovered, then epistemology is, subject to the law of diminishing returns, likely to shrink in importance. The ancient sceptics, in particular the followers of Pyrrho of Elis, provide us with an outstanding example of this law at work,[4] and in the last chapter I discussed this issue as a fulcrum of post-Kantian scepticism. Epistemology exists, therefore, in a not always very well-defined limbo between the blatantly obvious and the hopelessly obscure. Scepticism makes it possible, but unleavened scepticism can also destroy it. *Id quod scepti dant idem quoque recipiunt* – what the sceptic gives, the sceptic takes (back).

I think the reader can see where this is going. Given the strong connection between metaphysics and epistemology, the wave of philosophical suspicion that has swept over metaphysics in the past century and a half, the sense that metaphysics refers either to non-realities or to hopelessly remote ones, has inevitably spilled over into epistemology. Bluntly put, if metaphysics is a shadowy misconception, then so, too, is epistemology, as it has hitherto been understood. Thus, the options for this 'first philosophy' can, for the purposes of this exegesis, usefully be reduced to two and laid out in stark (if somewhat artificial) opposition to one another: either epistemology is fundamental to all investigations of the cosmos – an inquiry into a basic method of procedure for the recognition and acquisition of knowledge – or it is not, because no such basic procedure is either possible or necessary. (I add 'necessary' here because one option is that there is nothing, *in general*, to know.) In the latter case, epistemology will be a more limited, local, historical, and shifting enterprise. The first option, the one suggested by the appearance-and-reality structure of Xenophanes' realist metaphysics, is called *foundationalism*. The second, fundamentally anti-metaphysical, or at least anti-realist, one, is called *naturalism*. We shall take a look at each of these in turn.

Foundationalism

A foundationalist, like the naturalist who follows, is an ideal type to which no actual philosopher will ever absolutely conform. Having said that, a foundationalist begins from the contention that knowledge must rest on a pedestal of certainty, on a set of indubitable (or *indefeasible*) ideas. From this base of immediate, or *intuitive*, knowledge, the truth of other, superstructural,[5] ideas can then be inferred. The result is, in theory, a method for evaluating all inferences – that is, all *defeasible* (i.e., falsifiable) claims about the world. The foundationalist therefore works from the inside out. He first tries to understand how the mind produces ideas about the 'external world,'[6] and then he tries to establish, on the basis of that understanding, a reliable method for evaluating those ideas. If successful, a foundationalist will be able to recognize which ones accurately, or at least adequately, represent the world – which is to say, accurately represent what is outside the mind. Failing that, he will at least have a heightened sense of how much trust can be put in particular ideas, how open they may or may not be to error. From this perspective, epistemology is a reflexive and general 'first philosophy,' capable of developing 'indefeasible criteria' that will make possible the adjudication of knowledge claims made by all other parts of philosophy and indeed all other disciplines.[7]

A foundationalist epistemology is anchored to a realist metaphysics with respect to an 'external world.' By this I mean that epistemology comes with a strong commitment to the existence of an 'objective' reality that the knower seeks to know. I do have to note that the case of Berkeley's idealism may well seem to qualify this assertion, but it is not clear that it does. Even Berkeley traced the ideas in the human mind to their source in an 'external world,' albeit the rather unusual one of God's mind. So, with this half-caveat, I shall retain my assumption about the connection between foundationalism and realism. Readers may already have discerned this assumption in my treatment of Descartes in Chapter 2. Indeed, if not the modern initiator of foundationalism (probably he is), then Descartes is at least an excellent representative of it.

Foundationalism is a powerful theory so deeply rooted in modernity that it probably looks a lot like common sense to most readers. We are quite used to the image of a disengaged knower[8] standing opposite an independently existing world-to-be-known. All I need add is that the disengagement is twofold. First, the knower must be, as I have said above, reflexive, a psychologist able to investigate in the first instance not the world but the workings of her own mind. She must, in other words, begin by becoming an object of knowledge to herself. This entails initial understanding both how her mind constructs ideas about the world and how to assess their credibility. The next step – the investigation of the world that is 'external' to her – proceeds on the basis of this understanding, which enables her to separate signs of truth from those of (possible) error. The first step is the biggest, and without too much distortion, it can be said that the most important part of modern foundationalist epistemology takes place in the mind and is about the mind. It is in the disengaged mind of a transcendental knower – that is, a being who stands apart from the world – that the foundation is established.

It is no easy task to delve into the human mind and discover there a set of indubitable ideas that will serve as the bedrock of the quest for knowledge. A solid starting point can be frustratingly elusive. At least since Aristotle, philosophers have been aware – in some cases have feared – that only what is called deductive reasoning[9] can yield certainty, and even then only if it proceeds from true premises. Consider the following basic, and perhaps familiar, deductive argument: *If* all humans are mortal and *if* Socrates is human, *then* Socrates is, indubitably, mortal. The truth of the conclusion – the 'then' statement – follows necessarily from the truth of the two 'if' statements, or premises. It is impossible for the premises to be true and the conclusion false. This means, as I shall explain in the next chapter, that the argument is *valid*, or formally correct. The argument has, that is, a structure that can *support* truth. But how do we know whether the premises actually *are* true? This is the crucial issue that scepticism raises. For if we do know that, then we know something new – that Socrates is mortal – but if we do not, then we do not know anything beyond the fact that the syllogism is valid. I imagine it's a fairly safe bet that most of my readers are pretty certain that in this case the premises are true. But, if we adopt a Cartesian attitude of radical doubt – and here it is useful, philosophically circumspect, in fact, to do so – we cannot *definitively* say that they are. There are still humans to be born and maybe one or more of them will turn out to be immortal.[10] There is, as well, the less difficult but nonetheless important problem of reference: Perhaps the 'Socrates' I refer to here is not a human at all but my pet cat. So, *probably* the premises are true but – this is the fulcrum of Descartes' radical doubt – *probability is not necessity*. Because it is not, this is an insistent question: How can we guarantee the end point of our reasoning unless we can guarantee the premises that lead to it? And how can we do that in a way that defeats radical doubt or even less extreme forms of scepticism?

Philosophers, both ancient and modern, have certainly felt the need to propose answers. The Socratic method of the *elenchos*, of the close examination and refutation of ideas,[11] was based on Socrates' conviction that self-contradictory ideas, and on a larger scale inconsistent sets of beliefs, are necessarily false – or at least are shot through with falsehoods. Working from that axiom, the elenctic (or Socratic) method was designed to strip away false beliefs (for *they* can be identified – as contradictory) until – perhaps – only true ones remained. These *elenchos*-resisting ideas could then constitute the foundation for reasoning that would produce 'real' knowledge. Of course, Plato tried to improve upon the *elenchos*. In his 'middle' dialogues[12] – where, perhaps, Socrates' voice yields to Plato's own – the Forms were held up as positive standards against which all human knowledge claims were to be measured. To be in possession of (or in the presence of) them, was to have knowledge from which other bits of knowledge – other true statements – could then be produced. For example, if I know the Form Justice, I can decide, with certainty, whether action X is just. I can produce a syllogism that is valid *and* true: All and only just acts have the Form 'J'; action X has the Form 'J'; hence, action X is just.

The problem, as we know, is that humans cannot approach these Forms in their lifetimes and, consequently, are condemned to live in the shadowy half-light of opinion. On Plato's account, no epistemological method could produce absolute knowledge – or, perhaps more accurately, knowledge of the absolutes. Descartes tried to overcome this limitation by positing the epistemological bedrock of innate ideas that were clearly and distinctly (i.e., self-evidently) true. This is an interesting reformulation of Plato, who thought that knowledge of the Forms lay within our *psyches*, but that it was well and truly hidden behind layers of bodily – shadow-producing – appetite. In the *Meditations*, Descartes essentially does what Plato said we could not do: He sheds the prisonhouse body, takes a good unobstructed look at his transcendental mind, and discovers – so he tells us – if not Forms, then pure and trustworthy innate ideas. Once these ideas are identified, a true argument can be developed from them. If I know innately – clearly and distinctly – that I am imperfect and if (again, clearly and distinctly) an imperfect being cannot generate an idea of perfection, then I know with certainty that the idea of perfection which I (clearly and distinctly) have did not originate with me.

Unfortunately, the existence of innate ideas was not clearly and distinctly revealed to all philosophers. For the English empiricist philosopher John Locke, and some of the ancient empiricists as well, the concept of innate ideas was a mere fiction. In Locke's opinion, not even the idea of God fits the bill, and 'I imagine there will be scarce any other idea that can pretend to it.'[13] It is, rather, the evidence of the senses that anchors knowledge, although necessarily in a much less secure way than Platonic Forms or Cartesian innate ideas. Locke's argument is roughly that since the mind clearly does not control the comings and goings of the sense-dependent ideas that it manifestly has, these ideas must necessarily have an outside source. There must be some 'brute input' to which they can be traced,[14] and there must, therefore, be a path or a bridge between the mind's ideas and the world. The difference, as we shall see below an important difference, is that the path is not deductive – because it does not start from self-evidently true ideas – and hence it cannot aspire to the certainty of Cartesian epistemology. This inevitably steered many Lockean empiricists away from foundationalism.

Plato, Descartes, and Locke are hardly in agreement on the issue of how knowledge is achieved, but they do share the postulate that if one can manage to begin from some point or points of certitude – Descartes' Archimedean point, for example – it will then be possible to construct a method of procedure that will end in an accurate representation of the world. The mind, if only we understand it correctly, if only we can trace the genesis of its ideas, is a mirror of nature.[15] The history of philosophy, however, seems to have given us many different mirrors and some of them – like Locke's – are none too clear.

Descartes' Foundationalism

We now have the outlines of foundationalist epistemology. It begins with a disengaged knower who first turns inward to herself, taking her mind as the primary object of investigation. When such investigation yields up a trustworthy starting point, and hence a store of trustworthy ideas, she can, by examining how she arrived at them, develop a method for distinguishing true ideas from false. She can, in other words, recognize what she knows with certainty about the external world – mindful of Berkeley, we can call this the 'world' outside, and independent of, her mind – because she now knows which trains of ideas are trustworthy. Ideally, this method will serve as the basis for judging all knowledge claims, and epistemology will be established as the foundation of all knowledge-producing disciplines.

For a working example of this process, we can return to Descartes' *Meditations*. The radical doubt with which he begins them was designed as a Xenophanean prophylactic against the assumption that knowledge is easily attained. By making Descartes excruciatingly sensitive to error, radical doubt wards off the seductive sirens of custom and prejudice. In its weaker form, radical doubt entails doubting everything that it is not logically impossible to doubt, but in its stronger form the introduction of the Evil Demon gives Descartes momentary warrant to doubt even logical truths. (It may be that I am simultaneously taller and shorter than you, but that the Evil Demon is hiding this knowledge from us.) As we also know, the first trustworthy, or indubitable, idea that Descartes rescues from the clutches of the *Malin Génie* is the existence of himself *qua* mind. Descartes then discovers in his mind certain other 'clear and distinct' ideas that the 'light of nature' (i.e., human reason) assures him are true. (A clear and distinct idea is roughly one whose truth is apprehended intuitively – i.e., without going through a chain of inference.

For example, 'I must exist in order to be deceived' is self-evidently true. I don't reason my way to it.) As we know, these ideas are innate as opposed to 'acquired,' which means that they are – like Kant's transcendental ideas – not derived from experience. (Descartes' rule is that experience is always fuzzy.) Beginning with the certainty of the mind's existence, Descartes traces a deductive path through a series of innate ideas – clearly and distinctly, the greater cannot come from the lesser; an imperfect being cannot, therefore, be the source of an idea of perfection; a perfect being must, therefore, exist – until he arrives first at God (the perfect being) and then at the 'external world.' (A perfect God would not deceive him about the existence of the world because that would, contradictorily, be a sign of imperfection.)

Starting from the bedrock certainty of the mind's existence, a certainty rescued from the clutches of the Evil Demon, Descartes is able to develop a method of logical inference that he believes can be used to adjudicate all knowledge claims. By applying the intuitively derived 'clear and distinct' criterion, Descartes is, he maintains, able to establish when a judgment is sound and when it is not – which is equivalent to saying, 'when it is certain and when it is open to doubt.' One must recognize that there is a very strong claim underwriting this assertion, and without it Descartes' method would never get off the ground. It is this: Because of its *immediate access* to the 'light of reason,' the human mind is capable of recognizing a certain kind of truth. In short, we do not simply know that we *have* innate ideas – we know that about all our ideas. We also know that these innate ideas are true. It is almost impossible to overemphasize how important this concept of innate ideas is to Descartes' method. By contrast, consider Plato. Because Plato sees no possibility for similar, immediate access to the Forms (except in the philosophical dream of the ex-prisoner gazing upon the sun) – his God is not so accommodating as Descartes.' We might say that Plato's foundationalism is more hypothetical than actual, because he respects, as Descartes' does not, the extreme difficulty, if not impossibility, of the foundationalist epistemological circle: that you have to have knowledge in order to get knowledge. While Plato is willing to take the metaphysical step of designating certain ideas as innate, he is (like all good Freudians) not willing to suggest that we have immediate access to them. His tripartite soul, burdened with obfuscating appetites, is less accommodating than Descartes' more transparently rational Stoic soul.[16] The light of reason will never completely penetrate it.

In face of this circularity, it is worth underlining how strange Descartes' argument is. Why, if the Evil Demon can apparently deceive us even about logic – if he can make 3 + 2 equal to something other than 5^{17} – can he be defeated by what is, apparently, 'only' a logical argument? Descartes' reason for rejecting the demon's omnipotence is roughly as follows: for any possible object, X, either X exists or it does not exist. If X does not exist, nothing can be done to it (because, obviously, *there is no X*). But to deceive is to do something to some thing. Hence, if X is the mind, and if something can be done to the mind (it can be deceived), then the mind necessarily exists. This argument *is* valid. This argument demonstrates that it is logically contradictory to assert that one is deceived and yet one does not exist. But why, if the Evil Demon can defeat logic, if we accept *that* as an axiom, is it necessarily true as well? If we accept as a metaphysical premise the Evil Demon's absolute power, logical validity is manifestly not the harbinger of truth. Nothing is. Therefore, Descartes' argument is *not* clearly and distinctly true, and if so, his method never gets off the ground.

Descartes circumvents this objection by exempting intuition from the power of the demon. If the foregoing is not an argument but an intuitive insight, then it is an innate idea, and Descartes does not need an argument to show that it is true. What he grasps in this immediate *noninferential* way just is true. Once Descartes knows that his mind necessarily exists, and that he (who is this 'he': a meta-Descartes?) can trust its clear and distinct ideas, the rest follows. But why, then, does Descartes offer an argument? More to the point, why can the Evil Demon *not* deceive us about our intuitions? It would seem to be just the sort of thing he would be able to do. Locke may have a point: Descartes' reliance on innate ideas may be arbitrary, although metaphysically necessary if he is to retain hope of achieving certainty. It is all a bit tortuous, though, and perhaps it shows why some of the Humanist scholars of the Renaissance had already turned away from asserting a connection between formal logic and empirical truth towards methods of argument that accepted that we cannot, strictly speaking, *guarantee* the truth of our premises.[18] They had, it seems, decided to live with precisely the sort of uncertainty that Descartes refuses to accept.

A Kantian Re-statement of the Problem

Even if we set aside such doubts (however legitimate they may be), it still needs to be noted that with the progress of the Enlightenment Descartes' procedure, and indeed all foundationalist procedures, became vulnerable to a serious objection. I shall state this objection in Kantian terms. If one insists on maintaining a strict realist stance, asserting the existence of an objective – a *noumenal* – world, and if one further insists, *as Kant did not*, that that world is the proper object of knowledge, then the site of Kant's human knowledge, the *phenomenal* world grasped by the mind, may look like little more than a disappointing consolation prize for a being who is incapable of 'true' or 'absolute' knowledge. (Recall Nietzsche's history of an error.) In other words, the foundationalist must take care not to collapse the world-to-be-known too completely into the mind of the knower, unless he is willing to concede that human knowledge falls short of absolute, objective knowledge, or alternatively, that the world exists only in the mind – which raises some interesting Berkeleyan questions about the nature of reality. This threat to the god's-eye view seems to haunt Descartes' epistemology every bit as much as the Evil Demon does. One can argue that Descartes does 'no more' – and without, as Kant did, admitting the fact – than delineate the way (or *a* way) in which the mind grasps the world by acting on its impressions. If one takes the not entirely unreasonable step of refusing to elevate those impressions to the status of innate ideas, of insisting, as John Locke did, that the mind is instead a *tabula rasa* awaiting the imprint of experience, a blank slate that may have an innate capacity to learn but no innate knowledge, then Cartesian epistemology becomes self-validating. Humans know as humans know. Therefore, Cartesian epistemology is empty. In John McDowell's trenchant phrase, the Cartesian mind is left 'spinning in a frictionless void,' responsible to nothing but itself.

These comments underline why innate ideas are so crucial to Descartes' foundational method. Innate ideas are the material from which Descartes builds his metaphysical bridge (one that goes through God) between the mind and the world. But a century and a half after Descartes, Kant thought that the bridge had begun to crumble, especially the crucial arch that connected Descartes' mind to God. By the end of the Enlightenment, passage from the mundane to the transcendent no longer seemed a legitimate metaphysical move. As Kant argued in the fourth of his antinomies,[19] there can be no conclusive proof that there is a God to connect with.

Insofar as an epistemological foundationalist is a metaphysical realist about the external world, and she pretty much always is, all of this is a cheerless prospect since what she wants is a sure-fire way to assess the relation between her ideas and that elusive world. The loss of God as a bridge to the world or, more generally, the loss of self-standing intuitions as a foundation of knowledge, is a serious blow to the hope of doing so. In a foundationalist schema, a world-related idea – in Descartes' parlance, an acquired idea – is true only if the claim it makes about the world is, in whatever way we define the term, accurate. One way (although not the only way) to think about this is as follows. If I say, 'My car is red,' that statement is true just in case I exist (let's be Cartesian and grant that), I have a car, and that car is red. Thus, the truth of Descartes' acquired ideas, like the truth of all 'sense-dependent' ideas, is independent of the mind that formulates them, decided by the existence or non-existence of what they depict. (I should note that there is no end of controversy over just what that is: objects, facts, states of affairs, sense-data, phenomena.) The same could be said of innate ideas, but with acquired ideas there is no appeal to the self-evident light of nature, no appeal to the doctrine of clear and distinct ideas, in effect, no appeal to God, that can pre-empt the appeal to the world. In order to have knowledge of the world (as opposed to knowing it exists), we have to be able to decide which of our statements – which of our ideas – match up with it and which do not.

Here, I am describing something called the *correspondence theory of truth* (although this term is anachronistic in that it is a twentieth-century one). It is an epistemological theory that presupposes the existence of an objective external world and the ability of the mind to represent that world in its ideas. A statement – such as 'My car is red' – that describes a part of that world is true if the *corresponding* fact – my red car – exists. (I must warn readers that more than a little ink has been spilled over the issue of just what a 'fact' is.) Because it looks outward to the world and seeks to match ideas to the world, the correspondence theory is unmistakably foundationalist in tone but – and this is the point where all the complications begin to arise – it is the product of an *empiricism* that can (although not necessarily will) actually undermine foundationalism. It is sad but probably true that the more one looks for correspondence between one's ideas and the world the less one finds it. (This is another version of the moral that the more closely a philosopher looks at the world the more insistently it disappears.)

My point is that Cartesian rationalist philosophy inevitably bumps up against empiricism. That should not be surprising, as Descartes is essentially trying to provide a basis for empirical (experimental) modern science. Indeed, when he is acting the part of the scientist, his outlook is quite strongly empiricist. Empiricism, as we know, is an epistemology in which knowledge is deemed to be the product of sense experience. As such, it stands in opposition to Cartesian rationalism, which sets knowledge on the foundation of innate ideas. That rationalist version of foundationalism consists, as we have seen, in a trail of logical inferences that begin with innate or intuitively clear and distinct ideas and lead outward to God and finally the world. The empiricist, by contrast, *begins* with an acceptance of the *fundamental* fact that the senses imprint the external world on our minds (as images), albeit – we can never escape Plato's cave – not always accurately. (In Kant's case, of course, the consistency with which we perceive phenomena makes accuracy more or less beside the point.) For an empiricist, the assumption that an 'outside world' is at work on us is axiomatic, although, again, the example of Berkeley reminds us that it may be a rather surprising world. It is also axiomatic that the external world is an epistemologically remote world, since in most versions of empiricism what we are directly in touch with is not the world but *our perceptions of the world*, perceptions we may never get beyond and which may, therefore, render the very notion of an 'external world' moot.[20] Faced with this 'veil of perception,' an empiricist can very easily end up as a phenomenalist for whom the world is never more than a collection of 'sense-data,' Kantian bits of phenomena that we somehow piece together. This is the dilemma: By rejecting innate ideas, empiricists forego hope of a secure route to the external world. One effect is to undermine the foundationalism that empiricists, too, seem to accept. We need to take a closer look at this problem.

Truth and the World

In its more robust incarnations, the correspondence theory and the empiricism in which it is encased, has generated energetic attacks on the metaphysical conception of a transcendental world – ones that look, therefore, to superannuate Cartesian epistemology. In the words of the English logical positivist A.J. Ayer, disputes about a metaphysically transcendent world are 'as unwarranted as they are unfruitful.'[21] There is, insists Ayer, no world, certainly no available world, beyond the one that is grasped by 'science and common sense.' Hence, Ayer's assertion of the *verification principle*: 'A sentence is factually significant to any given person, if, and only if, he knows how to verify the proposition it purports to express – that is, if he knows what observations would lead him, under certain conditions, to accept the proposition as being true, or reject it as being false.'[22] In short, the meaning of a proposition lies in its method of verification. If a proposition can be verified empirically or logically, it is true; if it can be falsified empirically or logically, it is false; and if it is susceptible neither to verification nor falsification, it is meaningless. On this principle, I can decide whether the statement 'My car is red' is true (or false) but not whether 'God is good.' As the latter statement admits of neither logical nor empirical verification, it is meaningless.

This is all very neat but, unfortunately, the story does not end here. Logical verification essentially refers to tautologies such as, 'propositions "p" and "not-p" cannot be simultaneously true.' It need not detain us here. More important for our purposes is the empirical claim in which Ayer and many other logical positivists[23] became entangled. The vexing question is this: Just how much strength needs to be accorded to the principle on its empirical side? Given a 'strong' reading, scepticism has its say; what, after all, can ever count as irrefutable empirical proof? The very idea of such proof is that it is available to us – knowledge is available to us – only after the evidence is in, and as Hume points out the evidence never really finishes coming in. Tomorrow's experience may confute today's. Where sense experience is concerned, there is therefore always room for doubt and hence for scepticism. The rule is that experience occurs in the realm of *probability*, which means that no proposition can be empirically verified or falsified *with absolute certainty*. As Hume argued, very probably the sun will rise in the east tomorrow but, strictly speaking, we will not know that until it does. Only when day breaks will be able to refute the sceptic, who will then shrug and tell us that tomorrow is another day.

On this kind of strong reading, all empirical propositions are meaningless because they can never be conclusively verified. But if we retreat towards but a 'weak' reading of the principle – roughly that standard or accepted practices which accord reasonably high degrees of probability can serve as standards of verification – anything, any accepted piece of common sense, could conceivably count as proof for an empirical proposition. That, however, means that the very thing that often needs to be tested – the habitual trust of common sense – is set beyond doubt. So, the principle is always going to be either too strong or too weak, the world-to-be-known either too remote or too near at hand.

If one is strongly attached to the idea of correspondence, this is a glaring weakness, one that was more or less fatal to logical positivism, and one that helped point many empiricists towards a naturalized epistemology. We shall see below why that is so. For now, I shall say only that logical positivism provides a good example of the difficulties that arise as a foundationalist epistemology and a realist metaphysics push philosophers towards the position that, *somehow*, the truth of what one says depends upon how well it matches up with the world; in which case, knowledge depends on being able to demonstrate this match-up. While there is much good sense in this – when we talk about the world it is perfectly reasonable to want to do so accurately or truthfully – the difficulty is that we often seem to be squeezed between the shoals of scepticism and the weeds of naivete. Think how obvious it is, based on the experience of the naked eye, that the sun orbits the earth. For much of our history it would have required a greatly exaggerated scepticism to doubt this 'fact.' Yet, the claim that the sun orbits the earth is false. There is no corresponding fact, and to think otherwise today would be, at best, hopelessly naive. When the knowledge of one age is but the naivete of another, and one age's scepticism is another's knowledge, the verification principle, and behind it the correspondence theory of truth, is bound to seem less helpful than common sense might suggest.

The correspondence theory of truth, and even more generally, the belief that experience gets us in touch with the world, is thus the locus of a series of empiricist-generated issues that have bedevilled foundationalist epistemology. Descartes tells us that if epistemology is to be foundational, the path between the knower and the world-to-be-known must be clearly delineated – and it must be infallible. There must be the bedrock of a detached but reflexive 'knower' who understands how his mind generates ideas and how to assess them once they are generated. This is the apparent strength of Cartesian rationalism, in which the mind proceeds logically and inexorably from a foundation of clear and distinct ideas. Once we get to the world, however – once we satisfy ourselves that the world exists – things begin to go awry. As the empiricist never tires of reminding us, the particular nature of the external world will always be less than fully clear and distinct.

So, with experience comes a lack of clarity, with a lack of clarity comes doubt, and with doubt comes scepticism. Once he has managed to reach the external world, even Descartes cannot eradicate doubt, however much he may try to suppress or minimize it. Descartes begins the *Meditations* with radical doubt, and when he overcomes it what still remains is a weaker (reasonable) doubt that, as Plato taught, is the companion of all beings with limited powers of understanding. The possibility of error, on this admittedly smaller scale, cannot be made to go away. And neither, therefore, can scepticism. Furthermore, despite its smaller scale, this remaining scepticism cannot be dismissed with a Cartesian shrug at the fact that humans cannot be perfected, that we always want to know too much, too quickly. This is precisely where the phenomenalist tincture of empiricism becomes more insistent. If our connection to the world is mediated through perception, it is just hard to see how we can get beyond perception to the world.[24] If what we apprehend immediately is not the world but our perceptions or ideas or sense-impression (there are many terms) thereof, then the images we derive from perception have to be interpreted or judged by the mind. To use an old philosophical trinket, we may clearly perceive a stick partly immersed in water as bent even though it is not. Hence, we cannot assume that the ideas of the world that we build up from perception are necessarily accurate copies of it. In a strict phenomenalist account, they may not be copies of it at all, and it may be no more than a prejudice to assume that they are. It is, as Locke tells us, the quickness of the acts of judgment, the way they move through the well-worn ruts of habit, that induces us to overlook these possibilities and proceed towards a comfortable realism.[25]

So, in some sense the Cartesian rationalist takes the long way around (through God) to the point where he will allow experience to have its say, and when he arrives there he finds the empiricist waiting for him with a simple but potentially devastating question: How do we ever know with certainty that any *particular* idea we have is correct – an accurate copy of some thing or event in the world? Even if we accept Descartes' proof for the existence of the world, how do we know whether we can know (be certain of) anything *about* that world? *How,* in other words, does Cartesian rationalism help us to know that world *in detail?* Cartesian rationalism advises us to take care not to let our desire to know the world outstrip the limits of our understanding, but good advice does not an epistemology make. Once we move beyond intuition to inference, beyond the mind to the world, the ground begins to tremble beneath us. It seems that the method Descartes so diligently sought – 'rules so clear and simple that anyone who uses them will never mistake the false for the true'[26] – ends, when it finally bumps up against experience, in an unsettling uncertainty.

Yet, if Descartes' foundationalist project begins to crumble before the phenomenal nature of experience, it is, as we have seen, far from clear

that the empiricists – who, after all, insist on the primacy of this experience – can save the day. For empiricism raises two possibilities, which I
have already alluded to but which now need to set out more clearly.
The first is the anti-realist and thoroughly phenomenalist (not to mention Berkeleyan) possibility that *all we have are our perceptions and ideas*,
the 'world' from which they allegedly come being little more than a
metaphysical assumption. Ayer's brand of logical positivism pivoted in
this direction. The second, and realist, possibility is that our ideas are,
as Hume tended to think, copies of a world against which they can be
tested. But to reiterate Hume's point, we can never insist that the tests
produce knowledge, because although we can falsify our ideas we can
never absolutely verify them, since every day brings new experience.[27]
Knowledge is a chimera that may disappear with the dawn. Neither the
realist nor the anti-realist can be certain whether, how far, and how
accurately our ideas correspond to that entity we call the 'external
world.'

Kant's Last Stand

We have come back to the moment when Kant appears on the scene,
determined to save empiricism from Humean scepticism by preserving
the certainty of knowledge. We have already seen Kant take a unique
phenomenalist tack and argue that the human mind – with its intuitions
and categories – imposes a consistent structure on the world. Since
the *phenomenal* world – the world of experience grasped through the
senses – will always take the same shape (for example, it will always
be three-dimensional), we can achieve certainty about this world
because rather than the mind conforming to the structure of the world,
the world conforms to the structure of the mind (or, at least, the structure of experience). This epistemological turnabout is what Kant refers
to as his 'Copernican Revolution' in philosophy, and it truly was a
revolution.

The core of the position is perhaps to be found in his concept of the
synthetic a priori.[28] The reader will recall that *a priori* judgments are
known to be true or false in advance of any empirical evidence, whereas
the truth or falsity of *a posteriori* ones is known only after such evidence
has been consulted.[29] Kant also divided judgments into 'analytic' and
'synthetic' types. Analytic judgments, in which 'the predicate is included in the subject,' are essentially definitional: 'All bachelors are
unmarried' and 'If equals be added to equals the wholes are equal' are

two of Kant's examples. Synthetic judgments, in which the predicate is not included in the subject, are experiential, or empirical: 'My car is red,' for example. So far, this is simple: if you know what a bachelor is, you know, by definition, that he is unmarried and don't need to ask him whether he is. But even if you know I have a car, you do not, by definition, know that it is red. The concept of 'my car' does not contain the concept 'red' in the way that the concept 'bachelor' contains the concept 'unmarried.' So, the truth of analytic judgments is known *a priori*, which means that they are absolutely certain. The truth of synthetic judgments, on the other hand, is known *a posteriori*, which means that they cannot be certain *when we make them*. They are by definition open to doubt and, therefore, to the attacks of sceptics like Hume, who remind us that experience can always reverse itself. Thus, Kant's empiricist dilemma is as follows: Knowledge of the external world has to be based on experience (it has to be synthetic), but if it is truly knowledge it also has to be certain – it cannot be changing from one moment to the next – which means that it has to be known *a priori*. Hence, the unique Kantian category of the *synthetic a priori*: judgments based on experience – not true simply by definition – but which we know with certainty to be true.

Let's consider two of Kant's examples.[30] The first is that the shortest distance between two points (on a flat surface) is a straight line. According to Kant, this statement is not self-evidently true – as Hume would say, it can be contradicted without absurdity – *until one considers the way the human mind intuits space*. Then it will be understood that *for such a mind* – by extension, within experience – this statement will always be true. The evidence as grasped by the human (or any experiencing) mind will always bear it out because human perception, which takes place within experience, is not capable of grasping a world in which the shortest distance between two points on a flat surface is not a straight line. So, too, with the statement, 'Seven plus five equals twelve.' There is, Kant argues, nothing in the concept of 'seven plus five' that necessarily entails the predicate 'equals twelve' any more than 'my car' entails 'red.' We don't think that someone is illogical if he asserts that 'seven plus five equals eleven.' We simply think he cannot add. (This is what Hume meant when he said that 'matters of fact' – which are roughly analogous to synthetic judgments – could be contradicted without absurdity: to deny the truth of '7 + 5 = 12' is not illogical, it is just wrong.) The point is that the sum has to be worked out. But once it has been worked out, indeed, even before it has been worked out, it is easy to see that, given the immutability of quantitative judgments, the numbers will always add up to that sum. Take the more difficult 267 × 422. The answer is almost certainly not immediately obvious. You really do have to work it out. But what you do know with certainty is that there is just one answer, and it will always be the same answer.[31] Hence, you can trust the method of multiplication to lead you to it. It will produce that great and much sought after redundancy, 'certain knowledge.'

From the perspective of most of the philosophers who preceded him, Kant's revolution would probably look like a retreat. Kant sets metaphysical limits to the concept of knowledge that Descartes or Hume or Locke or Plato would have found unwarranted, restricting it to a 'human' or 'experiential' knowledge that comes up short of the 'absolute' or transcendental knowledge of a god's-eye point of view.[32] But that, perhaps limited, knowledge will at least be *certain* knowledge of the external world that *we*, phenomenally, inhabit. The intuitions of time and space and the categories of judgment will always produce the same sort of phenomenal world and so, necessarily, a knowledge of it that can be trusted. (In a way, this is tantamount to saying that while Descartes' *noumenal* Evil Demon might deceive us, he cannot alter the structure of either our experience or our deceived minds, so all deception will at least be uniform. Insofar as knowledge is tied to consistency – and in a fundamental way it has to be – there is no *human* distinction to be made between knowledge and consistent deception.) Anyway, Kant's lesson is that if knowledge entails certainty, it can extend no further than the phenomenal world.

What Kant does is to preserve certainty by inserting the world-to-be-known into the experiential structure of the mind of the knower – or at least by establishing a symbiotic relationship between them. (Perhaps Kant is doing explicitly what Descartes had done implicitly.) By doing so, he solves the problem of the fundamental uncertainty of the relation of our ideas to the world by making it moot: For us, appearance just is reality. This is a brilliant solution, but one that almost certainly contributed more to the attack on foundationalist epistemology than to its defence. Once the knower and the world she knows are joined in this symbiotic manner – once the world-to-be-known becomes parasitically dependent on the mind of the knower – a drift towards naturalism would seem to be inevitable. (Although naturalism has perhaps the opposite tendency of collapsing the knower into the world-to-be-known.)

In summary, foundationalism is a method for attaining knowledge based on the metaphysical postulate that there is a mind-independent world-to-be-known. To reach that world, we require an infallible method that begins from an infallible starting point. Cartesian rationalism establishes that method as a set of deductive inferences proceeding from an infallible stable of innate – clear and distinct – ideas. By attacking the existence of such ideas, empiricists such as Locke and Hume undermine the contention that there is any settled epistemological method by which one can achieve certainty about the state of the world. Kant attempts to save empiricism from the resulting scepticism by providing it with a rationalist-looking foundation of intuitions of time and space and categories of judgments that introduce stability into our experience. The effect, however, is less to preserve the possibility of a god's-eye view of the world that opens out onto absolute knowledge than to set what we humans know at one remove from such a view. Humans are now locked into *their* world, and this new symbiosis of the knower and a world-to-be-known takes us to the borders of naturalism.

What Naturalism Is

In contrast to foundationalism, naturalism locates the knower in a specific (cultural, historical, disciplinal) context, or web of contexts, from which there is no escape or, in less-prejudiced language, to which there is no outside. The naturalist's epistemological idiom, therefore, differs from the foundationalist's: The 'objects of knowledge' are not 'out there,' but 'all around one.' The working image is not of discovering a world but of exploring one in which we are engaged, or to which we are spontaneously connected – an image of involvement rather than contemplation. While, with respect to its metaphysical commitments, naturalism can spread out in both directions along the continuum of realism and anti-realism, it is not generally associated with the strong realism we get in foundationalism. For the naturalist there is no god's-eye view and no ready-made world awaiting our discovery. As Hilary Putnam has pointed out, this is not necessarily to insist (in the strong anti-realist way of many neo-Nietzscheans) that 'we make up the world,' only that it is not 'mind-independent.'[33] It is enough, however, to nudge the naturalist towards the anti-realist end of the continuum, because it forces her to refrain from asking, in the manner of a committed realist, which ideas are objective and which are subjective. To do so is, from her perspective, to commit what Putnam has called the 'fallacy of division.' According to Putnam, 'What we say about the world reflects our choices and interests. To try to divide the world into a part that is independent of us and a part that is constructed by us is an old temptation, but giving in to it leads to disaster every time.'[34]

This is a warning worth heeding. We have seen that the rationalist (or Cartesian) strategy of rigorously separating the mind from the world is rife with epistemological problems. But so, too, is the empiricist response, which essentially tosses the mind back into the world. The American philosopher Wilfrid Sellars famously gave expression to a problematic form that that response could take when he accused realists of being seduced by the empiricist 'myth of the given': the idea that we have distinct and incorrigible sense impressions (perceptions) from which to construct an objective portrait of the world. In recent years, John McDowell has elaborated this accusation, arguing that if our ideas were absolutely governed by what is given in experience, we would have no control over them. Our minds would simply be slaves to experience. But, alternatively, McDowell points out, if our minds were detached from what is given in experience, then experience would contribute nothing to, and in no way constrain, our thinking. The first horn of the dilemma, where our ideas just are the product of nature, McDowell calls 'bald naturalism.' The second, where we spin in the 'frictionless void' of our own reasons, he calls 'rampant Platonism.'[35] As these are unsatisfactory versions of, respectively, empiricism and rationalism, McDowell has attempted to elucidate a third option, which he has dubbed 'naturalized Platonism.' Although I want to be careful to try not to amalgamate this subtle and difficult position too much into these remarks – it is really a mixture of foundationalism and naturalism – naturalized platonism is a description that evokes a naturalist-looking image of a mind that is, in its nature, part of the world and yet retains a free and rational space of reason where the world cannot intrude. The difficulty is to see how this can be, how the mind can be 'engaged' in the world – how it can be responsible to it – without being ruled by it.

The Threat of Relativism

So, we know roughly what naturalists want to do. In evoking an image of involvement rather than contemplation, they express their commitment to tearing away the veil of perception and putting the 'knower' back in touch with the world. This is a task ill suited to strong varieties of realism. One reason this is so is that there may now (this is Rorty and not McDowell) be a plurality of worlds to be known – at the extreme, as many as there are knowers – none of which can claim precedence as the 'original' or 'true' world. From a naturalist perspective, given the effects of culture, history, and different fields of study, it may well be more accurate to speak of 'knowledges' than knowledge. As one commentator has pointed out, a philosophy freed from foundationalism 'would not need to derive the legitimacy of various fields of knowledge from the same unique source.'[36] The naturalist may feel no need – no obligation – to construct a single epistemological method, a single way of knowing, as the foundation of knowledge. (I think, however, that this would be anathema to McDowell's direct realism, but see note 33.) Certainly, the naturalist will feel no need to believe that any particular way of knowing will remain forever unchanged. The 'world' is always the world-someone-knows, or is-engaged-with, and to that extent (as Nietzsche might remind us) it does not exist in all its fullness – awaiting discovery – in advance of the activity of knowing. Berkeley controversially declared that *esse est percipi:* To be is to be perceived. A naturalist motto might be, 'to be is to be known.'

This *is* strange. Indeed, at first glance, naturalism may seem a more elusive and less satisfying position than foundationalism, just because it rejects the strong realist distinction between the knower and the known. (To that extent, naturalism is more Hegelian, more historically fluid, than it is Kantian.) The problem, as I have said above, is that most of us do instinctively make that distinction, imaginatively setting ourselves at one remove from the world we claim to know. This contemplative image is a deeply ingrained one. Platonic realism – 'But that's not what justice is!' – is part of our everyday talk about both objects and ideas. If we really are detached from the world, however, our gaze may be contemplating nothing but our own freedom, and we may know nothing but our own will. If so, what began as objectivity collapses into the subjectivity of a mind spinning in the void created by the myth of the god's-eye view. To be freed from this illusion, the naturalist denies that knowledge is 'obtained' by a correct epistemological method. Rather, an epistemological method creates, or helps to create, a particular kind of knowledge. However, if this frees the naturalist from the clutches of the god's-eye view, it seems to lock her into a claim to godlike creativity that will make all good Platonists – and not a few naturalists – cringe. This is the problem: The naturalist accuses the foundationalist of wanting to see as God sees, whereas the foundationalist accuses the naturalist of wanting to create as God creates. To this second charge, many naturalists (with the exception of the Nietzscheans) respond with

Putnam's caution that we do not – or not completely – 'make up the world.' We are engaged in it, we work on it, but we do not create it. As I have said, it is not clear just how this compromise is to be worked out. Put differently, it is not clear that we are *not* on the slippery slope to claiming a godlike creativity.

Certainly, the foundationalist's charge and the naturalist's 'Putnamist' response suggest that this slope is never far away. One gets the distinct feeling that both sides fear it. The problem (which is also present in the weak version of verificationism) is that naturalism can make knowledge look just a little too relative, a little too malleable to be – well, knowledge. (Hence, McDowell's anti-Nietzschean determination – and Putnam's, too – to retain a role for 'the given.') Nowadays, most of us are used to hearing that morality is relative (whether we believe it is another matter), but far fewer of us consider 'harder' scientific knowledge in the same light. This attitude might lead readers to reject naturalism out of hand. The world, they will insist, just is, independent of our ideas about it. Therefore, it is important to point out that this is not necessarily the case in the philosophical and scientific communities. Almost forty years ago, in his seminal work, *The Structure of Scientific Revolutions*, Thomas Kuhn adopted a naturalist position – and one that looks very relativist, too. Kuhn argues that all scientific theories are true because, in essence, they all establish their own criteria of truth. He concedes what I have: that most people more or less instinctively adopt a realist stance towards scientific theories, assuming that one is superior to another 'because it is somehow a better representation of what nature is really like.' Kuhn contends that this realism is impossible to sustain: 'There is, I think, no theory-independent way to reconstruct phrases like "really there."' The idea of 'a match between the ontology of a theory [what it asserts is real] and its "real" counterpart in nature' is 'illusive in principle.'[37] In this strongly anti-realist brand of naturalism, theories do not constitute an externalization of what Rorty has called 'inner representations of reality':[38] On the contrary, what we call 'reality' is largely a projection of the theory. Consider, for example, how the concept of gravity structures our sense of what is going on universe, or how genetics determines the way we understand why we are as we seem to be. Given the extent to which such concepts and theories construct our images of the world, it should, the naturalist tells us, come as no surprise when the world matches up with them. If that is so, then a theory has to be assessed in some way other than in terms of its 'representational capacity' – which is fundamentally how a found-ationalist wants to assess it.

If there is substance to this view, if, as Charles Taylor has argued,[39] our representations of the world are grounded in the way we deal with it, then the god's-eye perspective of foundationalism and of pre-Kantian metaphysics, is indeed an impossible fiction. According to Taylor, the foundationalist's error consists in 'ontologizing' an epistemological pro-cedure – which is to say, in presenting a particular line of reasoning as if it were part of 'the very constitution of the mind.'[40] (Of course, I sug-gested in Chapter 2 that it is in the nature of metaphysics to do some-thing like ontologizing reason by inserting logic into the very heart of human existence. We shall come back to this issue in Chapter 5.) The naturalist will argue that this error has to be remedied, in the first instance, by something like Locke's – or the empiricist's – scepticism about the innateness of ideas,[41] since that at least gets us back to the world and away from 'rampant Cartesianism.' Once a philosopher loses sight of the fact that we actually *inhabit* (as opposed to contem-plate) the world, she will also lose sight of the possibility that there may be many worlds to inhabit and many ways, therefore, to skin the cat of knowledge. Having done so, this philosopher will see no viable alterna-tive to the foundationalist's 'ontologized' image of a logical mind, stocked with innate ideas, mirroring an equally logical world. Once the naturalist has availed herself of the therapy of empiricism to free her-self from the grip of innate ideas, however, she has to be careful not to turn around and surrender either to the 'givenness' of experience or (this is less likely) to a too-rampant Nietzschean creativity. This was Kant's great insight, and the one McDowell has tried to elaborate: Neither unbridled empiricism nor unbridled rationalism can satisfacto-rily explain how the mind interacts with the world. Descartes' specula-tion on how the immaterial mind might be embodied is a torturous affair, while Hume's empiricism turns it into something approaching a ghostly fiction. Yet, Kant is not the last word, either. Many philosophers would make the same point about Kant's transcendental idealism that he made about earlier versions of empiricism and rationalism. At best, the argument might go, Kant's philosophy brings us to the edge of the world, where the frictionless void, the myth of the given, and Nietzsche's godlike creativity are all spread before us. There are still steps to be taken, and decisions to be made, if a satisfactory epistemology is to be constructed from the ruins of the Enlightenment.

Post-Kantian Naturalism

Given these possibilities, naturalism is a strong, if diverse, current in the anti-metaphysical rivers of post-Kantian philosophy. It is one that has gathered strength in the twentieth and twenty-first centuries. One very important source of naturalism – although scarcely the only one – is the broadly influential work of Martin Heidegger. The concept of *Dasein* (literally 'being-there,' his term for human existence), which is so central to Heidegger's thought, posits an engaged and historical 'being-in-the-world' who deals with her surroundings on the basis of what she discovers, 'ready to hand.' She does this, first, in the context of what Heidegger called 'pre-understanding,' an inarticulate but practical, somewhat intuitional, somewhat experimental relation to things that only an engaged being can have. We come, for example, to know what a hammer is – to have a *concept* of it – by hammering. Since a hammer is a hammer only if someone hammers with it, the knowledge encased in the concept is inextricably tied to – or emerges from – the doing. In other words, there is no Platonic possibility of recognizing a pre-existing Form and certainly no possible god's-eye view of the matter.

Sartre – who was influenced by Heidegger – expresses a similar sense of the human condition in the credo which I have already quoted (and which Heidegger rejected): 'existence comes before essence.'[42] As we know, this famous little slogan tells us that there is no 'original' human essence or nature that precedes and shapes an individual's life. *We* are the architects of our lives, and neither innate ideas nor innate logical circuitry provide us with *a priori* knowledge about how to live them. We work that out as we go and, as such, we never stand outside the world in the way that objects do. A hammer may be said to stand outside the world, to have an essence, because it is the planned creation of someone for the preordained purpose of hammering – Sartre's angle of vision is different from Heidegger's here – but we humans have no similar preordained purposes, and so there is no essential knowledge to be had either of us or of the moral worlds we inhabit.

In the generation after Sartre, Michel Foucault used the dyad 'power/knowledge' to examine, in a manner analogous to Kuhn, the way in which procedures for doing things – institutionalized practices, political strategies, and the like – are correlated with knowledge. Foucault sees no possibility for treating the concepts in isolation from one another – as if knowledge could be extricated from the history (or context) of its birth and application. In the words of his American interpreters,

Hubert Dreyfus and Paul Rabinow, 'we have no recourse to objective laws, no recourse to pure subjectivity, no recourse to totalizations of theory. We have only the cultural practices that have made us what we are.'[43] There is no History, no grand meaningful course of human development, only genealogies that preclude foundational theories of knowledge.

If we look in the other direction, towards the nineteenth century and the early parts of the twentieth, we can discover an important source of naturalism in the work of the American pragmatists, principally, C.S. Peirce, William James, and John Dewey. James proposes that truth is the product of what experience compels us to believe, famously asserting that: 'Truth *happens* to an idea. It *becomes* true, is *made* true by events.'[44] Our ideas – what we claim to know – can be categorized as true or false only in relation to how well they work as descriptions of the world we experience. Once again, the idiom differs from foundationalism. Ideas are not *copies* of reality but *descriptions* of it that, as Quine would remind us, either hold up or fail to hold up to the scrutiny of 'the tribunal of experience.' This means, of course, that the truth of an idea can come and go as the world unfolds.

In this very quick sketch of naturalist tendencies – it is really no more than an incomplete list – the reader should note that the various positions could be distributed along a kind of Putnam–Nietzsche continuum. Heidegger and the American Pragmatists stand closer to Putnam. Their images are ones of being engaged in a world that is something more than clay in the knower's hands. By contrast, Sartre is closer to the freedom of Nietzschean creativity, less hemmed in by history and context. Foucault is harder to place, because his work has, I think, more to do with liberating us from a particular form of the myth of the given, the pseudo-objectivity of power.

Wittgenstein and Naturalism

There is one source of naturalism that I want to dwell on in some detail. It is both a paradigm of the position and a very powerful and subtle critique of the foundationalism that it opposes. This source is the 'later' work of Wittgenstein, which is in part a critique (not necessarily a hostile one) of his *Tractatus Logico-Philosophicus*, in which he had espoused a kind of correspondence theory of truth according to which language and the world are isomorphic.[45] In what follows, freely adapted from remarks in his posthumously published *On Certainty* and parts of the *Philosophical Investigations*,[46] I shall try to convey the sense – or sensibility – of that critique.

The premise that I want to advance is straightforward but counter-intuitive, and certainly anti-Cartesian: It is that I can know you have a headache but you cannot. Imagine the following scene. I am teaching a philosophy course and you are my student. Just before the final exam you inform me that you have a terrible headache and cannot write the test. I respond by asking, 'How do you know you have a headache?' If you are like most people, you will respond with a half-dazed, 'Well I just do.' So, let us assume that is your response. I note, politely, that you have simply reasserted the original proposition, which is that you have a headache. 'All right,' you say, 'my head hurts.' 'That's just what a headache is,' I reply. 'You are still reasserting the proposition.' Here, despite the pain in your head, you need to stop and take stock of the discussion. If you do, you will notice that the problem lies not so much in your answers as in the fact that you *tried* to answer. *For it is a very strange question*, and you have to recognize and then respect – with dignified silence – that strangeness.

Here is the naturalist's point. When asked how you know you have a headache, all you can do, really, is reassert the proposition, because in this instance knowing is, from a naturalist perspective, a tad redundant. Compare these two statements: (1) I have a headache; and (2) I know I have a headache. As Wittgenstein points out, the addition of 'I know' in the second statement adds nothing to the message in the first. That is because your headache is so immediate, so much a part of you, that you cannot possibly doubt that you have it. (You would never say, 'I think I have a headache,' although you might say, 'I think I'm getting a head-ache.') Your headache is something like an *ontological condition*, by which I mean that you are in no way *disengaged* from it. There is no room for doubt about its existence because – to speak metaphorically – there is no space between you and it. Its being is part of your being. The pain is an 'inner' state that, in Saul Kripke's words, 'God could find if he looked into [your] mind.'[47] Put differently, it is an utterly primitive state that (unless there is a Cartesian demon at work) is immune to sceptical challenge by the person who has the headache. For you, there is no need, in fact no possibility, to follow the epistemological route from doubt (or appearance) to certainty (or reality). You cannot say, 'I appear to have a headache,' run some tests, and then conclude, 'Yes, I really do have a headache.' No one would know what to make of that. To put the matter as plainly as I can: You do not *know* that you have a headache; you *just have* a headache, and you report this fact by uttering the appropriate sentence.[48]

By contrast, imagine my position. I have to decide whether to make you write the exam or to let you go home. From my perspective there is plenty of room for doubt. Students have been known to fake headaches to get out of exams, after all. So, I look at you. Your face is pinched, apparently in pain; your pupils are dilated, and you seem overly sensitive to the noises around you. Moreover, you have an 'A' average, have done all your work on time, and are, so far as I know you, an honest person. I decide to let you go. As you are leaving, another student asks me why you do not have to write the exam, and I reply that you have a headache. The student then asks me, 'How do you know?' Now, do you see? The question, when asked *of me about you*, is not strange. The student's scepticism directed at me is perfectly plausible, and I readily respond, 'Because she looks to be in pain, she is sensitive to noise, and she has always told me the truth in the past.' The student may not like my reasons, may not agree that they are, or can be, definitive.[49] Nevertheless, the fact remains that I can give them: I can lay out the *epistemological path* that I took from doubt to certainty. I can do that because there is an *ontological space* between your headache and me. Unlike you, I do not have immediate, or intuitive, access to it. Knowing is an issue for me precisely because I have to draw inferences.[50]

First lesson of naturalism, then: ontology before epistemology. We can know only what we are capable of doubting, and we are not capable of doubting everything. Descartes also said that we are not capable of doubting everything, *but he took those indubitable things to be precisely the things we know.* In other words, we know what is clearly and distinctly beyond doubt. So, in Descartes' argument, *you* will know you have a headache, but *I* never will. For me, scepticism continues to hold sway, and since most of our knowledge concerns facts about the world – entails, so to speak, questions about your headache rather than mine – it cannot be eradicated. Wittgenstein takes an opposite tack designed – perhaps – to save the world from scepticism by embracing it. In Wittgenstein's view, it is redundant to claim to know what is beyond doubt because – as Descartes would have to agree – knowledge is about overcoming doubt. So, *pace* Descartes, knowledge is not an intuition. Knowledge is a process that begins with doubt and that, because it also ends with a lesser but still-present doubt, can always be revised. You may be fooling me, and I may find out that you are. In such a case, I will shrug and say, 'Well, I thought I knew she had a headache.' This will never happen with your own headache, which is, to reiterate, why something as immediate to you as your headache is does not require knowing. No process, no knowledge. Knowledge, like language, is a public, not a private, thing.

So, Wittgenstein has reversed Descartes: Epistemology is no longer the 'first philosophy.' All our inquiries take place in a world that contextualizes them by providing an ontological framework. We distinguish, therefore, between what is epistemological and what is ontological by distinguishing between what can be doubted and what cannot.[51] For Wittgenstein, the ontological framework does not consist of innate ideas or even of immediate sensations like pain; rather, ontological ideas are historically conditioned and subject to change. There is a Humean point here: Today's certainty may be tomorrow's doubt and vice versa. These are very powerful frameworks. Our epistemological job is to find our way around within them, but Wittgensteinian ontology cannot, to recall Taylor, be *fully ontologized as a permanent structure.* That is what I meant by 'embracing scepticism.' For Wittgenstein, doubt is not a sign that the possibility of knowledge is under threat – *but that it is in process.* Therefore, when we find ourselves in a position to doubt a piece of our ontology, it becomes epistemology. An astronomer in thirteenth-century Europe would, for example, have based his labours on the indubitable proposition that the Earth was the unmoving centre of the universe. (More or less: Ptolemy's system entailed offsetting Earth from the centre of an eccentric circle.) Everything this astronomer did would have proceeded from that *ontological* foundation. When Copernicus showed how that proposition could be doubted, the Earth's position and movement became a 'knowledge issue.' Today, the matter has long been settled, and a different ontology awaits the young astronomer. For her, without doubt, the Earth moves. She could prove that it does, of course, but there would be something very *pro forma* about such a proof. It would lack suspense because we really cannot imagine how it could be wrong, and if it is, *everything* is. We are, quite simply, not in a position to doubt its veracity.

Therefore, it is not *despite* but *because of* its historical mutability that the world we find ourselves in just is, with its passing certainties, the space within which a theory of knowledge can develop. Put differently, for the naturalist, epistemology is immanent rather than, as the foundationalist would have it, transcendent. The things that are beyond doubt frame knowledge, in a manner reminiscent of Kant's metaphysics, perhaps. They determine *what* can be known – your headache but not mine – but they do not determine *how* it can be known. That is the work of epistemology. Foucault wrote that 'since Kant, the role of philosophy is to prevent reason from going beyond the limits of what is given in experience.'[52] By restricting knowledge to the realm of doubt, Wittgenstein was doing something like that – restricting knowledge to the realm of public experience. To underline the point I made above, Wittgenstein transformed scepticism from knowledge's poison to knowledge's fundamental condition. In a strange new way, the world beyond doubt is, like Kant's *noumena*, a world beyond knowing. The search for knowledge is just the attempt to solve the problems *our* world brings to our attention.

Second lesson of naturalism, then: Once an issue has been identified as epistemological, the tests, the routes to certainty – which are no longer quite so certain – are, as in a weak form of verificationism, often a bit conventional and even *ad hoc*. That is because the naturalist is willing to decide that you have a headache, not on the basis of an infallible set of tests – there is no god's-eye view, and certainly no intuition, available to him – but on the basis of the standard (or best available, whatever that means) assessment of the evidence. This is, in part, because of the first lesson. The standards, the tests, and our attitude towards them – our sense of how fallible they are; what new and better ones have arisen, etc. – are subject to change over time, precisely because they come from a community and not from God. Never mind headaches; even the apparently unshakable certainty of the Earth's central position in the universe was eventually overthrown. From this perspective, a foundationalist epistemology does look – to recall Charles Taylor's phrase – like an attempt to ontologize epistemology, to render permanent a particular way of investigating the world based on a particular set of assumptions about that world (and, therefore, as against James's warning, to see truth as an accurate copy of the world instead of a description that works). If, however, the borders between ontology and epistemology are permeable, if the naturalist principle that what is foundational today may be conjectural tomorrow (and vice versa), is sound, this is, philosophically speaking, a dangerous – or at least a misguided – thing to attempt, because no theory of knowledge is ever absolute. To echo James, theories are always being made and remade. And, a naturalist might add, that is what makes science, science: constant criticism and revision of its standards. In Otto Neurath's memorable naturalist metaphor, we are like sailors constantly rebuilding our ship on the open sea. If so, our knowledge can hardly achieve the solidity the foundationalist seeks. Descartes wants to establish 'rules for the direction of the mind.' By contrast, Wittgenstein suggests that we cannot even be certain what a rule is, how it works, or whether one is following it. Hume tells us that the future cannot be tied to the commitments of the past. Wittgenstein tells us that the past may contain no commitments in the first place. We just go on as we see fit.

From a naturalist perspective, to ontologize epistemology is, to the extent that it erases the admittedly permeable borders between ontology and epistemology, necessarily to epistemologize ontology, as well. Put differently, a naturalist will argue that the attempt to produce a foundationalist epistemology eradicates either epistemology or ontology. The result is a murky condition in which either everything can be known (and so there is no ontological framework) or nothing need be known (because everything is ontologically obvious, and there is no need for epistemology). In this context, Kant's insistence that the 'self' has to be treated as an ontological entity, whose unified existence is assumed *without being known*, can be understood as an attempt to re-establish borders Descartes and Hume had perhaps tried in their different ways to erase. When Descartes 'proves' that his mind exists, or when Hume 'demonstrates' that the existence of the 'self' as a unified entity cannot be demonstrated, they are epistemologizing an ontological proposition, opening up to doubt things that cannot be doubted, if one is to go on with the business of asking questions. They are doing something that is either (in Descartes' case) redundant – because 'I exist' is an ontological proposition, and you cannot doubt an ontological proposition – or (in Hume's case) impossible – because you cannot refute a concept (the 'self') that you cannot, metaphysically speaking, do without, if you are to make the refutation. (This, of course, makes Hume's refutation self-refuting.)

A Short Summary

To summarize, a naturalized epistemology begins with a contextualized being, a knower who is already *in* the world. All knowledge, such as it is, arises out of this fundamental fact of engagement. Knowledge is, therefore, historical. Like a great but sluggish river, knowledge will twist and turn, never freezing into an epistemological bed of ice on which all other disciplines can stand. Our worlds – or at least the ontological assumptions on which they are founded – will come and go, as will our knowledge. On this account, the transcendent 'knower,' the godlike surveyor of reality, whose epistemology (as incorrigible as my student's headache) has been frozen into an unalterable ontology, is only a metaphysical conceit. Wittgenstein's naturalism thus constitutes a rejection of the traditional sceptic, who denies that knowledge can be attained because he denies that we can ever achieve the absolute certainty of the god's-eye view. My strange question to my hypothetical student – How do you know you have a headache? – can perhaps be classified as one a traditional sceptic might ask insofar as it is a way of asking how we can know anything. He might therefore be interested in it as a particular form of the general question: How is knowledge possible? From a naturalist's perspective, however, the general question makes no sense because absolute (i.e., ontologized) standards of knowing have been ruled out of court. The naturalist – the Wittgensteinian version thereof, anyway – will only ask particular questions: How might one come to know whether someone has a headache? This can be generalized into a class of questions – how might we come to know whether claims about internal states are true? – but the Wittgensteinian naturalist will not necessarily commit herself to the idea that there is only one answer to all such questions. Each particular case may have to be considered on its own merits. This takes us to the borders of an ontology of extremely variegated everyday life, which is where ordinary language philosophy (which, through G.E. Moore, had some influence on Wittgenstein) makes its entrance. If we are going to do ontology from the perspective of ordinary language, we shall not ask, 'What is real?' but 'What do our ways of speaking set beyond dispute?' The student's access to her headache is beyond dispute and so is not a matter of knowledge.[53]

Coherence Not Correspondence

We might say that what a naturalized epistemology produces, then, is not 'certainty' or 'objectivity' – that is the idiom of foundationalism which naturalism seeks to replace – but a kind of *commentary* on ways of unpacking the world. (And repacking and repairing it, if we adhere to Neurath's image of rebuilding a ship at sea.) One thing such commentary will reveal is that while the correspondence theory of truth always *appears* to be at work in our epistemologies – the idiom will be invoked, utterances will be compared with the world – upon close inspection these utterances will have a circular look to them insofar as our theories and ideas – our ontology – will already have established what counts as a good, or *true*, description and arrangement of the 'facts.'

To elaborate something I touched on above, the theory of gravity constitutes a good explanation for a range of phenomena, including why neither the Earth nor we soar off into the great beyond. But other explanations *might* work equally well. One reason we think this cannot be so is that we often blur the border between fact and theory, treating bits of theory as facts that have independently arisen from experience. In other words, we confuse different kinds of conceptual entities. This is largely the result of a loose employment of 'facts.' When we refer to something as a fact, we generally take the expression to mean that what we are saying is true. (Logically: statement S – 'My car is red' is true because fact F – my red car – exists.) But we have to be careful. The fact that the moon orbits the Earth is based on a very different order of observation from the 'fact' that gravity is responsible for this movement. Quine has argued that the objects to which a theory is committed are often 'mythical' – let's say they are non-observational or conceptual things wrapped up in language. Taking a few liberties with this idea, I want to suggest that our ways of speaking often turn gravity into something like a mythical 'fact.' What I mean is that we speak of gravity *as if* it were a fact, when in fact it's not; gravity is a concept (or theory) that explains why, among other things, large bodies orbit one another in particular ways. In other words, there is no 'fact' of gravity that *corresponds* to a theory of physics; there is a concept of gravity (expressed in laws) that *is part of the theory*. What may or may not correspond to the theory is the observed behaviour of objects under certain conditions. But the possibility remains that another set of laws embedded in another theory of physics could explain (and predict) the same behaviour equally well, or – this is a more radical proposition – divide up the behaviour of the universe in a different but equally workable way.

I am not, here, recommending that we go for a spin in the frictionless void: The theory must answer to the observations. But the theory is not the same thing *as* the observations, and a set of observations do not automatically generate a particular theory. If theories and observations intersect at those mysterious and sometimes mythical junctures that we call 'facts,' this, a naturalist will argue, is because the theories generate the 'facts' as much as the observations do. Put differently, theories structure observation. The relation between concepts and experience, the naturalist will tell us, cannot simply be read from a foundation up, and we have to take care, therefore, to understand where our 'facts' come from and what they are.

This position owes something to pragmatism. If we accept William James's argument that 'truth' just means something like, 'it works,' then the theory of gravity is true (assuming that theories can be 'true'; perhaps only sentences can be). It does not, however, have a monopoly on truth because it is possible that other theories could work, too. It owes more to Quine's insistence that the correspondence between bits of language and bits of the world is anything but self-evident.[54] Statements of fact, he argues, 'face the tribunal of sense experience not individually but only as a corporate body,'[55] which is to say, as parts of a theory or some such linguistic agglomeration that carries with it its own, generally unstated, ontology – its own sense of reality. We do not experience gravity. The laws of gravity, encased in a larger theoretical framework, explain *and structure* our experience. Most of us, most of the time, are so wrapped up in that framework that we can imagine no other world save the one it gives us. So, the facts of pure observation – if there are such things – meld into the 'facts' generated by our theoretical gaze. To return to James, as long as it all works, we are quite properly happy with the arrangement.

There is a hint (perhaps more than a hint) of circularity here, which returns us to what I have taken Kuhn's work to imply: That all theories are true insofar as they all establish their own criteria of truth. In other words, our ideas correspond to the world because to a very significant degree that is the world our ideas have constructed for us. This makes it very difficult to speak of the way the world 'really' is, or even of the way we are – in a Kantian sense – constrained to describe the world.[56] In the more extreme forms of naturalism, all realist bets are off, as *the* world gives way to a whole bunch of individually created worlds. In its more restrained (and probably more responsible) forms, experience has its say, although it is not always clear just how, and how far, it does. In either case, there is no brute 'given' at the foundation of our thought.

So, in either case, the correspondence theory of truth has to make room for something like a *coherence* theory of truth. A coherence theory rests on the assertion that a statement is true if it hangs together with other statements that are also assumed to be true. Although exactly what it means for statements to 'hang together' is difficult to say – the phrase is purposely vague and could range in intention from a strong 'is entailed by' to a weak 'is consistent with'[57] – Quine's comment that they face the tribunal of sense experience as a corporate body is an evocative metaphor. In a coherence theory, truth is a function of the experiential and/or logical consistency of a set of statements. The problem is that 'experiential consistency' falls into the quagmire of the self-validating circularity of the correspondence theory, as well as all the snares of naturalism set out above, while 'logical consistency' is positively medieval. However difficult it is to match theory up with independent facts derived from experience,[58] there is nonetheless an irreducible empiricist bent to modern science – or to the idiom of modern science (take your choice) – that leaves little room for a *purely* logical account of truth. A theory has to be *logically coherent*, or non-contradictory, since an incoherent theory says nothing testable about the world, however true its observation statements may be.[59] This makes logical coherence a necessary but not a sufficient condition of truth. To make it sufficient, some other criterion, some algorithm for connecting the statements in a theory to 'the world,' has to be added to the mix. For an epistemological naturalist, a pragmatic criterion, one that backs a safe step or two away from the strong empirical naivete of the correspondence theory, might fit the bill. This gives us a pragmatic version of coherentism: *a coherent theory that works*, that does not break down in the face of what we take to be 'experience.' After all, to the extent that a theory shapes our experience, such a breakdown would be a damning criticism, demonstrating that the theory's construction of experience is self-contradictory.

As usual, Rorty has fashioned a more radical option by adding a rhetorical touch to his pragmatism, advising us to stop worrying about experience, to stop making it a grand metaphysical issue. Rorty is fond of quoting Nietzsche's aphorism that 'truth is a mobile army of metaphors,' by which he seems to mean that a statement or idea becomes true through 'the literalization of novel metaphors.'[60] In other words, as new ways of talking about the world prove their worth *in whatever ways*, as they become, for whatever reasons, convincing, they come to be treated *as true*. The 'as true,' of course, opens a whole can of metaphysical worms: as true in relation to what? Since, for Rorty, they are not true *in relation* to anything but their own use – in other words, he suffers no relativist guilt – Rorty can effectively drop the 'as' and argue that the metaphors simply come to be true, with 'true' meaning, I think, something like 'taken literally.' This is very much in the spirit of James's assertion that truth *happens* to an idea. As a radical naturalist, with perhaps Nietzschean leanings, Rorty lives in this fluid space where all talk of 'final vocabularies' has to be set aside on the ground that no set of statements can be absolutely, irrefutably true.[61] Vocabularies come and go, into and out of fashion. The world – or the human conception of it – has no intrinsic nature,[62] and so there is no intrinsic or necessary way of talking about it. It 'does not provide us with any criterion of choice between alternative metaphors.'[63]

Still, however unhelpful the world may be in this regard, choices of vocabulary *are* made. Indeed, almost everything I have said in this chapter can be construed as an argument about choice of metaphors: copying versus describing, discovering versus creating, corresponding versus cohering, 'in' versus 'outside' the world, and so on. Each of these choices expresses certain metaphysical assumptions about 'reality.' Each, in fact, evokes a certain picture of reality. The emergence of any new vocabulary – including an epistemologically naturalist one to replace a foundationalist one – is signalled by removing the quotation marks from the new metaphors and placing them round the old ones. Let me offer a hypothetical example somewhat removed from the concerns of epistemology. The English historian of political thought, Quentin Skinner, has written that in the Italian city states of the Renaissance the term 'liberty' 'meant first of all [the city's] independence from the Emperor,' and second, the 'right to maintain their existing form of government.'[64] Imagine this in the narrowest sense. Imagine that the terms 'free' and 'unfree' are exclusively used to describe cities or states, but not individuals. If so, the first applications of the concept of liberty to the individual are consciously metaphorical. To say that an individual is 'unfree' (for in this example the term would almost certainly arise in the negative, as a complaint) is to compare his condition with that of a city or state that is not self-governing. Imagine, now, that the metaphor sticks. A mode of speech, thus, arises in which people come to be treated 'as if' they were oppressed cities. As time passes, people come to think of themselves in terms of the metaphor, and political philosophers eventually drop the quotation marks. It is now – literally – true that individuals are free or unfree. A new vocabulary has emerged with a new set of statements ('I'm free'; 'I'm not free') that are now true or false.

All of this forces on a knower the tricky demand that she understand when a metaphor is a metaphor – when the quotation marks are on – for only *naturalized* metaphors, ones with the quotation marks removed, have truth values and are matters of knowledge. For Rorty, this entails understanding the force of idioms or what he calls 'vocabularies' – in particular, understanding that they tell us not what a mind-independent world is like but what our particular perspective on it is. For naturalists who wish to remain in closer contact with the 'outside world,' the problem of the difference between the literal 'that' and the figurative 'as if' is less easily dismissed. Wittgenstein worried about the deceptive 'outward similarity' between metaphysical and experiential statements,[65] and I think we can transfer this concern to the relation between metaphorical and experiential ones. There is, notes Wittgenstein, a difference between 'seeing as' and 'seeing that' (the former is perspectival) which is easy to overlook, but which needs to be respected if we are to understand the difference between a metaphor and a statement of fact and also to understand how hard it often is to distinguish the two in practice.[66] (It is like distinguishing 'facts' from facts.) Rorty has eradicated this distinction by reducing all statements to 'seeing as' status, but with an overlay of historical dispensation that allows for the possibility of what I can only call a figurative transition from the figurative to the literal. Thus, Wittgenstein's distinction becomes, in Rorty's idiom, something like a distinction between 'living' and 'dead' metaphors. One way of 'seeing' the world can be replaced by another without any gain or loss of truth or, consequently, of knowledge. This takes Rorty beyond the positions taken by Wittgenstein or Quine or Kuhn. They may think there are not many theory-independent observational 'seeing-that' statements to be made, not many points at which theories match up with a 'brute factual reality,' but there are some. In Rorty's radicalized naturalism, there do not seem to be any. Even naturalism itself is only another metaphor-shift, signalled by the transition from the literal, 'The mind is the mirror of nature,' to the figurative, 'Foundationalists see the mind as the mirror of nature.' One can pose a McDowellian question here: Is this a liberation of reason or is it going for a spin in the frictionless void?

The Winds of Relativism

I have thus far trod carefully around the edges of the question of whether naturalism sails *too* close to the winds of full-blown relativism. Certainly, in its more radical versions, naturalism does seem to edge up against relativism, and when it does, truth may seem to fall victim to the pure subjectivity of someone who blurts out, 'Well, it's true for me.' Few philosophers would actively espouse such philosophically disheartening naivete. Nevertheless, versions of naturalized epistemology as radical as that of someone who, like Rorty, suggests that truth may be nothing more than a compliment we pay to a statement, may be open to the charge that truth has been reduced to something like this condition. Few naturalists will follow Rorty down that road. But insofar as they are committed to the proposition that the truth of a statement depends to a significant degree on the vocabulary or theory in which it is embedded, they have to accept that different vocabularies and different theories *can* produce different sets of true statements. These statements never really carry the naive subtext, 'Well, it's true for me.' This is because, as Wittgenstein so persuasively argues, languages are not private affairs. (In short, such a statement is actually incoherent: We cannot say what it means.) Such statements are nonetheless only 'true within the vocabulary,' which is to say, true for 'us,' for the community that uses the vocabulary. If there is no 'real world' 'out there,' independent of vocabulary-users, that can act as the final arbiter of vocabularies, this is, or so the argument goes, as true as a statement gets. Truth is not embedded in the world but in the speaker's ontological commitments. For the foundationalist and metaphysical realist this is unlikely to be true enough. He will complain that coherentism tells us not what statements are true but what statements the speakers of a language *take to be true*. That, he will insist, is not the same thing as truth, because there is, logically, a distinction to be drawn between what X thinks is true and what is true – unless, of course, X is an infallible god.

On this point, the foundationalist will have lots of support. Most philosophers seem at least a little discomfited by the spectre of even this less radical community-based relativism. Even it can look like a slippery slope towards unbridled subjectivism and, as I have said, no respectable philosopher wants even to be in the neighbourhood of someone who blurts out, 'Well, it's true for me.' Perhaps that is why philosophers such as Foucault and Derrida have tried in different ways to anchor their non-foundational thought in impersonal and shifting language structures that are less open to individual innovation than Rorty's vocabularies or Donald Davidson's languages. At one point, Foucault advances the idea that discourses (or 'discursive practices'), which mutate for a variety of not always discernible reasons, most of which lie outside human control, act as a limit to what the historically conditioned and determined individual can say.[67] As the French psychiatrist Jacques Lacan (echoing Samuel Beckett) reminds us, such a being does not speak; he is spoken. Insofar as subjectivity resides in the realm of frictionless choice, such 'spokenness' would defeat it. But at what cost?

Epistemology has thus become something of a philosophical Scylla and Charybdis, with movement in either direction – towards the un-changing rock of foundationalism or ever-moving whirlpool of natural-ism – evoking danger and a good deal of debate. Because our ways of speaking are at least foundational *in tone*, based on a strong sense that we are articulating real truths about a real world, what we say inevita-bly has a correspondence *feel* to it. We *feel* that the truth of what we say is a function of how well it matches up with the world. On close inspection, the naturalists argue, this turns out to be a very loose, indirect, and circular kind of correspondence, comforting because it is bound to work out but ultimately unenlightening. On the other hand, naturalism's tincture of relativism is neither comfortable nor, in terms of our vocabularies, even very natural. Foundationalism holds out the carrot of objective, value-free knowledge, the kind of knowledge we generally think of as scientific. Naturalism strikes at the root of that knowledge, turning it into, if not a subjective, then a limited and histori-cal product lacking secure foundations. For an epistemological natural-ist, knowledge is the product of a Hegelian history with one twist: It betrays no sign of progress towards absolute knowledge.[68] A foundationalist might point out that if this is so, if naturalism is true, it is self-refuting, since its truth cannot be permanent. Naturalism can be true only in the sense that it represents either, à la Rorty, a changing of the metaphorical guard in a world that no longer 'believes in' the sanctity of 'objective knowledge' or a recognition that we cannot get outside language and history. Naturalism cannot be true in a way that absolutely refutes foundationalism, because foundationalism, like any other vocabulary, is eternally capable of a return to centre-stage. A naturalist might reply that a foundationalism understood as one vo-cabulary among others is itself self-refuting because it now has to accept the inescapable truth that there is no absolute truth – which is what foundationalism denies. If so, then epistemology is, like meta-physics, the reduced enterprise that I have described as a commentary rather than a pursuit.

In this context, we may find ourselves driven towards what Alexander Nehamas has described as the truth-negating 'perspectivism' of Nietzsche.[69] Contra Socrates, Nietzsche argues that even if there is absolute truth (and he does not think that there is), we are in no way bound by it. Reasons for believing something count for more than truth. How we view things is more important than how things are. Nietzsche prefers, as a matter of principle, the frictionless void of self-produced reasons and the 'mobile army of metaphors' to the implacable reality of hard truths. Thus, he takes us to the untamed edge of naturalism, which is also the border of the new scepticism: We do not know whether there is any truth, and even if there is, we have no reason to pay particular homage to it. This is a good place to end. Both sides can be left to their arguments, which are many, varied, and often enormously subtle, far more so than I have been able to indicate in this chapter. I hope only that I have said enough to demonstrate that if epistemology is not, as Charles Taylor fears, in a bad way, it is at the least navigating perilous straits, which threaten to take it far from the glow of Plato's sun.

Addendum I: Ancient Epistemology

Before closing this chapter it is necessary to append a few remarks about the ancients whom I have, after the opening paragraphs, largely neglected. The neglect is judicious, for the epistemology of the ancient philosophers is in many ways distinct from modern concerns, and to delve into it would take us too far afield into a 'specialist' area. Anyway, the ancient world, like the modern, is hardly uniform in its epistemologies and not easy to characterize quickly. To speak somewhat anachronistically, versions of foundationalism and naturalism can be found among the Greek and Roman philosophers. There are rationalists, empiricists, and sceptics, too, but the setting is sufficiently different from the modern – in part because of the tremendous influence of science since the Renaissance[70] – that it is difficult to know how to connect the two worlds. Aristotle, for example, seems to hold a foundationalist view of knowledge insofar as he thinks that human beings just are fitted to know the world and that they therefore have trustworthy intuitions about it. But as he seems unable to decide precisely what those intuitions are, or how, exactly, we employ them, there is also a naturalist feel to his epistemology.[71] In the end, however, it might better be described as 'participational,'[72] which is to say that for Aristotle the human mind participates in – moves through – the great structure of being. This looks a little like the oxymoron 'naturalized foundationalism,' in which knowledge consists in understanding how we and other things fit into this structure of being. Plato's epistemology, in which knowledge is ultimately knowledge of the Forms, can also be described as participational. What Plato supplies is not a method for attaining knowledge – certainly nothing as detailed as Descartes' method – but a more static sketch of what knowledge is (knowledge of the Forms) and where a person must be (in the immediate presence of the Forms) in order to attain it. To be sure, there is also, particularly in his account of Socrates and his method, a great deal of emphasis on the justification of claims, just as there are a lot of procedural considerations in Aristotle's *Nichomachian Ethics*. The Socratic *elenchos*, with its relentless testing of the consistency of sets of claims, comes close to a coherence theory of truth, and Aristotle's insistence that the search for knowledge of the good life must begin with a consideration of what one's society considers good has a pragmatic feel to it. We can, in short, read theories backward as well as forward, but only with a great deal of circumspection and a great deal more consideration than I can give the matter here.

Addendum II: Epistemology and the Philosophy of Mind

Many of the concerns of this chapter are closely connected to the branch of philosophy – a rather large one in current analytical circles – called philosophy of mind. This is not surprising, because a central concern of philosophy of mind is how to work out just what the knower – the epistemological subject – is like. We often refer to ideas *in* the mind but what exactly do we mean by 'mind' as opposed to 'brain'? Do both entities exist, or only one? If we make an ontological commitment to both, how are they related? Such questions remind us that the ghost of Descartes haunts us still. Descartes' dualism, that thorny relation of mind and body (and therefore brain), has yet to be dispatched to its final rest. Not that attempts have not been made to do so. Philosophers have espoused both reductionist and eliminative theories – which is to say, physicalist (and therefore monist) theories that seek either to reduce mental events to physical (i.e., brain) events, to make the one a translation of the other, or, more radically, to eliminate mind-talk altogether. By contrast, non-reductionist theorists often argue that the mind only 'supervenes' on the brain – which is to say that there are legitimate mind operations. A supervenience theorist will accept that these operations could not exist without corresponding brain ones, but will insist that the two are not, as the reductionists would have it, mirror images of one another.[73] In their various ways, such theories try either to disperse or to make peace with the last vestiges of Descartes' great transcendental ego.

The bedevilling difficulty is that we usually end up with either too much mind or too little. Reductionist and eliminative theories flirt with the latter problem by veering towards a brain/nature model that reduces thought to brain functions, many of which remain, of course, to be discovered. In this view, 'mind' is essentially a word for those as yet undiscovered functions. Non-reductionist theories, on the other hand, risk preserving the mind at the cost of nature by detaching it from brain function. It is, after all, difficult to step back from physicalist theories without granting the mind *some* freedom. This is the 'seesaw' that McDowell describes in *Mind and World*, one that has us alternating between the 'rampant Platonism' of a mind that works in splendid isolation from nature and the 'bald naturalism' of a mind that has succumbed to nature, to the point, perhaps, where it ceases to exist. In the first case, there are only free-standing, self-given *reasons*, thoughts beholden to nothing but the mind's logic. In the second, there are only natural *causes* that move us no matter what a now-impotent reason may have to say about the matter. In neither case does there seem to be such a thing as knowledge. In McDowell's opinion, the trick – and it is not by any means an easy one – is to imagine how to dismount the seesaw and put mind and world back together. Insofar as that entails putting mind and brain together, it may be an impossible task. Understanding our consciousness may be, as Colin McGinn has argued,[74] something that evolution has simply not equipped us to do. The mind may be as McGinn describes it: a 'mysterious flame' that will always elude our grasp.

5

Logic and Its Place in the Universe

SUMMARY

Here, we do two things: introduce logic and consider the current debate concerning the place of logic in philosophy. The sceptical reaction to metaphysics has generated suspicion about the foundational nature of logic. However, before we can assess this, it is necessary to get some grasp of the fundamentals of, in particular, deductive reasoning. Readers are introduced to the laws of reason and the concept of validity as a way of understanding these fundamentals. We then turn to the question of the primacy of logic as opposed to rhetoric – philosophy as science as opposed to philosophy as literature. In this context, some of Derrida's arguments, as well as the non-arguments of a Zen master, are briefly presented.

Nietzsche *Contra* Plato

We may as well let the next domino fall. The anti-metaphysical, naturalist, and neo-sceptic trends running through contemporary philosophy cannot be without implications for logic, which I shall define as the formal expression of the *logos* that has long sat at the heart of the discipline. For, if as I argued in Chapter 2, logic fuels the metaphysical impulse, and if that impulse, the desire to see – behind appearances – a clear, coherent, and objective reality, fuels foundationalist epistemologies, then all that I have been saying so far must circle back to logic. The question put to it is this: What does logic – in particular deductive logic – have to do with truth? Can it be, as Descartes assures us it is, a *road* to truth?

Nietzsche uses the Greek gods Apollo and Dionysus as metaphors for reason and passion, order and chaos, announcing that in the modern age Dionysus has arisen to challenge the supremacy of Apollo.[1] Apollo is the beautiful sun god of straight-shooting archers, far-seeing prophets, and musicians who are the keepers of the great harmonies. Apollo is the god whose priestesses at Delphi announced to the world that no one was wiser than Socrates.[2] In short, Apollo is Plato's god, if ever there was one. For Nietzsche, however, Apollo is the god who 'reigns also over the fair illusion of our inner world of fantasy.'[3] The illusion is that the universe is as orderly a place as the Apollonian vision and the Platonic Forms suggest it is: as orderly as *logos* suggests. So, Nietzsche sets down beside Apollo the frenzied wine-god Dionysus, who is responsible for the poetic emanations of tragedy and comedy and who embodies, so Nietzsche tells us, the true and passionate soul of music, and therefore, of the universe.[4] In short, Nietzsche proclaims *poiesis* as our liberator from the chains of *logos*.

I mention music advisedly, because it is one of the grounds on which Nietzsche first engages Plato and Platonists. He does so with good reason, I think. One of the seminal influences on Plato were the Pythagoreans, whose school Plato visited in the early fourth century BCE. Pythagoreans viewed music as an expression of the great mathematical harmonies of the universe.[5] Plato tries to express that order in his own philosophy, to unpack it so far as he can, and write it down – not musically but 'mathematically,' in the precise philosophical language of *logos*.[6] In other words, Plato tries to bring the inner mathematical harmonies out of the music. This, the young Nietzsche informs us, is a futile exercise, for when language imitates music – and this is what Plato's elegant mathematical *logos* does – rather than giving expression to the 'innermost core' of music, it simply produces a superficial copy: a simulacrum. Nor will Plato's myth-making help, for 'no amount of poetic eloquence will carry us a step closer to the essential secret of that art.'[7] Plato – or Socrates; Nietzsche almost always refers to Socrates in these matters – claims for *logos* the beauty and the 'insight' of music. But it was a false claim, and the result is to make 'a tyrant of *reason*.'[8]

As I have indicated, Nietzsche's comment about 'poetic eloquence' suggests a link not only between music and *logos* but also between music and Plato's great myths. This is interesting. The poetry of Plato's myths is, perhaps, his 'real' music – or, at least, what most of his readers would think of as such. Yet, the great philosopher produces it a little shamefacedly. Or does he? Plato often apologizes for resorting to myth – 'I don't know but I have heard that the truth is something like this' – but his irony is as difficult to unpack as wisdom itself. It seems Plato is somewhat uncomfortable in using myth as a substitute for what a precise, mathematical *logos* ought to have been able to say directly, but could not. One could argue, as I have, that Plato's poetic eloquence masks the failure of reason. Nietzsche appears to be suggesting as much. He argues that, rather than going beyond reason and extending its insights, the myths serve instead to reveal the limits of reason, and, therefore – implicitly – the myths also reveal the tyranny of the claims that Plato makes for reason. In Plato's hands, the reputedly supreme *logos* always falls short of its goal, absolute truth, and is forced to take refuge in the simulacrum of *mythos*. The poetic extension of the insights of reason is, in reality, their truncation. If one were to accept this criticism, then Plato's understanding of music is wrong in two ways. First, he tried to reproduce music as a higher *logos*. Second, when he could not do so, he reduced music to poetry, in order to hide its limitations. All of this was done to promote the pre-eminence of reason, which, as any philosopher knows, stands above poetry.[9]

Here, as so often in his works, Nietzsche was throwing down the gauntlet, not only to Plato but to Descartes, Kant, Hegel, and all other defenders of the majesty of reason. One effect of the challenge is to open up the role of logic to critical scrutiny. We can use the language of Chapter 4 to set its terms. From a foundationalist perspective, logic – the formal rules of reasoning – is essentially a portrait of the human mind. In being logical, we are, in a very central way, being human. That humanity is, moreover, a kind of microcosm or mirror (choose your metaphor) of the rational universe. This view can be traced *at least* to Plato for whom *arête* (i.e., 'virtue,' which is a kind of 'care of the psyche' or nourishment of one's soul) just was the proper pursuit of reason. The development of one's powers of reason was essential to one's development as a person. So, too, did Descartes and Kant assume the sovereignty of reason. Indeed, until the end of the Enlightenment, those philosophers who had the temerity to reject this position – Machiavelli, Hobbes (the man Locke refers to as 'the justly despised Mr Hobbes'), Hume, and a few others – were always something of a *succès de scandale*. By contrast, we have seen that from a post-Nietzschean and naturalist perspective, logic is, or may be no more than, one mode of thought. Logic is one of a number of rhetorical (i.e., persuasive) strategies available to speakers and writers. If so, the fault, the great sin of philosophers, lies not – in the first instance, anyway – in their use of logic but, rather, in the status they accord it. The pre-eminence that philosophers have traditionally granted to logic, its role as the foundation or even embodiment of reason, is from this perspective an ancient rationalist bias that needs to be abandoned or, at least, greatly modified. In reply, a contemporary foundationalist might take as her *leitmotif* Wittgenstein's somewhat Kantian assertion in the *Tractatus* that 'we could not *say* what an "illogical" world would look like.'[10] We are, as Aristotle put it, 'life that speaks.' We are souls that bear the ineradicable mark of language, and language is inherently bound by the laws of logic, which is to say by what I shall soon define as the laws of contradiction and tautology. If there is 'sense' or 'meaning' or 'knowledge' beyond logic, we do not have access to it. If there is a world that transcends logic, it is a *noumenal* one, and we cannot get at. Like Descartes' Evil Demon, the non-logical lies beyond our ken. That explains why Parmenides is entirely serious when he decides that the assertion that there is a multifaceted world of time and space is illogical. For a foundationalist, to study logic is to explore the contours of the world and to allow it, so far as one can, to be enlightened by the glow of Plato's rational Apollonian sun.

Although I like this slightly overlit image, I am afraid I must dim it somewhat by inserting the following caveat: This perspective, spun from Wittgenstein's dictum, can be accorded varying degrees of strength. In the strongest version – of which Cartesian foundationalism is an expression – the human mind just is logical, as is the universe it mirrors. In Kantian terms *phenomena* and *noumena* coincide. If so, it has to be said, this is a happy coincidence. A weaker, or middling, version will retain the claim that the human mind is logical without extending it to the universe itself. This restricts us to the *phenomenal* side of the argument. Under its auspices, we describe ourselves – with distinct echoes of Kant – not as *seeing* the order of the universe but as *imposing* order on the universe. The weakest, possibly pragmatic, version of the argument externalizes the ground of logic completely. It asserts not that we necessarily are, in our natures, logical – which is what the first two versions do assert – but that our experience in the world demonstrates the usefulness of logic to human enterprise.

For our present purposes, there is no need to choose among these perspectives. Right now we need to focus on what they have in common, rather than on how they differ. What they have in common is the contention that logic occupies a central place in philosophy because of the role it plays in framing the world for us. To this extent, logic stands, potentially, in judgment of the entire philosophical enterprise. An illogical argument or a self-contradictory philosophical discourse is, by definition – *by Socrates' definition* – a bad one. (Presumably a pragmatist would find logic useful, in part, because illogical arguments are useless.) Rhetoric, which values persuasive arguments over logical ones, is therefore, as it is in Plato's works, to be rejected as a non-philosophical – certainly a *less* philosophical – mode of discourse that seeks not knowledge, but power.[11] Plato's myths are conceivably a type of rhetoric – stories that aped the sun and persuaded by their brilliant imagery. For that reason, Plato has perhaps from his own perspective, reason to apologize for telling them. In any event, Plato's his myths appear both to have raised and suppressed a question that later sprung to Nietzsche's lips: Is logic the most fundamental form of language, the foundation of all knowledge, or, is it simply a form of rhetoric, a kind of logical poetry that pretends to a truth it cannot deliver? Do we, in other words, accept logic because it is the truth of *logos*, or do we accept it because Plato and other tyrant-makers have persuaded us to do so? (Let's think about what is going on when the unnamed guardians release the prisoners in the cave.) Like all the other philosophical issues I have tried so far to raise, this one can be safely left to the reader's judgment. What I need to do to assist that judgment is outline the rudiments of the deductive logic that is at issue.

The Laws of Reason: Identity

Logic, or at least the deductive branch of it, is, essentially, the expression of three fundamental laws: the law of identity, the law of the excluded middle, and the law of non-contradiction.[12] These laws, which are the embodiments of the principles of contradiction and tautology, are interconnected such that any one of them can be derived from any of the others. Let's consider each in turn.

At first glance, the law of identity is no more than a piece of common sense: *When reasoning, identify (define) your terms clearly, and then stick to those identities.* Reasoning requires clarity, and good reasoning just is clear: To parody Kant, the predicate 'clear' is included in the subject 'good reasoning.' Unfortunately, the issue is not quite as simple as that, primarily because the law of identity comes in two parts: a clarity demand followed by a consistency demand. Moreover, the clarity demand, however commonsensical it is, broaches a suppressed epistemological issue – which is to say, the extra-logical one of how to determine the *correctness* of a definition when it is mapped onto the world. The point is that to be clear is to indicate what a term picks out or identifies, and we generally think it a semantic virtue if it picks out the 'right thing.' If someone is talking about widgets, he ought, from an epistemological point of view, not to be referring to small furry quadrupeds. This is because epistemologists, the frustrated scientists of the philosophical community, have a tendency to be reaching out to the world. They want to know the truth (or rather, they want to develop procedures that will allow them to know the truth): Is that really what a widget is? The logician, for better or worse, is less interested in truth. She has nothing against truth. She is perfectly happy if a term picks out the 'right thing' in the world, but she will point out that, strictly speaking, *all* the law of identity requires is clarity – which is to say, that a term be defined in such a way that what it identifies can be picked out from among all other things. (And, given the difficulties inherent in reference, that is in itself no small thing.) It is perfectly possible to produce a clear but incorrect identification for a term, so long as it allows you to pick out *something*. I can teach someone to identify the word 'widget' with gerbils, and if that person goes on to use the word 'widget' every time he sees a gerbil, I will have satisfied the clarity demand. What we are bumping up against here is the *formal* nature of logic, which is to say its concern with procedure, or form, as opposed to truth, or content.

This formality is also the hallmark of the second part of the law of identity, where a *consistency* demand is added to the clarity criterion: Once a term is identified, do not alter that identification in the course of the discussion. Nothing is said, or even implied, about the correctness of the identification, which now seems to have been forgotten. On the contrary, if anything is implied, it is that one ought to stick with a clear but incorrect definition once it has been made. We can label this the 'don't change horses in mid-stream' rule. I sometimes introduce students to this criterion by consistently, and without explanation, referring to books as calculators. Very quickly, they begin to respond to my command to 'take out your calculators' by producing their texts, and business proceeds as usual. Problems arise only when I switch the identifying word for book before each class, or worse, each time I want to refer to a book.

The point is that in a discussion about chairs or any other object in the world, it is a good idea to make a correct identification if you can, but to do so is not, strictly speaking, fundamental to deductive logic. What *is* fundamental is the demand that the identification, however accurate or inaccurate it is, be clear and consistent. If we parcel out responsibilities, correctness (and therefore truth) is the province of science (*episteme* in Greek), clarity of grammar and syntax, and consistency of logic. Insofar as logic is linguistic, it owes a debt to clarity. But since – or if – *pace* Descartes, logic owes nothing to epistemology, it has no debt to correctness. (And so, logic begins to recede from the world, which is one of the points I want to make in this chapter.) Moreover, many terms cannot be identified as easily as 'chair' or 'gerbil' or 'widget,' for these are concrete nouns that admit of ostensive definition. Someone can point to an article of furniture and say, 'There, *that's* a chair,' and in doing so pretty much satisfy the law of identity.[13] But abstract nouns such as 'justice' or 'knowledge' or 'beauty' – the very terms that philosophers are often concerned with – do not admit of ostensive definition. They admit of definition, but not of extra-linguistic identification. (I pointed this out at the end of Chapter 3.) Someone may indicate a painting and exclaim, 'Now, *that's* beautiful.' But she is not picking out beauty in the same way that she would pick out a chair – for the chair is literally a chair, while the painting is not literally beauty (or is it?).[14] To recall a point I made at the end of Chapter 3, we define these metaphysical-looking terms only through reference to other terms, only *in* language. Therefore, it is seldom possible to say, absolutely, that the definitions are *correct*. Indeed, it may not even be useful to think of them *as* correct or incorrect.[15] Nevertheless, we can at least hope to achieve clarity and consistency – although we have to remember that philosophy is full of unfulfilled hopes. (In a sense, clarity just is consistency: a definition that does not send us off in different directions.)

Because the logician aims at a clear and consistent identification of the terms in her argument, the law of identity is violated principally, although not solely, through *equivocation* – using a term in different and perhaps contradictory ways in the course of an argument. Consider the following, rather silly and sexist, but logical argument that a student gave me a long time ago: *Only man is rational; no man is a woman; therefore, no woman is rational.* Logically, which is to say 'formally,' this argument is fine. It is what we call a valid argument. If we map it against experience, however – that is, if we turn to epistemological concerns – problems arise with respect to the *identification of terms*. Most experienced English speakers will take the first instance of 'man' to refer to 'humankind' and the second to refer to 'male,' in which case 'man' has two definitions, or identifications, in the argument. This is equivocation; and this argument works only insofar as we fail to notice the equivocation. If we decide to correct it by substituting the different definitions for the word 'man' in the argument, we get the following: *Only humankind is rational; no male is a woman; therefore, no woman is rational.* Now the argument manifestly lacks sense; it is a *non sequitur* and invalid to boot. The possibility of this invalid reading was always there, but papered over by the equivocation on the term 'man.'

So, on one reading (two actually) the argument is valid, while on another (two) it is invalid. Everything depends on whether we hook 'man' up to one or two identities. I stress, once again, that truth is not at issue here. *If* there is an equivocation on 'man,' the argument falls apart, *if not* it is valid – although almost certainly untrue. If someone prefers a logical argument to an illogical one – the first reading to the second – our grounds for condemning her cannot be logical ones. We may do so on the epistemological ground that the valid argument is untrue – not only men are rational – but here the logician stands beside jesting (*pace* J.L. Austin) Pilate and asks, 'What is truth?' When you think about it, this is quite surprising. Although our preference for the second, un-equivocal but illogical, reading is based on sound experience, it is not logically necessary. Let's give this a strong statement: It is merely a prejudice to assume that logic must bow before the demands of 'the world.' Of course, a neo-Nietzschean would respond, it is equally a prejudice to assume that the world must bow before the demands of logic, and is that not what Platonists have been ordering us to do all these many years?

To help us ponder this point, let's consider a slightly subtler example of equivocation: *Power corrupts, and knowledge is power, so knowledge corrupts.* Here we have to focus our attention on the term 'power.' In the first instance, power appears to refer to the ability to control people, in the second, to the ability to control one's environment or situation in life. These are overlapping identifications, but they are not identical, and it is the suppression of this potential lack of identity – the potential equivocation – that allows the argument to appear to make sense. If I control the equivocation by writing (as I think experience dictates), *'the ability to control people corrupts, and knowledge allows us to control our environment, so knowledge corrupts,'* that 'sense' disappears, just as it did in the first example. I remind you, however, that the logician, *qua* logician, does not care which reading is enforced. She is content to point out that one is valid and one invalid. If she takes on the role of an epistemologist, however, she does care. As Robert Brandom points out,[16] knowledge claims (post-Cartesian ones, anyway) must be part of an 'inferentially articulated network' that commits us to those claims and entitles us to make them. This would seem to be the point at which logic becomes responsible to the world. In the case of both the 'power corrupts' and the 'only men are rational' arguments, entitlement would seem to be lacking for the surface, or literal, reading. Let's focus on the 'only man is rational' argument. In it, there would seem to be no entitlement to the first claim if 'man' is understood as 'male' and there would certainly be no entitlement for understanding 'man' as 'humankind' in the second claim. This reminds us of an important naturalist lesson: the use of terms involves, as Brandom puts it, 'adopting a complex, essentially *socially* articulated stance or position in the game of giving and asking for reasons.' In this light, consider how 'unnatural' the argument is on first reading and how easily most people will accept the equivocation explanation for the unnaturalness. Only a Martian or an excessively committed logician will refuse to be moved by it.

If the logician does refuse to be moved, it is because she pulls logic up short of a fully realized semantics. Questions of reference are to be sorted out in the world, and that is somebody else's business. (And presto, a *logos*-world dualism appears.) For her, the law of identity invokes a primary and highly formal condition of meaningful discourse, *one that is prior to truth:* that we be (as far as possible) clear and consistent in the use of our terms. Quine, who was sceptical about the ability of logic to touch an objectively real world, asserted the rule, 'No entity without identity.' Quite so, but everything depends on how we interpret this rule, whether we understand it as reaching right out to the world. In logic, a term must have one (and only one) identification. If we treat this as a formal demand, the truth or correctness of the identification does not matter. Apply the law of identity to a term, give it a clear and non-contradictory definition, and it becomes a logical entity.

The Laws of Reason: The Excluded Middle

Next is the law of the excluded middle. This law – *for any term 'X,' everything in the universe is either X or it is not X* – reduces choice to a basic two options, excluding all third (fourth, fifth, etc.) – or 'middle' – possibilities. Since everything begins with identity, think of it this way: When a term is deployed in an argument, either it has a clear identification or it does not. If it has, then a listener will be able to pick out instances of it – even if, because of an incorrect definition, they are incorrect instances. If you grasp the identity – understand the definition, in effect – of the term 'chair' then you will be able to pick out individual chairs in the universe. (If 'chair' is defined as 'small, furry quadrupeds,' that is what you will pick out, and you may find yourself sitting on a gerbil.) You will also understand that, since identity individualizes an entity, everything in the universe either is a chair or is not a chair. There is no middle option. This is the principle of *tautology*: In the case of every entity (i.e., everything that has an identity), the universe divides into two and only two classes – the 'is' and the 'is-not.' A tautological statement is always true, because it encompasses all the possibilities in the universe. Moreover, we know tautological truths *a priori* – in advance of any evidence. I know, for example, that there are only two classes of people who will read these words: people-named-Jane and people-not-named-Jane. No other possibility exists. I leave it to the reader to assign herself to one of these classes.

What the law of the excluded middle does, then, is introduce 'identity' to its constant companion 'difference,' for a term has an identity only insofar as it is *differentiated* from other terms. As Quine put the matter, 'we cannot know what something is without knowing how it is marked off from other things.'[17] There can be an 'is' only if there is an 'is-not,' which is why negation is such an important logical concept. A green traffic light is a sign that has meaning only because it is 'not-red' and 'not-yellow' – which is to say, it is 'not "not-green."' If neither of the other signs existed in the traffic light system, the green light would be meaningless. It would amount to the message: 'Either go or go.' (There would, that is, be no 'not-go' option. Of course, our traffic signals are not strictly binary, since they have three options.) In logical terms, it would say, 'either X or X,' whereas the law of the excluded middle requires us, in support of identity, to be able to say, 'either X or not-X.' Of course, green could be set out in opposition to no light at all – 'green on' (go) or 'green off' (don't go) – but the point, *pace* Parmenides, is that there must be at least two possibilities to create the context of meaning. If everyone in the world were named Jane, no one would really have a name at all. Names make sense only in the context of other names. In a Jane-only world, the question, 'What's your name?' would never be uttered. In short, to be able to identify an entity 'X,' 'not-X' must exist, at least as a possibility. (Parmenides is spinning in his grave!)

Tautology may seem to represent a rather trivial kind of knowledge. In fact, though, tautology can be very useful when it comes to focusing thought and imposing order on the world. This of course follows from what I have been saying – without the law of the excluded middle, the whole universe would collapse into a Parmenidean oneness. As illustration of the utility of tautology, let us consider a couple of examples that are not so much logical puzzles as puzzles that logic, or to be specific, the law of the excluded middle, can help resolve. They will also serve to underline how the concept of 'identity and difference' is at work in this law.

In the first puzzle, you are confronted with a set of eight coins and a balance scale (and a lab assistant to do the weighing for you so you don't cheat). Seven of the coins, you are told, weigh the same. However, the eighth is either slightly lighter or slightly heavier than the others. Your mission is to use the scale to isolate the unique coin and determine whether it is heavier or lighter than the others. But here is the catch: you only get three weighings to accomplish the task. The first imperative is, therefore, 'do not waste weighings.'[18] Every time you put coins on the scale, you have to learn something from doing so. The law of the excluded middle will help you do this. You implement it by asking yourself the following tautologically astute question: When I place a certain number of coins on the scale, will *one of only two possible things happen*? For example, suppose you decide to begin by weighing all eight coins, placing four on each side of the scale. Will one of two things happen? The answer, strictly speaking, is no, not if you understand the options you are looking for. Only one thing will happen: the scale will not balance. One side will go down and one up. Since you do not yet know whether you are looking for a heavier or a lighter coin, this tells you nothing. This move is useless because you know *a priori* what will happen. Realizing this, you divide the coins in half, weighing four (two on each side) and leaving four aside. Now, indeed, one of two things will happen: either the scale will balance or it will not and – this is also crucial – you cannot know in advance which of the two possibilities will occur. *If* the scale balances, the unique coin is patently not among the four on the scale; *if* the scale does not balance, it is.

In either case, there were two and only two options and whatever happened narrowed down your search – from eight possibilities to four – for the unique coin. So, this was a good move. As you consider the options for the next weighing, you have to keep the law of the excluded middle securely in mind. You must, once again, make a move where you know *a priori* that one of two things will happen. But, again, you do not know which of the two will happen. (That you will know only *a posteriori*.) If, for example, you simply divide up the group of four coins containing the unique one (putting two on each side) and weigh them, you know *a priori* what will happen – the scale will not balance. Since you do not know whether you are looking for a lighter or heavier coin, this is, as before, absolutely useless knowledge. So, after much thought, what you do is take three coins from the group where the unique coin is and three from the all-normal group and weigh them against each other. *Now*, one of two things will happen. Either the scale will balance or it will not balance – and you do not know which it will be. If the scale balances, then the fourth coin from the 'unique group' is the coin you are looking for. Simply weigh it against any other coin and you will know – in three weighings – whether it is a heavier or a lighter coin. If the scale does not balance, then the unique coin is among the three you set on the scale. If that side has gone up, the coin is lighter; if it has gone down, it is heavier. Now all you do is weigh any two of those three coins. I hate to beat the idea to death, but, once again, one of two things will happen: the scale will balance or the scale will not balance. If the scale balances, then the third coin in the group is the one you want, and you already know whether it is heavier or lighter. If the scale does not balance, then, since you already know whether the coin you are looking for is heavier or lighter than the rest, you simply take either the one that went down or the one that went up, as the case may be. Again, you have isolated the coin in three weighings.

Throughout this process, the law of the excluded middle directed your thought by containing possibilities and making options manageable. This is the model for all binary systems, and it is a very powerful intellectual tool. Should there still be sceptics among my readers, I ask you to consider this puzzle. It may seem more daunting than the previous puzzles, and it takes us a step closer to the binary heart of this logic. You are ushered into a room where there is a very long table on which 10,000 blank slips of paper have been laid out in a line. You are told that on the underside of each slip a sum of money is written. No two sums are the same, and the slips are set out randomly on the table, so there is no orderly progression of sums. All is chaos. Here is the question: If you were instructed to start turning over the slips of paper, beginning on the left and working your way along, and if you were instructed to stop when you thought you had turned over the slip with the largest sum of money written on it, what would your chances be of actually doing so? (You cannot turn them all over and then go back and look.)

In my experience, most people go for the basic 1 in 10,000. In fact, however, you have a much better chance than that if you, once again, put the law of the excluded middle to work on the problem. To begin with, while you do not know precisely where the slip you want is, by the law of the excluded middle you do know *a priori* that it is *either* among the first 5,000 slips *or* it is among the second 5,000. There is no third option.[19] Moreover, the chances of it being one place or the other are fifty-fifty. This doesn't help much, but it would if you had one more piece of information – if you knew what the second-highest sum is. Indeed, if you had that bit of information, you would be absolutely guaranteed to get the highest sum. The problem, the fly in the logical ointment, is that you don't know what the second-highest sum is any more than you know what the highest sum is. But, what you do know *a priori* is that it is *either* among the first 5,000 slips *or* among the second 5,000. The chances here, as before, are fifty-fifty. So, there are four possibilities for the distribution of the highest and second-highest sums. I have set them out below, with (1) standing for the highest amount and (2) the second highest: Each of these distributions has a 25 per cent chance of actually existing.

	1st 5000	2nd 5000
a)	1 & 2	
b)	1	2
c)	2	1
d)		1 & 2

From this it is possible to derive a strategy that will greatly improve your chances of finding the highest sum. What you do is play option (c): You bet that the second-highest sum is in the first 5,000 and that the highest sum is in the second 5,000. Then, you simply turn over the first 5,000 slips – keeping track of the highest amount that appears – and continue through the second 5,000 until you get a higher amount, which is, by definition, the highest. Since the chances of each option being the actual one are equal, you have a 25 per cent chance of stopping at the highest amount – hardly a guarantee, but a lot better than 1 in 10,000. Besides, you are not done yet. Consider option (d). If it represents the actual distribution, and you are playing (c), then when you come to the second 5,000 slips, you still have a shot – because the highest amount is still there. Here, things get a little more complicated. I will not continue, but a quick glance should suggest that you will still have about a half of a 25 per cent chance of stopping at the highest amount – that is, a 12.5 per cent chance. Added to option (c), this gives you virtually a 37.5 per cent $(3/8)$[20] chance of finding the highest sum, which is a lot better than most people think. If (a) or (b) represents the actual distribution of the two highest sums, you are, of course, dead in the water.

Mathematicians and statisticians have told me that this method of solving the problem is crude beyond belief, and I am willing to accept their judgment. But that is the point: The law of the excluded middle, which seems so trivial, is the foundation of much deeper thought, and a foundation, therefore, that can often be put to much good use. This law is also the foundation of the truth table, which contains the essence of all binary logic, including that of computers.[21]

The Laws of Reason: Non-contradiction

Finally, there is the law of non-contradiction: *Nothing can simultaneously occupy contradictory states.* Essentially, this serves to remind us that we can never exercise the Parmenidean option of collapsing identity and difference into one another. I cannot, for instance, claim simultaneously, and in the same world, to be named Andrew and not named Andrew, because these are different and mutually exclusive states. The law of non-contradiction can be linked to the law of the excluded middle by saying that an entity can occupy only one side of a tautology at a time. Otherwise, we would not be able to identify it, and the whole foundation of logic would, once again, collapse.

I must add the following brief discussion about time. (Although this may seem somewhat tangential, it is not.) If we reflect on the law of non-contradiction, it will reveal how logic depends on us adopting a segmented view of time, in which there are these strange metaphysical entities called 'instants.' We often think of time this way, especially when we are measuring things – such as the 'time' of runners in a race – or in some other way dividing the world into distinct temporal parts. We also, sometimes, think of time in a quite different way – as a kind of Heraclitian river that flows along without breaking up into distinct parts. Consider the second hands on analogue watches. Most modern ones move, somewhat jerkily, from second to second. They are the perfect embodiment of 'instant time,' pausing just enough – insinuating a 'blank space' between seconds – to allow us to distinguish one second from another. Imagine a hand, however, that swept around the 360 degrees of the face in one smooth motion. That would be 'flow time,' bereft of metaphysical inter-second spaces. A flow time-watch is not terribly good for measuring things, because each unit of time (a second in this case) disappears far too smoothly into the next one. To measure things 'by time' we need to be able to identify discrete units. The jerky movement just described does this for us by creating the necessary illusion of a gap – a small, but metaphysically indispensable pause – between seconds.[22] Given this gap, we are able to apply the three laws of reason: Either it is 10:22.56 or it is not, and it cannot be both. (Note how the fundamental law of identity is encased in the other two, which essentially specify what the first means.) However satisfying this is, and however inept the sweeping 'flow-time' watch would be at measuring discrete units of time, it needs to be pointed out that the latter undoubtedly catches the way we phenomenally experience time – which is to say, as a continuous and undifferentiated Heraclitian flow of events.

I will not push this metaphor, which threatens to force me to concede how artificial the imposition of logic on the world is, any further. I will simply add that it shows how our ontology – our catalogue of what sorts of things exist – often enters into our thinking without our quite noticing it. Logic and certain kinds of measurement require us to enter into an 'instant-time' ontology as a condition of doing logic or of making those measurements. This seems to be an example of the thesis that the truth of what we say is decided in advance by our metaphysics. The logic I have been outlining – which, being above-board and honest, I have referred to as 'binary' – rests on a dualist ontology: Things are or they are-not, and all 'maybes' are excluded as illegitimate refusals to play the game. Nothing sweeps; nothing is indefinite. This should be borne in mind when considering my comments in the latter part of the chapter.

Let us return now to the law of non-contradiction. Essentially, this law is a signpost that marks the boundary of logic. To step beyond it is to step beyond logic into another, in many ways unimaginable, world. Paradoxes are prime examples of this 'stepping beyond,' little forays into the unknown. A paradox is a statement whose truth value (true or false) will not stand still; if it is true, it is false and vice versa. (In short, paradoxes refuse to live by the laws of binary logic.) But, since, by the binary law of identity, the statements in a logical argument are identified by their truth value (i.e., as 'true' or 'false' although no good logician really cares *which* they are), and since, by the law of the excluded middle, a statement is supposed to be *either* true *or* false, and since, by the law of non-contradiction, it cannot simultaneously be both true *and* false, this amounts to an impossible statement: a non-statement, therefore. Consider Bertrand Russell's 'Barber of Seville paradox.' In it, Russell asks us to imagine a *man* who is a barber in Seville. This barber shaves all, and only, the men in Seville who do not shave themselves. That is the fundamental rule. Now, Russell asks, does the barber, a man of Seville, a citizen in good standing of that fair city, shave himself? Well, if he does shave himself, then by rule he doesn't – and if he doesn't, then by rule he does! The lesson? The man described here is paradoxical and cannot exist – or at least we cannot, within a binary ontology, imagine how he can. There is no identity for this non-entity, unless we apply a version of set theory in which the barber is treated as a kind of 'meta-man' who stands outside the domain of 'all the other non-barber men of Seville.' (The 'I am lying' version of the well-known liar's paradox can thus be resolved by making that statement into a meta-statement about every other statement the speaker makes. This means that it stands above them as the one true statement the person utters. So long as the statement belongs to the same class as the speaker's other statements, the paradox remains.)[23]

In the same vein, there is a well-known intellectual trinket which consists of asking what happens when the irresistible force meets the immovable object. Using the law of non-contradiction, we can predict that they will in fact never meet, because they are defined, or identified, in a way that makes their simultaneous existence contradictory. An irresistible force would, by definition, be able to move all objects. Hence, if such a force exists there are, by definition, no immovable objects. On the other hand, an immovable object would, by definition, resist all forces. Hence, if such an object exists there are, by definition, no irresistible forces. Of course – to underline the ontological point made above – this is true only in the binary world. If we transfer our residence to the sweeping currents of the 'flow world' where time and other 'quanta' dissolve in the never-ending, infinite river where an inhabitant of the instant-world cannot swim, we can then define an irresistible force as an arbitrarily large force and an immovable object as an arbitrarily heavy object. In this case, there is no paradox, because there is no necessary reason why an arbitrarily large force cannot coexist with an arbitrarily heavy object.[24]

Taken together, the three laws of reason frame a binary universe and instruct anyone living in it to define her terms clearly and to use them consistently in a non-contradictory fashion. In this universe, a tautology is always true, and a contradiction is always false – we know these things *a priori* – and in between, in fine anti-Parmenidean fashion, is the 'real' world of possibility, where statements may be true or false. Having framed this difficult world, the logician, given her druthers, will leave it to the scientist or, at least, the epistemologist to figure out what is actually true and false. But she knows that they will be a lot more efficient because she has set out the guiding *a priori*'s of necessary tautologies and impossible contradictions.[25]

Deduction and Induction

Earlier, I distinguished between the *a posteriori* world of possibility and the *a priori* world of tautology. In doing so, I was essentially distinguishing between, respectively, inductive and deductive reasoning. As I noted, what I had to say applied to deductive logic. I must now add a few comments about the distinction between deductive logic and induction, because this is germane to grasping the problematic relation between logic and the world. Induction, which starts roughly from experience, entails drawing conclusions that are, if the reasoning is sound, *probably* true. In a nutshell, induction is thinking about the content of the world. In the most fundamental sense, one moves from the evidence to a conclusion: If 90 per cent of the tested models of a given car manufacturer's product have faulty transmissions, then it's a sound bet that if you buy such a car you will be visiting your mechanic. But a sound bet is not a sure bet. For all of their recorded history, Europeans could observe only white swans, and so they drew the quite reasonable and sound inductive inference that all swans are white. Then some Europeans went to Australia, where they discovered black swans. That's the point of induction: One draws a conclusion based on (one hopes) good evidence. But no matter how good the evidence is, the chance remains that it is wrong. One is never absolutely entitled to one's commitments. This is because induction entails basing an inference about very large or unbounded classes, like swans, on experience of something less than the whole. A person projects from what he has experienced to what he will experience in the future. It is possible to achieve very high degrees of probability about what will happen, but never certainty. That is where Descartes' (and Hume's) scepticism about empirical evidence is rooted, and that accounts for his completely deductive route to the world.

Deduction is a formal method of reasoning. Deduction is concerned not with truth but with validity – which is to say, with the formal

connection between ideas. Hume calls this the 'relations of ideas,' pointing out that it has nothing to do with what the world is really like.[26] In
this respect, deduction is like a mathematical proof: To accept some
statements *as* true entails accepting others *as true*. Deduction is a process of reasoning, or argumentation, in which premises are set out such
that *if* they are true, then a conclusion properly drawn from them is also
necessarily true. A sample *syllogism* – a deductive argument with two
premises – will show what I mean:

Premise 1: *If* philosophers are abstruse;
Premise 2: *And if* Plato is a philosopher;
Conclusion: *Then* Plato is abstruse.

One cannot, without violating the law of non-contradiction, accept the
premises as true and then reject the conclusion.

So, the process is fundamentally simple. In a deductive argument
you draw a conclusion based on premises, which, if true, demonstrate
that it is true. *The truth of the conclusion follows necessarily from the truth of
the premises.* Despite this, the point at issue is never truth: In the above
case we don't really know whether philosophers are abstruse or even,
strictly speaking, whether Plato is a philosopher. We need to understand just how heavily the little conditional 'if' weighs on the argument.
If the two premises are true, *then* so is the conclusion. *If*, however, either
of the premises is false, *then* all bets are off, for then the conclusion
could be either true or false. It bears repeating: 'Truth,' strictly speaking, is an epistemological judgment on the *content* of an argument (i.e.,
that what is being said is true), but deductive arguments are really
about *form* rather than content. As I have said, what this means is that
the primary issue is not whether deductive arguments are true, but
whether they are *valid*.

The idea that arguments can be valid without being in the least true is
a rather important point when one is considering the role of logic as a
foundation stone of philosophy. Consider the following syllogism:

Premise 1: *If* all Martians are Texans;
Premise 2: *And if* all Texans are Canadians;
Conclusion: *Then* all Martians are Canadians.

In this case, anyone with sufficient experience of the world will recognize that all three statements are false. Yet, the argument is valid, for *if*
the premises were true then so, *necessarily*, would the conclusion be, as

well. In other words, the argument has the correct deductive form. By contrast, consider the following invalid syllogism:

Premise 1: *If* humans are mortal;
Premise 2: *And if* Socrates is mortal;
Conclusion: *Then* Socrates is human.

These premises could be true – humans could be mortal (they seem to be) and so could Socrates, upon whom the hemlock had a deleterious effect – but that does not *necessarily* mean that Socrates is human. Nowhere has that been stated. Socrates could be another kind of mortal – my pet cat, for example – since the argument does not restrict mortality to humans. So, although the argument is, in all likelihood, comprised of true statements, it is invalid – which is to say, those particular true statements do not add up to a proof that Socrates is human. By contrast, had I written 'only humans are mortal' for the first premise, the argument would have been valid but false. Again, the correct form does not guarantee truth.

The point is that deduction is a type of calculus, a manipulation of various kinds of logical operators.[27] There are a number of deductive calculi, possessed of varying degrees of power, but they all adhere to the same basic principle of validity, and however closely validity may cosy up to truth, it never quite gets there. In this context, Hume's distinction between 'matters of fact' – reports on experience – and 'relations of ideas' would seem to hold fast. When we talk about the world, we are asserting matters of fact (swans are white) that are, if we have carefully considered our experience, very likely to be true. When we talk about relations of ideas, we are talking about logical connections (If A>B and B>C then A>C) that are governed only by the definitions that set them out. Casting another glance at the Martian argument above, I have said that the content, which concerns Martians, Texans, and Canadians, is almost certainly false. The form that emerges from the logical words that connect the false claims nonetheless makes the argument valid. But I used a hybrid logic when I stated it above, so let me restate the argument in more rigorous sentential form:

If someone is a Martian *then* he is a Texan, *and if* he is a Texan, *then* he is from Canada. *Hence, if* someone is a Martian *then* he is from Canada.

Now, the point is that when we have our eye on validity, sentences are just sentences. In this syllogism there are three sentences: (1) Someone is a Martian. (2) Someone is from Texas. (3) Someone is a Canadian. These are simple declarative sentences, no different in type from 'The car is red' or 'Bananas are fruit': just so much content, we might say. We are uninterested in content, and, therefore, we simply replace the sentences with variables – 'p' for sentence (1), 'q' for (2), and 'r' for (3). Now the argument can be symbolized such that its form is highlighted: 'If p then q and if q then r, hence if p then r.' The only words left – they are in italic print in the sentential form given above – are the logical ones, which is to say, the *form-giving* ones. They, too, can be replaced by symbols: $[(p \rightarrow q) \cdot (q \rightarrow r)] \rightarrow (p \rightarrow r)$. The arrow means 'if ... then' and the dot means 'and'; the square brackets mark the two premises off from the conclusion. (For simplicity's sake, read the arrow between the square brackets and the conclusions as 'hence.') Now we have what amounts to a Humean statement of the relations of ideas: If one event (q) is conditional on another (p) and if a third event (r) is conditional on it (q), then the third event (r) is conditional on the first (p). Hume would emphasize that the world need not obey this apparently causal law – that we are only describing how things *appear* to work – but I think all we need do to get this effect is remind ourselves how the conditional 'if' marks deduction off from the world, because what it says, of course, is that the relation imagined between p, q, and r need never apply.[28] All that the statement asserts is that *if* a certain relation *were* to apply between p and q and between q and r, it would apply between p and r, as well. In short, this is simply a statement of the logical concept of transitivity.[29]

The Return of Rhetoric

To summarize, inductive reasoning reaches out to the world, but it always falls short of the certainty that Descartes and others craved. Deductive reasoning achieves that certainty, but only because it never touches the world. (That's why, in its way, Descartes' *Meditations* is so ingenious: it makes deduction touch what by definition it cannot touch.) I must add that this description is debatable, because philosophers do debate it. Given the role of logic in the tradition of philosophy, it would be surprising, indeed, if philosophers had nothing to say about the interface (or lack thereof) of deductive logic and the world. For it is not too great an exaggeration to say that philosophy was in its origins a kind of *logos* worship, in which truth and meaning were understood to be, if not the products of logical consistency, then very closely tied to it. The categorical logic that Aristotle first formulated and that has since been developed in a variety of ways was a formal expression of this *logos*. Virtually until the end of the Enlightenment of the eighteenth century, the place in philosophy of logic, if not undisputed (for it was hardly that; one need only read Hume to see that there were strong challenges), at least secure. Kant, as much as Plato, could magisterially appeal to the dictates of an essentially deductive process of reason. Until Kant's subtle redescription of the role of reason, his deft repositioning of Plato's sun in the philosophical cosmos, philosophers could indulge themselves in the panorama of the god's-eye view, which was, after all, what *logos* seemed to afford them. Philosophers could seek the purity of a perfectly consistent metaphysical account of things and believe, as Descartes did, that in such an account there was something transcendent and absolutely true.

In the present day, however, certain philosophers will insist that the story of *logos* is the impossible fabrication that Nietzsche said it was. These philosophers have to be taken seriously, for reasons that go right back to Plato. The problem is the following. Insofar as a set of 'absolutely true' Platonic statements would also be absolutely abstract – all form and no content, lacking the concrete ephemera, the necessary shadows of this world – they would be pretty much unsayable. With the approach of the Forms, language, and therefore philosophy, comes to an end, yielding to silent contemplation. In this context, Kant's insistence that there is no knowledge divorced from experience – the conditional proposition 'p $\rightarrow$ q' is epistemologically empty until the variables are given content, and content is not innate – can be set in opposition to Plato's theory of recollection, in which knowledge of the Forms is innate, although too deeply buried to get at.[30] For Plato, as for Descartes, experience gets in the way of *logos* and, therefore, of knowledge. That is what Kant began to reverse. Kant believes experience is absolutely essential to knowledge, the ground upon which reason does its work. Without experience, without the shadows of the cave, there is no human knowledge, and reason produces only empty abstractions. (That is why the philosopher who has gazed upon the sun is something more than human.)

Nevertheless, Kant did not go all the way with this idea. For Kant, every bit as much as for Plato, *logos* is indispensable. For example, judgment – which Kant describes as bringing a particular thing under a concept (such as the hypothetical relation) – is crucially important in the pursuit of knowledge. This is because knowing entails abstraction, moving from the particular 'thing' to the general concept, and then connecting it to other concepts and other things. It does no good to know that you have a virus, and that you are ill, unless you can grasp the conditional antecedent-consequent[31] relation between them, which takes the general form: 'If it is a virus, it will make you ill.' This sense that the world is knit together by the connections of logic remains (despite Hume's criticisms)[32] a very powerful idea in our culture. We still tend to adopt, as the most important measure of intelligence, the ability to think abstractly, to move confidently around the conceptual realm, to go beyond 'mere' facts. Intelligence quotient (IQ) and aptitude tests are, principally, tests of the ability to do math, logic, and grammar, which is to say, of the ability to grasp relations in the abstract.

Many contemporary philosophers would argue that logic is an empty abstraction whose pre-eminence is a more politically determined condition than we generally imagine it to be. (Certainly, few experts now seem willing to argue that IQ tests are neutral, objective tests of something called 'intelligence.') Plato went to war, waging a pitched battle with the rhetoricians, the dread Sophists who sought – so he tells us – the power to persuade rather than the wisdom to seek truth.[33] To the degree that Plato won this battle (the fact that we consider Plato to be one of the great figures of the ancient world indicates that he won most of his battles), rhetoric was, thereafter, judged in the court of a foundational logic and, by definition, found wanting. This is the judgment that is being reconsidered by those anonymous beings to whom I have given the label 'new sceptics.' Alongside the conceptual arguments, there is some good historical warrant for their doing so. Plato's victory was never as complete as some might have us believe. Among the ancients, Aristotle and the Stoics both paid serious attention to rhetoric and, to that extent, are less logically partisan than Plato. The same could be said of the pedagogues of the later Roman Empire and Middle Ages, for whom rhetoric was a central part of education. Aristotle, for example, is sure that logic is an important element in the construction of a persuasive argument, but one that can carry conviction only to the degree that one's audience shares one's initial premises. (We saw as much in the 'only man is rational' argument.) In other words, given that it is so difficult to ascertain the truth of one's premises – especially in the matter of abstractions – logic could scarcely constitute a framework for epistemology, at least not without a little boost from rhetoric. This admixture of logic and rhetoric raises important questions about priority and contamination, the most central of which is this: While logic can be an element of rhetoric – that is, as Aristotle says, the force of logic can be used to persuade – can logic ever be fully separated from rhetoric and made prior to rhetoric? Can logic be severed from the act of persuasion and attached solely to epistemology, which is the search for truth as opposed to persuasion?[34] If it cannot be, if none of our premises are self-evidently true, then logic is so much less powerful than has been assumed. It is as if the little word 'if' has ruined everything by forcing logicians to pull their discipline up short of the world, making everything 'merely' formal.

That is why philosophers long looked so carefully for a foundation of certainty – for what Descartes calls an 'Archimedean point,' a beginning assertion immune to the destabilizing 'if' – upon which to build their arguments. As we know, at the dawn of modernity, Descartes found his in innate ideas, which he claims can be known by intuition, an instantaneous, clear, and distinct grasp of their truth. However, as the historian of ideas Stephen Gaukroger has pointed out,[35] the tradition of rhetoric that descended from Aristotle and the Stoics was (in part for the reasons I have just set out) centrally concerned with the *strength* of images – the Greek word was *phantasma*, the word that I translated as 'simulacrum' in Chapter 1). A vivid image will convince, a confused or bland one will not.[36] A good rhetorical argument will therefore rest on 'images' so strong that they, and not logic, carry conviction along with them. Gaukroger points out that this notion is likely a direct ancestor of Descartes' clear and distinct ideas but, as is usually the case, the child is not exactly like the parent. In Descartes' hands, the point of clear and distinct ideas is not to convince others, but oneself. This conviction is, moreover, now said to derive from intuitive, and, therefore 'objective,' clarity, rather than vivid rhetorical images. It is not illegitimate to suggest that what Descartes does is insert a rhetorical ghost into his psychology of intuition to shore up his epistemology. In a sense, Descartes disperses the shadows of the cave by turning some of them into epistemologically impeccable intuitions. Plato, instead, resorts to a *deus ex machina*, the 'rough hands' that turn a chosen few away from the persuasive shadows. And, while we don't know who the owners of those hands are – and therefore, while the danger of rhetorical contamination remains[37] – it is a way of separating us, at least imaginatively, from our convincing images. At the end of the day, however, in Plato's case and in Descartes,' the unsettling presence of rhetoric as a kind of anti-*logos*, although it is suppressed, is not eradicated.

The Metaphysical Implications of Rhetoric for Logic

Important and enduring for philosophers is the issue of the metaphysical implications of rhetoric for logic. In the twentieth century, in the absolutely famous case of the *Tractatus*, Wittgenstein argued compellingly for the fundamental importance of logic. Like Kant with metaphysics, however, he does so in a rather strange way. Logic, he tells us, frames the world, providing it with a metaphysical scaffolding of necessity and impossibility within which possibility – the world itself – unfolds. Yet, the world that logic frames in this work is startlingly cleansed of traditional metaphysics. A transcendent logic sits 'outside' the world and walls it in. Inside those walls are only contingently connected facts, possibilities that are not susceptible to any kind of metaphysical – and therefore in Wittgenstein's estimation, logical – analysis that will unveil their meaning. However necessary it is to our view of the world, logic does not *touch* the world. All logic can do is *show* – or picture – what the world is like. Logic cannot, for example, say *why* the world is like that or *why* the way the world is might have any value. Logic can show us that the world can be this way but not that way – that, for example, descriptions of contradictory 'states of affairs' or mutually exclusive 'possible worlds' cannot simultaneously exist. But logic cannot explain why logic works (*why* contradictories cannot both coexist). Anyone who did not simply 'see' that would, in effect, be alien to the world. So, logic is the Atlas – the inexplicable, primitive ontology – upon which our sense of the world rests, and it is no good asking what *it* rests on. Take logic away and the world disappears. That is why, contends Wittgenstein, those who have understood his point will also understand that it is a point that he cannot make.[38] Wittgenstein violates his own prohibition and discusses what logic does. But this is like an eye watching itself watch the world. (It seems to me that one could apply this principle to Descartes and say that we can use intuitions, but we cannot justify that use.)

There is, then, a kind of shrugging 'this-is-just-what-we-do' foundationalism in the *Tractatus* (which can be opposed to the naturalism of Wittgenstein's later work). Logic is set up as the framework for language and our grasp of the world. If a sentence does not state a fact about the world, if it steps outside the bivalence of true and false and the restraints of tautology and contradiction, it is really only an empty pseudo-sentence. In reaction to this position, a naturalist will take a step towards rhetoric and set language outside logic, rejecting the idea that the latter has metaphysical priority over the rest of language. Against the *Tractatus*, a naturalist will argue that worlds can be meaningfully framed in all sorts of non-logical, non-rational ways. This claim can be viewed either as nihilist (since there is no longer any absolute guarantee of order) or liberating (since there is no longer any absolute imposition of order) or both. (After all, Nietzsche reminds us that all nihilistic scenarios are potentially liberating, for they open up the possibility of creativity.) A foundationalist would take the first position, a naturalist the second, and a thoroughly anti-metaphysical philosopher would probably add that logic – or better, the metaphysical attachment to logic as the foundation of truth – facilitates rather than cures the pseudo-communication that Wittgenstein seeks to exorcise from language by creating the illusion that we can talk about the world in unambiguous ways. To that degree, the anti-metaphysical philosopher would tell us, logic has always been a metaphysical but rhetorically vivid fraud – incapable of reaching out to the world and establishing absolute identities. Logic cannot adjudicate meaning. Perhaps nothing can.

I have now returned to the central concern of this chapter, expressed this time in a kind of naturalist neo-sceptic idiom. I have suggested that, despite its undeniable usefulness, logic is unconcerned with truth, because it is incapable of assessing anything other than its own tautological truth. That was the point of the 'only men are rational' syllogism, and I want now want to return to it in order to underline the charge a radical naturalist might level against a foundationalist view of logic. There is, I said, no formally *definitive* way to decide between alternative readings of the argument: Any competent English-speaker can, without logical absurdity, read 'man' as 'male' both times, 'humankind' both times, as 'male-humankind' or as 'humankind-male.' (This is not to deny that 'any competent English-speaker' will almost certainly note the difference between 'man' and 'a man' and prefer the 'male-humankind' reading and hence accept that the argument is invalid and *non sequitous*.) All that the different readings do is create four arguments, two valid and two invalid. Logic – deductive logic anyway – judges validity, but it cannot tell us which identities to choose. Logic cannot, in other words, tell us whether to give the argument a valid or an invalid reading. Only experience, which creates a context – Robert Brandom's 'socially articulated position' – for our reading, does that. I take seriously the parenthetical point above: On inductive (i.e., experiential) grounds, most of us are likely to think that the invalid reading, with the equivocation on 'man,' is probably the best one. But experience is, so to speak, *extra-textual* (after all, it's what we bring to bear on the argument), and from the point of view of a 'pure logician,' amounts to a kind of metaphysical prejudice that we impose on the text. (The reader should consider carefully what her 'instinctive' reading of the argument was and whether it was prejudiced.) Strictly speaking, the logic or illogic of the syllogism is – to use a Derridean term – *undecidable* because it follows from the meaning that one attaches to the terms. Hence, there is nothing for logic to pronounce on definitively, except to say that, in defiance of its own laws, the syllogism is, across all the possible universes created by different readings, *simultaneously valid and invalid*. Only by taking seriously the 'as' in 'reading "man" as "male,"' and so on, which is to say, only by accepting that logic cannot go to work until a metaphorical and, therefore, metaphysical world has been chosen, can this contradiction be dissolved. In that case, the important question, the question that saves logic from itself, is obviously rhetorical: By which reading, by which set of identifications, are you most persuaded? This is to decide which world you will assume is in place – one, for example, where 'man' refers to humankind or one where 'man' refers to men. Once this rhetorical issue has been decided, logic can render its judgment concerning the suitability of the argument in that world.

I can now parody Kuhn and say that all our readings are 'true ones' because they are all our metaphysically chosen readings. This amounts to saying that truth – what we believe or know the world to be like – trumps validity. One answer to the question 'How do we understand one another in the absence of a foundational logic?' is, therefore, that we do so on the basis of shared perspectives (or ontologies or, perhaps, Kuhnian paradigms).[39] These determine the terrain – the content of the world on which a now less-than-transcendent logic will be set to work. Disagreements over meaning and truth are, thus, at least in the first instance, resolved not by logic but by anthropology. Disagreements over meaning and truth are resolved by the different contexts – including the 'private' context of what any individual has read up to the point of her confrontation with a text – which produce different persuasive readings. Contexts throw up the metaphysical framework within which logic can – although it need not – come into play. What logic cannot do, or cannot be guaranteed to do, is play across frameworks. What is valid within one set of assumptions is invalid within another, and there is no absolute way – although there are many 'ad hoc' ways – to decide which is the better set. What's more, to apply the lessons of Chapter 3, our metaphysical frameworks are seldom so clear or unitary in their systems of identification that they will necessarily give rise to just one reading of a text. Indeterminacy is part of the pattern. So the dilemma, once again, is that every reading is a true one, but it is also a misreading of another reading, and there is very little that logic can do about that.[40] What logic *can* do is metaphysically local rather than metaphysically absolute. This is, perhaps, another way of stating a basic distinction between foundationalism and naturalism: one world versus many worlds.

Let me now try to ratchet the pressure on logic up another notch. My argument has moved towards the conclusion that logic is not only subservient to metaphor, it is based on *a* metaphor. The law of non-contradiction, first formulated by Aristotle, is historically the original of the three laws of reason. It derives its power from a concept of simultaneity: Nothing can be *simultaneously* 'X' and 'not-X.' However, as I pointed out in my outline of the three laws, for such a concept to have meaning, time has to be seen *as* a series of discrete instants – as opposed to, say, an uninterrupted 'flow' – for without distinct, and distinctly illogical, gaps between 'instants,' it would be impossible to decide whether two events are simultaneous. (Einstein has assured us that it is indeed impossible, if for other reasons.) Without 'instants,' the concept of the 'same time' just evaporates into thin air. Aristotle – the first philosopher to formalize logic – did, in fact, see time in this way – or at any rate, it is inherent in the kind of logic he developed. But, this is scarcely the most 'natural' view of time. Obviously, other metaphors, other metaphysical views, are also abroad. One way to put this is to say that all descriptions of time are pretty much guaranteed to be metaphorical. The metaphor of 'instants' is simply the one that is necessary to two-valued logic. Drop that metaphor, adopt another metaphysics of time (something we do constantly, just never when we are doing two-valued logic), and that logic will disintegrate. In a flow-time metaphor, with its river imagery, event X is neither here in time nor there in time (because 'heres' and 'theres' cannot be delineated). Therefore, it is impossible to make contradictory claims about where X is. With this in mind, let me essay a syllogism: If rhetoric generates our stock of metaphors, and if one of these metaphors generates logic, then rhetoric generates logic. We accept logic – believe in its power – just because, and just insofar as, we live under the sway of a particular set of metaphors, a particular metaphysical construction of reality. Why do we live under them? The answer may lie in history or anthropology rather than in either human nature or the laws of nature. Certainly, when Hegel imposed what I have called a flow metaphor on logic, applying his dialectic to make each instant, each 'quantum of being' constantly dissolve into the next – as if contradiction were the motor of logic (and therefore of history) rather than a brake applied to it – the nature of logic, and philosophy itself, was bifurcated. On one side is a bivalent, and perhaps Kantian, analytical stream (which runs through a lot of 'Anglo-American' philosophy), and on the other is a dialectical and Hegelian 'continental' stream (which we find on the mainland of Europe).[41] In recent years, and to analytical eyes, the latter stream has often come to look more like a kind of anti-logic: not a framework for understanding the world so much as a means of dissolving understanding. Insofar as the 'dialectical stream' is often filtered through the strange prisms of Nietzsche and Heidegger, this is not an unreasonable observation. Neither is it, however, a damning criticism.

Local Logic

Yet, the ghost of bivalent logic is not so easily laid to rest. Philosophers have, understandably, a great deal of trouble getting along without logic, and for good reason. Logic is an extremely useful, and probably indispensable, instrument. As the American philosopher Stanley Cavell notes, even Jacques Derrida – the philosopher who has apparently done more than any other in our age to undermine the pre-eminence of logic – has been known to express impatience when he feels that his work has been misunderstood.[42] But how, wonders Cavell, can it be misunderstood once the laws of logic have lost their domination, once our only transcendent understanding of 'understanding' has been ruled out of court, and once, therefore, even apparently contextualized words can simultaneously carry contradictory meanings? Three possible replies may come to mind. First, the misunderstanding consists in thinking that there has been a misunderstanding (i.e., in taking Derrida either seriously or without irony; at his word, so to speak). Second, logic has paradoxically been reinstated as the ground of higher judgments about rhetorical devices. Third, by insisting on an unambiguous context for reading *his* texts, Derrida is claiming for himself a privilege he will not accord to others.

My suspicion is that none of these 'replies' captures what Derrida is doing and, therefore, what his complaint is. I think Derrida's deconstructive readings of texts are, in the best tradition of Socrates, instructively negative. They are intended to lay bare the contradictions and unresolved tensions that Derrida believes exist in all texts and, therefore, to expose the metaphysical myth of a consistent, clear, and unambiguous meaning. The 'truth' that Derrida is asserting is not that texts say everything and, therefore, no one thing, but that texts do not say *only* the 'one thing' (whatever it is) that their authors and readers often think they do. (This is what Socrates often tries to demonstrate to his interlocutors.) All the logic in the world cannot stitch a text together so tightly that the seams do not show. That, it seems to me, is what Derrida's elenctic and *logical* readings are intended to demonstrate. As Kant taught, it is no easy thing to undermine logic – at least as a regulative principle, which is to say, as a principle that structures experience (and, we might add, reading) – and continue to philosophize. In the spirit of this teaching, I would submit that Derrida is less undermining logic *in toto* than using logic as a local and regulative tool to undermine the myth of its metaphysical *imperium*.[43] Derrida is not discarding logic so much as relocating it within the narrower, more naturalist, metaphysical surroundings that I have been outlining. This suggests – and I think Derrida says as much[44] – that it is not metaphysics that we ought to escape – which we cannot do. What we ought to escape is the illusion that metaphysics can be absolute, that it can be what traditional metaphysicians want it to be. There is, as Quine once put it, no 'cosmic exile,'[45] no place outside time and intellectual frameworks where the philosopher can go to attain the god's-eye view. Derrida appears to think that philosophers have long used logic as the Wittgensteinian ladder that would take them to that exile. In a sense, Derrida tries to demonstrate what Wittgenstein himself admitted: This is logically impossible, a trick of language, and therefore, a wasted effort.

Logic and the Zen Master

I want to make one more remark concerning the traditionally central place of logic in western philosophy. If that place is historically determined – which is to say, if logic is the contingent result of our past, rather than a necessary consequence of our nature – then, if we look in another direction, in this case to the east, we should not be overly surprised to discover different histories governed by different metaphors. In these different histories and metaphors, logic – or more generally, *logos* – is not always the pathway to knowledge and knowledge to

wisdom. On the contrary, on some views, logic is the cloud that ob-
scures wisdom from view. Western philosophers have taken such east-
ward glances and seem to have learned from them. Both Heidegger and
Derrida, in their subversion of the *imperium* of logic, reveal resonances
of Zen, or *something* non-western – or non-Platonic, which might be the
same thing.[46]

In this light, I am obliged to draw attention to the elision of the
difference between knowledge and wisdom that I have permitted in
these pages. Knowledge, as it appears to be defined by most of us in the
west, entails 'knowing-how' or 'knowing-that'; it has a mechanical,
'seeking' aspect (in Chapter 4, I noted that a hunting metaphor seemed
naturally to emerge) for which logic provides, as it were, the impetus –
as it did in the puzzles I set out above. This should not be surprising;
techne – empirical, teachable craft knowledge – is something of an ideal
for Plato. *If only* knowledge of the great abstractions – wisdom, justice,
holiness, or knowledge itself – could be mapped onto this model, the
philosopher's troubles would be at an end. Wisdom, on the other hand,
always seems to have more to do with an orientation towards life and
an ability to reflect on what one is. Wisdom is, perhaps, a blend of deep
experience, sound judgment, and unflagging ethical concern. Under the
aegis of wisdom, puzzles are not solved but dissolved. Knowledge is, or
is principally, 'science'; wisdom is, or is principally, 'art.' (I apologize
for this lengthy insertion, but the preceding sentence cries out for
comment: 'Knowledge is science' is a tautology, insofar as the Latin
scientia is the equivalent of the Greek *episteme*. Furthermore, the word
that the Greeks commonly used for 'art' was *techne*, which is also linked
to 'technology' and the teachability of science. It is as if the craft aspect
of the plastic arts struck the Greeks more forcefully than the 'art' aspect.
We have here an example of overlapping, although not identical metaphysical frameworks: the Greeks' and ours.) Described in this way,
there is no reason to see the pursuit of knowledge as a direct route to
wisdom. Heidegger holds something like this attitude in his later work,
I think, and Wittgenstein as well.

Yet, much in the 'western tradition' encourages one to see knowledge
as the path to wisdom. Plato views knowledge in this way, and his
influence, of course, has been considerable. Plato, like Socrates, is an
inveterate logician, who dedicates himself to the development of an
epistemological route that would guide him towards the one thing he
knows he lacks. In that sense, wisdom would either be the outgrowth of
techne, of a craftsman's skill, or it would be eternally elusive. A Zen

master might hint – because he is too polite to speak directly – that this is a mistake, the point at which Plato and Socrates turn away from wisdom. From the Zen master's perspective, the irony may be that Plato, Socrates, et alia, try to use *logos* as the pathway to wisdom, when, in fact, there is no path – *because there is no place to go*. Wisdom cannot be pursued. The metaphor is all wrong, if indeed, a metaphor can be wrong.[47] Wisdom is elusive precisely *because* it is pursued. Indeed, insofar as we can discern his presence behind Plato,[48] Socrates does seem to get this a little. Socrates' discursive path leads inward towards meditation on what, innately, he knows. Socrates' whole *logos*, in fact, is an ascetic, difficult discipline. And, of course, Plato's myths are departures from *logos*. Yet, in the end neither Socrates nor Plato is silent.[49] Neither philosopher is able to await the approach of wisdom. As logical craftsmen, they pursue wisdom by pursuing knowledge. Like Descartes, they are hunting for a method. Some critics – Heidegger, for example – might say that their metaphysics gets in the way such that it all ends not in wisdom but in a technological science. Hence, the elision I have been considering: Knowledge becomes wisdom, art becomes craft, and scientists become the Great Magi.

At the beginning of the last chapter, I quoted Charles Taylor's remark, which noted in part that epistemology was once the pride of modern philosophy. Since the triumphs of science have been the pride of the modern west, this is not surprising. Yet, it seems to me, many of the 'deepest' philosophers of the modern age have been more concerned with ontology – with, in one way or another, the debate about metaphysics. It seems as if knowledge might be a consolation prize, and one that we have not much understood. The 'neo-Nietzscheans,' and the ordinary language philosophers and the analytical philosophers, as well, have spent a great deal of time pondering the question of how we *are* in the world, of what it is to live as a human being. As philosophers, they cannot, of course, take a Zen master's advice and cease their talking and writing – their arguing. What they can do, though, is turn language back on itself. They can place its slipperiness, its apparent unreliability, and its illogical logic under the philosopher's microscope. Thus, if logic has been shifted from its place at the centre of the philosophical universe, the vacancy has been filled by considerations of language in general. We have become, once again, Aristotle's 'life that speaks,' beings for whom, as Hilary Putnam explains, 'elements of what we call "language" or "mind" penetrate so deeply into what we call "reality" that the very project of representing ourselves as being "mappers" of something "language-independent" is fatally compromised from the start.'[50] For the logician – perhaps we can say, for the traditional metaphysically minded philosopher – the displacement of logic might therefore seem to reduce one's choices to a tautological two: silence or elegant, post-modernist, deconstructive babble. (I think my remarks on Derrida and logic suggest, more kindly, that the babble is really a form of therapeutic analysis of metaphysical pretensions.) Reflections on language may, however, represent an attempt to find a third way – indeed, a whole lot of third ways – that will allow us to go on talking meaningfully, although perhaps not in the way we once did.

In Conclusion

I shall leave the discussion here and take it up again in Chapter 7. Before that we will have considered Plato's wisdom question about how to conduct our lives. This is the question that subverts, perhaps more thoroughly than any other, the pre-eminence of logic. All I can say now is that, like any other calculus, logic can be a powerful intellectual tool. What the meaning or implication of the use of logic is may be a deep metaphysical issue, a practical issue, or even no issue at all. When queried, perhaps philosophers can do no more than answer à la Wittgenstein: Logic is just (part of) what we do. If that seems too dismissive of opposition, too unphilosophical, I can add – taking from Wittgenstein again – that perhaps the trick really is in knowing when to stop one's explanations.[51] For this much is clear: In questioning the pre-eminence of logic, philosophers risk their world. (Such questioning seems, therefore, to go hand in hand with announcements of the end of philosophy.) Yet, as I have already noted once or twice in these pages, philosophers seem peculiarly driven to take that risk. In doing so, philosophers could prove to be foolhardy or egocentric, but, and to reiterate *my* position, I suspect they are merely being honest or, at least, sincerely attempting to be honest.

6

Ethics:
The Good, the Bad, and the Beautiful

SUMMARY

More uncertainty: in this case not about what ethics is but about how it fits with what has gone before in this text. That said, the chapter is oriented around two poles: ethics as the 'aesthetic' pursuit of the good life and ethics as the moral concern with right and wrong. We see that because the ancient concept of arête *– which can be translated as 'virtue' and 'excellence' – contains both notions, a certain vagueness underlies our conception of 'good.' When our conception of good is brought to the surface, the possibility of holding irreconcilable notions of a good life and a moral life comes with it. This is the tragic possibility that much of modern ethics has suppressed. We also consider the question of realism in ethics: Are there moral absolutes, or must ethics be naturalized – if not relativized? If so, how do we compare different ethical systems? The chapter ends with a brief consideration of politics in relation to ethics.*

First Thoughts and Last Confessions

A Peripatetic philosopher[1] by the name of Aristocles famously said that Plato divided philosophy into three parts: physics (metaphysics, really), logic and ethics. With this chapter, and granting that epistemology is strongly rooted in metaphysics, I can, perhaps, claim that this book is, in basic outline, true to that observation. This is not a bad thing for a work in which the great philosopher's cave image has been so central. Yet, I am somewhat reluctant to make the claim, because I am uncertain how well I can accommodate ethics to its companions, logic and metaphysics. In contemporary philosophy, it often seems that there is a disjunction between the vagaries of ethics, or moral philosophy, on one side, and the 'harder-edged' pursuits of metaphysics and epistemology,[2] on the other. I am not sure whether I can span this disjunction well enough to make a smooth transition from the concerns of previous chapters to those of this one. Given this uncertainty, I think it is necessary to consider briefly the relation among these parts of philosophy.[3]

Aristocles gives me some comfort, because he appears not to have thought that the relation among the subdisciplines of Plato's division was either particularly close or necessarily hierarchical. Each was, thought Aristocles, distinct and theoretically separate from the others.[4] There is obviously some truth in this (or else I could not write this book as I have!). It is also true, however, that some intertwining of these areas has always existed, as has some sense – by no means always the same sense – of their relative importance. Philosophers are hardly neutral about such things. They do, *pace* Aristocles, have opinions and they make claims. Usually, philosophers accord one of the 'parts' primacy, even if an important place is set aside for the others. Let us take as an example the great Roman man of letters and Stoic-cum-Academic-cum-Epicurean philosopher, Cicero. Ethics, according to Cicero, was the most important part of philosophy – but, he argued, logic was required to secure its insights and metaphysics to see everything as part of a cosmic whole. So far, this book has carved an un-Ciceronian path from metaphysics, through epistemology, to logic, insisting that logic and metaphysics (and epistemology)[5] have long sat at the centre of philosophy in the western world. I have used different metaphors on different occasions. Metaphysics and logic are foundations, the two stoutest branches of the tree of philosophy, the heart or core of it. What all of these metaphors represent, however, is the assertion that philosophy devoid of logic and metaphysics is either very different from what has for a very long time gone on under the name or, possibly, is not philosophy at all. Those who follow Nietzsche and Heidegger will likely make the opposite claim: Only when philosophy has been cleansed of its metaphysical and logical illusions will it become – I am not sure what tag to use here – either 'true philosophy' or 'true, philosophy transcending thought.' As already noted at the outset, this claim defines much of the 'new scepticism' and 'neo-Nietzschean' philosophy of this young century and its predecessor. From this perspective, as from its inverse, questions of logic, metaphysics, and epistemology are very important insofar as they contain ancient philosophical attitudes that have to be combated if the discipline (or its successor)[6] is to be turned onto a better path. We cannot, it would seem, be indifferent to Plato: We either pay homage to his vision or betray it.[7] But that was the case even in the ancient world.

Ethics – which the Stoics and, indeed, many, perhaps most, Hellenistic philosophers saw as the core of philosophy[8] – I find harder to locate. Certainly, I do recognize the legitimate presence of ethics. In any consideration of philosophy's subdisciplines, ethics is always there, accorded its place as an undeniably important part of philosophy. But just where is 'there'? At the beginning of Chapter 1, I referred readers to the 'map' of philosophy included in the appendix to *The Oxford Companion to Philosophy*. This map consists of three circles. In the inner circle is epistemology, metaphysics, and logic, just what we have so far found in this book. The line drawn around these disciplines is solid, marking them off as the substantial inner core. Philosophy, we learn from this map, is about what we can know and what the world must be like for these things to be knowable. Ethics, actually, is not included in any of the circles. However, its very close relative, moral philosophy, is in the second circle, which is separated from the third and outer circle only by a permeable dotted line. These outer parts of philosophy, we are told, are 'less general and concern limited areas.' They also are dependent on the items in the inner circle, and this is a one-way, or non-reciprocal, relationship. I offer here two comments about this bit of philosophical cartography: First, it would not look right to the ancients. Second, if we accept it nonetheless, we have now left the inner circle of philosophy. (I should add here that the philosophy of language, the subject of the next chapter, is also located in the second circle.) I have to confess that I am far from certain that I *would* accept this distribution. Yet, I am equally far from certain that my treatment of ethics does not implicitly accept it. (I can slot language into the inner circle much more easily.)

This disquietude underlines what I said at the close of Chapter 1, and which I am, in essence, repeating here: *I* am telling a story around the fire in the cave, taking a particular view of philosophy, one which, we have now seen, gives pride of place to metaphysics in a way that makes it easier to incorporate logic and epistemology than ethics into any schema that I might wish to produce.[9] Perhaps, to recall Rorty,[10] this is because of the way philosophy came to me. In other words, ethics was taught to me as part of the outer circle or, to change the metaphor, as something like an important tributary to the mainstream of metaphysics, epistemology, and logic. It may be, therefore, that I have trouble locating ethics in any other way. Or, perhaps, there is a more objective reason that really does have to do with the nature of philosophy, as opposed to the 'nature of philosophy as it was taught to me.' Perhaps I have got the place of ethics just about right. I am not really sure. Because of that, readers would be well advised to take my comments in note 9, above, seriously. To parody Kant, I do not know to what degree we are dealing with things phenomenal and to what degree with things noumenal.

Given this, all I can do is make my present views – or suspicions – clear. I do think that ethics is both a fundamental concern of philosophy and one that is, I suspect, intimately connected to the metaphysical issues that run through this book.[11] (Certainly, Nietzsche's critique of metaphysics is entwined with a critique of ethics in a manner that leaves little doubt as to their intimate connection.) Therefore, in what follows, I shall try to elucidate some ethical versions of these issues. They will, however, be intertwined to the point where it may sometimes be difficult to view them separately. So, in an attempt to create some initial clarity (which I can then proceed to muddy), let me enumerate the three principal issues with which I shall be concerned. First, there is, as there has been in every chapter, the question of realism. Are moral values foundational expressions of some sort of moral facts (or Platonic Forms) that exist independently of any 'knowing mind,' or, in a naturalist vein, are there only localized moral vocabularies? We might restate this as: What is ethical discourse *about*? Second, and closely connected to the foregoing, is the question of whether there can be something like a scientific account, if not of ethics then (at least?) of moral reasoning. After all, the original 'science' of metaphysics was linked to the certainty that there were real and universal entities to be discovered. The more mind-independent these entities are, and the more objective the great truths of the world are, the more securely, perhaps, ethics, or some part of it, can be set down as a science. To the degree that this does not hold, we have to look in other, more naturalist, directions. This issue can be expressed as: What *kind* of discourse is ethics? Third, we need to take some account of a division I have just insinuated into the discussion: Are there two parts to ethics? Put differently, is ethics broader than moral reasoning? Does (or should) ethics contain a view of 'the good life' that is distinct from and, perhaps, prior to 'the moral life'? Hence, is the concept of goodness fundamentally a twin-pronged one or, if you prefer, is goodness a broader, and therefore different, category than virtue? This question is important insofar as it raises issues concerning the identity of our ethical concepts. In particular, it raises the issue of whether there is a kind of equivocation in them – I shall say between 'virtue' and 'excellence' – that needs to be clarified. This is, I think, a second way of asking what ethical discourse is about. In particular, is ethics always about moral issues of right and wrong or is it sometimes about something other than that? I shall begin with a mix of the first and last of these issues, which take us back almost to the birth of ethical thought.

The Problem of *Arête*: Excellence and Virtue

In the *Republic*, Socrates reminds his listeners that, in their consideration of the structure of the just *polis*, 'it is no ordinary matter we are discussing, but the right conduct of life.'[12] The right or proper conduct of life – what we know as ethics – is, the great philosopher tells us, no ordinary matter. Part of me nods assent, of course. What to do, what choices to make, how to steer one's life? These are difficult matters, full of perplexity. Yet, another part of me wants to withhold that assent. Most of the time, the conduct of my life is very ordinary, indeed. It is guided by rules, habits, and dispositions that seem beyond dispute, and hardly worth discussing, except, perhaps, in a philosophy class. But that is the point. The conduct of our lives is, for the most part, ordinary – until it is put under the microscope of Socratic examination. Then, what Marx said of commodities can be applied to our actions: What 'appears at first sight a very trivial thing, and easily understood,' turns out to be 'a very queer thing, abounding in metaphysical subtleties and theological niceties.'[13]

   The key to this transformation of the ordinary into the extraordinary, the mundane into the puzzling – which, by the way, is the particular magic of philosophy, Plato's sun casts a queer but always fascinating light on the world – can be found, as a kind of historical palimpsest, in the Greek word *arête*. The most common English translation, which can be traced, I think, to the Jowett translations of the nineteenth century,[14] is 'virtue,' But *arête* also carries another, often forgotten but lately rehabilitated, connotation, and that is 'excellence.'[15] Once we distinguish these ideas, we begin to separate, so far as we can, ethics from morality – broad questions of how to conduct one's life from narrower ones concerning moral right and wrong. Right now, it is important to see that the two English connotations are entwined in *arête*, giving the word a resonance that exceeds the translation capacity of either 'virtue' or 'excellence' on its own and a range, therefore, that encompasses both morality and ethics.[16] Alexander Nehamas has made the comment that *'arête* has an immensely broader range of application than its conventional English translation "virtue" while ... "excellence" strikes me as too vague and weak.'[17] It is a useful reminder of the limits of translation, ones that the reader would be well advised to bear in mind throughout what follows. Part of the problem stems from the fact that 'excellence' is ambiguous. It can refer both to measurable skills and capacities. Indeed, *arête* was used by the Greeks to refer to the skills of humans and the capacities of non-humans and even inanimate objects[18] – as well as to qualities that reflect a more general and aesthetic sense of accomplishment or refinement. Deployed in the latter range, *arête* certainly has ethical connotations and *may* also, although it need not, bear moral connotations. The *Oxford English Dictionary* defines 'excellence' – 'possession ... of good qualities in an unusual degree; surpassing merit, virtue, etc., dignity, eminence' – echoing these different shadings of meaning. 'Virtue,' however, is, or would certainly seem to be, unambiguously *moral*: the *OED* opens its definition of virtue with 'moral goodness.'

The first distinction we need to make between 'excellence' and 'virtue' can be brought out by contrasting 'good at' with 'good.' Let us imagine that an ancient Athenian has just commented to his friend that no one was as good (had as much excellence, as much *techne*, or skill) at killing his enemies as was Achilles (who was an excellent warrior), and the friend responds, 'Ah, but is that a good (virtuous) thing to do?' In other words, is killing one's enemies an activity that promotes or bespeaks *arête*?[19] This response, which may seem equivocal, adds the manifestly moral dimension of what we call 'virtue' to the sheer skill of 'excellence' in the consideration of what 'good conduct' is. It moves the meaning of *arête* into a different, and for us more recognizably moral, range. Unlike 'technical excellence,' 'virtue' *explicitly* requires that the something one is good at be good in itself. Therefore, that something needs to contribute to the goodness of the person, rather than simply indicate possession of a particular skill – which *just is* the goodness of the person, or alternatively, just is what the person is good at. (For many moderns, the first of these expressions indicates an ethical judgment, whereas the latter does not.) Put differently, in the 'virtue' translation, *arête* begins to look like a natural name for some undefined metaphysical quality – 'goodness.' We may often fail to recognize this quality, either in a person or an activity, but (in appropriate cases) it is there nonetheless. Thus, the word draws attention to the nature (or something in the nature) of the activity, as much as to the skill of the actor carrying it out. Insofar as it also draws attention to the actor, it draws attention to an elusive quality of the actor's character – a difficulty which stimulates Socrates' ruminations on whether virtue is teachable. As 'excellence,' that is, as a skill, *arête* might be teachable. But as 'virtue' – as the content of one's character, for example – how can it be, if we do not quite know what it is? Of course, and this cannot be overemphasized, Socrates' 'confusion' is possible mainly because he holds what we call virtue and excellence in a single definition – *in a single word*. The effect is necessarily to blur the distinction between our 'excellence' and 'virtue' translations. I say 'blur,' because the distinction is there. The hiddenness of virtue and the public, teachable nature of excellence are both present in Socrates' idea of *arête*, but unpacked. What Socrates does, *qua* philosopher, is to begin to unpack them, to separate them, and bring them into sufficiently sharp relief that they can begin to stand in opposition to one another, albeit an uncertain opposition.

It is important to say the obvious: One unpacks what is already there. Even for Achilles, certain activities (including killing one's enemies) were obviously virtuous, whereas others (betraying one's friends and family, for example) were not. *Arête* was not, even for Achilles, simply a matter of excellence. It was not simply a warrior's skill in action. The action was intimately related to a code of conduct. In common with all of us, Achilles founded excellence on virtue: No one can be an excellent coward, because cowardice is not a virtue. The difference that arises from Socrates' philosophical treatment is that Socrates begins to examine the virtue element of *arête*. Socrates considers it in a way that would not have occurred to Achilles – in something like the way that Xenophanes began to unpack the sceptical element of knowledge that was necessary to the development of epistemology.[20] Nehamas argues that *arête* makes something 'justifiably notable' and that the word refers to 'the inner structure and quality of things, their reputation, and the audience that is to appreciate them.'[21] This would, indeed, seem to suggest that *arête* has both an 'internal' – moral – and an 'external' – ethical – connotation, which I have distinguished, however roughly, as virtue and excellence. Achilles certainly has a grasp of 'external' *arête*, or excellence – that is, I think, his main focus – but he also has some sense of its relation to an 'internal' virtue, however unexamined that concept may be for him. Socrates, by contrast, has a grasp of excellence, which confuses him insofar as he has a stronger concern with examining the much more elusive 'internal' virtue aspect of *arête*. (Socrates is, perhaps, a moralist, whereas Achilles is an ethicist.) Socrates is, in short, doing what a philosopher is supposed to do: examining the hitherto unexamined concept.[22] In bringing a heightened emphasis to bear on the virtue aspect of *arête*, Socrates is signalling his determination to consider, or reconsider, the question of *which* activities are good (*agathos*, generally translated as 'good,' is an adjective of *arête*) and *what* makes them so. He is directing his scepticism at dogmatic claims to know what virtue is,[23] and in expressing and developing this scepticism, he brings epistemology to bear on ethics.

We need to keep in mind that Socrates' assertion that the conduct of our lives is no ordinary matter is made to men who, for the most part, are not sceptical. Like Achilles, they are quite certain how to lead their lives. In fact, they are dogmatically certain that they know which activities they ought to strive to be 'excellent at.' Like Achilles, and perhaps most men and women everywhere, they see no need to unpack the virtue aspect of *arête* and set it under the microscope of the *elenchos*. They, therefore, see no need of epistemology either. To the philosophical and sceptical question: 'How do you know what it is right to do?' they answer either with a quasi-philosophical shrug or with an everyday reference to what is, in fact, done in Athens.[24] Thrasymachos's defence of a 'might is right' view of justice, in *The Republic*,[25] may seem extreme to a modern reader (and even to some of his fellow Athenians). Essentially, however, he is saying that a man who is able to defend the interests of family and friends displays *arête*, because this is what a man ought to do. It is what well-bred Athenians do and, hence, it is virtuous. In response, Socrates points out that Thrasymachos's certainty that defending one's friends and harming one's enemies is good (I am using 'good' as a marker for *arête*, but here the emphasis is on the virtue aspect of it), no matter what the circumstances, is unfounded. His point, or one of his points, anyway, is that *arête* is an elusive quality. This is not simply because excellence is difficult to achieve, which it is, but also because it is difficult to know what to be excellent at because we do not really know what virtue is, even if we sometimes are quite certain what kinds of things are virtuous.[26] Protecting the interests of an evil friend may not be a virtuous thing to do, no matter how 'good at' it one is. One has to decide whether the evil or the friendship takes precedence in one's consideration (and, in addition, whether the idea of an 'evil friend' is a coherent one).[27]

Nor do the problems end there. In forcing his interlocutors (in *The*

Republic and elsewhere) to examine more closely the question of what a good activity is, or more precisely, what it is that makes an activity good, Socrates also raises the question of *will*, of whether we will always *want* to do what is virtuous in a context where it seems to diverge from accepted notions of good (or excellent) conduct. (For his part, Socrates is an epistemological determinist who argues that if a person knows what it is good to do he will do it.)[28] Perhaps we will want to exercise our excellence at killing our enemies, even if it is not a virtuous (good) thing to do. Socrates has, we can see, muddied the waters by insinuating into ethical discourse a dichotomy between two kinds of goodness. This is the new ethics of Greece: a reasoned consideration of how to conduct one's life in a context in which 'mere' skill or excellence at traditionally sanctioned activities does not provide *sufficient* warrant for saying that its bearer has *arête*. After Socrates, moral questions sit at the heart of ethics and make it a much thornier subject.

The Vagueness of the Good

It must seem that our consideration of *arête* has, once again, catapulted us into the great philosophical realm of the vague, where we wander endlessly in search of metaphysical entities that are always just beyond our reach. For with 'virtue' all sorts of metaphysical niceties threaten to come into play. In Socrates' Platonic hands, a moral realism that extends, as I have said, beyond the traditionally sanctioned activities of the community and that threatens to annul some of them as virtues, appears on the stage.[29] In comparison, 'excellence' is, or seems to be, straightforward.[30] To discuss being *'good at'* a particular activity, knitting, say, we simply need to know how to measure, or judge, the relevant skills – which we can learn to do because we can examine the activity. But what if someone claims that Achilles was 'good at goodness'? 'Goodness,' or 'good' understood as 'virtue,' is an abstraction – for Plato a Form. Unlike knitting, it offers us nothing that is literally available for inspection. If there are relevant skills, we are not sure what they are.[31] So, while we can work out what it means to be a good knitter (that is, good at knitting), we cannot be equally certain that we can ever work out *with the same clarity* what it means to live a 'good,' in the sense of a 'virtuous,' life.[32] We do not know precisely what quality or qualities make an activity or a life virtuous. Therefore, we do not always know what skills to cultivate, nor whether we will have the strength of character to want to cultivate them.

In this way, the two aspects of *arête* help us to understand the 'paradox' of the epistemological determinism that emerges from Socrates' questioning of his accuser, Meletus, in the *Apology:* If anyone knows what it is right to do – if one knows what is really good – one will do it.[33] Socrates is insisting that *arête* is a product of knowledge and vice a product of ignorance. Insofar as it is a skill, this is necessarily so. Questions of virtue aside, why would a knitter not want to knit in the best possible way? But insofar as it is virtue – something other than a skill, something more mysterious and less teachable than a skill – we may have to accept that we are condemned to the shadows of perpetual ignorance. Lacking knowledge of virtue, we may not necessarily want to be good, not because of a failure of will but because of a failure of knowledge that sets us off in a wrong direction. We will want the wrong things. And, sceptically, how can we trust anyone else's claims to know what *arête* is? Therefore, how can we trust our would-be teachers? The same perplexity is abroad as in my treatment of the 'Allegory of the Cave,' where I had to confess that I am uncertain just why someone would want to leave the comforting fire and continue the arduous pursuit of knowledge and wisdom. This perplexity is, in both cases, well founded. Consider Plato's tripartite version of the *psyche*,[34] in which the will is tugged in one direction by a higher reason and in another by a baser appetite. We can begin to see how difficult this question was for Plato himself, how perplexed *he* was. What reason is there to be reasonable?[35]

Given the metaphysical difficulties that surround us, we need to exercise some caution. To try to elucidate *arête* according to the Socratic and Platonic model is a difficult task, and one might wish for some assurance that the effort of doing so is worthwhile. If so, one is not alone. Julia Annas points out that Plato's concept of the Good, which connects *arête* to a grand metaphysical vision of reality, 'was from the start ridiculed for its obscurity' and its extravagance.[36] In a modern age, suspicious of the very value of metaphysics, the reaction may be even stronger. We may well feel the need for some assurance that 'good' qua *arête* is, with all its apparent vaguery and equivocation, a meaningful term and a useful aid to understanding the conduct of our lives. Over the years, I have watched many of my students, confronted with a plethora of competing ethical systems in their multicultural classrooms, transform themselves into determined moral relativists and epistemological sceptics who, when they consider the issue, decide that 'good' is an approbatory word meaning roughly, 'This is what *I* like.' To seek a

larger, all-embracing 'Good,' a universal set of 'real' virtues or good
activities, is, they tell me, a waste of time because there can never be
knowledge of such things. They have a point. I think they have instinctively understood that in a democracy, especially a multicultural one
such as Canada, agreement generally stands above – and stands in for –
knowledge. They seem to have accepted, if not fully appreciated, John
Stuart Mill's assertion that 'all combination is compromise: it is the
sacrifice of some portion of individual will, for a common purpose.'[37]
The important question is not 'What is right?' but 'What can we agree
on?' It is not 'What do we know?' but 'Which opinion shall we accept?'[38] Hence, these young men and women will often accept certain
standards, of 'political correctness,' say, without debate because they
feel that these standards have been 'agreed on.' There is literally nothing more to be said. I am often left with the feeling that my students
find the world too ethically confusing for comment and that they present
public relativist faces to mask private absolutist ones.[39]

Plato would disagree with the public stance my students take and
perhaps endorse their private one. For him, 'Good' was *something*, a
teleological Form – *the* Form, really, the extravagant shining of his great
sun – which drew everyone to it and of which the philosopher, necessarily, sought knowledge.[40] Aristotle was critical of Plato's theory of
Forms.[41] He thought ethics was a practical science rooted in the habits
and traditions of a community. Nevertheless, Aristotle, too, held a
teleological view of 'Good' as something that draws us towards it. Like
Plato, he rejected any narrow hedonist conception of goodness that
would reduce people simply to reporting on what they like. Like Plato,
Aristotle thought that human beings were drawn by a higher sense of a
good that expressed a universal human nature. It seems to me that
there is wisdom here and, therefore, some value in pursuing the idea,
despite its metaphysical haziness. We need not accept Plato's or
Aristotle's teleology, or indeed, their sometimes narrow sense of what
is 'universal' (where, for example, 'free men' rather than 'free people' is
their concern) to see that the question of how we ought to live our lives
is an important one that cannot easily be reduced to a shallow hedonistic perspective or simply left to the tastes of popular opinion. Pleasure,
as Annas points out, is in Plato's estimation 'an elemental response to
good.' Pleasure indicates what we feel is good, just as pain indicates
what we feel is bad, but it is *only* an indication and an indistinct one at
that.[42] In plotting the conduct of our lives, we have, therefore, to think
directly about what is good, as well as what is pleasurable or popular:

This is what ought to guide our conception both of virtue and excellence.[43] This means that we have to think beyond notions of excellence understood as 'mere' skill to ones that contain a deep sense a life properly lived. We must also think of virtue as something more than merely what has been agreed upon by the community. At the very least, we ought not to *assume* – not as students of philosophy, anyhow – that 'good' is simply some version of the pleasurable, the popular, or the blind pursuit of traditional behaviour.[44]

The Aesthetic Aspect of *Arête* and the Threat of Tragedy

Ethics is that part of philosophy concerned with questions of how we ought to live our lives. That is what ethics is about. This may at the outset have seemed clear enough – especially if we add 'in the company of others'[45] – but we have now seen that ethics contains an inherent ambiguity insofar as concepts of 'excellence' compete with concepts of 'virtue' within a tradition of *arête*. Ethics is about both of these things, and they do not always go easily together. That is why, like many other bits of philosophical language, 'how we ought to live' is so difficult to identify clearly. To do so, we need perhaps to sharpen or develop our sense of 'excellence' as an ethical term. In particular, we may need to accept that the old notion of excellence as 'skill' may no longer have a terribly strong hold on our ethical imaginations, at least not in the democracies of the West. By bringing out the virtue element of *arête*, Socrates may have – as Nietzsche constantly complained – killed it off. There is, however, a related and equally ancient notion of excellence that may still have some hold on us. This is an *aesthetic* idea of excellence. According to the aesthetic idea, ethics can be understood to refer both to something like the rules for determining right conduct in given situations (doing one's duty, say) *and* to something like an overarching vision of a life (living well). Put differently, ethics can bear a rigid *moral* and a less rigid *aesthetic* connotation.[46] We need to give this excellence-based notion closer consideration.

To do so is really just to look at the two sides of *arête* in a slightly different light than we have been. 'Aesthetic excellence' is just one of the senses we can give to excellence – a kind of shading of the term. It is an important, skill-transcending shading that refers us to the vision of a life that is fully satisfying for a human being.[47] As such, aesthetic excellence extends the idea of a good life beyond the range not only of skill, but of morality as well. We have already seen that, while virtue and excellence may overlap, they are not coextensive, and to introduce an aesthetic element is to indicate a particular, and very important, way in which they are not. I *may*, for example, accept that it is always aesthetically good (excellent; or even, a beautiful thing) to do what is right (virtuous). But I may be less convinced that it is always right to do what is good.[48] Cultivation of the arts, or of my garden, may be an integral part of my idea of the good life. But there may be circumstances – times of national crisis, for example – when I would think it wrong to pursue this activity. Julia Annas has persuasively argued[49] that Plato's ethics, to the degree that they are tied to his theory of Forms, contain – in one case, I think she would say, 'suffer from' – this disjunction. If *arête*, including the practice of virtue, is a kind of skill that one can perfect or entity that one can come to know (and we have seen that Socrates was not sure this was so, but he kept the option open), then insofar as someone, the philosopher presumably, perfects the skill or attains the knowledge, she will scarcely be inclined to return to the cave and take up the governance of her fellow-citizens. This is because, in Plato's view of the matter, as she develops her understanding of *arête*, she also comes to understand more clearly what the 'good life' consists in: in a nutshell, contemplation of the Forms.[50] Insofar, therefore, as Plato insists that it is the philosopher's[51] moral duty to return to the cave, Annas sees the following contradiction in his position: 'The more successfully I reflect on why I am virtuous, the less inclined I am to act virtuously.' She suggests that in *The Republic* the contradiction is re-solved by the philosopher understanding that the duty to go beyond the 'self-interest' of her own life trumps the enjoyment of the private life of theoretical pursuits in the same way that, for a limited period of time, public service might trump private cultivation of the arts. 'There is,' notes Annas, 'nothing paradoxical, or fundamentally objectionable, in the idea that a skill might be self-undermining in this way.' But, she adds, it is a problem in the *Republic* precisely because that work is supposed to be a model for the individual *psyche*. It is as if the more one understands one's soul, the more one understands the intimate way it connects virtue, ethical skill, and an aesthetic appreciation of the good – the less inclined one is to serve it.

I am not convinced that the dilemma ever quite disappears, even in circumstances that do not involve the philosopher and her heightened sense of duty. However, it can sometimes be resolved through choice, which is to say, through an act of will. One may have a well-grounded conception of what is, aesthetically speaking, the good life, but recognize that the moral duties that arise from particular circumstances will prevent one from pursuing it. Plato's philosopher would probably be most content doing geometry, just as a god might prefer eternal contemplation of her own 'mind.' Yet, some sense of duty moves her to return to the cave, just as something moves the god to create a cosmos.[52] And something may move lesser mortals to do their duty, too. In any case, this shows us that the life of virtue is not necessarily coextensive with what is aesthetically the good life (perhaps not even for a god), and until someone can refute this assertion,[53] the assumption that a virtuous life just is a good life is little more than a (deeply held) prejudice. As Thomas Nagel has written, while there is 'something deeply unsatisfying about conflict between the good life and the moral life,' we cannot maintain that it is 'a necessary truth that the best life is realized by doing everything right.'[54] Of course, because it is deeply unsatisfying, because the paradox that Annas sees may exist not so much in Plato's presentation of ethics as in our response to it, because, in other words, this paradox may violate some of our deepest intuitions about goodness, it is worthy of serious sceptical attention.

Contemporary western – largely Christian – minds have, as a matter of fact, often seemed haunted by this distinction and have, as a result, put a great deal of effort into eradicating it. Modern deontological theories of ethics, for example, tend to collapse 'good' into 'right' or, in Kant's case (which is the most famous), into the dictates of moral reason. Deontologists are moral realists insofar as they argue that certain acts just are right or wrong. To take a well-known example, Kant argues that it is always wrong to break a promise, for if it were ever right to do so then the whole act of promising would disappear.[55] Thus, to keep one's promises is a 'categorical imperative,' a duty derived from a conception of a universal moral law.[56] This sort of argument is usually accompanied by the holistically induced inference that the good life just is doing what is right. Within ethics, morality – which is primarily concerned with virtue – trumps, or even subsumes, aesthetics – which is primarily concerned with an extra-moral kind of excellence.[57] To re-describe this in terms that are perhaps friendlier to deontology, what deontologists are doing away with is a teleological conception of 'good,' according to which 'good' and '(morally) right' can be seen as separate entities, with the former constituting the goal of human life. In other words, a teleologist will see the right as serving the good – like Thrasymachos, he will have trouble understanding how it can be wrong to act in an 'excellent' manner – the deontologist, however, will see the good as coterminous with the right. Alternatively, from a deontological point of view, the good may simply be irrelevant to morality.[58] In that case, not all of what I have called ethics can be housed under the same roof. In this view, all that resides in the house of ethics are moral duties. In either case, deontology ushers us into a virtue world in which the idea of aesthetic excellence is, if not banished, then placed under strict controls. Kant, for example, has a concept of natural perfection which the categorical imperative enjoins one to pursue and which consists in developing one's powers of reason, imagination, and other talents. This can, I think, be read as an idea of an aesthetically good life tied to a conception of what it is to be human. However, it strikes me as either being divorced from the conception of moral perfection or as being a dictate of moral reason – a form of moral duty. In other words, either this natural perfection is distinct from ethics or, if not, it is subsumed by morality.

Other minds, older minds, respectful of both virtue and excellence, may want to resist the usher's hand. They may feel that the two – from their point of view, equally legitimate – senses of *arête* stand in a non-teleological and non-hierarchical relation to one another. And, to complicate matters, they may view morality itself as internally inconsistent in a way that Kant most certainly did not. Let's return to Classical Greece, where the tragic heroes are confronted with two sets of moral imperatives (demands on their virtue) that leave little or no room for resolution, in part, because the demands are equal and contradictory and, in part, because their conception of a good life gives them no grounds for choice.[59] Whatever they do, whichever moral demand they accede to, the good life is destroyed.

In Aeschylus's *Agamemnon*, the eponymous king, pressed by the need to be a good (excellent, but also virtuous) leader, and so to ensure victory over Troy, sacrifices his daughter Iphigenia in obedience to the goddess who commands him to do so. At the same time, he knows that a good (virtuous) parent will refuse to carry out the sacrifice. Martha Nussbaum succinctly describes his dilemma: 'Pious service to Zeus is inseparable from the murder of his child; protection of that child would have been inseparable from impiety and from cruelty to his suffering soldiers.'[60] Agamemnon's crime is not so much that he sacrifices Iphigenia, but that he vainly persuades himself that he has made a correct choice, that in this context he *can* make anything like a correct choice, do something that is not a moral crime. Nussbaum, imagining Aristotle's response to Agamemnon's dilemma, suggests that we might pity the king rather than blame him if 'he had behaved more like a good character, with more sense of the tension and constraint that was forcing him to go against what he would sanely choose.'[61] Because Agamemnon fails to display such character, because, in essence, he fails to tremble before his humanity, he is destroyed, as is the nobility of the Trojan War itself. The just punishment of Troy becomes, in the words of one pair of commentators, 'a sacrilegious destruction of an entire city with its temples.'[62] The aesthetic possibility of a good – a beautiful – life, full of glory, is for Agamemnon and for most of the others in the Greek camp, frittered away in a now useless war – in a war that lacks virtue. One might argue that this possibility began to be frittered away the moment Artemis forced Agamemnon to choose between irreconcilable moral demands: From that moment on, either the war was lost or the leader was corrupted. *Tuche* – chance or luck; *tuche* is what happens to someone, as opposed to what he brings upon himself – had begun to work its awful magic, including the magic of making the king maim his own soul. A wise person, which in this instance Agamemnon evidently was not, will recognize that he has to bow before *tuche*. This entails recognizing that the good life may not be guaranteed by reason or, indeed, by any human quality, including virtue, because virtue may fracture into competing and irreconcilable demands.

Even if all moral imperatives do coincide, *tuche* may still intervene, destroying the best-laid plans. Chance – being sold into slavery or a crippling illness – may short-circuit the development of character, of what Aristotle called *megalopsychia*, greatness of soul. As Nussbaum suggests, in lives that are thus interrupted, the *energia* (activity) that never gets to burst from potentiality to actuality 'is only in a shadowy way itself.' The person who is deprived of this 'actuality' is to be pitied, although not, like Agamemnon, with all his opportunities, blamed.[63] The greater the soul, moreover, the more vulnerable it is to the ravishes of *tuche*. A brave and honourable man such as Oedipus is at greater risk than a lesser person, because of what the expression of his greater character requires. His desire and his ability to do what is right (virtuous), added to his excellence, his abnormal ability to act in and on the world, can conspire to destroy him more easily or more dreadfully than in the case of a lesser mortal. 'Excellence,' Nussbaum writes, 'diminishes self-sufficiency and increases vulnerability.'[64] This lesson was not lost on the Epicureans, who advocated a quiet retiring life, as free from the tentacles of chance as possible, as if excellence could be cultivated only if it were shielded from the public demands that virtue makes upon it. They refused, we could say, ever to return to the cave.

Iris Murdoch has written that 'Kant's view of ethics contains no place for the idea of tragedy,' and hence, he was unable to account for it in his aesthetics.[65] Deontology, with its emphasis on duty, turns ethics into a comedy – which is a very different thing from a travesty! Properly understood, things cannot turn out badly. In this, Kant is a Platonist, for Plato, too, tries to ward off the threat of tragedy. In many ways, Plato's work is an expression of the hope that the power of reason – in a sense, that a scientific understanding of the good – can reduce chance to nothing. In the *Euthydemus*, we are told that 'when wisdom is present, whoever has it needs no more good fortune than that.'[66] *Tuche* is the *aporia*, the yawning gap that stands between a human actor and the aesthetically good life, either by throwing up competing and incompatible 'right actions' or by forcing one to choose between what is 'right' and what is 'good.' In either circumstance, the ethical actor, summoned by two masters, finds himself in a position where the right may not be, indeed, cannot be, the pathway to the good life. Alternatively, there may be no single right action. Either way, there is a great deal of trouble lurking. Incompatible virtues render incoherent the deontologist's holist insistence that there are actions that ought to be done and disjunctions between right and good subject his grand rational vision to the ravishes of chance. Looking back at Agamemnon's dilemma, where both of these cases come into play, we might say that if there is tragedy, deontology is incoherent, and, if deontology is coherent, then tragedy disappears from our universe like a shadow from the wall of the cave. This may help us to understand the deontological thrust of Plato's – and I think Aristotle's – ethics. To ward off the threat of tragedy, ethics had to be formulated, by definition, as a non-contradictory science. The inherent scepticism of the tragic point of view had to be tamed using a moral algorithm. From a philosopher's perspective, Agamemnon is not stuck; he simply (!) lacks knowledge and the proper moral skills.

The dilemma of the tragedian, and the modern deontologically conditioned reaction to it, was dramatized in an interesting way in a very good movie called *A World Apart*. It is, so I understand, the more or less autobiographical story of a young white girl growing up in race-torn South Africa in the 1960s. Her father, a communist and member of the African National Congress,[67] has to flee the country. Her mother, a radical journalist, stays behind to continue the fight against apartheid. The girl, who is about thirteen, and her younger sisters live with their mother and feel very much abandoned by her, even as their need for her increases. Like Agamemnon, the mother finds herself torn between two sets of moral imperatives. One demands that she be a good parent, the other that she fight for social justice. She cannot satisfy both. Because she chooses to fight apartheid, the mother is torn from her family and imprisoned. This was a foreseeable result of her choice. Therefore, in effect, she becomes a bad parent, and there is no doubt that she does so in the opinion of her older daughter. If we apply the standards of Greek tragedy, there does, indeed, seem to be guilt. In pretending that her decision to fight apartheid is obviously, if regrettably, the right one, in assuming that it is deontologically given, and in ignoring, perhaps, the desire and ego that has encouraged it, and the vanity that made her believe that she could control the situation, the mother failed to appreciate the impossibility of her choice. The fact is, neither choice could have led to a good life. Whatever the mother chose, whichever version of right (virtue) she decided to pursue, her life was going to be diminished. She was going to suffer privation, hatred, guilt, and, perhaps, death.[68] *Tuche*, in the form of a racist homeland, did not provide the mother with a way out.

Having brought the viewer to this point, the movie then proceeds to an upbeat and entirely untragic ending. Apparently, its makers decided that their audiences would want right actions to be rewarded by 'good' results. In other words, the audiences would want a Kantian good will to be rewarded[69] – which is to say, they would prefer melodrama (not to mention the assurance of a 'scientific ethics') to tragedy. I am aware that I appear to be suggesting that the goal of a deontological ethics is to reduce tragedy to melodrama (an oxymoronic form of comedy: tragedy with a happy ending), and I do not want to push the idea too far. Nevertheless, it *is* a fruitful one insofar as philosophical ethics often seems to be directed towards rendering coherent what *ethos* – a person's character – and circumstance could not. To expand Nagel's comment noted above, the modern mind seems entirely unsatisfied by the prospect of a moral world that is so inherently irrational as to punish what everyone believes is good behaviour.

Shame and Guilt

One way to throw some more light on the distinction between virtue and aesthetic excellence, and to show how they operate in our lives, is to relate them to the categories of 'shame' and 'guilt.' As with the other terms in this chapter, these are not a mutually exclusive pair – one can, no doubt, experience shame *and* guilt in relation to the same action – but, in the context of ethics, I think it is possible to argue that shame carries the greater aesthetic and guilt the greater moral connotation. Roughly speaking, guilt stems from a failure to do what is right, whereas shame stems from a failure to achieve 'excellence.' As Bernard Williams has put the matter, guilt looks in the direction of others, whereas shame, even though it is felt most intensely in the presence of others, looks 'to what I am.'[70] Thus, guilt arises from failure to *do* what ought to be done, whereas shame results from failure to live up to a vision of what one feels oneself to *be* in the world. In Aeschylus's *Prometheus Bound*, Hermes says, 'It is shameful for a wise man to make mistakes.'[71] If this is so, it is not because the wise man does something morally wrong by committing an error, but because he falls short of what he feels himself to be. And because he has done nothing morally wrong, there is no reason to insist (or at least it is not immediately obvious why one would insist) that he ought to feel guilt as well. His ethical lapse (if that's what it is) is aesthetic, not moral.

In keeping with Williams's distinction, it is important to note that shame can be, and perhaps most essentially is, a private emotion in which I am the 'other' who judges 'me,' but guilt is public, and intimately connected to the presence of others. The other may be God, for those who practise some religions, but guilt resulting from an offence against the divine still involves another, even if no human knows of the act. If I commit a crime or tell a lie, the act may occasion both guilt (because I have harmed others) and shame (because I have failed to live up to my sense of myself – a sense which others may or may not share – as an honest man). This distinction is caught in the fact that we often refer to ourselves as *feeling* shame but *admitting* guilt. (A 'guilty' conscience – *feeling* guilty – would, in this account, be a misnomer; what one would feel is shame.) Someone may, therefore, be shamed by her guilt – that one can easily imagine – but it is harder to understand how she might be guilted by her shame. Insofar as shame betokens the existence of aesthetic sensibilities that express our strongest sense of who we are, it encompasses guilt, for without those standards there would be no foundation from which the latter could arise. To recall my comments on Wittgenstein in Chapter 4, shame is the ontological foundation from which guilt arises. A failure to do one's duty or obey a law is addressed in the context of a sense of who (one feels) one is. This suggests, in opposition to the deontologist, that the fundamental, or foundational, element in ethics – the basis of all moral positions – is the aesthetic, the vision of a good life which its bearers must try to actualize.[72] As Iris Murdoch has written, 'man is a creature who makes pictures of himself and then comes to resemble the picture.'[73] Insofar as this is so, she adds, the goal of moral philosophy (I would say, of ethics) is to 'give a satisfactory or sufficiently rich account of what we unphilosophically know to be goodness.'[74]

Realism Returns

Of course, even if we accept this relation between the right and the good, guilt and shame, virtue and aesthetic excellence, even if we agree that ethics is, at bottom, a kind of aesthetics – or, failing that, that ethics is shot through with aesthetic issues – a deeper question of origin remains to be answered. At this point, the metaphysics of realism – in this case, moral realism – comes back into play. Where do our visions of the good life come from, and what validates them? For the sake of simplicity, we can reduce the options to what are by now a familiar two: Our visions of the good life are either 'this worldly,' naturalist in some way, arising from experience, or 'other worldly,' absolute and foundational emanations of a universal nature or universal truth. Among philosophers, there has never been general agreement as to which is the more convincing option. Plato thought values were other-worldly entities that existed independently of experience. Aristotle insisted that there was a strong this-worldly aspect to them.[75] In contrast to Plato, Aristotle insisted that, even if a certain way of living could ultimately be classified, absolutely, as 'the good life,' the ethical values that we have are socially generated, and they have to be, in the first instance, examined as such.[76]

Difficulties arise with both positions. The 'this-worldly' approach may seem far too relativist, incapable of supporting anything grander than a sociological description of what different peoples, in fact, do. On the other hand, if ethical values are absolute and transcendent, we are thrown, once again, into the metaphysical agony of pursuing abstractions that seem to defy specific definition. In the *Tractatus*, Wittgenstein made values transcendent – and then solved the problem by dismissing the possibility of ever talking about them. 'The sense of the world,' he wrote, 'must lie outside the world.'[77] If ethical values exist, then they transcend the contingent facts of the world, and, since facts are all that can be talked about (or so Wittgenstein argues in the

Tractatus), ethical values necessarily lie beyond language.[78] I am tempted to comment – and so I shall – that one conclusion to be drawn here is that the 'higher' the standards of value, the more elevated one's ethics, the less that can be said about them. The danger, once again – and these just are, I think, waters that philosophers have to navigate – is that we are forced to find a way between relativist chatter and dignified but, perhaps, unenlightening transcendental silence.

As with metaphysics, epistemology, and logic, so, therefore, is it with ethics: The shadows of relativism and naturalism that haunt the contemporary world seem, inevitably, to fall across our discussions and obscure thereby an earlier metaphysical clarity. Ethics is an attempt to think about what is good or important in our lives. But since Kant released philosophers from the constraints of a dogmatic reason, which insisted that it is possible to delineate the 'good life' and left them free, within the limits of their reason, to construct their ethical positions,[79] they have been at something of a loss. However universal Kant's moral laws are in application, however binding once enunciated, they are given by *human* reason alone. Our freedom as moral agents just is the result of the limits of our reason. 'Good' is, therefore, a metaphysically useful, but ultimately indefinable concept. Lately, however, we have become even more earthbound than that. Many post-Kantian philosophers are unable to share even *his* dogmatism, which is to say, his insistence that even if reason cannot unveil the *noumenal*, we ought, nonetheless, given the commonality of reason as a human trait, to be able to think our way to the same moral conclusions: We ought to be able to agree on what is a good and so to understand what are binding moral laws. Against Kant, contemporary philosophers point to such things as culture, circumstance, and evidence of human individuality as ethics-forming aspects of our lives that stand between us and the articulation of moral laws that *all* humans can accept.

In short, when reason is applied to an aestheticized ethics freed from the constraints of moral realism – and that is pretty much what naturalism does – it need not point in any particular direction. Reason, then, has ceased to bind us together. The thrust of what can be described as a kind of Nietzschean naturalism that runs through much contemporary thought is that we do not search for the 'good.' Rather, we reflect on what we deeply – 'instinctively' in Nietzsche's parlance – value as 'good.' A few paragraphs ago, we saw that Iris Murdoch has said much the same thing. Sometimes, such reflection may change what we value. It may alter our idea of 'good' and, indeed, our idea – or perhaps 'presentation' – of ourselves. The fact remains, however, that we do begin, as Aristotle would have us do, with some deeply ingrained notion of what is 'good.' The difference between Nietzsche and Aristotle on this point is whether any amount of contemplation or reflection will bring us any closer to knowledge of an absolute 'good.' The difference between Nietzsche and Kant is whether it will bring us closer to anything that we can agree on as a universal moral law. For Nietzsche, life is *poiesis*, an aesthetic fashioning that has no universal mould.[80] To echo Socrates, or perhaps Chilon of Sparta,[81] there is nothing to know but oneself – and, contra Socrates, every self may be different. (This was also Kierkegaard's message.)

In this view, to attempt to define the 'good' life in anything more than a contextual and perhaps highly individual manner is to fall victim to what the English philosopher G.E. Moore, following Hume, called the 'naturalistic fallacy.' Moore's point is that however important a word 'good' may be, and he thinks it is a very important word – in fact, that it is *something* – it lacks *necessary* content. To think that the word 'good' has such content is to make the mistake of treating an abstraction as if it were an ostensively identifiable thing.[82] The same could be said of the term 'right' as it is used in certain contexts. There is currently a lot of talk in some quarters about 'human rights' – and since the seventeenth century, 'natural rights' – but it is no easy matter to explain why certain rights are 'human' or 'natural,' which is to say, why they are an essential part of the human condition. (To put this in terms of the naturalistic fallacy, the fact that we value certain rights does not demonstrate that we *ought* to value them.) If these rights – of life and liberty, say – belong to us *as* humans, that is, if they necessarily belong to us absolutely and universally, they are transcendent. If *that* can be demonstrated, the burning issue is then no longer whether these rights exist – for that is what has been demonstrated – but whether they are universally respected. This is, in point of fact, the way most politicians in the western world speak of 'human rights': as if their existence is, at least potentially, obvious to everyone. Individuals who fail to recognize or respect human rights are either recalcitrant or in need of education. A philosopher might want to educate such politicians in the subtleties of the naturalistic fallacy. From another direction, we might do well to recall the nineteenth-century English utilitarian, Jeremy Bentham, who rejected natural rights theory with the blunt comment that, if the world were anything to go by, the rights of humankind were fundamentally the rights to be 'starved and conquered.'[83] Put differently, rights are the creation of power, and power is anything but transcendent. Power creates what it can and, within that range of capability, what it wants. In Bentham's view, unlike in Plato's ideal city, rights are nowhere laid up in heaven.

Even if they are not Benthamites, contemporary philosophers seldom espouse an absolutist or other-worldly theory of ethical values. They are, at best, reluctant moral realists. Yet, the words we use in ethics – value, right, good – are hard to keep earthbound. As humans, we inhabit what we might call 'value-space,' part of which is 'ethical value-space,' and there is something inherently absolutist about it. That's how it *feels* to us. Let's look first at a non-ethical example. If I assert that Plato is a great philosopher, I am asserting a value. The question then is: What is the standard of greatness? What message do I mean to convey here? Am I asserting that Plato is, in some absolute (and realist) sense, a 'great' philosopher – am I pointing towards the Form Greatness – or am I simply asserting that, as a matter of fact, most contemporary philosophers hold a high opinion of Plato's work? The second alternative of course begs the question why philosophers hold this opinion. After all, in contradistinction to my ethically relativist students, I appear to be doing something more than simply reporting the outcome of a poll among philosophers. I think my students would be disappointed if I told them that is all I meant by the remark. I might, therefore, provide a list of reasons why philosophers think Plato is a great philosopher, although it is hardly likely that all philosophers will set down the same reasons (or even agree that he is great). At any rate, I shall then have to explain why whatever reasons philosophers come up with are definitive of greatness. The answer, I fear, may be a Rortian-sounding one – 'because philosophers say they are' – which means that I am not justifying my remark so much as introducing the students to the culture of philosophy. If I reject this possibility, the eternally recurring issue of transcendent standards once more awaits me. I may back off somewhat and argue that I am appealing only to certain recognizable 'craft standards' of 'excellence.' Philosophy, I might note, is a *techne*. It is a skilled activity at which, demonstrably, Plato was very good (which is true, I think), but it is likely that I and my listeners feel that I am doing something more than simply asserting this rather banal fact. Like looking at a 'great' painting, in making the claim about Plato's greatness as a philosopher, I feel myself to be appealing to 'excellence' as a concept that picks out not just technical skill, but less definite aesthetic considerations, as well. (Think of two pianists, both equally adept. One, however, has a feel for the music he plays, whereas the other does not.)

To recall Murdoch, once again, I feel I am trying to give a philosophical account of what I already know. This is an important feeling, one I ought to heed. For even if I do not wish to assert that there are absolute values, I may have to recognize that I feel values *as if* they were absolute, or other-worldly, and, therefore, both real and beyond definition. We inhabit 'value-spaces,' including what Charles Taylor has referred to as a moral space.[84] I think these value-spaces are shaped by an aesthetic sensibility that we, perhaps, cannot fully articulate. Concepts that describe these spaces ('excellence,' the 'good life,' 'greatness') include, along with measurable or quantitative (skill) elements, qualitative (taste) ones as well. And however much they are related, the latter cannot be reduced to the former. I teach my students philosophy. I bring them along until they begin to 'see' why Plato is great: I *initiate* them in the manner, perhaps, of the unseen personages in Plato's cave. (That initiation may, of course, be indoctrination.) In this context, Taylor argues that a problem inherent in modern forms of naturalism is that they restrict ethics to producing guides to moral action. 'In this conception,' writes Taylor, 'there is no place for the notion of the good in either of two common traditional senses: either the good life or the good as the object of our love and allegiance.'[85] In a related manner, the American moral philosopher John Rawls has distinguished a 'thin' conception of good, in which 'the concept of right is prior to the concept of good' and good must not circumvent right, from a 'full' theory, which is a well worked-out concept of good. In essence, we use a stripped-down, thin theory of good as a foundation for developing principles of justice, and when this has been done, we can then apply the principles to the development of the full theory.[86] This is, I think, similar to my earlier distinction between deontological theories of ethics and aesthetic theories of ethics.

This value-talk is vague. Yet, even though that vagueness places a limit on Plato's dream of ethics as science, it is not necessarily (I want to say, 'by no means') a bad thing, something to be excised from our ethical discourse. The vagueness may well be a frustrating but essential quality of ethics: frustrating because it means we can never have the last word on value issues and essential because the aesthetic remains, at least partly, elusive and, thus, resistant to dogma. Taylor's assertion that we live within moral 'horizons' that are 'constitutive of human agency,' suggests this inherent tension in ethical discourse. Moral horizons may fall short of clear and distinct delineation – almost certainly they do – but to attempt to step outside them 'would be tantamount to stepping outside what we would recognize as integral, that is, undamaged personhood.'[87] In a similar vein, when Iris Murdoch writes that we are oriented in a world that is animated by our 'indicating a moral dimension,'[88] we need to pay attention to the subjectivity, the fundamental *poiesis*, in her choice of the word 'indicating.' In these accounts, we are, as moral beings, necessarily concerned with the question of how we ought to live our lives. We value – people, activities, and things – and, ultimately, we value valuing. In the process, we construct something like moral horizons or, more broadly, ethical spaces. The questions we ask – how to value, how to decide what it is right and excellent to do, how to relate these notions – and the answers we give to them, will do much to define these spaces. They *may* turn out to be (look) other-worldly and absolute, or they may remain securely within the this-worldly realm of cultures and societies. In either case, these are the spaces within which we think about how we ought to live our lives.

Are There Moral Absolutes?

Depending on one's point of view, there are both rewards and pitfalls to other-worldly and this-worldly theories of ethics. I have suggested what some of them are, but I think it will help to provide some summary here. The realism of other-worldly theories is, I think, satisfying insofar as such theories manage to avoid a relativism that can leave one feeling as if the words 'good' and 'virtue' are scarcely worth the effort of enunciating.[89] But absolute, transcendent values are difficult, by many accounts impossible, to verify. They are, therefore, open to the attacks of scepticism. We may be talking about nothing. Just how does one demonstrate that a human right enjoys more than the sanctity afforded it by power and communal agreement? Socially rooted, naturalistic this-worldly values are, by contrast, easier to grasp, and their origins easier to explain. But, of course, the shoals of relativism threaten. Long before Moore articulated the naturalistic fallacy, David Hume established his version of it by arguing (perhaps in the face of Aristotle's hopes) that we cannot logically infer what we *ought* to do from what we, in fact, do.[90] Hume's conclusion is that ethical standards have no rational, or scientific, justification. (This is also part of Wittgenstein's point.) We are, said Hume, guided by a 'moral sense,' a kind of psychological sympathy with others, an instinctive reaction to their pain and pleasure. Hence, while morality is universal – we all possess the moral sense – it is not transcendent. Rather, morality is a matter of human psychology.[91] As John Rawls has said, in comparing the sceptical Scot with earlier, god-infused versions of moral sentiment theory, 'with Hume we are in another world altogether.'[92]

Almost two centuries later, Jean Paul Sartre caught the thrust of the dilemma that is implicit in Hume's argument[93] when he argued that, even if God existed – and Sartre did not think that 'he' did – he would be irrelevant to the process of defining morality because we all must make our own choices, including deciding whether God is speaking to us. Of course, Sartre's lonely individuals are scarcely united by anything so strong as a moral sense. They choose alone, *as individuals*. However, since they are social beings inhabiting moral spaces, each choice is, nonetheless, a signal to all others concerning how they ought to act.[94] There are thus approximately six billion gods on the planet Earth sending out moral messages – many of which are conflicting – in every direction. The upshot is a lively moral debate without guidelines. As the Marquis de Sade might have said, human is as human does; by definition, nothing a person chooses to do is un-human or unnatural, and so everything must go into the discursive pot. To quote Nietzsche, 'There are no moral facts, only phenomena capable of moral interpretation.'[95]

If we follow Hume, Sartre, Nietzsche, and others, and abandon the transcendent in ethics, a plethora of competing this-worldly theories ensue. There is 'emotivism,' which is a development of Hume's moral sense theory and according to which the wellsprings of morality, our determinations of right and wrong, good and bad, are external to reason. There is 'prescriptivism,' which presents moral theory as a set of rules – commands really – intended to guide conduct. On this account, terms such as 'good' and 'right' are designed not to describe a quality, but to tell humans what to do.[96] Both emotivism and prescriptivism are *non-cognitive* theories insofar as they stand outside the sphere of rational knowledge in much the way that God's commands do. On these theories, no rational account of the origin of morality is possible. By contrast, there is the cognitive ethics of 'consequentialism,' according to which actions are judged in terms of their results. Utilitarianism, with its insistence that actions ought to maximize happiness, is an example of this sort of theory. If an action contributes to the happiness of the individual or, in social terms, the greatest happiness of the greatest number, it is good; if it detracts from it, it is bad. Bentham famously developed a 'hedonic calculus' that measured such things as the intensity, duration, certainty, and immediacy of pleasures as a way of deciding on their comparative rationality. Indeed, this is probably one of the best examples of an ethics that is, in theory, reducible to a science and reproducible as an algorithm. Of course, Bentham's calculus exasperated the other great utilitarian of the nineteenth century, John Stuart Mill, who did not think that all pleasures are quantifiable. Moreover, Mill believes that some pleasures are of a higher quality than others. There is his famous comment on Benthamite ethics: 'It is better to be a human being dissatisfied than a pig satisfied; better to be Socrates dissatisfied than a fool satisfied.'[97] Each of these theories – or varieties of them – will have a concept of good lurking somewhere in the background (in the case of utilitarianism, in the foreground). They all, nonetheless, deny, or certainly seem to deny (except *possibly* in the case of emotivism, which *can* be made to appeal to a universal human nature), the existence of transcendent moral values. As such, they seem to stand in opposition to a foundationalist ethics such as Kant's, which, you will recall, asserts that there are actions that ought to be done just because they are right: not because they will lead to 'good' consequences or because they will promote a 'good' life, but because they are, *by the standards of reason*, right.[98]

But note that, in a deontological theory such as Kant's, the moral life – doing what it is right to do – just is the good life. In that sense, doing what it is right is also doing what is beautiful; certainly, it is analogous to the beautiful.[99] But, with this conflation, his ethics collapses into the kind of procedural morality that Taylor warned against: Reason properly and you will reach the right conclusion, because the right conclusion is the one that comes at the end of a proper line of inference. This simplifies matters in some ways – transcendence has now been abolished – but it also creates problems. As I pointed out above, procedural moral reasoning suppresses any tragic possibilities that may await us, for, as Alasdair MacIntyre has noted, there is now only one set of things we ought to do – the moral set.[100] The dilemmas that give rise to tragedy thus disappear, and one may be forgiven for suggesting that life is thereby flattened out and made much less testing and interesting. But, perhaps this is the salutary boredom Plato and all other writers of ethical comedy have been searching for. Since few of us want to be on the receiving end of tragedy, this may seem more a gain than a loss. It may, in fact, be the prime moral directive of modernity, as it was of Epicureanism. Even so, there are other issues that need to be addressed.

Among them is the charge that a moral theory empty of transcendent-looking concepts of good and right tends to look amoral. As writers such as MacIntyre, Murdoch, Taylor, and Rawls have pointed out, moral activity is virtually impossible to imagine without a prior set of values that includes some notion of the 'good' life, even if that notion resists definitive articulation[101] or is 'only' a cultural artefact. It is, in other words, difficult to understand how a moral theory can be purely *procedural* – how it can be methodical, scientific, but not aesthetic. *But*, if it can be, then such a theory can be universalized as a sort of logical calculus, and for many theorists that must be part of the allure of procedural ethics.

Consider Descartes' apparently crystalline example of procedural reasoning. Applying his 'clear and distinct' rule to human thought, he generated a proof for the existence of a God who is the guarantor of both our existence and that of the world. I argued in Chapter 2 that that argument is circular, although not viciously so. If we focus solely on Descartes' proof for the existence of God, however, the circularity is more troublesome, because Descartes seems all along to assume what he has set out to prove: that God exists. It is, I think, perfectly plausible to say that his argument is not so much a proof as a reminder to his contemporary readers that God is a necessary scientific and moral concept that bonds the world and humankind together. Bluntly, and too crudely: We can trust innate ideas because they are innate – that is, because they come from God, who has provided us with sufficient powers of reason to grasp their truth. Hence, we know that God exists because God exists. And because God exists the world exists. One lesson this Cartesian circle may have to teach is that moral thinking has, as Murdoch has suggested, more to do with seeking clarification of our values, with seeing distinctly what our 'goods' are, than with discovering absolute and transcendent values. (In other words, Descartes does not know how to think without God, and he has shown clearly and distinctly why this is so.) It can be read as confirmation that all moral procedures take place within, and are animated by, already existing ethical frameworks that may be perfectly natural but that, nonetheless, come to us as a ghostly teleological presence. What we think is other-worldly is, not too surprisingly, of this world. As it is with metaphysics and epistemology, so too is it with ethics: The ghost of the god's-eye view is always with us.

To a thoroughgoing proceduralist this may seem a tad narcissistic, as if ethics is mainly about gazing into the mirror of a culture it cannot transcend. We can develop procedures just because we have beliefs. But, from the other side, procedure without a contextualizing sense of the good life is aimless. Still, a proceduralist – Socrates included – would remind us that context *without* procedure may amount to little more than a blind following of the traditions that provide our visions of the good life. Ethical discourse is self-conscious, and that is what procedures, even though they begin with one's beliefs, poke away at by providing ways of thinking through our conduct, of presenting it to ourselves. Socrates was, in many ways, a traditional Athenian, believing in the gods, respecting the ways of the city. His refusal to escape prison and death because he thought it wrong, harmful both to his soul and to Athens, reflects a deeply conservative temperament. Yet, Socrates is subversive, too. His commitment to certain goods, his deep belief in his city and in the gods, was constantly sharpened, given focus, by his elenctic method of reasoning. Socrates employed the *elenchos* to question beliefs. If one could stand up to his questioning, his persistent attempts to refute it, it could be accepted as true, but if not it must be discarded.[102] By means of this procedure, Socrates hoped to increase his and his interlocutors' grasp of, among other things, the good life. This could not be done in a vacuum, however. It required something to work on, an already existing belief: For Socrates, any belief would do. Aristotle's ethics would seem to owe a debt to this method, as does Kant's assertion that 'pure reason' remains inert without the inspiration of experience. So, we need context – we need a life to think about. But we need procedure, too, for that is what liberates ethical discourse and its aesthetic visions from the tyranny of command and tradition and ensures that visions of the good life do not become ossified. Moral laws can, thus, become Kantian laws, formulated by reason, which we give to ourselves. Whether those laws can ever capture the beauty of a life well lived is another question.

Comparative Ethics

Based on the foregoing, we can now say that ethics is a *process of reasoned discourse* about what is good and what is right. Whether the 'good' reduces to the 'right,' whether these terms are in some way commensurable, what the hierarchy of goods might be and what the rights ought to be, are issues for this discourse to take up. In the process, one's sense of oneself and others, which includes one's sense of time and place, ought to be sharpened in such a way that direction and, if necessary, emendation of one's conduct becomes possible. As such, ethical discourse necessarily moves beyond a recitation of rules and becomes a finely textured and layered investigation into what we are and what we (feel we) ought to be, either by ourselves or in company with others. If this is done with proper care, we will also learn how to reflect on our ethical values and, perhaps, those of other cultures as well, in something like their own terms. That is, by learning how to question ourselves, we may learn how to question other cultures – from the inside, so to speak. And so, we may learn how far we can compare and evaluate one ethical system with another.

Since this last suggestion may be contentious to many in a naturalist-minded contemporary world, some clarification is needed. If ethical discourse is contextual, if it is framed by an already-existing concept of the 'good,' then what can be said about its relation to competing discourses? Since each discourse will surely be satisfactory in its own terms – unless it is in the process of disintegrating – competing discourses must be incommensurable, and any third discourse will simply judge the other two according to *its* terms. Where, then, is the possibility of an 'objective' judgment? The short answer is that there is no such possibility. The slightly longer answer is that, even if there is no such possibility, *some* comparison is nonetheless possible.[103] The basis for such a comparison is the experience of each discourse *in its own terms*. Since no culture is absolutely static or isolated, the capacity of a culture's ethical discourse to respond to change will provide a sort of litmus test of its authenticity. An inadequate response to change may be defined as one that represses or evades challenges and which, as a result, deforms the discourse, along with the culture that espouses it. The discourse, then, either maintains its hegemony by force or becomes irrelevant to those who formerly lived within it.

History is full of examples. To pick one at random, the early modern European theory of the Divine Right of Kings, which maintained that monarchs ruled by God's fiat and ought, therefore, to enjoy absolute power, simply could not withstand the forces of change in the sixteenth, seventeenth, and eighteenth centuries and was swept, along with a monarch or two, into Marx's dustbin of history. Today, the Roman Catholic Church's teaching on contraception is largely ignored by its flock in much of the western world, and one may wonder how long its positions on abortion and the ordination of women can withstand the currents of the early twenty-first century. However traditional the exponents of a culture and its ethics may try to be, one lesson of history is that things change, and, if they are to survive, ethical systems have to take account of, and reflect, that change. This is not to argue that ethics is merely a reaction to change, an effort to legitimize what has already transpired, but it is to argue that since ethics is articulated in a non-static context, it has to be understood as a reasoned response to what is going on in the world. One can, then, compare ethical discourses in terms of their capacity to adapt to, incorporate, and in some cases, initiate, change – in essence, by their capacity to remain relevant to those who live within them. If this is a science, it is, as Aristotle and Kant understood, a very practical one, and probably a very metaphysical one, as well.

On Politics

I shall conclude this chapter with some brief comments on the relation of ethics to politics. For Plato, politics was the highest activity since it was the one that aimed at producing the good life – or at least as good a life as human beings could produce. For most people (although, as we have seen, perhaps not for the philosopher), the good life was (insofar as it could be realized) a product of the *polis*. This is why the philosopher who has gazed at the Forms feels a moral duty to re-enter the cave – the city – with her guiding wisdom in hand. This intimate connection of politics to ethics runs throughout western thought.[104] Constitutions, both ancient and modern, have always attempted to enshrine values that the community considers to be necessary to the good life of its citizens. In the modern era – which is to say, since the sixteenth or seventeenth century – individual freedom has been very high on the list. As Taylor notes, in this era, 'ordinary life,' the quiet private life of the individual, underlies our 'bourgeois politics.'[105] This is virtually an Epicurean view. It is as if, in contradistinction to Pericles, politics exists not to fulfil us but simply to protect the private realm, where we can fulfil ourselves in whatever way we personally see fit. This distinction between the public and the private, thus, becomes an essential one, and indeed, it was a principal concern of John Stuart Mill in his magisterial *Essay on Liberty*.[106] So it is that in the West individual liberty has come to be treated, often simultaneously, both as a good in itself, as in Taylor's conception of the ordinary life, and as a condition of a good life, as it is in Mill's *Essay*. That is, individual liberty has been put forward as both an end and a means to an end. I think one can find this ambiguity in the bills of rights enshrined in some modern constitutions. Their declarations stand as elements of a certain concept of 'good' founded on the sanctity of the individual and as a protection for that individual in the pursuit of his private life – which is to say, of his private conception of 'good.' It is worth noting that many immigrants to the West seem to experience the individuality and public secularity of life in the liberal democracies as something of an ethical lacuna. In protecting freedom as a means to largely private ends, the state fails to reflect the more communal conceptions that these people have of the good life. (The same might be said for the *soi disant* social conservatives of the United States and Canada, who sometimes appear to want to impose a particular vision of the good life on their societies, while at the same time – and it has to be said, somewhat paradoxically – staunchly defending individual liberties.)

It may be that these immigrants (insofar as they are not merely my straw people) are alive to a certain irony in the democratic politics of the West. To enshrine private life (in whatever form it may take) as the good life is to divorce politics not only from religion but also, in certain fundamental ways, from ethical discourse itself. To do so re-presents politics as either the art of perfecting the 'night-watchman state' that oversees the pursuit of private goods or the science of the pursuit of power, which is just the ability to ensure one's private vision of the good. But, if politics is sealed off from transcendent notions of the good, it is to a certain extent sealed off from 'normal' ethical concerns. The night-watchman state is, supposedly, concerned only with ensuring fair play among its citizens, although given the inevitable differences in wealth and power, 'fair' becomes an excruciatingly difficult term to define. Perhaps because of this, the state can seldom be as impartial as the image suggests. As John Rawls argues at length in his *Theory of Justice*, the principle of 'justice as equity' always requires some restrictions on individual liberty. Political power, thus, moves inevitably beyond the scope of the watchman state and becomes a fundamental support for the individual's pursuit of her version of the good life. Insofar as these versions are varied and possibly incommensurable, one conclusion, drawn long in advance of the nineteenth-century conception of the watchman state, is that politics is, therefore, about the pursuit of power – the means to pursue one's version of the good.

The progenitor of this view is the sixteenth-century Florentine, Niccolo Machiavelli, whose ideas are sufficiently famous and influential that his name has – somewhat unfairly – entered English as a synonym for ruthlessness. In *The Prince*, a book of advice dedicated to (and ignored by) Lorenzo de' Medici, Machiavelli wrote that, above all else, a prince must 'maintain his state,'[107] and any action that contributes to that end is a 'virtue.' Although it may not represent Machiavelli's real thoughts on the matter, the ethical hierarchy in this work is excruciatingly clear (and for some readers, clearly excruciating): political virtue is whatever contributes to political excellence, which is just the ability to grasp and retain power. This virtue is a teachable skill – Machiavelli is trying to teach in *The Prince* – although it is not one that Plato or Aristotle would much have cared to put on the syllabi of their schools. Machiavelli's political theory, thus, has the shape of an ethics, but one that is particular, or local, to the activity itself (which by some definitions is just what makes it a science). Since the end of politics is power, and since the political virtues are often not (and certainly not necessarily) Christian ones, what the prince must abandon is the idea that politics is part of a larger societal or universal system of ethics. Political life is guided by its specific ends, and larger sets of values are to be taken into account only insofar as they have to – or can – be. Power, in other words, respects only power, and the science of politics is the science of power.

This is enough to make a Platonist weep, for no glorious sun illuminates Machiavelli's world. Even so, perhaps the worst that can be said of Machiavelli is that he was terribly insightful.[108] In understanding power he came to see that factionalism, not cooperation, was the inescapable fact of political life. Aristotle had also seen and feared this element of politics, but he thought that for the most part it could, for some time at least, be kept under control. Plato, too, had feared the addictive power of self-interest, so much so that in the *Republic* his philosopher-kings were not allowed to touch money or to raise their own children.[109] (The political structure of classical Athens, with its mixture of clans and townships and its allocation of all offices except generalships by lot, also reflected this fear of factions and self-interest.) Like Machiavelli, the ancients saw politics as an activity subject to certain social and psychological pressures that constantly threaten to deform the good that it is intended to produce. But unlike Machiavelli, the ancients thought – hoped? – that there were ways to avoid this deformation. For the great Florentine, however, the politics of power was not a deformation at all, just purely and simply politics. When one considers that, in the modern era, the writings of Marx may well most closely reflect the classical sensibility of politics as the foundation of the good, and when one reflects on what has transpired in Marxist societies in the twentieth century, when one considers how communist parties have appropriated and distorted this sense of good, one can see something of the danger of allowing ourselves to believe that politics can ever be about anything more than power. (In addition, one can understand why a non-Marxist Marx looked forward to the 'withering away of the state.') Closer to home, when one considers the often staggering venality and partisanship of politicians in democratic societies, it is possible to appreciate the strict controls to which Plato proposed to subject even wise leaders. I have often thought that the best metaphor for a good politician is Odysseus avoiding the sirens' song by lashing himself to the mast.[110] Like Odysseus, politicians will never be deaf to the seductions of office, and unless they (and their interests) are very tightly lashed to the mast of political probity it very often ends in tears.

Given these rather gloomy ruminations, we might say that the point of political philosophy is to consider how to rise above our lamentable humanity and enunciate a concept of good that is more inclusive (or if not, then less invasive) than a personal or factional idea and how, therefore, to institute a procedure that will ensure that politicians will pursue that good in contradistinction to their private goods. The answer, or at any rate the best answer that we in the West have, may seem both banal and contradictory because it places procedure before 'Big Concepts' of good: democracy. For much of the history of the West, democracy was considered unworkable for a reason that is of Platonic inspiration: Human beings are not sufficiently rational to be trusted to govern themselves. Put differently, their concepts of 'good' are likely to be so debased, so fundamentally appetitive, that no 'real' good will ever emerge from such a politics. Far better to have an enlightened despot, a philosopher-king who will rule wisely in the people's best interest. In the early nineteenth century, Bentham articulated the contradiction at the heart of this argument, which he himself had once espoused: Even philosopher-kings, who would after all be human, would look to their own interests if they were not carefully constrained. (Otherwise, why would Plato find it necessary to regulate their lives so carefully?) The best way to do this, Bentham reasoned, was not by regulations – since we cannot literally lash them to masts, none could be strict enough – so much as by the threat of recall, which is to say, by regular elections. And since no one person or group of persons could be trusted to look to the interests of all,[111] everyone must be allowed to express his or her interest in these elections. In short, suffrage should be universal.[112]

I find this reasoning interesting, if only because it goes against the

Millian ideology of democracy that I was taught as an undergraduate, in which, in fine Platonic fashion, the advent of democracy was tied to education.[113] In Bentham's formula, democracy is necessary (or in Mill's case, acceptable) not because (or when) people are rational and capable of altruism, but precisely because they are irretrievably self-interested. Few of Mill's fools will turn into Socrates. When we cannot find among us even a single philosopher-king, when we realize that this really is an ideal-type laid up only in heaven, we ought not to expect to find countless millions of them. In the Benthamite view, we do not, therefore, live up to democracy; in our self-interest we live down to it. Because there is no universal good, because, as Hannah Arendt once said, there is now only opinion, we have to be democrats. One is reminded of Winston Churchill's famous dictum that democracy is the worst system of government except for all the others.

That no form of government is either laid up in heaven or scientifically perfectible, the fundamental irrationality of the self-interest of both citizen and ruler: these are perhaps reminders that democracy is an act of *poiesis*, an open-ended journey of construction that cannot be enclosed in a static Platonic *episteme* (science). This is something that many anti-metaphysical or neo-Nietzschean writers have articulated in recent years. Simon Critchley has written that, for Jacques Derrida, 'there is an historical and systematic connection between literature and democracy. Literature is the public articulation of a sphere of private and intimate experience, on the basis of which "the realm of the political can be and remain open."'[114] If so, it may be that in 'living down' to democracy we are deconstructing the idea of a political rationality that we do not sufficiently possess – that we cannot even express – and opening up a political poeticism that we do not sufficiently recognize in ourselves. It may be that if we see that this is what is going on (or see this *as* going on), we may manage to inject into politics a much-needed dose of art,[115] which will help us, if not to articulate more clearly our sense of what a good life is, then to produce images and visions that make room for such a sense. If so, in politics, science may give way to, or at least make room for, much-needed metaphors of the imagination.

7

Philosophy and Language:
The House of Being

The page that was blank to begin with is now crossed from top to bottom with tiny black characters – letters, words, commas, exclamation marks – and it's because of them that the page is said to be legible. But a kind of uneasiness, a feeling close to nausea, an irresolution that stays my hand – these make me wonder: do these black marks add up to reality? The white of the paper is an artifice that's replaced the translucency of parchment, and the ochre surface of clay tablets; but the ochre and the translucency and the whiteness may all possess more reality than the signs that mar them.

Jean Genet, 'Prisoner of Love'

Language is the house of being. In its home human beings dwell. Those who think and those who create with words *are the guardians of this home.*

Martin Heidegger, 'Letter on Humanism'

SUMMARY
Suspicion about metaphysics seems inevitably to lead to a turn away from the world to language as the ultimate 'object' of thought. We orient our discussion of this issue around a consideration of two very important figures in twentieth-century linguistic philosophy (although one is not a philosopher!): Ferdinand de Saussure and the 'later' Wittgenstein. We conclude with some final thoughts about philosophy – what it may be and why, even if it is indefinable, philosophy is nonetheless a viable and even vibrant discipline.

A Language-World

The reader who has arrived at this point will be aware that philosophy is intimately concerned with issues of language. As the American philosopher Robert Brandom has said, 'the 20th century has been the century of language in philosophical thought.'[1] The reader will, in fact, be forgiven for wondering whether philosophy is concerned with anything but language. If this is her suspicion, it may help her to know that philosophy has indeed been much affected by what is known as the 'linguistic turn' of the twentieth century and that this book has been very much influenced by it. (Perhaps it has been corrupted by it.) The term designates philosophy's recourse to the anti-realist view that any world beyond language, beyond what it describes, discusses, represents, and analyses, is inaccessible. The reader will also be forgiven if she feels that, despite everything that has been said in these pages, such a view rubs against the grain of common sense, which is to say, against the realist assumption that we use language to communicate about *something* beyond language (unless, of course, language is the topic of discussion). The world, in other words, is 'there' before language gets to it, and only a philosopher could summon up the audacity to challenge the claim that there is an objective world 'out there' for human beings to experience. For the rest of humankind, the point is beyond debate, and the lesson is clear: One cannot say *just anything* about the world; one cannot talk worlds into existence. (Only a god can do that.) So, we hold to some version of the correspondence theory of truth, which asserts that what we say is true or false depending on whether it accurately depicts the part of the (experienced) world to which we are referring. In this view, language is a tool we use to communicate our experience. We may use language well or badly or anywhere in between but that, nonetheless, is why we use it. Wittgenstein's assertion in the *Tractatus* that language *shows* what the world is like seems eminently reasonable. The world shows itself to us, and we show it to others, using the medium of language.

In defence of philosophers, I remind the reader that because philosophers so often deal in abstractions there is seldom any obviously 'real' referent for them to pick out in the external world. 'Good,' we have seen, scarcely admits of the easy denotation of a concrete word such as 'chair.' Given that abstract terms are a fundamental part of their business, philosophers necessarily sail close to the winds of language. Consider the enormous difficulties encountered by Socrates in his endless inquiries. In the *Euthyphro*, he reminds his eponymous interlocutor that no one is going to get into a fight over concrete, or measurable, issues (such as which of two people is taller), but that even the gods may fall into discord over abstract questions such as 'What is holiness?'² The reason is precisely the one I have noted: Holiness does not literally exist *in the world* in the way a chair does. To discuss holiness, or any other abstraction, is to remain fundamentally within the confines of language, where a word has to be referred to other words. There is never a point at which we can stop, point, and say, 'There, that's what it is.' So, we go on talking – unless, of course, there are Forms. To gaze upon the Platonic Forms would be to pass from talking to seeing – it would be to render the intelligible world visible – in which case abstractions such as 'holiness' and 'goodness' would become as apparent to the philosophical eye as a chair is to the physical one. But this is a metaphorical moment of 'in-sight' that does not come to the living. We do not know, we are not always sure, whether we are talking sense or non-sense. The nineteenth-century German philosopher Friedrich Schlegel wondered about this, too, when he asked: 'Of all things that have to do with the communication of ideas, what could be more fascinating than the question of whether such communication is actually possible?'³

So, if the ancients recognised the problem of universals – and fundamentally, that is what their metaphysics is about: the way in which such abstractions can be present to us – the moderns have added a layer of difficulty which owes much to the suspicion of metaphysics that I described in Chapter 3. Socrates speaks and Plato writes as if holiness *is* something. They may not know what it is, but they are certain that holiness (like other abstractions) has ontological substance. Forms are 'solid' metaphysical 'presences,' natural names for some 'thing.' So, these ancient thinkers evince a certainty about the world that few contemporary philosophers can manage. Most of the latter group would be wary of saying that language names or describes discrete natural units, either in the world or outside it. This is not because they are idealists, who have given up on anything but the mental world, but because they deny that the world consists of what we might call discrete ontological units – certainly not abstract ones – that await our discovery and naming. There is, in other words, no one thing to which terms such as 'holiness' refer, and therefore no universally correct usage of such terms. Language, as anti-realists would remind us, imposes itself on the world, creating it in human terms. Richard Rorty's description of the matter is that 'modern European philosophy amounts to an attempt by human beings to wrest power from God – or, more placidly put, to dispense with the idea of human answerability to something nonhuman.'[4]

This is not a position shared by everyone. Many philosophers do adhere to realism with respect to great parts of the world, especially of the physical world. Still, it has to be said, even there the anti-realist stance has had a significant impact, and Rorty's description does catch the flavour of much that has gone on lately. To return to the issues of Chapters 2 and 3, many philosophers would argue that language – certainly philosophical language – is not a *tool* we use to announce discoveries about a mind-independent world but rather the *environment* that makes that world in the first place. It just is the world we move about in. No absolute reality, no teleology, no set of Forms, nothing of this sort awaits the philosopher's discovery; her world is a mass of raw material that language can shape – and, indeed, already has shaped – in a variety of ways. Even more, language is itself a raw material that can be bent this way and that. The world a philosopher knows is just the world she puts into words (or which has been put into words for her) and as the words change, whether by her fiat or someone else's, her world changes.

Now, it may seem equally realistic to say the reverse – that as her world changes her words will change – but we have to be careful. For, while she experiences the world, and while her experience may vary, the world does not dictate how she will describe her experience, how she will shape it in language: It has, we might say, no opinion on the matter. The human world in this sense is a *conceptualised* world as opposed to a *brute* one. Whether two experiences are the same or different, for example, is a linguistic, or at least, a human, matter. A friend who teaches the history of science and medicine once showed me the court proceedings in a patent case in which one drug company was suing another. At issue was whether company B's drug was the same as A's – whether B had copied A. The proceedings, which centred around long and very involved arguments concerning the concepts of 'same' and 'different,' constituted one of the best examples of high metaphysics that I have ever come across. The lesson? If experience were eloquent – in this case, if it were obvious what a copy is – we would never have to speak for it. But if 'copy' is a concept, it does not spring full blown (i.e., fully conceptualized) from experience. If there is substance to this argument, then rather than language being something that exists in the world (the common sense view), the world is something that exists in language – or comes to us through language. A philosopher's main concern is therefore not what's 'out there,' even though she will agree that there is something out there, but what we say about what's out there. She will not, for example, ask 'What is truth?' but 'What do *we* mean when we say something is true?' or 'How do we use the word "true"?'

To link these comments to earlier chapters, the attack on (or suspicion about) metaphysics that is so much a part of contemporary philosophy has tended to bring great stress to bear on the relation between logic and epistemology. As a result, many philosophers have come to feel something like the following: Logic can help us to set out what we (presume we) know with a certain – although perhaps misleading – kind of clarity. It can help us to see the implications of our claims to knowledge. *If* one is committed to the proposition that X leads to Y and if one believes that X is, as we say, the case, then one is required to believe that Y will ensue. But logic cannot in and of itself provide us with knowledge of any particular part of the world. Logic cannot tell us *whether* X is the case. Perhaps nothing can, for there may be no absolute truths, only an ever-morphing language. This means – or *may* mean – that when epistemology is set down in a naturalist environment, it is more than a little marooned and may not flourish. For, as Wittgenstein might wish to remind us, if reference is unstable and if logic is only formal, then knowledge-related issues seem, very often, to be little more than squabbles over the use of words. (I reproduced one such squabble in Chapter 4 when I argued that no one could ever know he has a headache.) But if these are the only squabbles she has, what is a poor philosopher to do but turn her face towards the world that language has created for her? What choice does she have but to accept language as the ontological framework of her world?[5] In short, she has to consider whether she ought to be more concerned with questions about the *meaning* or *use* of language than with questions about *knowledge*. In this final chapter, I want to consider two thinkers who did much to establish the context of this linguistic turn and so make us confront this extremely important question. One is the 'later,' or post-*Tractatus*, Wittgenstein. The other is Ferdinand de Saussure, who by most accounts is not a philosopher but whose effect on philosophy has been very great indeed. I shall begin with Saussure, whom we met briefly in Chapter 3.

Saussure's Linguistics

Saussure's *Course in General Linguistics*, which stems from three sets of lectures he delivered between 1906 and 1911 at the University of Geneva, had an enormous influence on twentieth-century philosophy, social science, and literary theory. The development of structuralism and post-structuralism,[6] including deconstruction, can at least in part, probably in large part, be traced to the influence of his work. At the heart of Saussure's linguistics is the concept I introduced in Chapter 3: the 'sign.' We saw that sign is comprised of two sub-concepts, the 'signifier' and the 'signified.' The signifier is a word – 'tree,' for example – while the signified is the 'thing' it refers to, in this case an actual tree. So, a sign is: {'tree' [referring to] a tree}. Of course, since a tree is not always present when we say the word 'tree,' the signified is more accurately a 'concept' – the idea of a tree – for which the signifier is a 'sound image.'[7] That is pretty easy: When we hear the word 'tree' it conjures up the idea of a tree.

Signs are thus the basic elements of meaning. It is important to note, however, that Saussure did not consider signs to be 'ready-made,' or natural, ideas, as Plato, for example, thought the Forms were.[8] On the contrary, for Saussure signs are arbitrary constructions – principally because there is no *necessary* connection between a signifier and a signified. At first glance, the signifier would seem to be the source of the problem, and indeed, it is insofar as any sound image can, in theory, be made to stand for any signified. This is not to deny that signifiers are chosen on etymological grounds or for the way they sound or for some other perfectly good reason. It simply is to insist that, with respect to any signified, another signifier could be substituted for the one that is used without loss of meaning. Reverse the significations of 'sheep' and 'horse' or 'good' and 'evil' and the world will remain in place. Some sound images may do better than others but, nonetheless, any one will do. But that is just what we might call a nominalist point: There are no Platonic entities that demand, as their right, certain names. A more important point is that according to Saussure the signifieds are not natural ontological units – discrete things which obviously exist independently of language and which, therefore, any observant person will pick out even if he does not know what to call them.

This is a strange, perhaps counter-intuitive, idea. So, let's create the 'What's that?' test to help us get a handle on it. According to this test, we shall be willing to consider the possibility that something is a natural ontological unit if virtually anyone, speaking any language, is capable of asking in its presence, 'What's that?' A tree would certainly *seem* to pass such a test. Certainly, a tree seems to be a 'natural signified,' something for which there should be a name, or signifier. But with larger agglomerations of flora, such as 'copses,' 'woods,' 'forests,' and 'bushes,' the impression of natural ontological unity grows quite a bit fainter. Rather than seeing a copse and asking 'What's that?' a speaker of the English language is likely to be given the word and taught what it signifies. Even then it may take some time for him to see a copse with any certainty. ('Is that a copse or a wood?') And when we turn to other languages, we may find it very difficult to translate the concept 'copse' because there may be no precise corresponding signifier – which means, of course, that there is not corresponding signified either.

So, 'tree' and 'copse' seem to tell us different things about language. A tree seems so obvious and natural a thing that we feel certain there must be a name for it in any imaginable language. The resulting sign may be arbitrary insofar as another word could be substituted for it – we could call it 'elmer' – but some word or term seems necessary. This is the nub of Plato's concept of an 'ideal name' in the *Cratylus*, where he accepts, if a bit grudgingly, that while one word may be exchanged for another, there are nonetheless things – discrete entities or correctly formed 'concepts'[9] (Forms, say) – that require names. From this perspective, the signified *generates* the signifier, much as the presence of the animals caused Adam to name them. The world, or some part of it, is thus prior to language, and so we are, *pace* Rorty, answerable to it. The trouble, as we have seen, is that, although this seems eminently reasonable, even obvious and necessary, with trees, woods and copses are far less demanding signifieds. Are *they* discrete, correctly framed natural, and universal concepts, or are they hazy conventional ones? Certainly, different languages group collections of trees and shrubs in different ways, and there is not in every language the same number of group signs. Saussure's anti-Platonic conclusion tilted in the direction of copses: He declared the sign to be an arbitrary construction both in terms of the choice of the signifier and of what it signifies. Whether we are talking about trees or woods, language 'follows no law other than tradition.'[10] The world is not waiting for an Adam to name its parts. The world may, however, be waiting for a god to create its parts by naming them – because gods can, apparently, talk the world into existence. *Res solum in nomine existit* (The thing exists only in the name).

Of course, since language has a social dimension, a history that sanctifies signs and suggests or determines how they may be changed and how new ones will be developed, the names do not exactly come out of the blue. The signifier 'computer' is, for example, scarcely an arbitrary choice for what it signifies; any competent English-speaker can pretty much see why that name fits that object. Other signifiers could have been chosen, but given the history of the English language most of them would have been far less suitable. The cultural history of a language also helps to determine what 'things' or concepts the language will pick out, and, therefore, how that culture will evolve. Without pushing the point too far, we can say that *very often* we will name things according to the history of our language, and we will see that which enables us to see.[11] Language anchors our 'seeing,' in other words. Yet, given the arbitrariness and conventionality of the sign, it also has enough flexibility to evolve and, therefore, allow us to see new and different things. Observation, as any good empiricist will tell us, is not completely in thrall to language. To put this in Saussurean terms, language has both a 'diachronic' aspect – it changes over time – and a synchronic aspect, which is to say that at any given moment language is a fairly definite and stable system of signs.[12] Viewed synchronically – without its history, so to speak – this fixed system of signs will necessarily appear to be arbitrary, as will our 'seeing.' Without its history, there is no reason 'chair' rather than 'chaise' should be the English signifier for a chair, and there is no reason we should see copses or woods, as opposed to some other agglomeration of trees. When considered diachronically, some of that arbitrariness will disappear into a more orderly sense of historical development. We will understand why a chair is a 'chair' and not a 'chaise' and how copses came to our ancestors' attention.

The Unbearable Lightness of Language

Let's think for a moment or two about the synchronic aspect of language. Drop a line through a language at a particular moment in time and it will seem to be that slightly paradoxical entity: a fixed system of arbitrary signs. That 'fixed system' is in effect a snapshot of the enormous pool of signs available at any given time to those who speak the language. This is simple: individual *speech* involves selecting and relating signs from among those that the *language* makes available. But speech, being individual, has its own special brand of arbitrariness. Therein, signifiers and signifieds are mutated in a variety of ways that create changes in the language itself. (Think of the effect of slang on a language or the way various regional dialects affect the 'standard' version of a language.) In short, the arbitrariness of language, and hence its capacity for change, is manifested in speech. This is, of course, because of the fundamental arbitrariness of the sign, the fact that the relation of the signifier to the signified is not a natural one. A sign can always be broken apart, in which case either the word-signifier and the idea-signified disappear from the language, along with the sign they constituted, or else one or the other (or both) is (are) reconstituted in combination with other signifiers and signifieds, creating new signs. In practice – which is to say, in speech – this happens all the time, because language is a diachronic system, not to mention one with a huge pro-clivity for metaphors. So, the meaning that a sign bears exists only so long as the sign does and is, therefore, as arbitrary and ephemeral as the sign itself. In other words, the meaning does not have some sort of independent existence in the absence of the sign. Hence, in 'reality' synchrony – which is to say, meaning-stability – doesn't exist (in the same way, perhaps, that 'instant time' doesn't exist), except as a theo-retical postulate that allows us to consider the 'meaning-bearing' na-ture of the sign.

An important qualification is necessary here. The meaning of a sign is not *simply* a product of the internal and unstable relation of the signifier to the signified, but also involves its external relation to other signs.[13] One such relation, probably the most central one, is the 'paradigmatic.'[14] As an example of it, consider the green traffic light (or even the term 'green traffic light'), which is a signifier for the signified/concept 'go.' The resulting sign – 'Green light / Go' – gets its meaning not simply from its internal unity – from the fact that green is a 'symbol' for 'go' – but from its relation to two other signs: 'Red light / Stop' and 'Amber light / Prepare to stop' (or 'Proceed with caution'). (Language is, as I have been saying, a system of signs.) This traffic light paradigm is obviously as arbitrary as the signs that constitute it. There is no *neces-sary* reason the system has to be set up in the way it is or the colours have to carry the signification they do. Nor is the copselike 'prepare to stop' / 'proceed with caution' nearly so obvious a state as the treelike 'stop' and 'go.' Now, we need to throw up a cautionary amber light here and point out that not all philosophers would accept that this example represents how language operates. Some would argue that the word 'go' refers to certain ('go-ing') actions in the world and, as such, is independent of other words such as 'stop' (although, as I shall make clear below, it would seem to require a concept of 'not-going'). In short, language is mapped onto the world and is therefore natural (i.e., non-arbitrary) in a way that systems of traffic lights are not. This view, which has some connection with my comments above about natural objects, asks us to do what Saussure says we cannot do: look beyond language, as an inter-related system of signs, to the world. From Saussure's perspective, when we consider the arbitrariness, or conventionality, of the signs at this systemic level, we are propelled into the heart of a meaning-problem that disjoins language and the 'world.' But, of course, this is a fundamental issue in the linguistic turn: Is language or 'the world' the foundation of our life?

To get a better hold on this Saussurean arbitrariness, we need to return to the three laws of reason outlined in Chapter 5. One way to understand the first step in establishing meaning is to understand that meaning entails being able to identify a 'thing.' One way to do that is to link a signifier to a signified. But, to do this is also to distinguish that thing – by the law of the excluded middle – from all other 'things.' To be able to say what a sign means in this sense, therefore, entails understanding what it does not mean, which further entails – according to the law of non-contradiction – that the sign in question cannot simultaneously bear and not-bear a particular meaning. Apply this to the traffic lights. The meaning of the signifier 'green light' is established, first, by relating it to the signified 'go' and then by distinguishing the resulting sign from those constituted by 'red light / stop' and 'amber light / proceed with caution.' Hence, to be able to say fully what the signifier 'green light' means, in this paradigm, we need to know not just what it signifies but also what it does not signify. If the non-green lights and their signifieds did not exist, the paradigm would disappear, taking the meaning of the 'green' sign with it. (Even if we confront a single light – a flashing red, for instance – its meaning is dependent on our familiarity with the traffic light paradigm. The point is that if there were only one thing drivers could do, there would be no need for lights or signals of any kind.)[15] So, the signifier 'green light' and the signified 'go' constitute a sign that has meaning only if there is, at the very least, a second sign consisting of a signifier and the idea 'don't go.' (It need not be a red light, of course. In fact, it need not be any second light: 'green light on' and 'green light off' would work.) The rule is this: Since identity (what a 'thing' is) depends on difference (what it is not), language as a system of signs is a system of identity and difference.[16] It is this system, and not the world, that generates meaning. Saussure is, in other words, a 'semantic holist' who argues that signs derive their meanings from their relation to other signs and not solely from reference to 'things.' Given this, and given the arbitrariness of the sign, it follows that language is a form of conventional social practice – a conventional rather than a natural system.

In post–Second World War thought, what came to be called 'structuralism' owed a great deal to the Saussurean conception of language as a synchronic system of signs, identities, and differences that could be read like traffic lights. All manner of cultural practices – the traffic lights represent cultural practice – came to be read as if they were meaningful languages with both a semantics and a syntax[17] encased in signs.[18] Deconstructionists, an altogether more mischievous lot than structuralists, responded by pointing out that language is a system of signs from which *many* meanings – what Derrida refers to as dissemination – can emerge.[19] Since 'many meanings' means no necessary meaning, deconstruction, insofar as one accepts it, undermines the stability that structuralists had found in applying Saussure's linguistics to cultural practices. It is as if deconstructionist readings are hyper-diachronous, whereas structuralist readings are hypo-synchronous. For the former, the idea of a single, solid (if momentary) linguistic meaning-structure is just one more doomed metaphysical 'presence' for how can there be *necessary meaning in an arbitrary system of signs?* Where could such meaning come from? What could anchor it and prevent it from meandering along its ever-changing path?[20]

These questions, which are thrown up by the fundamental arbitrariness both of the sign and its relation to other signs, hint at an interesting philosophical implication for the relation of the concepts of identity and difference. Recall Plato's project. The Forms he envisioned were ontologically absolute: *pure identity.* What is justice? The best, the unimpeachable, response would be to point to the Form, for *it* literally is Justice. In the absence of the Forms – we are never in their presence, but this remark would hold true even if we *had,* like the philosopher who returns to the cave, *been* in their presence – we are reduced to talking or writing about them. We are, in other words, reduced to employing a linguistic system of identity and difference, but in a very peculiar way, because *in the absence of the Forms there is no pure identity.* This is an aspect of language that is easy to overlook, for in normal parlance we employ – or feel we do – 'identity' and 'difference' all the time. We say to a child, 'There, that's a chair and that's a couch.' That's pretty much what a definition is: a *genus* (an identity) specified by *differentiae* (differences). A chair is a 'piece of furniture (genus) intended for sitting upon by one person (differentia: not a couch).'[21] In the ostensive definition I just imagined offering to a child, however, what is picked out are *instances* of 'chair' and 'couch,' or in less stilted language, actual individual chairs and couches. In the absence of the Forms, there are of course no 'absolute' chairs or couches to pick out – no 'chairness' or 'couchness' – but we, and indeed any earthbound Platonist, nonetheless want the child to master a concept that she will relate to the sound image 'chair.' We want her, in short, to master a sign in which the signified has no absolute or essential identity (except that it has to be a chair!) but which she can nonetheless use – conceptually – to separate the chairs from all other entities in the universe.

Because philosophy is inherently conceptual, we need to press this matter, for what it amounts to is this: Pure 'identity' always escapes language insofar as it can be alluded to, or marked off, only through 'difference.' This is doubtless confusing, for a reason that echoes the great Parmenides. If there is no absolute 'identity' how can there be 'difference' to anchor even a provisional identity? Put differently: How can negation – how can saying that 'that is *not* a good action,' for example – exist without identity ('*that* is a good action')? And if there is identity, why do we need negation? We can rest content with the irrefutable Parmenidean, 'What is, is.'

Let's go back to Plato. In the *Euthyphro*, Socrates is, quite typically, unable to say what 'holiness' is. The dialogue consists in his showing Euthyphro what holiness *is not*, as if he were drawing out a long string of differentiae. (What it is not, of course, is precisely what Euthyphro thinks it is.) The *elenchos*, the Socratic process of close questioning and refutation, essentially employs the law of non-contradiction as a stand-in for absent identity. If the *elenchos* can be applied, if, that is, a definition can be shown to be contradictory, there is no identity (for in a sense it is always different from itself). But, if the *elenchos* cannot be applied, if a definition cannot be shown to be contradictory (or different from itself) there may well be identity. In short, the definition *may* be correct. This is not a 'present' identity, however; not one that is 'right there' in front of the speakers. Rather, it exists only in the shadowy language of negation: 'Well, at any rate "holiness" is not that' or, 'Since this definition is not contradictory, it may be correct.' Knowledge of something is, as it were, glimpsed through the prism of contradiction, of all the things that it is not precisely – which may tell us precisely what it is not, which may, in turn, be the closest we can come to saying precisely what it is.

This is not caused by any failure in Socrates' admittedly rudimentary logic but by the fact that logic and language cannot express identity – not Plato's sort of pure identity, at any rate – except either vacuously or elliptically. Vacuously, pure identity amounts to saying, 'A is A,' as in 'A chair is a chair.' This is a tautology, which in ordinary speech amounts to a kind of admission of failure, a figure of speech that we resort to when we are too confused or intellectually adrift to dredge up a good definition: 'Well, a metaphysical absurdity is – you know, something that is, metaphysically speaking, absurd.' In the *Euthyphro*, Socrates ties his eponymous interlocutor up in just this sort of logical knot in order to refute his definition of holiness. Normally, the allegedly elliptical 'A is B' is more enlightening, as in: 'A metaphysical absurdity is a piece of philosophical nonsense in which one uses terms for abstractions such as "reality" or "pure being" as if they actually referred to some existing thing in the world.' Here we can usefully read from A to B and B to A: each expression points helpfully to the other. There can be no doubt that this is a better sort of definition. Yet, this is where logic can begin to make some mischief, although it is a mischief that is unlikely to bother the non-philosopher very much. Strictly speaking, these expressions are not identical, or at least their identity is very hard to pin down. In the first place, they play on different levels of generality. As the definition indicates, a metaphysical absurdity is only one type of philosophical nonsense, so left there 'A' (metaphysical absurdity) and 'B' (the more general, 'philosophical nonsense') are not identical. To say 'A is a type of B' is not the same thing as 'A is B.' That is why the definition must proceed to a differentia: 'metaphysical absurdity' may be the type of 'philosophical nonsense' that occurs when a person speaks of abstractions in the way described, but that is because the latter expression excludes other kinds of 'philosophical nonsense' – a term we have yet to define, by the way. If necessary, we can add more differentiae; we can go on specifying by excluding (or differentiating) until, ideally, we have excluded the whole of the universe but 'it,' *and that's what 'it' is.* Every differentia is generated by the need to exclude. Imagine throwing out, one by one, possible candidates for 'philosophical nonsense' – each time by appending a differentia – until you are left with nothing to exclude. (That is roughly what Plato's Socrates does.) Then, through the door of difference, you have come as close to identity as language will allow. It's what's left over, the residue of negation. The space between language and the world is never closed.[22]

We have now arrived at the frustrating, tantalizingly small, but nonetheless unclosable lacuna that is encased in Jacques Derrida's concept of *différance*, a word (it plays on the verbs 'to differentiate,' 'to differ,' and 'to defer') he coined to express the 'fact' that since meaning is always approached through something like the economy of difference I have been describing, it is never quite 'there' in the text.[23] In other words, since the relation of signs to one another is both arbitrary and constituted by the binary logic of difference, meaning – which is to say, the 'Formal' moment at which one can stop and say, 'There, that's the meaning; there is no more to say' – escapes language. Language cannot, as it were, achieve metaphysical fulfilment, because it can never quite close the gap between itself and the entities it appears to pick out. We seem to be caught here between the Parmenidean insistence that all being is one and unchanging and the Parmenidean impossibility of speaking of 'not-being.' But, unlike Parmenides, we gravitate towards the impossibility. Pure identity (A is A), which is absolute but uninformative and meaningless, gives way to the copula of simile and metaphor – to the endless procession of difference that so disturbed Parmenides. Put another way, metaphysics yields to language, and language is elliptical. Something is always *like* something else (A is a type of B), although, to be *like* it, necessarily, is to be different from it as well. In this view of language and logic, the lack of closure is unavoidable. The pure identity of 'A is A' is, essentially, a linguistic substitute for pointing, but we cannot point unless there are Forms – or *something* – to point to. Anyway, if there is something to point to we don't need a whole language, including the copula 'is': All we need are names for what is before us. (Point and say: 'Chair!' Of course, to identify one chair for someone is, however, no guarantee that he will never, in the future, suffer confusion over the 'chairness' of other objects.)

So, 'A is A' is either metaphysically illusory or linguistically redundant,[24] while 'A is B' pries open a (real or ordinary) world of virtually unlimited meanings. Perhaps this is one reason that Derrida directs our attention to writing as a primordial, as opposed to a derivative (from speech), form of language. Unlike speech, writing is free of such gambits as the pseudo-pointing (which we shall consider in the next section with respect to Russell's logical atomism) that induces us to believe in the metaphysical ghost of a pure identity that anchors 'Original' meaning. Both identities and meanings proliferate almost without end, because, to put the point metaphorically, language is a sea of metaphors – of identities in differences and differences in identities – that has no far shore.

Second Thoughts

There are, as usual, countervailing arguments to be made here. The position I have set out is aimed squarely at any variety of metaphysical realist who is willing to argue that there are real mind-independent entities that we can discover and that act as anchors for our grasp of the world. This roughly deconstructionist (and therefore 'new sceptical')[25] attack on identity contains a subtle and powerful critique of the illusions that metaphysics can throw up on the wall of the cave. But it has its illusions, too. If we return to Derrida's critique of Plato's use of the word *pharmakon*, which I outlined in Chapter 3, we can see that his argument depends on a mixture of 'instant' and 'flow' time to achieve the effect announced as *différance*. The Greek word simultaneously stands still as one or the other English definition ('remedy or 'poison') and constantly oscillates between them. To preview what I shall say in the section on Wittgenstein below, Derrida seems to be insisting that we do not know what the term means in the text, because two contradictory meanings are intertwined (in the way, perhaps, that the far less contradictory 'excellence' and 'virtue' are intertwined in *arête*). But, one might reasonably argue that it is more accurate to say that two contradictory *uses* of the term coexist in the word – and we seem to understand clearly what they are – and what we need to know is which one of them Plato intends. It does not seem beyond the realm of possibility that he intended one rather than the other – he seems to have had both concepts available to him, after all – and to know which would clear up the ambiguity. Or, perhaps, Plato intends to be ambiguous. To intend to be ambiguous is to claim that the ambiguity is under one's control, which is not Derrida's point. There is a difference between the wilful ambiguity of the writer and the unavoidable or inherent ambiguity of language, and as we saw in Chapter 3, Derrida thinks ambiguity is inherent in language. Writers are ambiguous because language is ambiguous.

To use, and perhaps abuse, some comments of the American philosopher Stanley Cavell,[26] concepts contain an 'indefinite number of instances and directions of projection.' There are a lot of different chairs in the world and a lot of possible metaphorical uses of the word 'chair.' Yet, we know (well, usually we do) what chairs are. We even know, most of the time, what the abstraction 'justice' is. Concepts have an inner 'stability' and an outer 'tolerance' that make them both comprehensible and usefully flexible. If we count context, syntax, and grammar as important elements in establishing – through use – these qualities, then much of the systemic instability of *différance* may begin to look like a form of linguistic intolerance, a stubborn refusal to accept the 'inner stability' of language. In this vein, Thomas Pavel has argued that 'there is no good reason why the metaphor of the differential system should still fascinate philosophers reflecting on language.'[27]

Perhaps there isn't. Perhaps Derrida and other deconstructionists overemphasize what is unstable and underemphasize what is stable in language. It would seem to be a new sceptic's temptation. Yet, I do not think that sceptical questions about identity, which are essentially questions about our ability to make the world hold still, are, as questions about meaning, idle ones. To say, as I did above, that there is no far shore of meaning is to say more or less what Nietzsche, the great progenitor of the anti-metaphysical movement, said: There are no metaphysical entities, no pure if absent 'identities,' to anchor what we say. Approached by a Saussurean pathway, the reasons for this are now cast in a slightly different light. After Saussure, Nietzsche's contention – metaphysical entities are illusions, like the shadows on the wall of Plato's cave – remains, but the *way* in which they are thrown up by language is seen from a somewhat different perspective. If, based on the idea of the Platonic Forms, we can describe metaphysical entities as 'pure identities' and if, following – or adapting – Saussure, we now argue that language cannot *articulate* the pure identities imagined by logic, then language simply cannot achieve metaphysical completion. It is not that metaphysicians are saying the wrong thing or, as in the case of the god's-eye view, trying to be what they cannot be. It is that metaphysicians cannot say what they *think* they are saying. Metaphysics is therefore a kind of linguistic conjurer's trick that philosophers play on themselves, one in which they convince themselves that they can discern, behind the shadows of difference, pure identities. But, they cannot, and because they cannot, they cannot stop talking and writing.

The Platonic dream of the Forms is a magnificent dream in which philosophy takes us to the point where we can escape language, where we can, in our wisdom, stop speaking or writing and simply *see* what there is to be seen. And then we can contemplate it. In the world of Forms, the only identification is *ostensive*: 'There, that is the Good. Now, look ye upon it.' Platonic philosophy ends in knowledge of the Forms, and that knowledge leads, decorously, to silence. A deconstructive version of the new sceptic, indeed, a new sceptic of any sort, might point out that there is a good reason why such silence comes only with death. Until then, even Plato's philosophers cannot see the Forms; even they must be content with discussing what these 'things' are like. No discussion of what things are *like* can lead to a statement of what they *are*. The stark lesson is that the living cannot transcend language because – a bad pun – they can never resolve their differences. This, by the way, is why philosophy will go on forever and will forever fall back on *poiesis*.

The Case of Logical Atomism

This point can be illustrated by a brief consideration of one famous attempt to make language answer to the world, Bertrand Russell's 'logical atomism.'[28] As an empiricist, Russell viewed language, essentially, as an instrument used to report on experience. He argued that in a *logically perfect language*, which is to say, in an absolutely efficient language, there would be a one-to-one correspondence between words and things in the world. 'Atomic propositions' (let's just call them basic sentences, although they are not quite that) would describe – match up with – 'atomic facts' (basic 'states of affairs' in the world). 'That is green' is an atomic proposition (or a reasonable facsimile of one), where 'that' is a linguistic pointer referring to some green thing. Unfortunately, this sentence, which seems so clear, is terrifically ambiguous: it can be construed either as predicating greenness of some thing – a car, for example – or as identifying what 'green' is. In the first case, the 'thing' in question is not precisely green. In the nicely metaphysical terminology of identity and difference, it can be identified *as* having the characteristic green because it is *not* essentially green: it is not what green *is*. Unless the hearer of the sentence understands that difference, confusion is possible. If someone utters the sentence 'That is green' in front of a green car, a person not well versed in English might be forgiven for assuming that the word (or name) for a car is 'green.' In short, he might get the identity (or reference) wrong and assume that the word picks out a thing rather than a property of that thing. In the second case, where the reference is to a property, the sentence means something like, 'That colour we call "green."' Once again, it works only insofar as one is identifying green against the difference of all other colours and has meaning, therefore, only in a system of colour-signs. Note, too, that in either case the proposition works only in the *presence* of something green. The speaker is pointing, or at any rate, with the aid of 'that,' pseudo-pointing. This lulls anyone who views the speaker as the shepherd of language into a false sense of security, for that good shepherd seems able securely to link the signifier 'green' with the signified 'concept-green': in general, to link signifiers with their 'meanings.' Whether he can is, we have seen, debatable insofar as the ostensive 'pointing' stands outside language. (These difficulties forced Russell into a phenomenalist position, according to which, names – or at least what he called 'logically proper names' – referred not to what we would normally recognize as objects but to 'percepts,' which are little bits of private sensation (a bit of colour or shape, for example) with which the speaker/perceiver is in direct contact. Objects are constructions out of percepts. The only terms Russell could supply for these percepts were 'this' and 'that.' This is a case of language collapsing under a too-rigorous demand for names that will absolutely identify their objects – in Russell's terms, identify them by acquaintance rather than by description.)

This is very peculiar. When speaking and writing, we use a whole range of what the American philosopher C.S. Peirce called 'indexicals' – pronouns, possessives, locators such as 'today' and 'yesterday' and so on. These indexicals seem secure in that – to use the terminology of Gottlob Frege[29] – they always have the same *sense*: We know what they mean. They do not, however, always have the same *reference*. They don't, in other words, always point to the same thing. If I say 'I am tired' and you say the same thing, the sense of the utterance is the same in both cases – an individual is expressing fatigue – but not the reference. In the first instance, 'I' refers (points) to me and in the second to you. It is also possible for the reference to be the same and the sense to vary. One example would be when I am standing beside a car and refer to 'this car' (i.e., the one near the speaker), and you are standing one hundred metres away and refer to 'that car' (i.e., the one at a distance from the speaker). So, sentences do not always, without help, securely conjoin sense and reference. Very roughly, what this means is that while we may understand perfectly well what a sentence *means*, we may not, without some extra-linguistic nudging, know to what, or whom, it refers.[30] (Of course, a neophyte English speaker, may not know what a sentence refers to because he does not know what it means.)

Derrida is probably right to insist that this disjunction does not become fully evident until we turn from speaking to writing. Writing effectively hands the text over to the reader, depriving the writer of the security of a speaker's 'pointing' presence. (He cannot, as it were, peer intently over the reader's shoulder. Insofar as she can, the reader ought to place the writer there by considering what the writer had in mind, but the text is not enclosed by that authorial intention and the reader is obviously not restricted by it.) What counts most now is what the reader thinks, how she understands the text – because 'she' is the only 'presence' left. Writing thus helps to bring out a simple but important truth about language: It does not literally point. 'That is green' cannot be as referentially successful in writing as it is in speech unless other pseudo-pointers are employed to stabilize it by fixing sense and reference. For example, 'Colours still confused her, so indicating a nearby car, he said, "There, that is green."' Even then the transmission of meaning from writer-sender to reader-receiver is far from assured.

Writing does not eradicate the sender – we retain a sense of someone saying something – but writing, perhaps, establishes a truer sense of the distance between the sender and the receiver, and in doing so (as any undergraduate who hands in an essay to be graded is well aware) shifts the balance of power to the receiver. What in speech can seem an intimate distance becomes in writing a virtually infinite one, and a comforting 'presence' becomes a disconcerting 'absence.' A spoken 'that' seems, for example, to be a powerful stabilizing and reassuring presence, and in speech it very often is. Translated into a series of markings on a page, it becomes, as Derrida so strongly argues, little more than the ghost of an author who may no longer count for very much. To the degree that this is so, the foundation of Russell's logically perfect language – the atomic proposition – is, with its reliance on the metaphysical guarantor of authorial presence – the indexical 'that' – only a pseudo-proposition that tries, unsuccessfully, to make language step outside itself. It 'bewitches' us, to borrow Wittgenstein's word, into thinking that language affords direct access to being.[31]

The Labyrinth of Language

Two lessons, neither of which finds universal acceptance among philosophers, can be drawn from Russell's 'failure.' The first is familiar by now: Philosophy, as conceived by Plato or Descartes, or most others in its long history, can never reach its goal because either the goal is unreachable or it does not exist. The Forms, the 'world,' 'reality' – all such absolute 'presences' are metaphysical illusions thrown up by language. Even though language works perfectly well to fix identities in a conventional way – to say, 'That is a car' is scarcely obscure to English-speakers – there is no pure identity to find. There is no metaphysical 'car-ness,' there are no universals, no absolutes. There is nothing that is the source or archetype of all the individual things that we identify. These absolutes are tricks of language, shadows that language casts on the wall of the cave.

The second lesson follows closely from the first. The logic that the philosophers have held up to the world as the universal language of clarity and truth – as a framework for pure identity, in essence – constantly deconstructs itself into a metaphorical language of difference. If A is B but B, by definition, is not-A, then A is not-A – which is contradictory. If A is not-B, then we escape contradiction but have 'only' a metaphorical identity expressed by difference: 'A is *like* B' or 'A is *expressed as* B.' Or, possibly, we may have, based on Frege's distinction between sense and reference, 'A and B are different names for the same thing.' Finally, we may have 'A is an instance of B.' These last two options are not metaphorical, but I shall argue below that they only delay, not solve, the problem we are dealing with. So, logic finds itself in the grave danger that we abandoned it to at the end of Chapter 5. This is the danger of being swallowed by rhetoric, which is to say, by the metaphorical language it was supposed to vanquish: in which case philosophy fails to escape *poiesis*. Worse, it may not even get to *poiesis*, for how can we say with certainty what A is *like* – how can we choose an appropriate metaphor? – if we do not know what 'A' is? Here we glimpse the bewildering poetic licence of the neo-Nietzschean sceptics, one that threatens to overturn the hitherto stately realm of philosophy. If language answers only to itself, what can control the endless shifting of signifiers over signifieds, the endless contingent creation and un-creation of signs, and the endless reorganization of the relation between signs? What is there to constrain the hyperactive and hyper-arbitrary tendencies of language? And, this is something that anyone – not just a philosopher – who is the least bit familiar with the way the modern media uses images, with the way a car can become a signifier for 'success' or 'virility' or the way different arrangements of signs can be used to convey novel messages, will understand.[32] In the post-modern world the inner stability of language (not to mention images) seems less and less assured.

This second lesson is a mouthful. I needed to express it in the way I have to give the reader a sense of the complication of the issue. Having done so, I think I can now gloss it a little. I can begin by pointing out that there are ways in which 'A is B' is uncontroversial and non-metaphorical. One concerns the Fregean case of A and B being different names for the same entity. Consider Frege's famous example of Phosphorus and Hesperus,[33] the names used by the ancients to refer to the morning and evening stars. When they turned out to be one and the same 'star' – the planet Venus, as it happens – it became possible to say, 'Phosphorus is Hesperus.' There is a rather large literature surrounding this example, so anything I say is risky. Nevertheless, it seems to me that we can decode this sentence as meaning something like: 'Phosphorus and Hesperus are actually the same (or 'a single') planet.' (Sentences about each one had different senses but the same reference.) This particular rendering of 'A is B' seems to work pretty well. But, when we extend identity beyond reference towards definition (or meaning) – which is what Socrates was interested in – things become more complicated. To say that 'A Buick is a car' also seems uncontroversial – we are in effect saying 'A (a Buick) is a case of B (a car)' – but we are beginning to indulge in a kind of 'semantic ascent,' although not, I think, the kind that Quine had in mind when he coined the term.[34] The point is, 'car' is a more general term than 'Buick' and with this generality – which is the second of the non-metaphorical instances of 'A is B' – we are beginning, in this case *only* beginning, to 'shift from talk of objects to talk of words.'[35] ('Is that a Buick?' is not a contentious question, but 'Is that a car? – as in, 'Is *that* really a car?' – could be.) Of course, 'Buick' is also a general term in its way, as in any term other than 'this' or 'that.'[36] We return to the problem of Russell's atomic propositions: There is a way in which we never get beyond the words – the descriptions – to the things.

Buicks and the like can at least be pointed out, or gestured at. When we ascend to terms such as 'truth' or 'justice,' however, we are getting into a more rarefied part of the linguistic atmosphere. We are beginning to ask philosophical (and metaphysical) questions about what makes something ('A') what it is. At the highest level of generality, all answers – all 'B's' – turn out to be not quite A's, and definitions are, as we have seen, either tautological ('A is A') or elliptical ('A is like B') or classificatory ('A is a case of B'). In the last of these cases, we know the universal only through the particular, which certainly suggests that semantic ascent can never bring us to the end point of 'real' contact with universals. We never find what Plato imagined in his Forms, an ontological anchor outside language.

These ruminations on language allow us to fix more securely what the neo-Nietzschean (and the Quinean) vision means for the Platonic sun. In previous chapters, I set out the argument that, if there are no Forms or metaphysical 'presences,' then the philosopher has to accept that, like all humans, he cannot escape the labyrinth of language. What

I have said above adds the second part of the double whammy: If language is truly a labyrinth, there never was any hope of escaping it, *not even if there were metaphysical presences.* Insofar as this is so, the philosopher has to accept that language has no solid ontological anchor, in which case philosophical language is fundamentally indistinguishable from the literary language it sought to escape. The philosopher's beloved logic can never be anything more than a form of rhetoric, or persuasive language, that works just as long as the content of the inference persuades us, and no longer. (Have you never said, in an effort to persuade someone, 'But it's *so* logical!'? There is a kind of desperation here born of the recognition that logic is not enough.) If, for example, I argue from the premise that 'if it's a cocker spaniel then it's a dog' to the case that 'that animal is a cocker spaniel,' you will likely be persuaded that that animal is also a dog. If, however, I reverse the first premise and argue that 'if it's a dog then it's a cocker spaniel,' nothing that follows from this false statement is likely to carry much weight with you.

One conclusion (I raised it in Chapter 5) is that logic is only as persuasive as its content, which is another way of saying that it doesn't touch the world. To borrow Robert Brandom's phrase, it simply makes our beliefs explicit – I shall add, 'in a particularly clear and persuasive way.' If, therefore, we feel that logic enjoys a greater warrant than other forms of language, that warrant is contextual or pragmatic or historical – anything but transcendent or absolute. The philosopher will thus have even more reason to consider whether Plato's opposition between *logos* and *mythos*, and his elevation of *logos* into a kind of first language, was either a philosophical delusion or a philosophical trick. If it was, then not only historians of philosophy but philosophers themselves have all along simply been telling metaphysical stories. As stories are never true or false (they are, after all, *stories*), truth, as the Platonic philosopher has understood it, must be set firmly to one side, along with absolute knowledge and wisdom. Plato's Apollonian sun of reason is thereby extinguished.

Wittgenstein's Early Philosophy

I could not possibly end the chapter here, with the loss of all meaning, truth, knowledge, wisdom and what have you. I feel I need to give the reader some hope, and I think perhaps Wittgenstein – the later Wittgenstein – can give it. Indeed, compared with the drama of the neo-

Nietzschean confrontation with metaphysics, which depends in large part on destabilizing Saussure's linguistics by emphasizing the diachronic and arbitrary aspects of it, Wittgenstein's later work seems a model of calm, work-a-day philosophizing. It is not, of course. It is enormously intricate and subtle; it simply – I often think, mercifully – lacks the *Sturm und Drang* of Nietzsche and his successors. Before discussing this work, however, it's necessary to draw together and expand remarks that I have made in previous chapters about Wittgenstein's 'early' work, the *Tractatus Logico-Philosophicus*. I apologize for any repetition, which in any case is not much, but it is better to collect everything in one place.

In the *Tractatus*, Wittgenstein argues that language can show what the world is like but not account for whatever meaning it might have. It is, one might say, a pure theory of reference. Following Bertrand Russell, Wittgenstein describes language as a set of propositions which represent (or picture) the facts of the world, ideally by establishing a one-to-one correspondence with the part of the world it represents. Like a picture, a proposition shares 'logical form' with what it represents.[37] If I show someone a photograph of my office, to determine whether it is accurate she must compare it with my actual office. For every object in the photograph there has to be a corresponding one in the office, and each one must stand in the same relation to all the other objects therein as it does in the photo. Similarly, for a city map to be 'true,' it must have map-streets that stand in the same relation to all the other streets as they do in reality. Finally, if a musician consults a musical score, she can play the music, because each note represents a corresponding sound. In each case, the relation is reciprocal; it is possible to work in the other direction, from the office to the photograph, the city to the map, and the music to the score. Somewhat more controversially, Wittgenstein insists that the same relation held true for propositions and the world. Hence, for 'My car is in my garage' to be a true proposition, there has to be a car in the world that is mine, a garage in the world that is mine, and that car must be in that garage. Note that here, too, the relation can be reversed: An English-speaker who observes the fact (his car in his garage) can generate the relevant proposition.

An important point that must be mentioned here, even though I cannot fully develop it. Saussure's concern is with the sign, in essence with the semantic relation of word to 'thing'; this is his fundamental linguistic unit. By contrast, Wittgenstein's basic unit is the proposition, or sentence. Words – signifiers, anyway – pick out 'things' or name ideas, but sentences describe 'states of affairs,' which is to say, relations among things. Signifiers name or pick out things, but propositional sentences show how these things stand in the world; in essence, they show us what the world looks like. Wittgenstein's propositions still represent the world, therefore, but how they do so is a more complicated – or at least a different – affair than the way in which signs do so. It is not difficult to imagine how a signifier picks out a signified, if only because we tend to be comfortable with the notion that words stand for, or name, things and ideas. Sentences, however, pick out facts – what a dismissive Peter Strawson called 'sentence-shaped objects' – and facts are, indeed, much stranger entities. In the first place, recalling what I said about trees and copses above, facts are scarcely natural units; to the contrary, facts seem to be linguistically dependent units that come into existence only when someone states them. That would seem to make the sentence-fact relation dangerously circular: A fact is something we state, and what we state is a fact. Consequently, all sorts of new conundrums about the nature of reference, meaning, and truth can arise once we ascend from the sign, or term, to the sentence as our basic unit of language. With respect to truth, Quine, for example, felt driven to argue that it is not sentences, but groups of sentences (or theories) that are accountable to the 'tribunal of experience.' At this point, we are more than halfway towards a non-representational coherence theory. This *can*, although it need not, be read as an admission that just how sentences represent, or picture, the world is less than obvious. The danger of stepping into language is that one may never step out of it again.

Still, let's grant that propositions do manage to represent the world and move on to the next point, that is, like other forms of representation, propositions can be accurate or inaccurate. This means that they can be true or false. But since propositions set out possible facts, or 'states of affairs,' then insofar as they are not self-contradictory, we can know only *a posteriori* which they are.[38] We can know their truth-value only once we have compared them with the part of the world that they claim to represent: 'A proposition,' Wittgenstein asserts, *'shows* how things stand *if* it is true.'[39] What a proposition cannot do is move beyond this blunt truth and show, or explain, what the meaning of that state of affairs (or fact) is. In other words, propositions cannot depict value. They have no metaphysical meaning, only the referential meaning, such as it is, that comes from representing or picturing. This rules out of court most of the great abstractions that so fascinated Plato. The very prosaic 'My car is red' represents a fact, but the more flighty 'My car is beautiful' does not. 'Beauty' is an abstract, aesthetic word, which, like ethical words, invokes a value for which we have no reference. As such it has no 'meaning' and no truth-value. That is the illusion that accompanies 'value-words': they seem to mean so much and 'in fact' mean nothing, because they have no fixed reference. Think of it this way: If a child points to a red object and asks 'Why is that (called) "red"?' most of us are satisfied to answer, 'Well, it just is.' But, if a child asks 'Why is that (called) "beautiful"?' we feel the need to offer a different, less assertive, and perhaps, 'deeper' answer. Or, at least, we don't feel that the bluntness of the 'red' answer will be very useful in the case of beauty. Part of the reason for the need for 'deepness' has to do with the fact that the child would, in all probability, not have used 'called' in this instance – which is to say, the child would probably not have adopted a nominalist stance towards 'beauty.' It is as if the child would already have learned, in the course of learning the words, that 'beauty' has a deeper metaphysical import than has 'red.' At any rate, we feel ourselves engaged here in a struggle to explain a word that has no fixed referent, or identity. Or better: We feel ourselves engaged in a struggle *because* the word has no fixed referent. (We generally find it much easier to say what a painting literally represents than what it means or why it is beautiful.)

So, the *Tractatus* restricts language to reference. Meaning, in the larger and somewhat ambiguous sense in which most of us understand the word (What does it all mean?), is beyond language, something metaphysical and unsayable. Propositions are the only bits of language not discomfited by this lack of metaphysical meaning, because they have reference: They show what the world is like, if they are true. But value-words like 'beauty' have no reference (they show nothing, we might say), and a sentence such as 'My car is beautiful' is, propositionally speaking, empty. It is a pseudo-proposition – a bit of pseudo-language, really – that identifies my car with 'something' that cannot be identified. Towards the end of the *Tractatus*, Wittgenstein summarizes this point as follows: 'The sense of the world must be outside the world. In the world everything is as it is, and everything happens as it does happen; *in* it no value exists ... If there is any value that does have value it must lie outside the whole sphere of what happens and is the case.'[40]

Language cannot deal with, *has not the capacity to talk about,* transcendental issues. Language 'can express nothing that is higher'[41] (i.e., that is beyond sense experience), because there are no discernible referents for the 'higher.' Insofar as metaphysical issues are transcendental, metaphysical language – indeed, any kind of 'meta-talk' that would explain why the world is as we find it – is logically impossible. To take logic itself as an example, Wittgenstein asserts that while we necessarily represent the world in proposition-pictures that are governed by the rules of logic, we cannot say *why* we *do*. That would require us both to speak about the possibility of an illogical world and to explain logically why only a 'logical world' can exist. Since, however, we cannot say what an illogical world would be like (i.e., since language is logical it cannot represent the illogical),[42] and since logic is a 'mirror-image of the world,' which cannot turn around and reflect itself,[43] we cannot do these things any more than a Kantian can hope to proceed beyond *phenomena* to *noumena*. This is why Wittgenstein insists that the propositions of the *Tractatus* are 'nonsensical.'[44] They constitute a metaphysical explanation of the way language works, of what it could say and not say, but an explanation that asserts as a condition of its truth that there could be no such thing as metaphysical explanations. Wittgenstein, thus, closes his masterpiece with the famous bit of advice that he had had to ignore in order to give: 'What we cannot speak about we must pass over in silence.'[45]

We have here the basis of a distinction – Wittgenstein's distinction, I think –between metaphysics and science. A scientist can explain why planets orbit a star insofar as she can provide evidence based on the facts of the matter. Similarly, a social scientist can explain why a given people consider burning witches to be a good thing to do. But a metaphysical philosopher cannot explain why an action is 'good' – in itself, so to speak. There is, despite Kant's best efforts, no way for a philosopher to inject necessity into the world – to be able to demonstrate that action X just is good and, hence, that the statement 'X is good' is true – and to bring meaning with it. When philosophers search for 'meaning,' in the sense of an explanation why something has value (which is to say, why it is what it is), they stumble into the illusory metaphysical world and get all tangled up in naturalistic fallacies. The solution to many of the great philosophical problems, therefore, consists, for Wittgenstein, as in a different way it does for the neo-Nietzscheans, in recognizing that such meanings just are metaphysical illusions created by language. The *Tractatus* is thus intended to dissolve rather than resolve these problems. Its closing request – 'What we cannot speak about, we must pass over in silence' – refers not to the silence of a philosopher who has found the Forms, but to the silence of one who has quit looking for them.

The Later Wittgenstein

If I may be allowed a little gentle cynicism, Wittgenstein, being a philosopher, could not let the issue rest there. After a ten-year hiatus, he returned to philosophy, in 1929, with the intention of investigating how language did in fact convey meaning. Although this may have been something of a *volte-face*, it was not, I think, a complete rejection of the *Tractatus*, which continued to set the terms of the later work. Most centrally, Wittgenstein continued to hold that that language-users could not transcend language. If non-referential meaning existed – and he now thought that it did – it had somehow to exist *in* language. Put differently: If philosophers could not expect to discover a transcendent meaning in what they said, they could nonetheless investigate the nature of meaning-in-the-world or, what amounts to the same thing, meaning-in-language. This is our ray of hope.

To find that ray, Wittgenstein had had to re-orient his attitude towards the problems of philosophy. In the *Tractatus*, he had thought through these problems in a more or less empiricist fashion, according to which a word had 'meaning' only insofar as it had an extra-linguistic referent – such as a car for 'car.' Value-words, bereft of reference – of correspondence to the world – were literally meaning-less. In the work that became the posthumously published *Philosophical Investigations*, Wittgenstein changed tack, taking a more naturalist and relativist course of inquiry that made room for 'meaning.' Language was no longer restricted to picturing the world. Now language was allowed to evoke a lot of worlds, ones that were, in effect, its creations. If it is possible to continue to use the metaphor of a mirror image (and really it isn't), the world of the later Wittgenstein is a mirror image of language. A particular way of speaking – what he dubbed a 'language-game'[46] – actually created the world it appeared to reflect. (In this sense, Wittgenstein is nearing Nietzsche's vision.) This is, of course, just what, according to Wittgenstein, most philosophers have failed to understand. In the *Tractatus*, language had delineated and pictured possible worlds, but now it made them as well, in the way that the rules of a game both delineate and create the game. This, to beat the metaphor to death, means that the game, when played, is a kind of mirror image of its rules. More important, it also means that there is no gap between language and its object, so there is no use in wondering whether language gives us access to the world of which it speaks. Do the rules of chess give us access to chess? By definition, yes, they do. Can chess exist without a set of rules? By definition, no, it cannot. In this sense, Wittgenstein seems to be less mesmerized than Derrida by the problem of metaphysics. Wittgenstein more or less brushes metaphysics aside by localizing questions of identity and meaning within language-games.

In essence, this entailed a shift of focus from logic as a kind of specialized meta-language to grammar, which reflected the workings – the usage – of 'ordinary' language in everyday contexts.[47] In the *Tractatus*, contradiction and tautology are used to construct a framework of necessity and impossibility around possible worlds. The car, once we identify it, can be 'all red' or 'not all red'; tautologically, one of these 'worlds' has to exist, but, in obedience to the law of non-contradiction, they cannot both exist simultaneously. As to which of these possibilities actually exists, one simply has to wait to see,[48] for although logic sets out the options, it cannot decide between them. Logic has no epistemological power. Nor does the showing-ground of logic bear any ethical implications: Logic provides no reasons for valuing one possible world over another. It was this fundamental meaning-inertness of logical language that Wittgenstein sought to address in his later work by emphasizing grammar. In the early 1930s, he wrote, 'The task of philosophy is not to create a new, ideal language, but to clarify the use of our language, the existing language.'[49] Renouncing the all or nothing, 'essence and meaning' or 'no essence and no meaning,' dichotomy of the *Tractatus*, he began to develop a theory of meaning-without-essences. Words, Wittgenstein pointed out, often lack concrete referents, but the grammar of their usage is sufficient to establish meaning. I am using 'grammar' in an extended sense here to refer to the formal and informal rules that govern the use of words in a language, rules that are, in turn, dependent on the 'language-game' from which they come.[50] Simply put, using language is an activity that, like games, is both rule-governed and context laden: what Wittgenstein called 'a form of life.'[51] This form of life can be broken down into those smaller, localized practices – also rule-governed and context-laden – that Wittgenstein called language-games. The impossible metaphysical meanings of the *Tractatus* were now brought to Earth and encased in these games.[52] In effect, meaning became *use*, and once one focuses on use, the problem of reference disappears. And the problem of meaning is thereby cast in a different light.

Some examples may help. First, let's remain for the moment outside language and consider an 'actual' game: football, say. As with all games, the rules of football govern what players can and cannot do. In the proper circumstances, for example, the quarterback can throw the ball downfield to a receiver. Left there, the action is sanctioned but has no *particular* meaning. We can break the game down into smaller contexts, however, and by locating the activity of passing in these contexts – by establishing its local grammar in effect – give it that meaning. If the quarterback throws a long pass on the first play of the game, it is a bold, assertive action; if he does it late in the game and his team is behind, it is an act of desperation; and, if he does it late in the game and his team is far ahead, it is disrespectful to his opponents and an action that signals poor sportsmanship. The context determines which of these mini-games is in play and therefore what the pass 'means.' Now, imagine a neophyte watching the game. On the first play, the quarterback 'goes deep' and the fans around him yell, 'Way to go, man! That took guts.' Then, on the last play of the game, with his team far ahead, he does it again. The neophyte, anxious to be part of the spectacle, leaps to his feet to yell, 'Way to go!' just as those same fans surrounding him scream, 'Ah, that stinks, man!' The play is the same, but in a different context its meaning is different and so, correspondingly, is the fans' reaction to it. What this neophyte does not know is that each pass was like a statement in a different language-game – the 'whole game' (think 'language') could be broken down into contexts with local, if unstated, sets of rules (think 'language-game'). Hence, even though the plays *appeared* 'grammatically' identical, they were not identical because they belonged to different language-games. They conveyed different meanings – in the first case exuberance, in the second insult – and therefore had different values. Value was determined not by the pass alone – on its own it has no particular meaning – but by its contextual use.

Now let's turn to language proper. Consider the vaudeville joke, part of the repertoire of the late Henny Youngman, 'Take my wife, please.' It is meant to be ambiguous, and in that ambiguity it represents the idea of language-games very well. Uttered in straightforward fashion, and without the 'please,' the sentence seems to be part of the language-game of 'examples': Take my wife as an example of, perhaps, a particular character type. In this game, you would expect whoever made the remark to go on to explain why his wife was a relevant example of whatever was under discussion. But, leave a couple of beats pause after 'wife' and then add, with emphasis, 'please,' and the sentence becomes a plea for someone simply to take her – part of a very different 'take-someone-off-my-hands' language game. (The joke turns on the pause, making the audience realize that they have been assuming the wrong language-game was in force. Like most jokes, it places the listeners in one context and then suddenly – by manipulating language – shifts them to another. The humour comes from realizing that you were in the 'wrong place' all along.) Alternatively, given the appropriate context, it could be a request to select my wife as a player in a game (the language game of 'selection') or even a desperate plea to the gods to relieve her of the pain of a serious illness (the language-game of 'prayer'). Just as in an actual game, the context in which an utterance is made determines its meaning by indicating which language-game is in force.

Sometimes, however, grammar narrowly construed just is the context that determines the game. Compare, 'two plus two is four,' 'Lorraine is a hothead,' and 'She is Valerie.' In the first instance 'is' is part of an 'equals' (or arithmetical) game, in the second a 'predication' (or qualities) game, and in the third a straightforward 'identity' game.[53] The words surrounding the copula – the syntax, in effect – alter its grammatical role and shift the nature of the game. In yet other cases, the utterance itself can establish the game. If I say, 'How are you?' to a friend, I assume that she will recognize this as the opening gambit of a 'greeting game' and respond appropriately, saying something like, 'I'm fine, thank you.' But, suppose you overhear someone speak this line to another who then replies, 'Go away!' Hearing this, wouldn't you adjust your sense of the language-game, and say to yourself something like 'Oh, they've been arguing' and then eavesdrop on the rest of their conversation, no matter how civil it was, with that assumption in mind? Wouldn't you, in other words, situate the conversation within a new – 'argument' – language-game?

This sense of the motility of language led Wittgenstein to adopt, in the *Investigations*, the anti-realist position that words are not names for things – symbols for Platonic essences. Words do not empirically pick out things in the world (or in our minds); rather, meanings coalesce around words in accordance with their usages in language-games. Meaning is, therefore, a property of sentences – or groups of sentences in a language-game – rather than a property of words. This is a direct result of the insistence that there are no essences, only uses – or, to employ Saussurean terms, that words are signifiers that can, in the context of sentences, signify a number of different 'things.' When philosophers try to ferret out non-existent essences (necessary signifieds of words in isolation from sentences and language-games), they get into trouble in the same way that the neophyte football fan did. Wittgenstein had already pointed out this trouble in the *Tractatus*, but there the solution was a judicious silence. In the *Investigations*, it was the therapy of bringing 'words back from their metaphysical to their everyday use,'[54] to, in other words, the language-games that give them their meanings. 'Goodness' or 'Beauty' may have no essences, but they do have meanings in the contexts of their employment in a variety of English language language-games.

Although the language may be 'ordinary' its uses are complex, so much so that philosophers often lose their way in the grammatical thickets surrounding them. In the *Investigations*, Wittgenstein lists various usages of the word 'blue.' Some of them are:[55] (1) 'Is this blue the same as that over there? Do you see any difference?' (2) 'Look, what different effects these two blues have.' (3) 'What's this blue called? Is it indigo?' To utter these sentences requires a fairly sophisticated grasp of 'blue.' It is necessary (a) to know what blue is, (b) to have mastered names for various shades of blue, (c) to be able to compare shades of blue, and (d) to understand that colours have aesthetic and emotional effects. It is, moreover, necessary to do all this in reference to a word that has no essence (that is not a natural name) and whose equivalent word (if there is one) in another language may be used quite differently – which is to say, it may not be equivalent at all. In fact, the word 'indigo' is unlikely to have an exact equivalent in many other languages, and so the existence of the colour is restricted to languages in which it exists. Only in them is it possible to 'pick out' indigo in the world, and even then there may be significant variations in the language-games into which it can be fit. Indigo may not, for example, fit into the same emotional language-games – evoke the same mood, or even any mood at all – in all languages. So, to be precise, what the speaker of the above sentences is demonstrating is a mastery of some of the language-games of colours in the English language.

It should now be clearer why Wittgenstein refers to language as a form of life. As language-users, we are initiated into language-games that govern how we use words and, therefore, what they mean. We are initiated into cultures. (The child who asks why something is *called* red but why something else *is* beautiful is displaying some mastery of our metaphysical language-games and a certain level of acculturation.) These games are necessarily conventional and of limited scope but infinite variety. In a passage that anticipates Derrida, Wittgenstein writes that 'language is a labyrinth of paths. You approach from one side and you know your way about; you approach the same place from another side and no longer know your way about.'[56]

The lesson should be clear by now: Wittgenstein's later work dispenses with the idea of a fundamental ontological structure of the world for philosophers to discover. There are only the structures language gives to it. The worlds we inhabit vary with the language-games we employ. These games, moreover, can be perfectly clear to their users and, as such, devoid of the vertigo of Derrida's philosophy. The problem is that since we live inside them we often make one great error: We take them to be absolute; we become 'bewitched' by them, and we begin to adopt metaphysical stances.

When my older son was beginning to talk,[57] I pointed to a dog and said, 'Dog!' He repeated the word, and I assumed he had learned the 'appropriate' lesson. Later, he pointed to the family cat and cheerfully announced, 'Dog!' Still later a squirrel was greeted with the same epithet. Was he wrong? It depends on how you view the matter. Based on his very incomplete grasp of English, or any other language, my son had roughed out a language-game in which 'dog' probably referred to small furry quadrapeds, or some such thing. He had not yet assimilated the normal language-game, but he had nonetheless employed one. (My point is that what is at stake here is learning a use, not recognizing an essence. To think otherwise is to make a metaphysical mistake, one which, as parents, we very often do make. When a child is given a toy and then uses it 'in the wrong way' – such as turning a tricycle upside down and spinning its wheels – very often the parent gently corrects the child, pointing out the 'proper' use. By eliminating some 'games,' we indicate the essential correctness of others.)

As his command of English developed, my son dropped his game in favour of the standard one, which, among other things, had the advantage of allowing him to communicate more easily with other people. It was also a more extended game than his personal one. In it, he could, for example, ask, 'What's this animal called?' whereas in his game they were all called 'dog.' (He could, of course, have pointed to a squirrel and asked, 'What's this dog called?' and waited for an answer like 'Matilda.') From a Wittgensteinian perspective, what must not be forgotten, however, is that neither for my son nor for anyone else does the word – 'dog' in this case – name, or 'pick out,' an essential entity or concept in the world. The match between word and concept (signifier and signified) has to be learned in the context of every game in which it is used. To say that my son's use was wrong is, in this view, a kind of metaphysical intolerance of the sentences he constructed in his language-game; it was, more charitably, a usage that lay outside the normal English language-game. (It also shows the limitation inherent in my concept of a 'natural unit' in that my son apparently did not see the different animals as 'different'; he saw them as 'the same.') What is true of concrete words like 'dog' (which, when used metaphorically, are not 'concrete' at all) is even more so of abstract ones like 'beauty,' where the rules, if they exist, are fewer, less detailed, and harder to master. 'That's a dog' and 'That's beautiful' *look* like identical kinds of sentences, but, as I have noted, 'beauty' is not present to the observer in the way 'dogness' is – and even the latter has to be learned. If 'dog' doesn't pick out an essence, 'beauty' certainly does not.[58] Alternatively, however, within a language-game, both can have, in equal measure, clear meanings derived from the way they are used.

Words owe their allegiance to language-users and not to the world. As language-users morph language, ontology – and, indeed, 'reality' – morphs with it. But because of 'the fascination which forms of expression exert on us,'[59] this sometimes happens to bad effect. As an example more central to philosophy than my son's child-speak, let's consider the word 'knowledge.' People – many of my students, certainly – often say that they are 'seeking knowledge' and in saying this insinuate into existence the metaphysical presence of something called 'knowledge,' as if from the utterance, 'I know how to split an atom' we can infer a second meaningful utterance, 'I have knowledge.' This, to adapt Gilbert Ryle's famous phrase, is to conjure up a ghost in the epistemological machine,[60] a shadowy essence that stands beyond language and beyond particular bits of knowledge, apparently awaiting our discovery of it. Wittgenstein issued a stern warning about these feats of ontological magic: 'Knowledge is not *translated* into words when it is expressed. The words are not a translation of something else that was there before they were.'[61] Like any other *word*, knowledge is simply one whose use is governed by the language-game in which it is employed; like any other word, it has no essential meaning – 'knowledge' does not exist really – until an encompassing game exists, and then it exists only in its use. We must, therefore, take care not to create pseudo-games that appear to allow words to escape language.

Recall the scenario I sketched in Chapter 4, in which I asked how you could know you have a headache. My point was that, while most people assume they do know they have a headache, they do not have to do the things that are generally considered necessary to knowing something – conducting tests and overcoming doubts, for example. If we adopt, as a somewhat arbitrary but naturalist-looking rule, that *to know something one must first be able to doubt what one asserts and then be able to overcome those doubts with evidence, thus demonstrating that one's assertion is true*, it is hard to see how any of us can know that *we* have a headache. *We just have it.* (We don't say, 'I know I have a headache,' but 'I have a headache.' That is, we don't insert the statement into a 'knowing-game.') The presence of the headache is ontological, which is to say, prior to knowledge, because it is beyond doubt. I then went on to point out that, according to these rules of the 'knowledge' language-game, I could know that you (or anyone other than me) have a headache. I used, as a criterion of my knowledge, what I shall dub the weirdness principle: If I ask you how you know you have a headache, there is no way to answer except to assert, 'Well, I have one,' because there is no way to prove it *to yourself*. The question should strike you as weird. But if I ask you how you know someone else has a headache, you will enumerate reasons: her pupils are dilated, she is sensitive to sound, her stomach is upset, and so on. You try to prove *to me* that she has a headache, and the effort doesn't seem at all weird. The point that I want to emphasize here is that 'knowledge' is a word, and as such its use is governed by the rules of the language-game(s) within which it exists. If you are in a context where you can apply the rules governing its use, where you can comply with the criteria for knowing that the game sets out, you can use the word; otherwise not. Otherwise you are creating a new language-game, which may or may not take root. In either case, behind the rules governing use lies precisely nothing.

Wittgenstein made language the creator (or the keeper) of ontology and the philosopher the guardian of language. What the philosopher guards against are the metaphysical presences – pseudo-entities such as 'knowledge' – that lurk like ghosts behind the use of words. The philosopher's role is to remind us that there are no foundational, or extra-linguistic, ontological entities – no 'Big General Beings.' What there are, are words that have sometimes ontological and sometimes epistemological uses; only language – with a little help from the philosopher – keeps them separate. To import some Saussurean language, viewed synchronically, the 'knowledge' language-game divides propositions into those that can be doubted (Wittgenstein calls them 'empirical,' but I shall call them 'epistemological')[62] and those that are beyond doubt (which I shall call 'ontological').[63] Viewed diachronically, however, propositions can change designations. Since the ontological propositions serve as the foundation of the epistemological ones (I can try to discover *why* I have a headache only if I *have* a headache), this can amount to a radical shift in what we know (and don't know). As I noted in Chapter 4, before Copernicus, most astronomers did not know how to doubt the proposition, 'The Earth is at the centre of the universe and does not move.'[64] An astronomer did his work – pursued knowledge of the heavens – based on that ontological proposition. Everything he did had to accord with it. Copernicus transformed the statement into an epistemological proposition that could be doubted and, therefore, disproved. (In other words, Copernicus taught others how to doubt what they did not know how to doubt.) Today, the movement of the Earth in a particular way is taken as fundamental, or ontological. I must emphasize that the point is not – at least not *always* – that an ontological proposition *cannot* be demonstrated (as was the case with your headache) but that it is, for the most part, *set beyond demonstration* because its users *cannot imagine how it could be wrong*. (The demonstration, we might say, is *pro forma* because we could not imagine it failing.)

According to Wittgenstein, the reason we need what I have called ontological propositions is that if we doubted everything, if, in other words, everything were an epistemological proposition, the language-game of knowledge would never get off the ground, since it requires some foundation of certainty upon which to work. Imagine that I get hit on the head and you want to make sure I'm all right. One quick test concerns my vision: Am I seeing straight? You hold up three fingers and ask me, 'How many fingers?' The epistemological issue here is my eyesight; the ontological condition of pursuing it is the existence of your fingers. To test what is in doubt – my eyesight – you have to hold beyond doubt the proposition that your fingers exist. (Imagine asking: 'How many fingers do you see if, indeed, I have fingers?') Now imagine that you have been in an accident and are afraid that your fingers have been severed. Lying on the ground, eyes clenched shut, you ask, 'Are my fingers still there?' I look and answer, 'Yes.' In this case, the epistemological issue is the existence of your fingers, and the indubitable ontological ground is my eyesight.[65] To test one proposition another has to be held beyond doubt, as the ground or possibility of the test. Once again, you can apply the 'weirdness' criterion. If you simply shrug at the strangeness of a 'how-do-you-know?' question, that is probably because you have been asked how you know an ontological proposition, and it is against the rules of *whatever* language-game you are playing to ask that. If, in the first scenario, someone asked you how you knew your fingers were there, just such a shrug would almost certainly ensue. Or, if you were playing bridge or chess or poker and a friend asked how you knew you were, what would you say in response? Some questions cannot really be answered because they are not, within the rules of the language-game, legitimate questions. As Wittgenstein said dismissively of some queries about how we know: If we don't know that then we don't know anything. This was his version of the weirdness principle and it serves, if you get my point, to keep what we say within the bounds of language.

Myth and Metaphor

To summarize, in the *Tractatus*, Wittgenstein argues that propositions show how the world is, if they are true. In his later work, propositions are confined within language and, in that sense, 'mean' or perhaps 'work' rather than 'show.' A language-game is a practice, a particular way of seeing the world, something like the way that Wittgenstein described in the *Investigations* as 'seeing as' rather than 'seeing that.' '"Seeing as ...",' he writes there, 'is not part of perception. And for that reason it is like seeing and again not like.'[66] 'Seeing as' is a metaphorical 'seeing' and if it is our principal way of 'seeing' we are not so far removed from Nietzsche's assertion that truth is a mobile army of metaphors. For the Wittgenstein of the *Investigations*, knowledge is not an absolute that one pursues but the outcome of a way of seeing the world, of a particular set of linguistic practices. As the practices change, as one comes no longer to see the world *as* this but *as* that – as one's metaphors change, in other words – knowledge (or the knowledge language-game) changes. (In the Middle Ages it was, apparently, possible to know that God exists, and so great philosophers developed proofs of his existence; but no longer.) I have said once or twice that if one is telling a story it is important to recognize that that is what one is doing. So it is with games, metaphors, and, therefore, metaphysics insofar as it too is a language-game. Metaphysics can thus be characterized as the practice of looking at things *as if* we could transcend language and experience. (This is why the *Tractatus* is a work of metaphysics.) I have the impression that Wittgenstein saw nothing wrong with metaphysics so long as the metaphysician recognizes, as Wittgenstein himself did in the *Tractatus*, what is going on. The problem is that it is easy to lose one's way in the '"philosophy of as if" ... this shifting between simile and reality,' to become, I suppose, too convinced by one's metaphors.[67]

Wittgenstein's comments on Freud are interesting in this context. He

ought Freud's work was more mythological than scientific, because it
onsisted of powerful stories (case studies) of unverifiable personal
histories rather than testable causal laws.[68] It lacked, in other words, the
scepticism that comes from the inherent falsifiability of a science. As the
French philosopher Jacques Bouveresse notes in his *Wittgenstein Reads
Freud*, Wittgenstein thought that one who insists, as Freud did, that
there must be a single correct explanation 'for the sort of phenomena
treated by psychoanalysis is not someone who is simply adopting the
dominant scientific attitude but someone who is already on the road to
producing a mythology.'[69] Hence, despite his obvious admiration for
Freud, Wittgenstein also thought that 'analysis is likely to do harm.
Because although one may discover in the course of it various things
about oneself, one must have a very strong and keen and persistent
criticism in order to recognize and see through the mythology that is
offered or imposed on one. There is an inducement to say, "Yes, of
course, it must be like that." A powerful mythology.'[70]

A mythology develops when people become convinced – or better,
convinced in the wrong way – by the metaphor. They come to think of it as
a correct or accurate description of the world as opposed to, say, an apt
or useful one. We thus encounter the scientist's claim without the
possibility of the scientist's test or, therefore, the scientist's scepticism.
This is one powerful way in which language can bewitch us, inducing
us to transform the 'as if' – in the spirit of Chapter 2, the hyper-
plausible 'as if' – of a metaphor into the 'that' of a scientific discourse.
This is also why, for Wittgenstein, attention to language is so important
to the practice of philosophy. Philosophical errors are essentially slips –
deep metaphysical slips – of the philosophical tongue.

Final Thoughts

There is an aspect, both ancient and Freudian, to Wittgenstein's work
that I want briefly to mention. It will ease us towards the end of this
book. In both its 'early' and 'later' modes, Wittgenstein's philosophy is
most often a matter of eradicating errors, of exposing pseudo-problems
rather than solving 'real' ones. In this respect, Wittgenstein's philosophy has certain cognates with Heidegger's 'de-struction' and Derrida's
deconstruction, insofar as it entails a constant attention to the labyrinth
of language – in effect a constant exposure of the illusions that language
throws up on the wall of the cave. As such, philosophy is a form of
therapy, an intense self-analysis on the part of the philosopher: *What am*

I saying?[71] In the 'linguistic turn,' which marks so much of contemporary philosophy, many philosophers have adopted a doubly introspective variant of this view of the matter, turning in on their own practices, struggling to come to grips with what they are doing as philosophers. (As Michel Foucault was so well aware, self-consciousness is a hallmark of post-Enlightenment thought.) Much of this *auto-critique* is concerned with the fundamental linguistic issue of whether philosophical discourse should seek precision and clarity or whether it should revel in ambiguity.[72] Throughout most of the history of philosophy, the Platonic-scientific-*logos* axis has dominated discourse, pointing to precision and clarity as the road to truth. Descartes' clear and distinct ideas are a paradigm of this attitude, as is the work of most of those who are known as analytic philosophers. Poets and other *literati* have been left to explore the other path. Those whom I have often referred to as the new sceptic (or neo-Nietzschean) philosophers – an unsettled mixture of deconstructionists and slightly radical pragmatists – have asked, for some time now, whether this should be so. They have asked, in effect, whether precision and clarity are 'real' or attainable or even proper goals for a philosopher. Are these, instead, metaphysical illusions, ghostly presences of the rationalist's dream? The new sceptic philosophers have wondered, in something like the words of Northrop Frye, 'whether ambiguity may become, not a mere obstacle to meaning, but a positive and constructive force.'[73] If philosophers are seeking absolutes – the Full and Final Discourse of Chapter 1, – then ambiguity is manifestly an obstacle. But, if there are no absolutes, precision and complete clarity are dreams that may cloud our vision.

I feel I must add that this is not a plea for bad writing. It is simply to ask how much philosophical or metaphysical clarity even very good writing can achieve. Wittgenstein's later work is in many ways a masterpiece of insight that is constantly clouded by a searing intellectual honesty that pulls him up short of a clarity that would disperse his puzzling wonder at the complexities of our linguistic muddles. He thought he had got that clarity in the *Tractatus*, and everything he wrote thereafter was fuelled by his belief that in fact he had not and could not. He had cured himself – slowly – of that particular disease of thought.

This brings us to the self-doubt of the new sceptics, wherein philosophy becomes a struggle with metaphysics, which is simultaneously a struggle with language – an enduring struggle to understand what we are saying. Such self-doubt has occasioned a period of meta-philosophy wherein concern for what philosophy is, what its goals ought to be, and how it ought to proceed, often threatens to push aside the activity of 'doing' philosophy, which is the activity that Wittgenstein and J.L. Austin, among others, so notably espoused. This should not be surprising. For if metaphysics has long been the stuff and substance of philosophy, its fall from grace, its exposure as an illusion, if that is what metaphysics is, is either a terrible embarrassment for philosophers, leaving them marooned between the propositions of science and the poetry of literature – or a grand liberation. (Of course, professions of freedom – 'That's what I wanted all along!' – may be made to spare oneself the embarrassment of non-existence.) Some philosophers have, effectively, raised flags of surrender, either by attempting, as the logical positivists did, to transform their discipline into a 'handmaiden' of science that works to clear away its metaphysical confusions, or by acknowledging it as a species of rhetoric, which is to say, of literature, and then getting on with the activity that Rorty recommends: telling stories (or writing poems). Hemmed in between two hostile forces, these philosophers seem to be trying to decide who to surrender to – except for the 'liberationists,' who don't need to surrender because they are not there any more. For them, the borders have come down, and everyone can get on with the business of writing what they want or feel compelled to write. Only university departments, which have to hire philosophers and literary critics and the like – and therefore have to check credentials – need worry about definitions.

As usual, I am tempted to say that I don't know what to say about all this. This time, however, so near the end of this book, I feel I ought to essay a little dogmatism in defence of the realm. So, let me say that philosophy is neither science nor literature. Let me, in fine circular fashion, put the matter as follows: If philosophy is either science or literature, then it is not philosophy, and philosophy does not exist. Since philosophy manifestly does exist, it cannot be either science or literature. I am well aware that I could be accused here of falling victim to the classical metaphysical error of attributing ideal reality to names, or of just plain tautological stupidity, so I had better elaborate a little.

If philosophy is either science or literature, there is no need for a distinct name that 'picks out,' however provisionally, the concept 'philosophy.' It will have finally yielded the last of its shrinking place in the language-games of western thought. In this case, the now-branchless trunk of the once-mighty tree will have shrivelled and died. Of course, it may not be a matter of dying. Perhaps philosophy has simply lost the cloaks that lent it a false visibility; perhaps it never really had life, except as the 'others' it was trying to become. There was, on the one hand, the cloak of science in which philosophy appeared as a discipline of discovery. Under its guise, dogmatic philosophers made progress towards truths great and small. Plato's dream of overcoming poetry and of installing reason as master of the cosmos is an important undercurrent in the development of western science. But Plato's dream is directed towards metaphysics and not nature.[74] To be blunt, you can have a science of nature – of protons and neutrons and electrons – but not of metaphysics. In the long run – a very long run, as it turns out – philosophers have had to admit that many of their most cherished philosophical concerns – justice, beauty, goodness – are matters of *opinio* (opinion, belief), rather than *scientia* (knowledge). There is no absolute meaning or truth to be ferreted out, nothing to look for beyond, as Wittgenstein puts the matter, what people say and do. It was left to the social sciences in the nineteenth and twentieth centuries to make sense of this welter of opinion,[75] but these are disciplines inhabited by non-philosophers.

If philosophy is not a science, then, by default perhaps, it might be a form of rhetoric or poetry or literature. Philosophy might be a form of storytelling, of spinning out and commending particular views of life. Like artists, philosophers struggle to fill their palettes with whatever interests them. After all, artists and novelists may give us more insight into beauty and justice and the like than philosophers ever do, so maybe joining their ranks is not a bad idea. This is of course aggressively anti-Platonist, a celebration of just the sort of thing Plato wanted gone from his ideal city. But it, at least, leaves the philosopher with *something* to do once the ideal city has gone from him, even if he has to learn to write in a different idiom.

We are flirting with philosophical nihilism here – with something beyond scepticism. Philosophers seem in danger either of abandoning themselves to the drudgery of a lab assistant's life or to the 'babble' of literature.[76] In either case, philosophy and philosophers disappear, because there are no philosophical thoughts to think and no philosophers to think them. In a book about philosophy, such self-betraying nihilism makes the question I set down at the beginning of this book – Is there anything uniquely philosophical for philosophers to do? – a serious one. My dogmatic answer remains: 'Of course, there is.' The nihilism is actually the epiphanous Nietzschean moment when philosophers realize that they never were scientists or poets and that what for so long shielded them from recognizing this was metaphysics: poetry disguised as science.

In the first place, even if philosophy, like literature, produces 'only' metaphorical truths (non-truths, really) and, therefore, mythic representations of our lives, these metaphors and myths – the ancient myth of reason, for example, which taught us to see ourselves as children of *logos* – have tremendous power. Even though, as Northrop Frye notes, 'the principle of implicit metaphor means among other things that when a "true" meaning is decided on for a word, it will usually be a choice among a number of metaphorical possibilities, and these other possibilities will still be there,'[77] the metaphors (and the myths they produce) have, during their lifetimes, the power to shape our worlds. All metaphors die away, all myths lose their power – so let their motto be *sic transit gloria mundi* – and all other metaphors are eternally ready to return, and in this stubborn refusal either to be immortal or to die, we begin to glimpse their necessity. In the Babel of metaphors, the competition of myths, the welter of explanations, and 'ways of seeing' that constitutes its practice, philosophy produces deep presentations of matters (such as what is good or right or true) without which a culture would be – well, uncultured and, certainly, un-conscious.

Some might argue that religion can deal with these issues, and indeed, it has. But philosophy is mythically secular, imbued with *logos* – even in its religious and anti-rationalist variants. It may sometimes hide behind metaphysics, but never, or at least not in the last instance, behind its own authority. Its secularity and its *logos* is, in part, a humble abdication of authority. The myths of philosophy (if that is what they are) are presented (metaphorically?) *as* arguments, and as such *invite* discussion. That inherently metaphysical *form* of presentation, which Iris Murdoch described as 'a delicately managed conversation that moves between degrees of generality to promote understanding of very general features of our lives,'[78] is worth something – a great deal, I should think – in its own terms, even if philosophers never quite get used to swatting at metaphysical ghosts that refuse to vanish. As Murdoch also argued, 'the development of consciousness in human beings is inseparably connected with the use of metaphor. Metaphors are not merely peripheral decorations or even useful models, they are fundamental forms of awareness of our condition.'[79]

Philosophy, then, exists for the nominalist reason that philosophers announce themselves as such, and constantly invent and reinvent philosophical language-games – metaphysical ones, but other ones, too: analytic, ethical, epistemological – important ones that no other self-defined group quite manages to duplicate. When philosophers examine the concept of 'mind,' for example, they do something different than a psychologist or a biologist does, and their work enriches those disciplines just as it is enriched by them. When philosophers examine knowledge, they do something other than trace the sociological path of what people think of as knowledge. This establishes the possibility of a useful dialogue between sociologists and philosophers. When philosophers develop theories of emotions and their place in our lives, they establish lines of contact with those who study literature, psychology, and other disciplines. To put the matter in pragmatic terms, philosophers analyse certain human practices and conditions in unique ways; they develop valuable and self-critical methods of understanding or describing these practices and conditions. Very often this activity seems worthwhile, not only to philosophers but to a wider public as well. Philosophy exists because, and insofar as, it can pay its way in our culture.

I have returned in these last pages to a suggestion I made in the first chapter: The philosophical conversation is most often a Babel of voices. I am now trying to assure the reader that the chaotic nature of the conversation vitiates neither its intention nor its value. As *logos*, philosophy is the self-conscious activity of trying to understand important aspects of our lives in ways that invite not only criticism and argument but also self-criticism. From this grows its sometimes profound analytical power and, one hopes, its subtlety and resilience. Even when philosophers 'restrict' themselves to the study of 'ordinary language,' they have the power to reorient our lives. It may, for example, seem a trivial thing to be told that we do not pursue knowledge, but simply use the word 'know' within the context of certain language-games. If you think about it, though, this little bit of analysis casts the issue of what you think is going on in the 'pursuit' of knowledge – which involves asking why the metaphor of 'pursuit' is being used in the first place – into clearer relief. It makes you think about what you are saying, and it makes you understand that what you are placing so much value on is a metaphor. As a result, the philosophical individual begins to look more closely, understand more clearly, perhaps, the context of his life. By the same token, when students tell me that they want to know '*the* truth,' my response is usually to get them to examine the metaphysical assumptions built into that demand. If they come away with a more restricted sense of truth, accepting, say, that there are truth-bearing propositions but that 'Abortion is wrong' is not one of them – because it is not a proposition at all. At least, it is not until 'wrong' is made sufficiently specific, and when it is, the utterance loses all the force that the students intended it to have. I feel that if I get students to consider such matters, their world may tilt, however slightly, on its axis. If students ask me what the 'meaning of life' is, I direct them to Kant but also to the Monty Python movie of that name, in which it turned out to be something like, 'Do your best and be kind to your neighbours.' If students begin to suspect that there are no Big Answers to their Big Questions, and certainly no easy ones, they may begin to look more closely at a lot of small ones. Socrates famously said that the unexamined life is not worth living,[80] but examination is a small and painstaking activity that takes place in the folds of the very ordinariness of our lives. Good philosophy – which is like good literature in this respect – constantly brings us back to ourselves.

So, look at it this way. Philosophers, like the admirably loyal, patient, and resourceful Penelope, spin and weave, and when they are done, they unravel their work and begin again. What they weave may be stories or myths built on metaphorical ways of seeing our lives, but they are also, in the folds of all that, critiques of ordinary life – and of knowledge and truth and consciousness – which, inevitably, unravel the myths and metaphors that shape it. Of course, my metaphor, like all metaphors, cannot to be pushed too far. When Penelope spun, wove, and unravelled, she bought time for her wayward but equally resourceful husband Odysseus to find his way home. She had a purpose that made sense of an otherwise meaningless activity. But what about philosophers? At the risk of stretching the metaphor beyond its breaking point, let me suggest that for them the point just is the activity. The unravelling, the unmaking, is as important as the making: the scepticism is as important as the dogmatism. In the activity, there is a discipline and a care (a therapy, perhaps)[81] that may bring its practitioners nearer to some condition that we can call wisdom. Not always – there are, as I said at the very beginning of this book, no guarantees – but sometimes. I am pretty sure that if there is an appropriate metaphor for wisdom (which would be the biggest metaphor of all) it is not some 'place' or 'thing' – a clearing that we enter or a cloak that we put on – but I don't know what it is. If the truth be told, I suspect that there is no good metaphor for wisdom. If it emerges, it emerges. Philosophy is about trying to find a way to let it do so. Philosophy is the aporetic exercise of trying to think the unthinkable and knowing that you are. And that is to bask in the sublime light of Plato's unextinguished sun.

The Twelve-Coin Puzzle and the Paradox of the Heap

The Twelve-Coin Puzzle

Let me restate the puzzle, which is an application of the law of the excluded middle. There are twelve coins, of which eleven weigh the same, but the twelfth one is either heavier or lighter than the others. Using a basic balance scale, the goal is to isolate the unique coin *and* determine whether it is lighter or heavier, in a maximum of three weighings.

Solution:

1 Divide the coins into three groups of four.
2 Weigh any two of the groups. One of two things will happen: (a) they will balance; (b) they will not balance.
3 Option (a)
   In this case, the coin must be in the third – unweighed – group. Here's what you do:
   i Weigh three coins from the third group against any three chosen at random from groups one and two. One of two things will happen: they will balance or not balance.
   ii If they balance, then the coin you want is the remaining one. Simply measure it against any other coin to determine whether it is lighter or heavier. You now have done two weighings.
   iii If they do not balance, then the coin you want is among the three you weighed. Since that side will have gone up or down, you know whether the coin you want is lighter or heavier. Suppose it is heavier: Now simply weigh two of the coins from this group of

three against one another. If they balance, it is the one you left out; if they don't balance, it is the coin that goes down. You have not done two weighings.

4 Option (b)

The sides don't balance. This is more complicated, but here's what you do.

i Note which side went up and which side went down. Let's suppose that side A went up and side B went down.

ii Now rotate the coins as follows: Move three of the A side coins to the B side, three of the B side off the scale, and three of the (hitherto unweighed) C group to the A side. One of two things will happen:

a *The sides balance.* This means that the coin you want is off the scale. Since it was from group B – the group that went down – it is a heavier coin. Now weigh any two of the three group B coins that are not on the scale. If they balance, you want the other one (which you already know is a heavier coin); if they don't balance, you want the heavier one (i.e., the side that went down). You have now done three weighings.

b *The sides do not balance.* In this case, one of two things will happen: either the tilt will remain the same (A up and B down) or it will be reversed. If it remains the same that means that the different coin is one of the two left in their original places. Weigh any normal coin against A. If A goes up (which is all it could do), that is the (lighter) coin you want; if the two coins balance, then the B side coin is the one you want, and you know it is a heavier coin. You have now done three weighings. If the tilt is reversed, that means that the coin you want was one of the three in group A that were switched to the B side – which means, it is a lighter coin. Weigh any two of those three: if they balance, it is the third coin; if they don't balance, it is the one that goes up. You have now done three weighings.

The Paradox of the Heap

This is one of a series of paradoxes designed to show that the world cannot be as it appears to be because that appearance is illogical. It goes as follows:

There can never be any such thing as a heap of sand because if there were then subtracting something as tiny as a grain of sand from that heap would never be enough to reduce it to non-heap status. By the same token if something is not a heap of sand, adding a grain will never be enough to make it a heap. Hence, it is impossible either to make or destroy heaps. The idea is, therefore, nonsensical and heaps must not exist – which makes the idea of destroying one moot – and it goes against the grain of logic to assert that they do.

This is really an argument against incremental change amounting to anything, and we can resolve it by applying the laws of reasoning. First, let's identify 'heap' as a quantity word. By the law of the excluded middle, quantity words are either specific or non-specific. Heap is non-specific. Now, the point about a non-specific quantity is that it cannot be measured with precision, but to talk about it in terms of grains of sand is to assert that it can be – to treat it as a kind of specific non-specific quantity. We don't add or subtract grains to make a heap; we just pile up a bunch of sand. But suppose a heap were a specific quantity, say, a million grains of sand. Then there would be a point at which adding a single grain would turn a non-heap into a heap and subtracting one would do the reverse. In short, since 'heap' is a non-specific quantity word, the issue of adding and subtracting grains of sand is irrelevant; but if a heap were specific, the claim of the paradox would simply be wrong. So the argument of the paradox is either irrelevant or wrong.

Ethics and the 'Other'

The relation of the self to others is a very difficult, and obviously central, ethical issue. It is implied in everything I have to say in Chapter 6, and here I want to offer a few additional comments.

That certain strands of contemporary philosophy are heavily indebted to Nietzsche is a point I have made in these pages, going so far as to refer to some of the anti-metaphysical philosophers as 'neo-Nietzscheans.' In ethics, as in so many other parts of philosophy, Nietzsche was – to parody his description of Socrates – a renegade who got himself taken seriously.[1] His attacks on traditional, Christian-influenced morality are among the best-known parts of his work (even if they are not very carefully read). Almost all undergraduates respond to his name with, 'God is dead.' Nietzsche is, to them, the great nihilist, the man who characterized the history of the West as a history of ever-increasing decadence, who saw its moral visions as expressions of slavelike *ressentiment* against nobler lives (of which Socrates' 'dialectic' is the first great philosophical expression)[2] and as attempts to extirpate all human creativity. This is true, so far as it goes. Nietzsche did reject what he saw as metaphysically dogmatic views that presented morality as a series of universal rules intended to restrict humankind to certain well-worn paths. 'A popular ethics,' wrote Nietzsche, 'wants to suppress bad expressions as far as possible, for the sake of the general welfare – an undertaking that is strikingly similar to the police.'[3] Since, for Nietzsche, there are no such paths, because there are no universal truths, these police moralities are merely expressions of a perverted will to power – attempts to impose one's views on others. By contrast, Nietzsche argues that a life is an individual thing – the life of *a* person. Attempts to rob life of its individuality by squeezing it into an ill-fitting off-the-rack morality are necessarily corrupt because they claim to speak the 'truth' – the moral truth – when all they really represent is a resentful power. They peddle the lie that there are moral facts out there in the universe to speak the truth about.

A person, Nietzsche argued, must learn to speak in the absence of such truth and, therefore, to fashion his own life. In Chapter 4, I commented on Richard Rorty's treatment of truth as a kind of literalized metaphor, noting his quotation of Nietzsche's expression that truth is 'a mobile army of metaphors.' Truth is also, according to Nietzsche, an army of 'metonyms and anthropomorphisms – in short a sum of human relations, which have been enhanced, transposed, and embellished poetically and rhetorically, and which after long use seem firm, obligatory and canonical to a people: truths are illusions about which one has forgotten that this is what they are; metaphors which are worn out.'[4] Here, and elsewhere, Nietzsche is trying to separate epistemology, what he sees as the scientism of western philosophy[5] expressed in its metaphysical attachment to truth, from ethics. (I noted in Chapter 4 that Socrates and Plato attach, subordinate, in fact, ethics to epistemology, so Nietzsche chooses his enemies well.) 'To be truthful,' Nietzsche says, 'means using the customary metaphors,' which is, in essence to 'lie according to fixed convention.'[6] That we can know what a life ought to be, that we can have a *science* of ethics, that there are truths upon which ethics could be founded: this is the great moral lie. Therefore, the secret – if that's what it is – to ethics is to take great care, in the manner of Nietzsche's mythical nobles, to fashion one's life according to one's instincts,[7] for then a person creates the value of actions and not the reverse.[8] To summarize: if truth is (to employ the terms I have been using) naturalized – and, according to Nietzsche, it is – then truth is nothing but the will to power hiding behind the lie that there is truth. All moulds, models, Forms, plans, procedures, and so on, for the 'good life' are also lies: what remains when one sweeps them aside is the individual, if only she has the strength to be that.[9] Ethics is therefore primarily an aesthetic activity directed towards the creation of a life that, if it is a 'good' life, *cannot be copied*. Ethics has to do, first and foremost, with oneself and not with others.

In *The Art of living*, Nehamas argues persuasively that in the last years of his life Michel Foucault also came to see ethics as fundamentally a 'care of the self,'[10] and, like Nietzsche, he found the roots of this attitude in ancient Greece. This is an important and influential view in contemporary philosophy, but one that raises the existential difficulty of just how the self-fashioning ethicist is to relate to other people, to other self-fashioning ethicists. To begin with the self, to look inward first, fits well enough with the aesthetic element of ethics, but it poses, shall we say, certain social and political problems, which can be summed up in the following question: How do we take others into consideration? This difficulty is reflected in different ways in different philosophers but, to take the case of one who has appeared in these pages, it shows up in Sartre's work as a profound, and perhaps, nihilistic struggle with commitment. Because Sartre begins by asserting the absolute ontological freedom of the individual – his complete responsibility for the life he fashions – the existence of others is, as he famously said, a kind of hell. The 'Other' is always there, her gaze a defining presence, a being who cannot be discounted but who is nonetheless the limit, the destruction almost, of 'my' freedom. Sartre's solitary moral agent, who cannot quite be solitary because so much of his 'personhood' resides in the Other, and yet who cannot quite accept that this is so, and who therefore reduces human relations to sado-masochistic contracts, led Iris Murdoch to characterize Sartre's work as 'the surrender to neurosis.'[11]

So, here is the issue. If the metaphors and myths that connect people are exposed as lies, on what basis can we constitute relations with other people? One answer, at one level the only answer, is to reject the antecedent of the conditional and insist that the myths aren't lies. In Emmanuel Levinas's work, for example, we find the self in what may be described as an instinctual, natural, anguished, but non-neurotic relation to the Other. In short, Levinas's self can never find itself in itself: hence, the 'care of the self' is, for him, essentially a form of care for others. To recognize another – and as 'intensional,' or outward-directed, beings that is what we inevitably do – is to recognize a moral relation, a sense of responsibility, for that being.[12] That cannot be avoided. Before Levinas, Simone de Beauvoir, in her trenchant feminist analysis of Sartre's concept of the Other as an objectification and alienation of women,[13] drew attention to the crucial importance of understanding this fundamental reciprocity. To recognize another consciousness is to recognize another person, and in that recognition there had to be a way back from the alienation of the woman as Other – as a kind of object-for-men (and hence for-herself) rather than subject.[14] Of course, all of this runs against the grain of such thinkers as Hobbes, Bentham, and Freud, all of whom argued in their different ways that the connection to others had to be created, crafted almost, by various forms of experience (usually painful), education, and sanctions. Modernity is not always a very chummy place.

How to summarize? As with the rest of philosophy, the anti-metaphysical currents of post-Enlightenment thought have brought enormous pressure to bear on the idea that we can ever speak the truth *about ourselves*. There is no truth to speak and no *logos* to speak it. Our lives cannot be epistemologized. In short, if the metaphysical domino topples, the epistemological one follows suit, and the whole enterprise of ethics, the whole sense of what it is to live a good life, has to be re-thought. What such re-thinking brings into question is the very notion of our relations to others.

Notes

Preface

1 Colin McGinn, *The Making of a Philosopher* (New York: Perennial Paperbacks, 2003), p. xi.

Chapter 1 What Is Philosophy?

1 The first philosophers, who lived in the Ionian city of Miletus, were generally referred to as *physiologia*, or 'nature philosophers'; the term came to designate those whose interests were primarily in what we would call natural science. The Heidegger quote is from his *What Is Philosophy?* trans. William Kluback and Jean T. Wilde (New York: Twayne Publishers, 1958), p. 35.

2 Those 'concerns' are metaphysics, epistemology, logic, ethics, and language. All have their origins in ancient Greece. For an interesting diagram of philosophy, see Ted Honderich, ed., *The Oxford Companion to Philosophy* (Oxford: Oxford University Press, 1995), pp. 927–9.

3 With respect to the lineage of 'dogmatism,' see Julia Annas and Jonathan Barnes, *The Modes of Scepticism* (Cambridge: Cambridge University Press, 1985), pp. 1–2: 'The word "dogmatist" in contemporary English has a pejorative tone – it hints at an irrational rigidity of opinion, a refusal to look impartially at the evidence. In its ancient sense the word lacked that tone; a dogmatist was simply someone who subscribed to dogmas or doctrines.'

Scepticism is traced to Sextus Empiricus (fl. ca. 200), a physician and philosopher who popularized the work of Pyrrho of Ellis, a philosopher who lived in the fourth to third centuries BCE and who argued that the

reasons for and against any position can never be definitive. The medical
community of the ancient world was also divided between 'dogmatists'
and 'empiricists' – between those who attempted to develop complete
theories of diseases, including their hidden causes, and those who concen-
trated on discovering, based on experience, what worked as a cure. See
Pierre Pellegrin, 'Medicine,' in Jacques Brunschwig and G.E.R. Lloyd, eds.,
Greek Thought: A Guide to Classical Knowledge (Cambridge, Mass.: Belknap
Press, 2000), and G.E.R. Lloyd, *The Revolutions of Wisdom* (Berkeley: University of California Press, 1987), pp. 158–71. Lloyd adds a third group, the
methodists, to the two I have mentioned here.

Kant delineates three philosophical standpoints: sceptical, dogmatic,
and critical. In Norman Kemp Smith's paraphrase, 'a dogmatist is one
who assumes that human reason can comprehend ultimate reality, and
who proceeds upon this assumption.' The sceptic, Kant tells us, 'is the
taskmaster who constrains the dogmatic reasoner to develop a sound
critique of the understanding and reason.' 'Critical philosophy' is the
designation Kant gives to his own work after Hume had 'awakened me
from my dogmatic slumbers.' *A Commentary to Kant's 'Critique of Pure
Reason,'* 2nd ed. (New York: Humanities Press, 1962), pp. 13–15.

4 Ancient scepticism tends towards the first of these views; modern
varieties – i.e., those that emerged in the sixteenth century and their
successors – are closer to the second.

5 By disputing the grounds for all claims to knowledge, the ancient sceptics
attempted to drive their dogmatic opponents into an 'infinite regress' of
arguments. For a good summary, see Jonathan Barnes, 'Some Ways of
Scepticism,' in Stephen Everson, ed., *Epistemology* (Cambridge: Cambridge
University Press, 1990). For more detail, consult Annas and Barnes, *Modes
of Scepticism*, ch. 3. We can characterize dogmatism as the attempt to discover what is real and scepticism as the discussion of what *seems to be real.*
See also Ewa Plonowska Ziarek, *The Rhetoric of Failure* (Albany: SUNY
Press, 1996), p. 27. One can propose substitutes for 'dogmatist' and
'sceptic.' 'Deconstructive' and 'constructive' might work, but the first of
these terms carries too much current baggage as the standard-bearer for
much of continental philosophy. 'Constructive' and 'diagnostic' have also
been suggested.

6 This began in the middle of the third century BCE. See Carlos Levy, 'The
Academy,' in Brunschwig and Lloyd, *Greek Thought.*

7 In the later Roman Empire philosophy was essentially training in public
speaking and letter writing. The historian Peter Brown notes that in late
antiquity philosophers 'tended to be peripheral figures on the political

scene.' *Power and Persuasion in Late Antiquity* (Madison: University of Wisconsin Press, 1992), p. 4.

8 See Annas and Barnes, *Modes of Scepticism*, Introduction, and also Myles Burnyeat, ed., *The Skeptical Tradition* (Berkeley: University of California Press, 1983).

9 For empiricism, see Chapter 4. See also, Martha Brandt Bolton, 'Locke and Pyrrhonism: The Doctrine of Primary and Secondary Qualities,' and Robert J. Fogelin, 'The Tendency of Hume's Skepticism,' in Burnyeat, *Skeptical Tradition.*

10 Burnyeat, 'Introduction,' in *Skeptical Tradition*, p. 3.

11 For an interesting and important treatment of dogmatic assumptions in contemporary philosophy, see Hilary Putnam's ruminations on his own development in *Renewing Philosophy* (Cambridge: Harvard University Press, 1992).

12 The idea of 'progress' is a lightning rod for this issue. The undogmatic American philosopher Richard Rorty sees 'intellectual and moral progress not as a matter of getting closer to the True or the Good or the Right, but as an increase in imaginative power.' *Philosophy and Social Hope* (London: Penguin, 1999), p. 87.

13 See note 10, above.

14 The American talk show host David Letterman has a bit where the curtain goes up on people performing strange vaudeville acts. Letterman and his bandleader then debate whether what they are watching 'is anything.' It's very post-modern.

15 A.J. Ayer, *The Central Questions of Philosophy* (Harmondsworth: Penguin, 1976), p. 1.

16 Roger Scruton, *Modern Philosophy: An Introduction and Survey*, 3rd ed. (London: Mandarin, 1996), p. 3.

17 Ludwig Wittgenstein, *Tractatus Logico-Philosophicus*, trans. D.F. Pears and B.F. McGuinness (London: Routledge and Kegan Paul, 1961), p. 3.

18 Ibid.

19 This will be discussed in Chapter 7. But see, Ludwig Wittgenstein, *Philosophical Investigations*, trans. G.E.M. Anscombe (Oxford: Basil Blackwell, 1978), part I, s. 122.

20 A.J. Ayer, *Language, Truth and Logic* (Harmondsworth: Penguin, 1971), p. 13.

21 Theodore Adorno, *Negative Dialectics*, trans. E.B. Ashton (New York: Seabury Press, 1977), pp. 3–4.

22 Martin Heidegger, 'Letter on Humanism,' in William McNeill, ed., *Pathmarks* (Cambridge: Cambridge University Press, 1998), p. 276.

23 Jacques Derrida, *Writing and Difference*, trans. Alan Bass (Chicago: University of Chicago Press, 1978), p. 79.

24 Richard Rorty, 'Is Derrida a Transcendental Philosopher?' in *Philosophical Papers*, vol. 2, *Essays on Heidegger and Others* (Cambridge: Cambridge University Press, 1991), p. 122. See also Derrida's comments in Raoul Mortley ed., *French Philosophers in Conversation* (New York: Routledge, 1991), pp. 94–5.

25 The diagram in the *Oxford Companion*, referred to in note 2, above, uses a series of concentric circles to separate the inner core from satellite areas of the discipline.

26 See Bruce Kuklick, 'Seven Thinkers and How They Grew,' in Richard Rorty, J.B. Schneewind, and Quentin Skinner, eds., *Philosophy in History* (Cambridge: Cambridge University Press, 1984).

27 A related issue concerns the Eurocentrism of philosophy, which Simon Critchley has expressed as follows: 'Must the Greco-European story of the philosophical tradition ... be accepted as a legitimating narrative by philosophers, even by those who call themselves philosophers only in remembrance? Must philosophy be haunted by the compulsion to repeat its Greek origin ... Could philosophy, at least in its European moment, ever be in a position to repeat another origin, announce another beginning, invent another tradition or tell another story?' *Ethics – Politics – Subjectivity* (London: Verso, 1999), p. 128.

28 This is Socrates' message to the jury at *Apology* 20d–23b. Its pretext is the story of a friend going to the Delphic Oracle and asking if anyone is wiser than Socrates. Socrates does not know what to make of the negative reply.

29 Depending on translation, Socrates' father Sophronicus was either a sculptor or a stonemason.

30 Plato, *Theatetus* 149a. The Greek *'aporia'* meant something like 'difficulty' or 'perplexity' or 'confusion.' Hence, the 'aporetic' method refers to Socrates' insistence that we really don't know the answers to the questions he asks. They are designed to make his interlocutors confront their ignorance of these matters.

31 Although Plato's 'Socrates' is the principal version of this remarkable man, his contemporary Xenophon also produced Socratic dialogues featuring a less philosophical, less enigmatic, and less irascible Socrates. My interest is in Plato's 'Socrates.'

32 Sophists were teachers who charged fees. At 20c of *Apology* Socrates expresses amazement that one can take money for teaching wisdom since, in his estimation, it is unteachable. Plato's *Gorgias*, *Protagoras*, and *Sophist* contain sustained attacks on the sophists. On the distinction between

philosophos and *sophos*, see Lisa Jardine, 'Lorenzo Valla: Academic Skepticism and the New Humanist Dialectic,' in Burnyeat, *Skeptical Tradition*, pp. 265–6.

33 See Plato's *Symposium* 201d and ff. See also Pierre Hadot, *What Is Ancient Philosophy?* trans. Michael Chase (Cambridge, Mass.: Belknap Press, 2002), p. 16: 'In general, since the time of Homer, compound words beginning with *philo-* had served to designate the disposition of a person who found his interest, pleasure or *raison de vivre*, in devoting himself to a given activity.'

34 This negative assessment of the Sophists is Plato's and not necessarily mine. In many ways, it is almost certainly an unfair assessment.

35 The Delphic Oracle was dedicated to the god Apollo.

36 I.e., to accept *aporia*.

37 This is known as *epoché*, or bracketing out one's beliefs. For a discussion of this act, see Myles Burnyeat, 'Can the Skeptic Live His Skepticism?' in Burnyeat, *Skeptical Tradition*.

38 For a discussion of the way in which scepticism contributed to the view of philosophy as a therapy designed to allow the individual to come to grips with her life, see, Martha Nussbaum, *The Therapy of Desire* (Princeton: Princeton University Press, 1994), esp. ch. 8.

39 See also Burnyeat, 'Can the Skeptic Live His Skepticism?' and Nussbaum, *Therapy*, p. 285.

40 The 'later' Wittgenstein was a practitioner of 'ordinary language philosophy,' which takes as its benchmark the way everyday speakers use a language. The Oxford philosopher J.L. Austin is another well-known exponent of this approach, although it is also associated with the Cambridge philosopher G.E. Moore.

41 Remember that the ancient sceptics held no positive doctrines. Their arguments were entirely directed against the 'dogmatic' schools.

42 E.g., how to underwrite moral values is a challenge for any sceptical philosopher. At the end of the *Tractatus* (6.54), Wittgenstein asserts that values lie beyond the world, by which he means that there is very little that one can say about them and certainly no way to demonstrate their 'veracity.'

43 The allegory is at *Republic*, 514a–521b. The quote about 'infinite controversy' is from J.N. Findlay, *The Discipline of the Cave* (London: Allen and Unwin, 1966), p. 22.

44 Readers of the allegory should take this idea seriously. Popular religious beliefs, for example, would almost certainly fall into the shadow category, although more 'elevated' conceptions of religion would be iconic. Heidegger states that the prisoners in the cave 'have no relationship to them-

selves at all.' In short, they lack self-consciousness, which is not surprising because they lack the capacity for doubt. Hence, scepticism is by definition an elevated, or philosophical, condition. *The Essence of Truth*, trans. Ted Sadler (London: Continuum, 2002), p. 21.

45 Plato's theory of 'Forms' is complex and requires careful study, esp. since he never explains it the same way twice. Aristotle rejects it and even Plato himself came to have reservations about it. See, e.g., *Parmenides*. Aristotle coined the term 'third-man argument' to refer to the objections raised there, ones with which he substantially agreed.

46 In *Republic*, the Allegory of the Cave is preceded by the Parable of the Line (509d–511b) which is about the stages of cognition. There, Plato imagines a 'visible' world and an 'intelligible' world of ideas. In the visible world, one begins in ignorance but advances to a higher stage of cognition just as the prisoner turns to see the fire. This is called *pistis* or 'confidence' in part because having overcome the illusions of ignorance the individual now thinks he possesses knowledge.

47 I shall return to this issue below.

48 One can read this as a birth allegory. Perhaps the philosopher's birth is simultaneously her death to the 'normal' world. Certainly, Plato thinks that anyone who has left the cave will not want to return to it. Also see, below, note 51.

49 Plato espouses the Pythagorean theory of 'metempsychosis' – the immortality and re-incarnation of *psyches*. In death, *psyches* had the Forms slowly revealed to them so when they were placed back in human bodies this knowledge would be within them, although buried beneath layers of appetite. See also *Meno*, esp. 81a–86b. Aristotle contends that wisdom is an essentially divine condition: 'Only God can enjoy this privilege.' *Metaphysics* I, 982b30. It is worth mentioning Heidegger's (*Essence of Truth*, p. 26 and ff) view that truth – the Greek *aletheia* – is 'unhiddenness.' To view the Forms is to have all shadows fall away.

50 They are, i.e., objects of understanding, grasped by the mind rather than the senses. See also *Republic*, 510a–d.

51 See *Phaedo*, esp. 66b–67b. I said above that the philosopher never gets to see the Forms. There is, however, the sage – and Socrates was generally accorded to be one, although he obviously did not consider himself as such – who has a kind of charismatic (i.e., god-given) wisdom that elevates him above the philosopher. Hence, as Hadot says (*What Is Ancient Philosophy?* pp. 46–7), philosophers are intermediate between sages and 'senseless' people.

52 *Republic* 595a–608b. Hadot suggests (ibid., p. 72) that Plato's dialogues 'can

be considered as works of propaganda, decked out with all the prestige of literary art but intended to convert people to philosophy.'

53 *Republic* 607b: 'There is from of old a quarrel between philosophy and poetry.'

54 A traditional description of the origins of philosophy (see Chapter 2) is as the separation of *logos* (reason) from *mythos* (stories): to be precise, from the stories of the poets.

55 There is no better book on this topic than Iris Murdoch, *The Fire and the Sun* (Oxford: Oxford University Press, 1977).

56 If we assign mathematics and logic to *logos,* we might say that Plato wants to transcend natural language because the highest truths must be expressed mathematically. A sceptical reader might consider that the highest expressions of modern science – its great laws – are mathematical and natural languages are poor substitutes that provide us with mere simulacra of these laws.

57 The idea of a 'hidden God,' beyond our capacity for knowing, is an important concept in western thought.

58 Rorty often gives expression to this view.

59 Stanley Cavell, 'Declining Decline,' in Stephen Mulhall, ed., *The Cavell Reader* (Cambridge Mass.: Blackwell, 1996), p. 332.

60 Richard Rorty, 'Charles Taylor on Truth,' in *Philosophical Papers*, vol. 3, *Truth and Progress* (Cambridge: Cambridge University Press, 1998), p. 39.

61 See Hubert L. Dreyfus and Paul Rabinow, *Michel Foucault: Beyond Structuralism and Hermeneutics*, 2nd ed. (Chicago: University of Chicago Press, 1982), p. 180.

62 Quoted in ibid., p. 107.

63 Rorty, I believe, expresses almost precisely this idea.

64 Michel Foucault, 'Nietzsche, Genealogy, History,' in *Language, Countermemory, Practice*, ed. Donald F. Bouchard, trans. Donald F. Bouchard and Sherry Simon (Ithaca, NY: Cornell University Press, 1977), pp. 151–2.

65 Sören Kierkegaard, *Philosophical Fragments*, ed. and trans. H.V. Hong and E.H. Hong (Princeton: Princeton University Press, 1985), p. 145.

Chapter 2 Metaphysics: The Search for the God's-Eye View

1 Hilary Putnam, *Representation and Reality* (Cambridge, Mass.: MIT Press, 1988), p. 58.

2 D.W. Hamlyn, 'Metaphysics: History of,' in Ted Honderich, ed., *The Oxford Companion to Philosophy* (Oxford: Oxford University Press, 1995), p. 557.

3 J.L. Austin, *Philosophical Papers*, 2nd ed. (Oxford: Oxford University Press, 1970), p. 117. Since to 'speak the truth' is just to utter 'true statements,' one could argue that 'truth' is both redundant and metaphysically seductive insofar as it makes one think of it as *something*.

4 This is Heidegger's view of the matter, one that has had a profound effect on the development of deconstruction.

5 Richard McKeon, 'Introduction,' in R. McKeon, ed., *Basic Works of Aristotle* (New York: Random House, 1941), p. xvii.

6 This is the most common version of the story.

7 Aristotle, *Metaphysics* IV: 1, 1003a21–25, in McKeon, *Basic Works*, p. 731.

8 D.W. Hamlyn, *Metaphysics* (Cambridge: Cambridge University Press, 1984), p. 1.

9 The reader can compare these remarks with my description of Stephen Hawking's 'weak anthropic principle,' in Chapter 3, note 11.

10 See Gottfried Leibniz, *The Monadology*, ss. 31–2, and *The Leibniz-Clarke Correspondence* (New York: Philosophical Library, 1956), L. III 2–6, L. IV 8–11, L. V 27–32, 36–65, 79–80, 104–6.

11 John Buridan was a fourteenth-century Paris philosopher. The parable is attributed to him; it is not among his extant writings.

12 According to Cambridge philosopher C.D. Broad, Leibniz contends 'that all talk of an undetermined event, in the sense of an event for which there is no sufficient reason, is nonsensical.' *Leibniz* (Cambridge: Cambridge University Press, 1975), p. 29. Einstein felt much the same way, famously asserting that 'God does not play dice with the world.'

13 Binding God to the dictates of reason is in the tradition of Greek philosophy, but it was a contentious issue for medieval Christian theologians who thought of God as omnipotent and unfettered. An omnipotent God raises many issues. Can he then limit his power in some way? Can he bind himself to the dictates of reason, or is he free to do the irrational? For a discussion of these issues, see Anthony Kenny, *The God of the Philosophers* (Oxford: Clarendon Press, 1986), esp. ch. 7.

14 Well, we put them together somewhere – in our mind or thoughts, or imagination or what have you. Philosophers argue over the exact 'location.' I have not chosen one but have instead left these ideas – colloquially – in our heads. For an interesting discussion, see Colin McGinn, *The Mysterious Flame* (New York: Basic Books, 1999), ch. 4.

15 E.g., see A.J. Ayer, *The Central Questions of Philosophy* (Harmondsworth: Penquin, 1976), p. 77.

16 I shall consider this issue in my remarks on Kant, below.

17 For introductions to this issue, see Jonathan Dancy, *Berkeley* (Oxford: Basil

Blackwell, 1987), ch. 2, 2nd J.O. Urmson, *Berkeley* (Oxford: Oxford University Press, 1982).

18 Indeed, since Berkeley distinguishes between 'real' ideas placed in our minds by God and 'imaginary' ones that we have 'made up' (think of the difference between the ideas of a horse and a centaur), he does have a realist view of the world. It's just that that 'world' was the mind of God. As I have said above, everyone has some conception of 'reality.' See George Berkeley, *Principles of Human Knowledge*, part I, ss. XXIX–XXXIII.

19 See Dancy, *Berkeley*, p. 39.

20 See Berkeley, *Principles*, part I, ss. XXIX–XL.

21 The Greek *atomos* meaning 'indivisible' or 'uncut,' is the alpha-privative of *tomos*, which means a part or a cutting and which gives us 'tome' in English in reference to a single book.

22 David Chalmers has expressed very succinctly this 'sense of self' that we seem to carry: 'One sometimes feels that there is something to consciousness that transcends all ... specific elements: a kind of background hum, for instance, that is somehow fundamental to consciousness ... This phenomenology of the self is so deep and intangible that it sometimes seems illusory. ... Still, there seems to be *something* to the phenomenology of self, even if it is very hard to pin down.' *The Conscious Mind* (Oxford: Oxford University Press, 1996), p. 10.

23 See my remarks on Parmenides, below. Interestingly, he does not deny the existence of the physical world, only that it is a world of time and space.

24 John Locke, *An Essay Concerning Human Understanding* (New York: Dover, 1959) vol. 1, II: III, s. 6. Reprint of A.C. Fraser edition, 1894; original published in 1690.

25 W.V. Quine, 'Ontological Relativity,' in *Ontological Relativity and Other Essays* (New York: Columbia University Press, 1969), p. 55.

26 'Constructionism' is the idea that a person is just the series of events that make up 'her' life. In that sense, 'I' am not there in advance of the events that make up 'me'; there is no underlying being to whom these things happen. See, e.g., Richard Wollheim, *The Thread of Life* (Cambridge: Harvard University Press, 1984), ch. 1, s. 6.

27 There is a famous complication of this example. Imagine that over the years the ship *The Golden Hind* has all its timbers replaced. The original wood is carefully stored and used to build a second ship. Which, then, is the real *Golden Hind*? This is probably the sort of thing Austin had in mind when he warned against the 'wile of the metaphysician' who toys with our sense of reality. Questions such as 'which is the real *Golden Hind*?'

2

2

may be metaphysically deep or they may simply be tricky. See also See J.L. Austin, 'Other Minds,' in *Philosophical Papers*, esp. p. 87 and p. 94.

28 Berkeley, *Principles*, part I, s. XVII.

29 This is part of the point Chalmers is making in note 22, above. It may be that throughout this section I have been trying to make more evident what is already as evident as it can be. In a famous series of lectures, the American Philosopher Saul Kripke argued something like this position, pointing out that we use the properties of an object to identify it – and do so very successfully – without worrying about which of these properties are essential to the object being what it is and which are not. This worry is a kind of hyper-abstraction (my term) that, in Kripke's opinion, bewitches philosophers into positing a false dilemma: Is the object a bundle of qualities or something behind the qualities? Kripke's answer is 'neither,' by which I think he means that both answers are too abstract to be useful and are at any rate concerned with the wrong question. The issue is not 'What is the essential identity of this object (or person)?' but 'How do I (or you) identify it?' This is an important distinction. Suppose there is an *ousia* behind all the qualities in my living-room chair: I might never pick it out – identify it – and yet I have so far always correctly identified the chair as *that* chair. In this view, identity does not reside in the chair alone; it is not a property of the chair. Identity has to do with how a conscious being picks out a chair and so it refers to *how* that being goes about doing such a thing. *Naming and Necessity* (Cambridge: Harvard University Press, 1972), pp. 52–3.

30 William Charlton, 'apeiron,' in the *Oxford Companion*. See also, G.S. Kirk, J.E. Raven, and M. Schofield, *The Presocratic Philosophers*, 2nd ed. (Cambridge: Cambridge University Press, 1983), pp. 108–22.

31 David Wiggins, 'Flux, Fire and Material Persistence,' in M. Schofield and M. Nussbaum, eds., *Logos and Language* (Cambridge: Cambridge University Press, 1982), p. 7.

32 I am using a simple version of modal logic here – which was not fully developed until the twentieth century. In it, the operator □ (or L) means 'it is necessary that,' and ◊ or (or L) means 'it is possible that.' Add negation (~) to the latter operator and one gets 'it is impossible that.'

33 For the 'complete' Parmenidean fragments, see Kirk et al., *Presocratic Philosophers*, 244–54. Closely associated with Parmenides is Zeno of Elea who devised a number of paradoxes designed to demonstrate that time and space were logically absurd concepts. The most famous concerns the swift runner pursuing a slower one. Before overtaking him, she must close half the distance between them and before she can do that she must close

half of that half and so on. The upshot is that the swift runner never overtakes the slower. Indeed neither of them ever moves because before they can cover a millimetre they must cover half of it ... and so on. Space, in other words, is an infinite series of points that can never be traversed. Therefore, it does not exist – at least not as we understand it. There have been many responses to Zeno's paradoxes. I shall only say that he seems to be talking not about space but about mathematics. Any finite distance can be divided into an infinite number of mathematical points (which, by definition, take up no space) but this is to talk not about space but *the measurement of space*. Aristotle famously took a run at refuting Zeno. For this, see his *Physics*, 239b5–7.

34 See G.E.R. Lloyd, 'Demonstration and the Idea of Science,' in Jacques Brunschwig and G.E.R. Lloyd, eds., *Greek Thought: A Guide to Classical Knowledge* (Cambridge, Mass.: Belknap Press, 2000), pp. 244–5. Lloyd notes that Parmenides 'appeals to what we might call the principle of sufficient reason.' See my remarks about Leibniz, above.

35 Try this: either the senses agree with the findings of reason or they do not. If they do not, they are by definition wrong, because reason has priority. If they do, they are irrelevant because reason has already spoken.

36 Of course, Copernicus's and Einstein's theories required the eventual support of empirical evidence. Indeed, in an interesting inversion of the principle of sufficient reason, one commentator has noted that Einstein built his theories of relativity 'on an extraordinary confidence in the exactitude of the art of experimentation.' In other words, since no experiments had ever managed to isolate the ether through which the earth supposedly moved, and against which its motion could be absolutely measured, he felt compelled to assume that there was no such ether and to redesign physics around that assumption. Hans Reichenbach, *From Copernicus to Einstein* (New York: Dover, 1980), pp. 51–2.

37 E.g., when Leibniz proposed the existence of monads – basic units of matter (and much more) – he deduced that such a 'basic unit' must be indivisible. But any unit of matter is by definition divisible. Hence, the monad must be immaterial! When we consider how in physics matter is convertible into energy, the idea may not seem farfetched.

38 E.g., see Dancy, *Berkeley*, p. 77. Lloyd notes that 'the dichotomy between reason and perception – even for reason to the exclusion of perception – has strong roots ... in the pre-Socratic period.' *The Revolutions of Wisdom* (Berkeley: University of California Press, 1987), p. 271.

39 See Lloyd, *Revolutions*, p. 272.

40 'To save the phenomena' means to fit appearances or 'perceptions' into a

general account of 'reality.' An example is the astronomy of Ptolemy, who accounts for the movement of the planets based on the assumption that the Earth is at the centre of the universe and that the planets (and the sun) move in circular orbits – this being, to his mind, the hallmark of rationality – around it. Since planets actually move in ellipses around the sun, Ptolemy has to create a very complex system of epicycles to make his system work. Yet he manages to do so and thereby to 'save the phenomena' of planetary motion. See Lloyd, ibid., pp. 293–5 and pp. 304–6. For a detailed account of the Ptolemaic system and its Copernican successor, I recommend T.S. Kuhn, *The Copernican Revolution* (Cambridge: Harvard University Press, 1957).

41 In a famous passage from *Phaedrus* (253c–256e), Plato likens the soul to a chariot in which 'reason' is the charioteer attempting to control the horses of desire and spirit. The horse of desire is especially recalcitrant, as if there is something, right in the midst of the human soul, that resists reason with all its might. Julia Annas notes in her short but insightful commentary on this passage and another from *Republic*: 'There is a kind of self-alienation at work here; part of me is regarded as being outside the self proper ... and as being always potentially disobedient to my real self.' *Ancient Philosophy* (Oxford: Oxford University Press, 2000), pp. 8–9.

42 The Milesians, e.g., often expressed their ideas in quasi-theological and anthropomorphic terms. These elements are only gradually excised from Greek science. See Kirk et al., *Presocratic Philosophers*, ch. I, esp. pp. 72–4.

43 The *Meditations* were published in Latin in 1641 and in French in 1647.

44 Descartes published works on a number of scientific topics, including optics, hydrostatics, and corpuscularism. Stephen Gaukroger's excellent biography makes clear the weight that has to be given to this 'side' of Descartes. *Descartes: An Intellectual Biography* (Oxford: Clarendon Press, 1995).

45 Descartes is, of course, a central figure in the development of a modern science based on an outlook quite different from Aristotle's. To that extent, scepticism is an important part of his outlook. For a detailed discussion of these issues, see Dennis Des Chene, *Physiologia* (Ithaca: Cornell University Press, 1996), as well as Gaukroger, *Descartes*. Des Chene argues (p. 2) that Descartes was attempting to construct 'from prime matter upward and from God downward, a functional equivalent to the Aristotelian philosophy of nature.' On Descartes' 'Aristotelian' education, see Gaukroger, *Descartes*, ch. 2, esp. p. 51 and ff.

46 Karl Popper, *Conjectures and Refutations: The Growth of Scientific Knowledge* (London: Routledge and Kegan Paul, 1963), pp. 36–7. Popper argues that

scientific theories must be testable. Each 'successful' test increases the reliability of the theory but no amount of testing can absolutely verify it. Unsuccessful tests can falsify it, however. For a good short explanation, see David Oldroyd, *The Arch of Knowledge* (New York: Methuen, 1986), pp. 300–12.

47 Bernard Williams, 'Descartes' Use of Skepticism,' in Myles Burnyeat, ed., *The Skeptical Tradition* (Berkeley: University of California Press, 1983), p. 344.

48 Although, as Gaukroger points out (*Descartes*, p. 311 and ff.), Descartes' scepticism is less strong than the ancient Pyrrhonistic version. In the *Meditations*, e.g., Descartes' sceptical voice accepts that there *is* something to know: the problem is whether one can ever know it.

49 Part of the problem lies in our understanding of 'certainty.' When the probability that a statement is true is very high, we adopt an attitude of 'moral certainty': simply put, we (justifiably) *feel* certain that the statement is true. But this is not the same as 'epistemic certainty' where there is *no possibility* that the statement is false. Here, we have moved beyond probability to necessity. So, we often 'feel certain' when, strictly speaking, we are not 'absolutely' certain. It is a philosopher's job is to keep an eye out for these kinds of distinctions.

50 Perhaps the most famous example of Descartes erecting barriers between our minds and the world is the 'wax argument' of the *Second Meditation*. It's an intricate passage that rewards careful reading. Not everyone is impressed by Cartesian dualism, however. The English philosopher P.F Strawson has written that 'one of the marks, though not a necessary mark, of a really great philosopher is to make a really great mistake.' In his view, dualism is Descartes' great mistake because it creates a misleading metaphysical picture in which minds and bodies do not quite fit together. What makes it 'great' is that its influence rolls down the ages. 'Self, Mind and Body,' in *Freedom and Resentment and Other Essays* (London: Methuen, 1974), p. 169.

51 See John F. Wippel and Allan B. Wolter, eds., *Medieval Philosophy* (New York: Free Press, 1969), ch. VI.

52 Aquinas (ibid., pp. 335–8) offers four other proofs: (1) Motion in the world demonstrates that there must be a first mover. (2) The chain of causality in the world demonstrates that there must be a first cause. (3) The temporality of beings demonstrates that there must be an infinite eternal being capable of generating them. (4) Gradations of perfection demonstrate that there must be a perfect being.

53 Regarding a vicious circle, see the glossary. Descartes is often accused of

proving the existence of God by assuming that there is a God. (God exists because we have an innate idea of perfection, which God implanted in us.) I am suggesting that, although Descartes proves the existence of the 'self' by assuming it, the original Cartesian 'self' is a mind only whereas the end product is a mind in a body. Hence, it is more accurately an arc than a circle.

54 That is fundamentally what a meditation is: thinking deeply about ideas one already holds to be true.

55 Thomas Nagel, *The View from Nowhere* (Oxford: Oxford University Press, 1986), esp. ch. 1.

56 See John McDowell, 'Singular Thought and the Extent of Inner Space,' in *Meaning, Knowledge and Reality* (Cambridge: Harvard University Press, 1998), p. 240. He argues that Descartes has introduced 'subjectivity into the realm of facts.'

57 Existence is, in other words, ontologically prior to characteristics: a condition of having characteristics. But see Colin McGinn, *Logical Properties* (Oxford: Oxford University Press, 2000).

58 See Immanuel Kant, *The Critique of Pure Reason*, trans. J.M.D. Meiklejohn (London: J.M. Dent, 1934), p. 43 and ff. (part I, s. I, of the Transcendental Doctrine of Elements). See also, S. Körner, *Kant* (Harmondsworth: Penguin, 1955), ch. 2. An intuition is grasped immediately (*spontaneously*, in Kantian language) and is incontrovertible. For Descartes intuitions are innate ideas; for Kant they are our grasp of time and space – i.e., of the external world. For a difficult but rewarding consideration of Kantian spontaneity, see John McDowell, *Mind and World* (Cambridge: Harvard University Press, 1994).

59 This is a *very* simplified version of the intuitions and categories. For an excellent outline of both, see Körner's, *Kant*.

60 Insofar as we focus on Kant's *phenomena* as the product of human psychology – i.e., as the result of the form imposed by the mind – he would seem to be taking an anti-realist stance. But he also appears to think that the categories and intuitions are in some way independent of the perceiver: conditions of experience. I find this difficult to comprehend but it does bring Kant closer to realism. *Noumena* then become, as I have suggested, a mere limit to the *phenomenal*. See *Critique of Pure Reason*, part II, II: III, esp. pp. 186–7. Here, Kant seems to distinguish between a 'positive sense' of *noumena* – the sense of it as a thing-in-itself – and a 'negative sense' as an absolutely empty 'world.' For a good summary of this issue, see Garrett Thomson, *On Kant* (California: Wadsworth, 2000), pp. 24–6.

Carol Rovane has pointed out that a condition of scepticism is that one has beliefs which one recognizes may not be true. Kant's concept of the *phenomenal* world precludes this recognition on a Cartesian scale. Hence, his metaphysics is anti-sceptical: whereas Descartes 'defeats' scepticism, Kant makes it a non-issue. 'The Metaphysics of Interpretation,' in Ernest LePore, ed., *Truth and Interpretation: Essays on the Philosophy of Donald Davidson* (Oxford: Oxford University Press, 1992), pp. 419–20.

61 On these issues, see McGinn, *Mysterious Flame*, ch. 5, esp. pp. 157–8, where he discusses split-brain patients who, to control epilepsy, have had the two hemispheres of their brain surgically separated such that they can no longer communicate with one another. McGinn asks, 'How many selves do these patients have?'

62 In *Critique of Pure Reason* (pp. 218–22), Kant acknowledges his debt to Plato's concept of 'Ideas' (or 'Forms').

63 See ibid., pp. 94–6: 'The *I think* must accompany all my representations, for otherwise something would be represented in me which could not be thought; in other words the representation would either be impossible, or at least be, in relation to me, nothing.' At the end of the passage in which this sentence occurs, Kant writes, 'I am, therefore, conscious of my identical self, in relation to all the variety of representations given to me in an intuition, because I call them all my representations.'

Before Kant, Hume, and after Kant, Nietzsche, rejected the unity of the self on the grounds that our thoughts, desires etc. are fundamentally incoherent. On Nietzsche, see Alexander Nehamas, *Nietzsche: Life as Literature* (Cambridge: Harvard University Press, 1985), p. 180.

64 Iris Murdoch, *Metaphysics as a Guide to Morals* (London: Chatto and Windus, 1992), p. 434.

65 Körner (Kant, p. 124.) suggests that 'far from being harmful this use of the Ideas may have not only great systematic but also great heuristic usefulness.' In short, it serves both an ordering and an interpretative function; it creates an individual and shows how she functions.

66 *Tractatus Logico-Philosophicus*, trans. D.F. Pears and B.F. McGuinness (London: Routledge and kegan Paul, 1961), 6.54. See also Ludwig Wittgenstein, *Culture and Value*, trans. Peter Winch (Chicago: University of Chicago Press, 1980), p 73: 'I might say: if the place I want to get to could only be reached by way of a ladder, I would give up trying to get there. For the place I really have to get to is a place I must already be at now.'

Chapter 3 Wittgenstein's Ladder: The Modern Reaction to Metaphysics

1 See, e.g., Thomas Nagel, *The View from Nowhere* (Oxford: Oxford University Press, 1986), esp. pp. 60–6.

2 Both quotes in *Renewing Philosophy* (Cambridge: Harvard University Press, 1992), p. 123.

3 Stanley Cavell suggests that Wittgenstein's ladder could be like climbing out of Plato's cave, that (if I understand him correctly) both are images for flights from ordinary life into illusions. But in Wittgenstein's image, the point is that one has seen the illusion and metaphysics comes to an end.

4 See Auguste Comte, *Auguste Comte and Positivism: The Essential Writings*, ed. Gertrud Lenzer (New York: Harper Torchbooks, 1975), p. 163. Cora Diamond suggests that since we need our ideas to make the distinctions that we do, we are led to insist that those ideas must point to something beyond us. This seems to apply to Comte's unconscious ontotheology. 'Realism and the Realistic Spirit,' in *The Realistic Spirit* (Cambridge, Mass.: MIT Press, 1991), pp. 49–50.

5 See Martin Heidegger, 'Letter on Humanism,' in *Pathmarks*, ed. William McNeill (Cambridge: Cambridge University Press, 1998), p. 276. Heidegger calls metaphysics 'a name identical to philosophy.'

6 There are also those who are either straddlers or crossover artists. A good example of incorporating both traditions is John McDowell's Hegelian reading of Kant in *Mind and World* (Cambridge: Harvard University Press, 1994). For this reason, among others, McDowell's book has been considered a revolutionary work in analytic circles.

7 See Heidegger, 'On the Essence of Truth,' in *Pathmarks*, pp. 151–2: 'The thinking of Being ... has since Plato been understood as "philosophy" and later received the title "metaphysics."' See also, Jacques Derrida, *Spurs: Nietzsche's Styles*, trans. Barbara Harlow (Chicago: University of Chicago Press, 1979), esp. pp. 109–19.

8 See 'Letter on Humanism,' p. 265.

9 I had better point out that it is debatable whether Plato thought there were Forms for concrete entities such as chairs and horses. He may have meant the concept to apply only to universal terms. As we shall see below, in the *Republic*, Plato applies the idea to beds – although, to be fair, it is hard to say exactly how seriously he intends the application to be taken. At any rate, he does not assume that there are Forms for everything – he exempts mud and dirt, e.g. – and seems to recognize that if there were he would merely have created a Formal world that is the duplicate of this one.

10 Kant famously compares subjectivity – the intuitions and categories of judgment – to coloured spectacles that we cannot take off. If they are blue-tinted, then the world necessarily appears blue. Richard Rorty has suggested that the deconstructionist philosopher Jacques Derrida – from whom I adopted the idea of 'presences' – is a committed anti-Kantian who is trying to show us what the world would look like if we took off these spectacles. 'Philosophy as a Kind of Writing: An Essay on Derrida,' in

Consequences of Pragmatism (Minneapolis: University of Minnesota Press, 1982), p. 98.

11 Readers may usefully compare Kant's views to Stephen Hawking's comments on the weak and strong 'anthropic principles,' which assert that intelligent beings will only exist in organized environments that can support them. There will necessarily be a fit between such beings and their surroundings. Kant uses the concept of regulative ideas to assert something like this, although he is perhaps looking through the other end of the telescope. His point is that rational beings will perceive only the world rational beings are capable of perceiving. *A Brief History of Time* (Toronto: Bantam, 1988), pp. 124–5.

12 An empiricist and sceptic, David Hume rejected the idea that one could move from experience to the demonstration of transcendental ideas. This is the 'naturalistic fallacy.' *Treatise of Human Nature* III, part I, s. III.

13 From *idion*, the ancient Greek word for 'private,' 'idiocy' bears the connotation of isolation or deprivation, from which the more common pejorative meaning is derived.

14 For the myth of the charioteer, see *Phaedrus* 246a–249d; on Cronos and Zeus and the tiller of the cosmos, see *Statesman* 269a–270b; on the Demiurge, see *Timaeus* 27c and ff.

15 See Iris Murdoch, *The Fire and the Sun* (Oxford: Oxford University Press, 1977), pp. 5–6. On Plato's use of painting as an analogy for poetry, see Alexander Nehamas, *Virtues of Authenticity* (Princeton: Princeton University Press, 1999), p. 251.

16 Roger Scruton, *Modern Philosophy: An Introduction and Survey* (London: Mandarin Paperbacks, 1996), p. 261.

17 Friedrich Nietzsche, *The Will to Power*, trans. Walter Kaufmann (New York: Random House, 1967), p. 608.

18 Richard Rorty, 'Solidarity or Objectivity?' in *Philosophical Papers*, vol. 1, *Objectivity, Relativism And Truth* (Cambridge: Cambridge University Press, 1991), p. 32.

19 Stanley Rosen, 'Remarks on Nietzsche's "Platonism,"' in *The Quarrel between Philosophy and Poetry* (London: Routledge, 1993), p. 187.

20 Stanley Rosen, 'Poetic Thinking in Nietzsche,' in *The Ancients and the Moderns* (New Haven: Yale University Press, 1989), p. 213.

21 Friedrich Nietzsche, *The Twilight of the Idols*, in *The Twilight of the Idols and the Anti-Christ*, trans. R.J. Hollingdale (Harmondsworth: Penguin, 1968), 'Reason in Philosophy,' 1–6, pp. 35–9.

22 Gilles Deleuze, *Nietzsche and Philosophy*, trans. Hugh Tomlinson (New York: Columbia University Press, 1983), p. 102.

23 *Twilight of the Idols*, 'How the Real World Became a Myth,' pp. 40–1.
24 See Friedrich Nietzsche, *Thus Spoke Zarathustra*, trans. R.J. Hollingdale (Harmondsworth: Penguin, 1969).
25 Friedrich Nietzsche, *Human All Too Human*, trans. R.J. Hollingdale (Cambridge: Cambridge University Press, 1996), s. 18.
26 J.P. Sartre, *Existentialism and Humanism*, trans. Philip Mairet (London: Eyre-Methuen, 1973), p. 23.
27 Regarding 'teleology,' see the Glossary of Terms. Sartre argues that while artefacts are teleologically determined by their makers, the same is not true for human lives. We are what we choose to be.
28 Michel Foucault, 'Nietzsche, Genealogy, History,' in *Language, Counter-memory, Practice* (Ithaca, NY: Cornell University Press, 1977), p. 142.
29 See above, pp. 21–2.
30 See note 62, Chapter 1.
31 Richard Rorty, 'The Pragmatist's Progress,' in Jonathan Culler (ed.), *Interpretation and Overinterpretation* (Cambridge: Cambridge University Press, 1992), p. 105. Since this description runs counter to our common intuitions about reading, I will point out that it crops up in all sorts of ways in twentieth-century philosophy. Gilles Deleuze and Félix Guattari, e.g., contend that 'reading a text is never a scholarly exercise in search of what is signified.' Rather, it is 'a schizoid exercise' of a 'desiring-machine,' a half-mad attempt to wrench from the text what we want or need. *Anti-Oedipus* (New York: Viking Press, 1977), p. 106. In her exposition of Derrida, Christina Howells castigates philosophers for reading him 'hastily and latch[ing] on to what they imagine is being argued ... because they are more interested in their own arguments than in the correctness of their reading of others.' *Derrida* (Cambridge: Polity Press, 1999), p. 71. Rorty seems to be suggesting that subjective reading just is the nature of reading. Deleuze and Guattari inject a note of madness into this subjectivity, and Howells simply finds it unforgivably sloppy. Still, Rorty's question can be asked of Howells: insofar as Derrida challenges the very idea of an original meaning in a text, just when is a particular reading of Derrida a misreading?
32 Similarly, the French philosopher Paul Ricoeur argues for the 'semantic autonomy' of the text, noting that its 'career escapes the finite horizon lived by its author ... It is part of the meaning of a text to be open to an indefinite numbers of readers, therefore, of interpretations. This opportunity for multiple readings is the dialectical counterpart of the semantic autonomy of the text.' *Interpretation Theory: Discourse and the Surplus of Meaning* (Fort Worth: Texas Christian University Press, 1976), pp. 29–32.
33 *Writing and Difference*, trans. Alan Bass (Chicago: University of Chicago Press, 1978), p. 82.

34 Jacques Derrida, 'Plato's Pharmacy,' in *Dissemination*, trans. Barbara Johnson (Chicago: University of Chicago Press, 1981), pp. 65–71. He is referring to *Phaedrus* 274c–275e. At 275d, Socrates says: 'You know, Phaedrus, that's the strangest thing about writing, which makes it truly analogous to painting. The painter's products stand before us as though they were alive, but if you question them they maintain a most majestic silence. It is the same thing with written words; they seem to talk to you as though they were intelligent, but if you ask them anything about what they say, from a desire to be instructed, they go on telling you the same thing forever.' Socrates then suggests, however, that some people are qualified to understand words, whereas others are not.

35 Jorge Luis Borges, 'Tlön, Uqbar Tertius,' in *Labyrinths: Selected Short Stories and Other Writings* (New York: New Directions, 1962), p. 13.

36 Rorty, 'Inquiry as Recontextualization,' in *Philosophical Papers*, vol. 1, p. 96.

37 Rorty, 'Texts and Lumps' in ibid., p. 82.

38 *Metaphysics as a Guide to Morals* (London: Chatto and Windus, 1992), p. 196.

39 Umberto Eco, 'Interpretation and History,' in *Interpretation and Overinterpretation*, p. 39.

40 I recommend Borges's 'Library of Babel,' in *Labyrinths*.

41 Jürgen Habermas, *The Philosophical Discourse of Modernity*, trans. Frederick G. Lawrence (Boston: MIT Press, 1987), pp. 190–9. On p. 189, he also rejects the Derridean contention that the philosophical text is '*in truth* a literary one,' as failing to respect a 'genre-distinction.'

42 *Interpretation and Overinterpretation*, p. 52.

43 Richard Rorty, *Contingency, Irony and Solidarity* (Cambridge: Cambridge University Press, 1989), p. 73.

44 Alexander Nehamas, *The Art of Living* (Berkeley: University of California Press, 2000), p. 86.

45 Christopher Norris, *The Deconstructive Turn* (London: Methuen, 1983), p. 42.

46 These ideas will be considered in more detail in Chapter 7. References will be supplied there.

47 Even ostensive definitions require a great deal of abstraction on the part of the person who is learning them. One has to look at a few chairs, e.g., and then extend the term to all chairs. For a difficult but exhaustive analytic consideration of how we manage to refer to the world see Gareth Evans, *The Varieties of Reference*, ed. John McDowell (Oxford: Clarendon Press, 1982).

48 See Rudolf Carnap, 'Overcoming Metaphysics,' in Michael Murray, ed., *Heidegger and Modern Philosophy* (New Haven: Yale University Press, 1978), pp. 32–3.

49 See Habermas, *Philosophical Discourse*, pp. 185–210.

50 *Thus Spoke Zarathustra*, part I, 'Zarathustra's Prologue,' s. 6.

Chapter 4 Epistemology: The Ghost in the Metaphysical Machine?

1 Charles Taylor, 'Overcoming Epistemology,' in *Philosophical Arguments* (Cambridge: Harvard University Press, 1995), p. 1.

2 Edward Hussey, 'The Beginnings of Epistemology: From Homer to Philolaus,' in Stephen Everson, ed., *Epistemology* (Cambridge: Cambridge University Press, 1990), pp. 12–19.

3 Ibid., p. 28. See also, G.S. Kirk, J.E. Raven and M. Schofield, *The Presocratic Philosophers*, 2nd ed. (Cambridge: Cambridge University Press, 1983), p. 180.

4 See Julia Annas and Jonathan Barnes, *The Modes of Scepticism* (Cambridge: Cambridge University Press, 1985), chs. 1 and 2.

5 See Thomas Nagel's warning against overplaying this opposition in his *The Last Word* (Oxford: Oxford University Press, 1997), p. 22.

6 Strictly speaking, non-subjective foundations could be proposed. If one rejects the sceptical aspect of the 'appearance and reality' opposition – as Aristotle does – then the subjective problem of how the mind's ideas relate to reality is very much less of a problem. The mind is in the world and its ideas just are trustworthy.

7 Regarding representing reality, see Richard Rorty, *Philosophy and the Mirror of Nature* (Princeton: Princeton University Press, 1979), p. 2.

8 I am not satisfied with the rather ugly 'disengaged' but it captures the image of a 'knower' who is a self-sufficient entity prior to her involvement with the world. Her mind is therefore a unique and distinct object of investigation – a transcendental ego.

9 Deductive reasoning will be outlined in Chapter 5. See also, Glossary of Terms.

10 Of course, if we say that humans are *by definition* mortal, no one who turns out to be immortal can be counted as human. A more serious point is William of Ockham's: we cannot infinitely extend the reference of a term to cover all beings that might, in the future, fall under its definition.

11 The *elenchos* is the core of the Socratic method. Socrates elicits from someone a definition of a concept and then proceeds, through questioning, to show that it is inconsistent, either in its own terms or in relation to some other idea that the discussant holds to be true. This demonstrates that the beleaguered interlocutor doesn't know what he claims to know.

12 Plato's dialogues are traditionally divided into early, middle, and late

periods. Although the exact order in which they were written is uncertain, the ones in which the Forms appear are generally considered to be from the middle period.

13 John Locke, *An Essay Concerning Human Understanding* (New York: Dover, 1959) vol. 1, I: III, s. 18, p. 106. Reprint of the A.C. Fraser edition, 1894; original published in 1690. On the ancient empiricists, see Annas and Barnes, *Modes of Scepticism*.

14 See Charles Taylor, 'Foundationalism and the Inner-Outer Distinction,' in Nicholas H. Smith, ed., *Reading McDowell* (London: Routledge, 2002), p. 110.

15 See Rorty, *Philosophy*, pp. 3–4.

16 The Stoics essentially reduced the human soul to the *hegemonikon* or rational ('leading') part of the soul. As A.A. Long explains: 'There is no ego or subject over and above the *hegemonikon*, no place for a self that has separate, quasi-Platonic constituents, a desiring part and a cognitive part. The *hegemonikon* provides the Stoics with a unitary self, actively engaged as a whole in all moments of an animal's experience.' 'Representation and the Self in Stoicism,' in Stephen Everson, ed., *Companions to Ancient Thought: Psychology* (Cambridge: Cambridge University Press, 1990), p. 107.

17 This example is from Descartes' *First Meditation*.

18 See Lisa Jardine, 'Lorenzo Valla: Academic Scepticism and the New Humanist Dialectic,' in Myles Burnyeat, ed., *The Skeptical Tradition* (Berkeley: University of California Press, 1983), p. 259.

19 See II: II, s. II of the 'Transcendental Logic,' in *The Critique of Pure Reason*, trans. by J.M.D. Meiklejohn (London: J.M. Dent, 1934). Kant delineates four 'transcendental ideas' that lead to contradictory theses that cannot be resolved. The fourth of these 'antinomies' consists in the contradictory pair of theses that (a) 'there exists either in, or in connection with the world – either as a part of it, or as the cause of it – an absolutely necessary being' (i.e., God) and that (b) 'an absolutely necessary being does not exist, either in the world or out of it – as its cause.'

20 The nub of Berkeley's criticism of Locke's empiricism is that it is a prejudice to assume that one's ideas are necessarily caused by objects in a physical external world.

21 *Language, Truth and Logic* (London: Penguin, 1971), p. 13. See Chapter 3, note 49, above.

22 Ibid., p. 16.

23 The logical positivists have different ideas about realism and the correspondence theory. Some, like Ayer, tend towards phenomenalism and are not very concerned with the 'external object'; others have moved away

from the correspondence theory towards something more akin to the coherence theory outlined below.

24 Berkeley uses phenomenalism to muster an argument against the existence of the physical world, but Ayer's point is that to be that there is no need (or way) to move beyond the analysis of objects as collections of sense-data.

25 Locke, *Essay*, vol. 1, II: IX, s. 9, p. 188. In the *Third Meditation*, Descartes warns against the 'spontaneous impulse' to believe what nature apparently teaches us.

26 René Descartes, 'Rules for the Direction of the Mind,' in *Philosophical Essays*, trans. Laurence J. Lafleur (New York: Bobbs-Merrill, 1964), Rule IV, p. 157.

27 David Hume, 'An Enquiry Concerning Human Understanding,' in *Hume's Enquiries*, ed. L.A. Selby-Bigge, 2nd ed. (Oxford: Clarendon Press, 1966), s. IV, pp. 25–39.

28 See Immanuel Kant, *Prolegomena to Any Future Metaphysics* (New York: Bobbs-Merrill, 1950), 'Preamble on the Peculiarities of All Metaphysical Cognition.'

29 For a famous revision of Kant's position, see Saul Kripke, *Naming and Necessity* (Cambridge: Harvard University Press, 1972), esp. Lecture 3. For an attack on the distinction between 'analytic' and 'synthetic,' see W.V. Quine, 'Two Dogmas of Empiricism,' in *From a Logical Point of View* (New York: Harper Torchbooks, 1963).

30 See *Prolegomena*, s. 20, and *Critique of Pure Reason*, Introduction, V.

31 But see Saul Kripke's ingenious (and debatable) argument regarding 'quus.' *Wittgenstein on Rules and Private Language* (Cambridge: Harvard University Press, 1982), ch. 2.

32 Rorty includes Kant among the 'inferentialist' philosophers, whom he contrasts with 'representationalists.' The latter see concepts as copies of the world whereas the former see them as rules of procedure. 'Introduction' to Wilfrid Sellars, *Empiricism and the Philosophy of Mind* (Cambridge: Harvard University Press, 1997), p. 9.

33 Putnam adheres to what he calls 'natural realism' as opposed to 'direct realism' or 'representational realism.' He holds that we are in touch with *certain aspects* of reality (perhaps ones dictated by interest or culture) and can therefore develop very different, but equally legitimate, accounts of it. *The Threefold Cord: Mind, Body, and World* (New York: Columbia University Press, 1999), Lecture 1. Putnam's also tells us that 'naturalism, is, to be sure, an extremely fuzzy label, covering a wide variety of metaphysical

and epistemological positions.' 'McDowell's Mind and McDowell's World,' in Smith, *Reading McDowell*, pp. 185–6.

34 *Renewing Philosophy* (Cambridge: Harvard University Press, 1992), p. 58.

35 *Empiricism*, esp. pp. 18–20. For McDowell, see his *Mind and World* (Cambridge: Cambridge University Press, 1994). ·

36 Thomas G. Pavel, *The Spell of Language* (Chicago: University of Chicago Press, 1989), p. 63.

37 Thomas S. Kuhn, *The Structure of Scientific Revolutions*, 2nd ed., enlarged (Chicago: University of Chicago Press, 1970), p. 206.

38 *Philosophy*, p. 371.

39 'Overcoming Epistemology,' p. 11.

40 Charles Taylor, 'Heidegger and Wittgenstein,' in *Philosophical Arguments*, p. 64.

41 *Essay*, I: I, s. 15.

42 See note 27, Chapter 3, above.

43 Hubert L. Dreyfus and Paul Rabinow, *Michel Foucault: Beyond Structuralism and Hermeneutics*, 2nd ed. (Chicago: University of Chicago Press, 1982), p. 204.

44 William James, *Pragmatism* (New York: American Library, 1974), pp. 132–3. James distinguishes his pragmatism from a foundationalist rationalism as follows: 'For rationalism reality is ready-made and complete for all eternity, while for pragmatism it is still in the making, and awaits part of its complexion from the future. On the one side the universe is absolutely secure, on the other it is still pursuing its adventures (ibid., p. 167). See also John Dewey, *Reconstruction in Philosophy*, enlarged ed. (Boston: Beacon Press, 1957), p. 156: 'If ideas, meanings, conceptions, notions, theories, systems are instrumental to our active recognition of the given environment, to a removal of some specific trouble and perplexity, then the test of their validity and value lies in accomplishing this work. If they succeed in their office, they are reliable, sound, valid, good and true.'

45 In the *Tractatus*, Wittgenstein argues that one can map language onto the world in the way one can project a map onto a city or a score of music onto a set of sounds. *Tractatus Logico-Philosophicus*, trans. D.F. Pears and B.F. McGuiness (London: Routlege and Kegan Paul, 1961).

46 Ludwig Wittgenstein, *On Certainty*, ed. G.E.M. Anscombe and G.H. von Wright, trans. G.E.M. Anscombe (Oxford: Basil Blackwell, 1969), esp. nos. 23–41, and *Philosophical Investigations*, trans. G.E.M. Anscombe (Oxford: Basil Blackwell, 1978), ss. 247–58.

47 *Wittgenstein*, p. 50.

48 I shall return to this example in Chapter 7. Here, I want to note Crispin Wright's characterization of this situation. He terms of statements such as 'I am in pain,' 'phenomenal avowals.' They have, he says, three characteristics: first, they are 'groundless,' which is to say, a request for 'corroborating evidence ... is always inappropriate.' Second, they are 'strongly authoritative,' in that they can be wrong only if the speaker is dissembling. In other words, one's doubts are not about the pain but about the sincerity of the speaker. Third, they 'exhibit a kind of *transparency*,' such that it would be absurd for the speaker to express doubt about her claim. The question I have raised is whether statements of this type fall under the rubric of knowledge or, more precisely, self-knowledge. I have suggested that they do not; that this sort of privileged – because non-inferential access – to a mind-state is not so much 'groundless' as 'deeply grounded': ontological rather than epistemological. 'The Problem of Self-Knowledge (I),' in *Rails to Infinity* (Cambridge: Harvard University Press, 2001), esp. pp. 320–1.

49 As Kripke points out (*Wittgenstein*, p. 100) we rely on the expression being uttered in the 'appropriate behavioural and external circumstances.' In his postscript, 'Wittgenstein and Other Minds,' he also notes how strange the ascription of pain (or any mental state) to another person can seem. My student who asks me how I know another student is in pain is in a sense recognizing the sceptical problem of how I know such a thing. What I see is behaviour from which I infer pain because I assume *analogically* that the student is a being *like me*. As Kripke says, this last assumption is central to the human community. I react as I do because I see the student as a person like me. He writes, 'We do not pity others because we attribute pain to them, we attribute pain to others because we pity them' (ibid., p. 142).

50 I am not attributing to Wittgenstein Russell's concept of *knowledge by acquaintance*. Russell argues that we know some things – such as perceptions – just because we are directly in touch with them. This is opposed to 'knowledge by description' which is built up through inference. Russell calls the former 'knowledge of things,' the latter 'knowledge of truths' – which I think makes it linguistic (knowing whether certain sentences are true or false). My point is that Wittgenstein does not seem to consider knowledge by acquaintance as knowledge but as something prior to knowledge. Hence, I call it a 'primitive state.' *The Problems of Philosophy* (Oxford: Oxford University Press, 1967), pp. 62–3.

51 Consider the question, 'How do you know she is X?' where X = a name. If 'she' is someone I have never met, it's a reasonable question, but if someone knowingly asks it in reference to my wife, say, it would be a very

strange question and would require extraordinary circumstances to make it a reasonable one.

52 Michel Foucault, 'The Subject and Power,' Afterword to *Dreyfus, Michel Foucault, and Rabinow*, p. 210.

53 See Barry Stroud, *The Significance of Philosophical Scepticism* (Oxford: Clarendon Press, 1984), esp. ch. 2. His discussion of J.L. Austin's 'Other Minds' is particularly to the point.

54 W.V. Quine, 'On What There Is,' in *From a Logical Point of View*, pp. 18–19, and *Quiddities* (Cambridge, Mass.: Belknap Press, 1987), entry on 'Truth.'

55 'Two Dogmas,' p. 37. This is one of the dogmas; the other is the validity of the analytic-synthetic distinction. See also W.V. Quine, *The Roots of Reference* (La Salle, Ill.: Open Court, 1974), p. 38: 'Most sentences do not admit separately of observational evidence. Sentences interlock.'

56 See George D. Romanos, *Quine and Analytic Philosophy* (Cambridge, Mass.: MIT Press, 1983), Chapter 4, esp. p. 97.

57 See Sybil Wolfram's entry on the 'Coherence Theory of Truth,' in Ted Honderich, ed., *The Oxford Companion to Philosophy* (Oxford: Oxford University Press, 1995).

58 Peter Strawson argues that facts are linguistic creations – sentence-shaped objects – that do not really exist. See also J.L. Austin's reply in 'Unfair to Facts,' in his *Philosophical Papers*, 2nd ed. (Oxford: Oxford University Press, 1970).

59 This point will be fully explained in Chapter 5.

60 Richard Rorty, 'Introduction,' in *Philosophical Papers*, vol. 2, *Essays on Heidegger and Others* (Cambridge: Cambridge University Press, 1991), p. 3.

61 See Rorty, *Contingency, Irony and Solidarity* (Cambridge: Cambridge University Press, 1989), p. 73.

62 Ibid., p. 8. It is worth noting Derrida's comment here, that 'metaphor is never innocent.' *Writing and Difference*, trans. Alan Bass (Chicago: University of Chicago Press, 1978), p. 17.

63 Rorty, *Contingency*, p. 20.

64 Quentin Skinner, *The Foundations of Modern Political Thought* (Cambridge: Cambridge University Press, 1978), vol. 1, p. 7. I am not suggesting that what follows is Skinner's view of the matter. Interested readers may also consult his *Liberty before Liberalism* (Cambridge: Cambridge University Press, 1998).

65 Ludwig Wittgenstein, 'The Blue Book,' in *The Blue and Brown Books* (New York: Harper Books, 1965), p. 55.

66 Ludwig Wittgenstein, *Philosophical Investigations*, trans. G.E.M. Anscombe (Oxford: Basil Blackwell, 1978), part II, s. xi. See also, Stephen Mulhall, *On*

Being in the World: Wittgenstein and Heidegger on Seeing Aspects (London: Routledge, 1993).

67 Michel Foucault, *The Archaeology of Knowledge*, trans. A.M. Sheridan Smith (London: Tavistock, 1972).

68 Hegel set human existence within history but he argued that history was imbued with a 'world-spirit' that moved inexorably towards a teleologically determined end. We might say that his history took place within History.

69 *The Art of Living* (Berkeley: University of California Press, 1998), pp. 145–9.

70 The science of Galileo and Newton emphasized quantity – measurement of masses and forces – in contrast to the qualitative science of the medieval Aristotelians. Descartes' foundationalism is an attempt to provide a logical basis for this science. The correspondence theory of truth reflects the determination of modern scientists to match their theories up with the world in a strict and measurable way. Pre-modern science was less occupied with these concerns and accordingly its epistemology was different. See Denis Des Chene, *Physiologia* (Ithaca: Cornell University Press, 1996). For an excellent short summary of medieval Aristotelian science, see Marcia Colish, *Medieval Foundations of the Western Intellectual Tradition* (New Haven: Yale University Press, 1997), ch. 24.

71 C.C.W. Taylor, 'Aristotle's Epistemology,' in Everson, *Epistemology*, p. 142.

72 Charles Taylor, 'The Validity of Transcendental Arguments,' in *Philosophical Arguments*, p. 31.

73 On this matter, I direct readers towards the work of David Chalmers, Paul Churchland, Jerry Fodor, and Colin McGinn.

74 In *The Mysterious Flame* (Oxford: Oxford University Press, 1977).

Chapter 5 Logic and Its Place in the Universe

1 Friedrich Nietzsche, *The Birth of Tragedy*, in *The Birth of Tragedy and the Genealogy of Morals*, trans. Francis Golfing (New York: Anchor Books, 1956), esp. ss. I–XII.

2 *Apology* 20d–23b.

3 *Birth of Tragedy*, s I, p. 21.

4 Ibid., s. VI, esp. p. 26.

5 On Plato and the Pythagoreans, see G.S. Kirk, J.E. Raven, and M. Schofield, *The Presocratic Philosophers*, 2nd ed. (Cambridge: Cambridge University Press, 1983), pp. 214–15. On the Pythagoreans and music, pp. 232–35.

6 On Plato and mathematics, see Gregory Vlastos, 'Elenchus and Mathemat-

ics: A Turning Point in Plato's Development,' in Hugh. H. Benson, ed., *Essays on the Philosophy of Socrates* (Oxford: Oxford University Press, 1992).

7 *Birth of Tragedy*, s. VI, p. 46.

8 *The Twilight of the Idols*, in *The Twilight of the Idols and the Anti-Christ*, trans. R.J. Hollingdale (Harmondsworth: Penguin, 1968), p. 33.

9 In his magisterial work of political philosophy, *The Spirit of the Laws*, the Baron de Montesquieu (1689–1755) distinguishes between the nature of governments (its structure of laws) and the principle which animates them – which he calls the spirit of the laws. Each form of government had its own animating principle: democracy had virtue, aristocracy had moderation, and monarchy had honour. Without these principles the various forms of government were empty shells awaiting corruption. Nietzsche's criticism of the rationalist tradition in philosophy is that it is, in a similar fashion, an empty shell of reason (or logic) bereft of the animating spirit of music – i.e., Apollo without Dionysus. *The Spirit of the Laws*, trans. Thomas Nugent (New York: Hafner, 1949), esp. III. Original published in 1748.

10 *Tractatus Logico-Philosophicus*, trans. D.F. Pears and B.F. McGuiness (London: Routledge and Kegan Paul, 1961) 3.031. See also, 3.03.

11 See, e.g., *Apology* 17–18a.

12 There is no general agreement as to what these 'laws' pertain to: are they laws of the mind, of nature, or simply of bivalent logic? In the last instance, they are more like rules for a game than scientific laws.

13 There is a very interesting process of abstraction going on here. A child who is taught what a chair is in this fashion will go on to apply the term to a host of other chairs that do not look much like the original 'paradigm' chair.

14 For Plato, though, it might well be a copy of Beauty. In the reverse direction, to say that it is 'not literally beauty' may be a piece of strident realism.

15 As we have seen, the Wittgenstein of the *Tractatus* thinks such statements are pseudo-propositions that lack truth-values. In the *Philosophical Investigations* Wittgenstein pretty much gives up on the idea of truth as correct reference. Trans. G.E.M. Anscombe (Oxford: Basil Blackwell, 1978).

16 Robert Brandom, *Articulating Reasons* (Cambridge: Harvard University Press, 200), ch. 3, s. 7, esp. pp. 118–19.

17 W.V. Quine, *Ontological Relativity and Other Essays* (New York: Columbia University Press, 1969), 55. He adds, 'Identity is thus of a piece with ontology.'

18 There is a more complicated version of this puzzle, in which there are twelve coins and – still – only three weighings to isolate the lighter or

heavier one. Interested readers may want to have a go at it. Appendix 1 gives a solution.

19 Tautologically, we can state this as 'the first 5,000' or 'not the first 5,000.'

20 As I understand it, the odds will come infinitely close to 37.5 per cent without ever quite getting there.

21 Truth tables establish the truth conditions of compound propositions based on the truth-values of elementary ones. Take any two elementary propositions p and q. They yield the following four possibilities:

p	q
T	T
T	F
F	T
F	F

Now take the logical constants that join these propositions to make compound ones: '.' = and (conjunction); 'v' = either ... or (disjunction); '→' = if ... then (conditional) and '↔' = 'if and only if' (biconditional). When we write these out along the top line, we can then fill in the truth conditions for each arrangement of the elementary propositions:

p	q	(p · q)	(p v q)	(p → q)	(p ↔ q)
T	T	T	T	T	T
T	F	F	T	F	F
F	T	F	T	T	F
F	F	F	F	T	T

What this shows is that a conjunction is true only if both (or all) elementary propositions are true, a disjunction is false only if both (or all) elementary propositions are false, and so on.

22 We can generalize this by saying that one can only measure precisely quantities that have precise definitions or calibrations. See Appendix 1, on the Paradox of the Heap.

23 In its simplest form, the Liar's Paradox is the sentence, 'I am lying.' If it is true, then you are lying – in which case it is false. But if it is false then you are lying – in which case it is true. The problem is that this paradox has no reference. When we lie, we lie *about* something and if we add in that something here the paradox disappears. If, e.g., I say 'It's Monday' and then add, 'I am lying' the second statement is true if it is any day other than Monday and false if it is in fact Monday. The original form of the paradox, however, seems to have come from a Cretan by the name of Epimenides, who said, 'All Cretans are liars' and in this form it holds up.

In the 'I always lie' version, if the statement is true then the person is lying, so it is false. If it is false, then all it means is that the person does not always lie and that is not contradictory, merely false. So it is half a paradox. Set theory is then necessary to make sense of the utterance although a person of good sense might simply conclude that the speaker is exaggerating.

24 I owe this point to my brother, Professor Jerald Lawless, who is a statistician and generally talks above my head.

25 See Bertrand Russell, *Our Knowledge of the External World* (London: Allen and Unwin, 1922), p. 54: 'In logic, it is a waste of time to deal with inferences concerning particular cases; we deal throughout with completely general and purely formal implications, leaving it to other sciences to discover when hypotheses are verified and when they are not.'

26 'An Enquiry Concerning Human Understanding,' in *Hume's Enquiries*, ed. L.A. Selby-Bigge, 2nd ed. (Oxford: Clarendon Press, 1966), s. IV, part I.

27 Sentential or propositional logic employs 'logical constants' (see note 21) to connect sentences (or propositions). Categorical and predicate logic employ the quantifiers 'all,' 'some,' and 'none,' attaching them (in various ways) to subjects which are then applied to predicates. See logical constants, existential and universal quantifiers, and modal logic in the Glossary of Terms.

28 Counter-factual conditionals are particularly interesting. These are cases in which the first term of the hypotheticalal proposition (the 'antecedent'), which is the condition of the second (the 'consequent') is manifestly false. Imagine a statement describing a situation that never existed and ask yourself how it might be true or false. If, for example, I say, 'If I were a wealthy man I'd give you all my money,' then since I am very definitely not a wealthy man, the condition upon which I would give you my money does not exist. Since, in bivalent logic, all propositions have to be true or false, this presents a problem. To assign a truth-value is necessary either to reduce 'true' to 'false' (i.e., true = not-false) or 'false' to 'true' (i.e., false = not-true). In logic, we do the former and define a false conditional as one in which the antecedent is true (the condition holds) and the consequent is false (the stated consequence does not follow). In all other circumstances, the conditional proposition is obviously not false so it is true!

29 This describes terms that can be transferred in one direction among subjects. One example is 'is taller than.' If Cordelia is taller than Ophelia and Ophelia is taller than Desdemona then Cordelia is taller than Desdemona.

30 See *Meno* 81e–84b.

31 See note 27.

32 'Enquiry,' ss. IV–VI.

33 See Socrates' description of rhetoric, the art of the Sophists, at *Gorgias* 462b and ff.

34 The point is that we can be persuaded by the truth if we recognize it as such but we can also be persuaded by what is false. As to whether truth or persuasion is more important to us, Nietzsche is in no doubt. In *Twilight of the Idols* ('The Four Great Errors,' s. 5, p. 51), he writes that the first principle of psychological explanation is that 'any explanation is better than none. Because it is at bottom only a question of wanting to get rid of oppressive ideas, one is not exactly particular about what means one uses to get rid of them: the first idea which explains that the unknown is in fact the known does so much good that one holds it for true.'

35 See Stephen Gaukroger, *Descartes: An Intellectual Biography* (Oxford: Clarendon Press, 1995), pp. 115–24.

36 Plato's Allegory of the Cave shows how important education is in deciding whether an image will be persuasive. One of the goals of his *paideia* seems to be to make strong images weak (turn them into shadows) and weak ones (abstract ideas which are hard to grasp) strong.

37 I suggested in Chapter 2 that we cannot know whether those hands belong to those who know the truth or simply to those who have power over the prisoners in the cave.

38 *Tractatus*, 6.54.

39 Thomas Kuhn defines paradigms as 'the entire constellation of beliefs, values., techniques, and so on shared by members of a given community.' He also employs a second usage of them as models for 'concrete puzzle solutions,' which is, in a sense, what reading is. *The Structure of Scientific Revolutions*, 3rd ed. (Chicago: University of Chicago Press, 1996), p. 175.

40 I am not convinced, in the manner of some deconstructionists, that there is always a variety of possible readings for a text. Sometimes, only one reading seems plausible. The reason may be, however, that our metaphysical world is so persuasive that we cannot imagine another reading. Restating in less deconstructive or radically naturalist language: it may be because the meaning/intention of the text/author is clear.

41 For a difficult but thorough exegesis of Hegel's logic, see Charles Taylor, *Hegel* (Cambridge: Cambridge University Press, 1975), esp. chs. IX and X. Certainly Hegel has influenced British and North American philosophers so this division is rough but not, I think, misleading.

42 Stanley Cavell, *A Pitch of Philosophy* (Cambridge: Harvard University Press, 1994), p. 42.

43 See Christina Howells, *Derrida* (Cambridge: Polity Press, 1998), pp. 2–3. Many of Derrida's works include textual analyses of other writers (in the

way that Socrates closely examines his interlocutors). This is a context in which a bivalent logic of contradiction can be deployed, but it is worth noting Thomas Nagel's reminder: 'However reasonable it may be to entertain doubts as to the validity of some of what one does under the heading of reasoning, such doubts cannot avoid involving some form of reasoning themselves.' *The Last Word* (Oxford: University of Oxford Press, 1997), p. 61.

44 See Howells, *Derrida*, pp. 36–7. Howell's statement of Derrida's position is that 'we have no language free from metaphysical presuppositions and are bound to use the very terms, concepts and logic we are contesting.'

45 W.V. Quine, *Word and Object* (Cambridge, Mass.: MIT Press, 1960), p. 275.

46 See, e.g., Heidegger's 'Letter on Humanism,' in William McNeill, ed., *Pathmarks* (Cambridge: Cambridge University Press, 1998), p. 265, where he asserts that 'meditation on being itself ... [which] alone reaches the primordial essence of *logos* ... [was] already obfuscated and lost in Plato and Aristotle, the founder of logic.'

47 Rorty might argue that we can reject a metaphor 'as' wrong on the pragmatic ground that it has gone out of fashion or has in some other way ceased to be relevant. See, e.g., 'Hilary Putnam and the Relativist Menace,' in *Philosophical Papers*, vol. 3, *Truth and Progress* (Chicago: University of Chicago Press, 1998), pp. 54–62.

48 Recall that we have two portraits of Socrates: Plato's and Xenophon's. Plato's is the more literary portrait; a better writer has produced a more subtle character, though perhaps not a 'truer' portrait. I direct readers to Alexander Nehamas's insightful *The Art of Living* (Berkeley: University of California Press, 1998), Part 1. On Socrates behind Plato, see Derrida's witty reversal of this relationship in *The Post Card: From Socrates to Freud and Beyond*, trans. Alan Bass (Chicago: University of Chicago Press, 1987), p. 14 and ff.

49 But see Nehamas's comments concerning Socrates' silence in *The Art of Living* and in particular his quotation of Kierkegaard's view as expressed in *The Concept of Irony with Continual Reference to Socrates*: 'What Socrates prized so highly, namely, standing still and contemplating – in other words, silence – this is his whole life in terms of world history. He has left nothing by which a later age can judge him' (ibid., p. 70).

50 Hilary Putnam, *Realism with a Human Face* (Cambridge: Harvard University Press, 1990), p. 20.

51 Ludwig Wittgenstein, *Zettel*, ed. G.E.M. Anscombe and G.H. von Wright, trans. Anscombe (Los Angeles: University of California Press, 1970), no. 314.

Chapter 6 Ethics: The Good, the Bad, and the Beautiful

1 That is, a philosopher of Aristotle's school, probably so named because the Lyceum (gymnasium) at which it was located had a covered parapet, or walkway, attached to it. I prefer the story that the name came from Aristotle's habit of walking about while he lectured. Nietzsche said that all the best ideas come while walking.

2 I would include here philosophy of mind, which is a mixture of metaphysics and epistemology. Philosophers such as John McDowell and Christopher Peacocke have also attempted to bring ethics closer to the heart of analytic philosophy. For 'Continental' philosophers, it has always been a central concern. See, e.g., the work of Emmanuel Levinas: *Totality and Infinity*, trans. Alphonso Lingis (Pittsburgh: Duquesne University Press, 1969) and *Time and the Other and Additional Essays*, trans. Richard A. Cohen (Pittsburgh: Duquesne University Press, 1987).

3 This is *one* way to divide up philosophy, and I am not insisting that it is 'true,' only that it is fruitful and convenient.

4 Julia Annas, *Platonic Ethics, Old and New* (Ithaca: Cornell University Press, 2000), pp. 111–12.

5 The reader will recall that I described epistemology as an original development out of metaphysics.

6 Many deconstructionist philosophers, as well as pragmatists in Rorty's mould, are rather impatient with the boundaries between academic disciplines. We shall see in Chapter 7 that they often erase some of them.

7 On the interpretations of Plato advanced by some important nineteenth- and twentieth-century philosophers, see: Catherine H. Zuckert, *Postmodern Platos* (Chicago: University of Chicago Press, 1996).

8 See Martha Nussbaum, *The Therapy of Desire* (Princeton: Princeton University Press, 1994). This work concerns Hellenistic philosophy, of which Nussbaum notes (p. 15): 'There is in this period broad agreement that the central motivation for philosophizing is the urgency of human suffering, and that the goal of philosophy is human flourishing, or *eudaimonia*.' In *What Is Ancient Philosophy?* (Cambridge: Belknap Press, 2002), p. 70, Hadot writes that for Plato 'knowledge is never purely theoretical. It is the transformation of our being; it is virtue.'

9 Women philosophers seem to have done much to reincorporate ethics into the mainstream of philosophy. In doing so, they may be reshaping a hitherto overly masculine analytic vision of philosophy. I have quoted Nussbaum and Annas in these paragraphs and I recommend their work to readers interested in the ethics of the ancient world. Regarding the map of

philosophy, see Ted Honderich, ed., *The Oxford Companion to Philosophy* Oxford: Oxford University Press, 1995), pp. 927–8.

10 See Chapter 1, pp. 10–11.

11 The reader may notice some circularity in this statement. I would also note that I am edging towards a holist version of philosophy that is open to a number of quite reasoned objections.

12 At 352d.

13 Karl Marx, *Capital* (Moscow: Foreign Languages Publishing, 1959), vol. 1, p. 71.

14 Benjamin Jowett was Master of Balliol College, Oxford, from 1870 to 1893. Noel Annan writes: 'his intellectual achievements were considerable; he introduced Hegel to Oxford, stimulated the study of early Greek philosophy and by his translations made Plato's spirit walk again in England.' *Leslie Stephen* (London: Weidenfeld and Nicolson, 1984), p. 185. On the merits of Jowett's translation of *arête*, see Alexander Nehamas, *The Art of Living* (Berkeley: University of California Press, 1998), p. 78.

15 See Alasdair MacIntyre, *After Virtue*, 2nd ed. (Notre Dame: Notre Dame University Press, 1986), p. 122, and Allessandro Ferrara, *Reflective Authenticity* (London: Routledge, 1998), pp. 30–1, and Nehamas, *Art of Living*.

16 Because of this, there is a risk of equivocation – of sliding between two ideas that are not quite the same – when we discuss virtue.

17 *Virtues of Authenticity: Essays on Plato and Socrates* (Princeton: Princeton University Press, 1999), p. 4.

18 Ibid., p. 4 and p. 319.

19 See John Rawls, *A Theory of Justice* (Cambridge, Mass.: Belknap Press, 1971), p. 403.

20 See the opening section of Chapter 4.

21 *Art of Living*, p. 78.

22 On Homer as a moralist, see Hugh Lloyd Jones, *The Justice of Zeus* (Berkeley: University of California Press, 1971), pp. 1–2.

23 See John Rawls, *Lectures on the History of Moral Philosophy*, ed. Barbara Herman (Cambridge: Harvard University Press, 2000), pp. 3–5.

24 I confess to oversimplifying a complex issue. And perhaps the shrug is not philosophical. In his *The Significance of Philosophical Scepticism*, Barry Stroud distinguishes (*passim*) between philosophical questions – which are often general (Descartes' 'How do we know the world exists?') and everyday empirical ones ('How do we know that Everest is the highest mountain?').

25 At 336b–347e. See esp. 341: 'The just is to do what is for the advantage of the stronger.'

26 See Gregory Vlastos, *Socrates: Ironist and Moral Philosopher* (Ithaca: Cornell University Press, 1971), p. 200. Vlastos notes that courage, temperance, justice, piety, and wisdom were for the Greeks 'incontestably ... terms of moral commendation par excellence.' Socrates accepts this, but disavows knowledge of their natures.

27 See *Republic* 335–336a. My example is adapted from this passage.

28 Aristotle disagrees: 'Wickedness *is* voluntary.' See *Nicomachean Ethics* III: 5, 1113b16 (McKeon, p. 972). But see his distinction between what is 'not voluntary' – actions done 'by reason of ignorance' – and what is 'involuntary' – actions done under the pressure of pain. Aristotle also distinguishes between acting 'by reason of ignorance' and 'in ignorance.' Ibid., III: 1, 1110b8–1111a2 (McKeon, p. 966). Richard McKeon, ed., *Basic Works of Aristotle* (New York: Random House, 1941).

29 To recall note 24, Socrates is asking his interlocutors for a philosophical – a general and consistent – account of virtue.

30 Anyone observing the skulduggery surrounding judged sports in the modern Olympics might wonder about this claim.

31 See, e.g., the conclusion to *Protagoras*, 360e–361d.

32 I like G.E. Moore's summary of this difficulty: 'Ethics is undoubtedly concerned with the question what good conduct is; but, being concerned with this, it obviously does not start at the beginning, unless it is prepared to tell us what is good as well as what is conduct.' *Principia Ethica* (Cambridge: Cambridge University Press, 1903), p. 2.

33 This is the 'Socratic paradox': the assertion that knowledge is equivalent to virtue. It turns moral questions into epistemological ones since acting virtuously automatically follows from knowing. Free will does not seem to enter the equation. A version of this emerges in *Apology* at 25–26a. See Nietzsche's comments in *The Twilight of the Idols*, in *The Twilight of the Idols and the Anti-Christ*, trans. R.J. Hollingdale (Harmondsworth: Penguin, 1968), 'The Problem of Socrates,' s. 10: 'Reason = virtue = happiness means merely: one must imitate Socrates and counter the dark desires by producing a permanent *daylight* – the daylight of reason.' But note Nussbaum's observation that 'philosophers have to believe, I think, that at least a part of evil is not innate or necessary, but that a good part of it is based on error, whether societal or personal.' Martha Nussbaum, *Sex and Social Justice* (Oxford: Oxford University Press, 1999), p. 241.

34 *Republic* 434d–441c.

35 See 'The Myth of the Charioteer' at *Phaedrus* 253c–254e, in which Reason is the charioteer attempting, with the help of a good horse (the Will), to tame the bad horse (Appetite) and make it amenable to its dictates. Reason is

unable to do so consistently and the ride is a wild one. For an interesting comparison, see Rawls in *Lectures*, p. 29. He notes that for Hume 'a passion does not *assert* anything' and cannot contradict the truths of reason. The passions just are a fundamental part of one's nature and, Hume tells us, reason must be a 'slave' to them.

36 Annas, *Platonic Ethics*, p. 96.

37 John Stuart Mill, 'Civilization,' in John M. Robson, ed., *Essays on Politics and Society*, vol. XVIII, *Collected Works of John Stuart Mill* (Toronto: University of Toronto Press, 1977), p. 122. Mill also argues (p. 136) that the two 'evils' of combination are that the individual is lost in the crowd and that individual character becomes 'relaxed and enervated.' The remedy for the first is 'greater and more perfect combination among individuals', for the second it is 'education, and forms of polity, calculated to invigorate the individual character.' 'Greater and more perfect combination' is a tricky (and vague) concept in a modern multicultural democracy, but nonetheless worth consideration.

38 For an insightful commentary on how the great truths that Plato sought have become matters of opinion in the modern world, see Hannah Arendt, 'Truth And Politics,' in *Between Past and Future* (Harmondsworth: Penguin, 1977).

39 It is important (as Mill understood it was) for educational institutions to confront this issue by creating forums for the debate and expression of 'private truths.'

40 In essence, the Form of the Good *is* the condition of knowledge and as such a kind of meta-Form. See Martha Nussbaum, *The Fragility of Goodness* (Cambridge: Cambridge University Press, 1986), p. 193.

41 See, Annas, *Platonic Ethics*, p. 96, and Nussbaum, *Fragility of Goodness*, p. 256.

42 Annas, *Platonic Ethics*, p. 141.

43 We shall see below (note 97), that this is the nub of Mill's criticism of Bentham's utilitarianism.

44 Regarding 'traditional behaviour,' see Nehamas's comments (*Art of Living*, pp. 134–5) on Nietzsche's 'nostalgic' defence of it. See also Aristotle's view in *Nicomachean Ethics* II: 1, esp. 1102b14–25 (McKeon, p. 952): 'Moral virtue comes about as a result of habit, whence also its name *ethike* is one that is formed by a slight variation on the word ethos (habit).' But what begins in habit does not, in Aristotle's opinion, end there.

45 See Appendix 2.

46 The Kantian idea of duty as given by reason seems to offer a moral reason for why one ought to be virtuous but perhaps one might wish to be virtuous just because it is a beautiful thing to be. See Rawls, *Lectures*, p. 1.

47 See Charles Taylor, *Sources of the Self* (Cambridge: Harvard University Press, 1989), p. 23. Taylor shows how this aesthetic notion has undergone a reversal from the ancient Greek world where the good life was the heroic one, to the modern western world, where it is often the 'ordinary' life.

48 To recall the logic of Chapter 5, the relationship is hypothetical, which is to say, it runs only in one direction. *If* an action is right *then* it is good but not the reverse.

49 *Platonic Ethics*, pp. 105–6.

50 Aristotle also thought that the best life was one of contemplation.

51 In Chapter 4 I argued that one who has gazed on the sun would no longer be a philosopher. I am not pushing that point in these remarks.

52 But see Plato's *Timaeus* 29d–30c. The creator, Plato tells us, being good and therefore free of jealousy, wished that everything else should be good as well – 'as like him as they could be' – so he brought order to bear on chaos. It is not unreasonable to say that the creator was moved by an aesthetic sensibility rather than a sense of moral duty. (Are gods subject to moral duty?)

53 Show, i.e., that an action is good *if and only if* it is virtuous.

54 *The View from Nowhere* (Oxford: Oxford University Press, 1986), p. 205.

55 Immanuel Kant, *Fundamental Principles of the Metaphysics of Morals*, trans. Thomas K. Abbot (New York: Bobbs-Merrill, 1949), pp. 20–1.

56 See ibid., p. 19. I am to act 'so that I could also will that my maxim should become a universal law.'

57 In his *Lectures* (p. 2), Rawls maps this distinction onto ancients and moderns as follows: 'The ancients asked about the most rational way to true happiness, or the highest good, and they inquired about how virtuous conduct and the virtues as aspects of character ... are related to that highest good, whether as means, or as constituents, or both. Whereas the moderns asked primarily, or at least in the first instance, about what they saw as authoritative prescriptions of right reason, and the rights, duties, and obligations to which these prescriptions of reason give rise.' Rawls warns against assuming that this difference is necessarily 'deep.'

58 For a good summary of deontological ethics, see Roger Crisp's entry in the *Oxford Companion*.

59 See MacIntyre's comment in *After Virtue*, p. 224. He argues that tragic heroes have to choose between rival but equal conceptions of 'good': 'By choosing one I do nothing to diminish or derogate from the claim made upon me of the other; and therefore, whatever I do, I shall have left un-done what I ought to have done.'

60 *Fragility of Goodness*, p. 334. See also, Bernard Williams, 'Moral Luck,' in *Moral Luck* (Cambridge: Cambridge University Press, 1981), esp. pp. 27–8.

61 *Fragility of Goodness*, p. 335.

62 Jean-Pierre Vernant and Pierre Vidal Naquet, *Myth and tragedy In Ancient Greece*, trans. Janet Lloyd (New York: Zone Books, 1988), p. 48.

63 *Fragility of Goodness*, pp. 324–5.

64 Ibid., p. 336. In making a place for *tuche* in his ethics, Aristotle – unlike Plato – makes a place for tragedy. On this, see David Farrell Krell, 'A Number of Houses in a Universe of Tragedy,' in Miguel de Beistegui and Simon Sparks, eds., *Philosophy and Tragedy* (London: Routledge, 2000), p. 88.

65 Iris Murdoch, 'The Sublime and the Good,' in *Existentialists and Mystics: Writings on Philosophy and Literature* (Harmondsworth: Penguin, 1999), p. 215.

66 At 280b.

67 I do not think this is the case in the movie. The screenwriter, Margaret Slovo, is the daughter of the late Joe Slovo, who was as I have described him here.

68 Margaret Slovo's mother Ruth First was assassinated in 1982.

69 I am uncertain whether the character of the mother in the movie has a good will in Kant's sense. For Kant, a will is good if it performs actions of moral value, which are actions the actor has no inclination to perform but does so because she recognizes it as a moral duty (a command of the categorical imperative).

70 Bernard Williams, *Shame and Necessity* (Berkeley: University of California Press, 1993), p. 92. Aristotle recognizes the intensely personal nature of shame when he characterizes it as 'more like a feeling than a state of character'; like fear it is almost a 'bodily condition.' *Nicomachean Ethics* IV: 9, 1128b10–14 (McKeon, p. 1000). 'The feeling,' he adds, 'is not becoming to every age, but only to youth.'

71 Line 1036.

72 Williams, *Shame and Necessity*, ch. 4. I have been using 'excellence' in two senses in these pages: as a skill (*techne*) and as an indicator of some aesthetic sensibility. Since the latter could be summed up as a kind of 'nobility' – a combination of the Greek *kalos*, with its connotations of 'good' and 'beautiful' and *agathos*, with its connotations of 'good' and 'noble' – *arête* has actually been bearing the weight of three English meanings: 'moral rightness' (or virtue), 'skill,' and 'nobility.' The word 'good' also plays across all three, although in a democratic age perhaps the last of these is somewhat muted.

73 Iris Murdoch, 'Metaphysics and Ethics,' in *Existentialists and Mystics*, p. 75.

74 Murdoch, 'The Sublime and the Good,' p. 205.

75 In Raphael's painting 'The School of Athens' (1510–1511), which hangs in the Stella della Segnatura in the Vatican apartments, Plato and Aristotle occupy centre stage; Plato is pointing to heaven while Aristotle lowers his hand as if to indicate earth. On 'this-worldly' and 'other-worldly' contrast, see Arthur O. Lovejoy's classic text, *The Great Chain of Being* (Cambridge: Harvard University Press, 1966), p. 75.

76 See, e.g., Nussbaum, *Fragility of Goodness*, p. 342.

77 *Tractatus Logico-Philosophicus*, trans. D.F. Pears and B.F. McGuiness (London: Routledge and Kegan Paul, 1961), 6.41.

78 Ibid., 6.421.

79 For a succinct comment on this aspect of Kant, and the twist given to it by Foucault, see, Ian Hacking, 'Self-Improvement,' in David Couzens Hoy (ed.), *Foucault: A Critical Reader* (Oxford: Basil Blackwell, 1986), p. 239.

80 See Nehamas's comments on Foucault in *Art of Living*, p. 179. The aestheticization of reason has been deplored by a number of writers on the left. In particular, see Terry Eagleton, *The Ideology of the Aesthetic* (Oxford: Basil Blackwell, 1990).

81 According to Diogenes Laertes, Chilon of Sparta was the one of the seven sages who wrote 'know thyself' over the main door of the oracle at Delphi. Others have attributed it to the Milesian philosopher, Thales. *Lives of Eminent Philosophers*, trans. R.D. Hicks (Cambridge: Harvard University Press, 1925), I, 40–2.

82 Moore, *Principia Ethica*.

83 Jeremy Bentham, *Economic Writings*, ed. W. Stark (London: Allen and Unwin, 1952), vol. 1, pp. 334–5.

84 *Sources of the Self*, p. 29.

85 Ibid., p. 79.

86 *Theory*, p. 396.

87 *Sources of the Self*, p. 27.

88 *Metaphysics as a Guide to Morals* (London: Chatto and Windus, 1992), p. 260.

89 Mill makes the following point in this regard: 'There is, I am aware, a disposition to believe that a person who sees in moral obligation a transcendental fact, an objective reality belonging to the province of "Things in themselves," is likely to be more obedient to it than one who believes it to be entirely subjective.' Yet, the utilitarian Mill adds, such belief is always urged by one's 'own subjective feeling.' John Stuart Mill, *Utilitarianism*, in *Utilitarianism, Liberty, Representative Government* (London: J.M. Dent, 1910), p. 27.

90 David Hume, 'A Treatise of Human Nature,' in H.D. Aiken, ed., *Hume's Moral and Political Philosophy* (Darien, Conn.: Hafner, 1970), III: I, s. I.

91 Ibid., III: I, s. II and Appendix I of 'An Enquiry Concerning the Principles Of Morals,' in ibid., p. 265 and ff.

92 *Lectures*, p. 73.

93 Sartre was not commenting on Hume in this passage.

94 *Existentialism and Humanism*, trans. Philip Mairet (London: Eyre-Methuen, 1973), p. 19.

95 *Twilight of the Idols*, p. 55.

96 See R.M. Hare, *The Language of Morals* (Oxford: Oxford University Press, 1952).

97 *Utilitarianism*, p. 9. Regarding Bentham's calculus, see his *An Introduction to the Principles of Morals and Legislation*, in *A Fragment on Government and An Introduction to the Principles of Morals and Legislation*, ed. Wilfrid Harrison (Oxford: Basil Blackwell, 1967), ch. 4, p. 151 and ff.

98 Recall, however, that in Kant's work the standards of reason cannot be understood as giving access to absolute knowledge of the good and right.

99 On this point see, Körner, *Kant* (Harmondsworth: Penguin, 1955), pp. 189–90.

100 *After Virtue*, p. 224.

101 See Taylor, *Sources of the Self*, part I, chs. 2 and 3.

102 See Alasdair MacIntyre, *Whose Justice? Which Rationality?* (London: Duckworth, 1988), p. 71. See also, Nehamas, *Virtues of Authenticity*, p. 16. 'The major burden of the elenchus is to test ... statements and Socrates assumes that no false statement can survive these tests.'

103 See Alasdair MacIntyre, *Three Rival Versions of Moral Enquiry* (London: Duckworth, 1990).

104 Henry Sidgwick, *Outlines of the History of Ethics*, 5th ed. (London: Macmillan, 1902), p. 2.

105 *Sources of the Self*, p. 14.

106 The essay opens as follows: 'The subject of this Essay is ... Civil, or Social Liberty: the nature and limits of the power that can be legitimately exercised by society over the individual. Instrumental in setting the limit was the "harm principle": 'the sole end for which mankind are warranted, individually or collectively, in interfering with the liberty of action of any of their number, is self-protection ... [The individual's] own good, either physical or moral, is not a sufficient warrant.' *Collected Works*, vol. 18, p. 217 and p. 223.

107 Niccolo Machiavelli, *The Prince*, in *The Prince and The Discourses* (New York: Modern Library, 1950), p. 65.

108 In 'Truth and Politics' (p. 227), Hannah Arendt wrote: 'No one has ever doubted that truth and politics are on rather bad terms with each other, and no one has, as far as I know, ever counted truthfulness among the political virtues.'
109 416b–417c.
110 Homer, *The Odyssey*, trans. E.V. Rieu (Harmondsworth: Penguin Classics, 1946), Bk. 12.
111 Jeremy Bentham, 'Constitutional Code,' in *The Works of Jeremy Bentham*, ed. John Bowring (New York: Russell and Russell, 1962), vol. 9, p. 61. Reprint of 1843 edition.
112 'Plan of Parliamentary Reform,' in *Works*, vol. 3, p. 452.
113 See John Stuart Mill, 'Rationale of Representation' and 'Essays On Government,' in *Collected Works*, vol. 18.
114 *Ethics – Politics – Subjectivity* (London: Verso, 1999), p. 107.
115 For an insightful discussion of this issue, see Martha Nussbaum, *Poetic Justice* (Boston: Beacon Press, 1995).

Chapter 7 Philosophy and Language: The House of Being

1 Robert Brandom, *Articulating Reasons* (Cambridge: Harvard University Press, 2000), p. 5. See Nagel's *The View from Nowhere* (Oxford: Oxford University Press, 1986), for a dissenting view. See also Alice Ambrose's lucid, half-century-old statement of the issue in her, 'Linguistic Approaches to Philosophical Problems,' in Richard Rorty, ed., *The Linguistic Turn* (Chicago: University of Chicago Press, 1970), p. 147.
2 *Euthyphro* 7b–7e. Socrates does not say that the gods would *necessarily* disagree about the meaning of such abstractions, only that it is a possibility.
3 Quoted in Alexander Nehamas, *The Art of Living* (Berkeley: University of California Press, 1998), p. 92.
4 Richard Rorty, 'John McDowell's Version of Empiricism,' in *Philosophical Papers*, vol. 3, *Truth and Progress* (Cambridge: Cambridge University Press, 1998), p. 143.
5 Nagel has lamented this tendency in analytic philosophy, describing it as a 'falling away from its origins in Frege's insistence on the fundamental importance of logic, conceived as the examination of mind-independent concepts and the development of a purer understanding and a clearer expression of them.' *The Last Word* (Oxford: Oxford University Press, 1997), p. 37.
6 As the names suggest, there is a certain symbiosis between the two perspectives. Below, I suggest that post-structuralism is a kind of Nietzschean critique of structuralism.

7 Ferdinand de Saussure, *Course in General Linguistics*, trans. Wade Baskin (New York: McGraw-Hill, 1959), pp. 66–7.

8 Ibid., p. 65.

9 See Simon Blackburn's entry on 'Language, History and Philosophy of,' in Ted Honderich, ed., *The Oxford Companion to Philosophy* (Oxford: Oxford University Press, 1995).

10 Saussure, *Course*, p. 74. To take one example, my French-English dictionary matches 'tallis' with 'copse.' My *Oxford English Dictionary (OED)* defines 'copse' as: 'A small wood of small trees grown for periodical cutting.' My *Micro Robert* defines 'tallis' as: 'Part of a wood or forest in which there are only small trees' (my translation). These definitions are close but not exact and could lead one to pick out different agglomerations of trees. See Hacking's comments on scholastic nominalism in his 'Five Parables,' in Richard Rorty, J.B. Schneewind, and Quentin Skinner, eds., *Philosophy in History* (Cambridge: Cambridge University Press, 1984), p. 122. Hacking argues that categories of people – criminals, lunatics, etc. – probably exist just insofar as words pick them out, and I think we can say the same of copses and woods. To extend nominalism to what I called 'natural units' – to trees, e.g. – does, as Hacking says here, seem to strain credulity. Our nominalism does not always go right down to the ground nor do our natural units ascend to the heavens. In *Ontological Relativity and Other Essays* (New York: Columbia University Press, 1969) (p. 80) Quine makes the same point about translation of sentences between languages, insisting that one cannot simply pair them off. One has, instead, to try to transfer the 'net empirical implications of a theory (or a language) to the new language.'

11 See Robert Kirk's entry on 'Sapir-Whorf Hypothesis' in the *Oxford Companion*.

12 Saussure, *Course*, p. 81: 'Everything that relates to the static side of our science [of linguistics] is synchronic; everything that has to do with evolution is diachronic. Similarly, *synchrony* and *diachrony* designate respectively a language-state and an evolutionary phase.'

13 Ibid., p. 114 and ff.

14 See Roland Barthes, 'The Imagination of the Sign,' in *A Barthes Reader*, ed. Susan Sontag (New York: Hill and Wand, 1982).

15 It would seem that, even in language, the concept of 'go' exists only because some form of 'not-go' does.

16 These concepts are more than a little indebted to Hegel. See Charles Taylor, *Hegel* (Cambridge: Cambridge University Press, 1975), p. 236.

17 Very roughly, semantics deals with the relation of signifiers to signifieds – i.e., with signs – and syntax deals with the relation among signs. Put

differently, semantics deals with the way words latch onto the world and syntax with the way we put them together in our sentences. Remember: 'Syntax bad garbled language is.'

18 The most famous pioneer of structuralism is the anthropologist Claude Lévi-Strauss, who certainly acknowledged his debt to linguistics. See, e.g., his *Structural Anthropology*, trans. Claire Jacobson and Brooke Schoef (New York: Anchor Books, 1967), ch. 2, esp. p. 32. Edmund Leach's *Lévi-Strauss* (London: Fontana, 1970) is an excellent introduction to his work.

19 For Derrida's comments on Saussure see his 'Semiology and Grammatology: An Interview with Julia Kristeva,' in *Positions*, trans. Alan Bass (Chicago: University of Chicago Press, 1981), pp. 17–23. With respect to 'dissemination,' Derrida seems to be pointing to both a semantic and a syntactic impossibility: signs are inherently unstable (as in the *pharmakon*) but so too, is the relation among them. See Christina Howells, *Derrida* (Cambridge: Polity Press, 1998), pp. 78–81, and 'Positions,' in *Positions*.

20 Here again we seem to be shifting between 'instant' and 'flow' time, between meanings that stand still *and ones that* evolve. In this sense, structuralists rely on traditional logic whereas deconstructionists 'deconstruct' it.

21 The *OED* definition for 'chair' is 'a separate, usually moveable, seat for one.' The differentiae here are 'separate,' 'usually moveable,' and 'for one.'

22 In his groundbreaking and extremely influential *Naming and Necessity* (Cambridge: Harvard University Press, 1972), Saul Kripke refers, somewhat disparagingly, to '[t]he hoary tradition of definition by *genus* and *differentia*' (p. 134). His concept of a 'rigid designator' (see the Glossary of Terms) is based on the proposition that we do not define everything – pick out the things that terms refer to in the world – by description. Sometimes we simply *designate* a thing – name it, in effect – thereby locking it into place. Think of yourself. On Kriple's argument, you are not identifiable as the sum of a bunch of attributes, of *differentiae* that we can trot out to distinguish you from other people. You are just *you*, the person designated by your name. Moreover, you are *you* in all possible (essentially, imaginable) worlds in which you could exist. You might be a philosophy student in one world and a downhill ski racer in another, but you are necessarily the same person in both. Hence, Kripke thinks that the 'tradition' of employing *differentiae* to produce complete descriptions is one that we can largely discard. We can cut the Gordian knot *differentiae* weave and just name things. If one accepts Kripke's argument, Derrida's concept of *différance*, which is explained in the next paragraph, will have less bite, because language will begin to hold still, if only a little. Kripke's argument has, of course, been the subject of much debate.

23 For a discussion of *différance*, see Derrida's interview, 'Implications,' in *Positions*, pp. 8–9. The concept is tied to 'dissemination' and 'undecidability.' Derrida also introduces the idea of the 'supplement' – remarks that are both unnecessary additions and essential complements to the text; ones, therefore, that deconstruct the distinction between what is essential and accidental. One could consider the many parenthetical remarks I have sprinkled throughout this book in this light. Are they essential complements to the 'main' argument or inessential but – kindly – interesting additions?

24 In *Virtues of Authenticity: Essays on Plato and Aristotle* (Princeton: Princeton University Press, 1999), p. 185, Nehamas has this to say about Plato's theory of Forms: 'If we accept [the] assumption that when Plato says that "beautiful" is a name of the beautiful, we are faced with a dilemma: either "beautiful" is a proper name of the beautiful and the self-predication reduces to the tautology "The beautiful is the beautiful"; or, to avoid this result, "beautiful" is a bona fide predicate of the beautiful, and beauty turns out to be ... a member of the class of beautiful things.' In short, we have the two options discussed above: the self-predication, 'A is A,' produces either meaningless tautology or else 'A' is a member of a more general class of things that happens to bear its name. Bertrand Russell called this a 'self-inclusive class.' The class of 'all sets with more than two members' would, e.g., include itself because there are more than two sets that have more than two members. But since it is difficult to see how beauty includes itself, in part because it is hard to see what else would be in the class, we veer towards what Aristotle called 'the third man argument.' See Glossary of Terms.

25 One defender of deconstruction has noted, 'The deconstruction of scepticism has notoriously been taken for the scepticism of deconstruction.' Ewa Płowanska Ziarek, *The Rhetoric of Failure* (Albany: SUNY Press, 1996), p. 2. Since this book might seem to be open to this charge will note that I have not argued that deconstruction is sceptical in a traditional sense. I have made deconstructionists part of my 'new scepticism,' which is directed not at the world but at philosophy – in particular, metaphysics – itself.

26 Stanley Cavell, *The Claim of Reason* (New York: Oxford University Press, 1979), pp. 185–6.

27 Thomas G. Pavel, *The Spell of Language* (Chicago: University of Chicago Press, 1989), p. 71.

28 Regarding 'logical atom,' see Glossary of Terms and Russell's 'Lectures on the Philosophy of Logical Atomism,' in *Logic and Knowledge: Essays, 1901–1950*, ed. R.C. Marsh (London: 1965), p. 179. In *Our Knowledge of the External World* (London: Allen and Unwin, 1926, pp. 13–14), Russell

divided the philosophy of his day into three types: the classical tradition descended from Kant and Hegel and carrying on the work of Plato, the evolutionary philosophy descended from Darwin and carried on, in different ways, by Herbert Spencer, William James, and finally, logical atomism, which incorporates the tools of mathematics. This is in essence the birth of 'analytical philosophy' and it looks to the spirit of Galileo: 'the substitution of piecemeal, detailed and verifiable results for large untested generalities recommended only by a certain appeal to the imagination.' Russell's hope is that this new scientific approach will reverse the reputation of philosophy as the discipline that 'has made greater claim, and achieved fewer results, than any other branch of learning.' See also Morris Weitz, 'The Unity of Russell's Philosophy,' in *The Philosophy of Bertrand Russell*, ed. Paul A. Schlipp (La Salle, Ill.: Open Court, 1971).

29 Frege is generally considered to be the founder of modern mathematical logic and was an enormous influence on Russell.

30 See Michael Dummett, *Frege: Philosophy of Language* (New York: Harper and Row, 1973), p. 84. Dummett's book is an exhaustive treatment of Frege's work. Russell distinguished between two kinds of knowledge: knowledge by acquaintance and by description. Acquaintance is basic, referring to the result of direct or immediate experience. Description is, by contrast, indirect or mediated, and subject to proof or disproof. One knows one's perceptions of colour immediately; one knows Julius Caesar by description. In a sense, Russell has the same problem as Descartes: if one kind of knowledge is basic and indubitable, how can we reduce other kinds of knowledge to that status? How can we show that description is anchored in acquaintance? This is to ask how we bridge the gap between private perception and public language. One question I have been raising is whether surety of reference can survive the transition from immediate acquaintance to public description. See also 'Knowledge by Acquaintance and Knowledge by Description,' in *Collected Papers* (London: Allen and Unwin, 1983) and *The Problems of Philosophy* (Oxford: Oxford University Press, 1967), ch. 5.

31 Moritz Schlick, a member of the Vienna Circle, who were strongly influenced by Russell's logical atomism, wrote that 'the meaning of a word must in the end be *shown*, it must be *given*. This is done by an act of indication, of pointing, and what is pointed at must be given, otherwise I cannot be referred to it.' 'Positivism and Realism,' in *Logical Positivism*, ed. A.J. Ayer (London: Allen and Unwin, 1959), p. 87.

32 See Saussure on 'syntagmatic' relations, in *Course in General Linguistics*, pp. 122–34. It's worth quoting Rorty here:'The modern revolt against

what Foucault calls "the sovereignty of the signifier" helps us think of the creation of new descriptions, new vocabularies, new *genres* as the essentially human activity – it suggests the poet, rather than the knower, as the man who realises human nature.' 'Is There a Problem about Fictional Discourse?' in *Consequences of Pragmatism* (Minneapolis: University of Minnesota Press, 1982), p. 137.

33 I direct readers to ch. 5 of Dummett, *Frege.*

34 See W.V. Quine, *Word and Object* (Cambridge, Mass.: MIT Press, 1960), pp. 270–6. Following Carnap, Quine describes this as an ascent from the 'material' to the 'formal' mode – i.e., from actual language to a logical or rule-setting meta-language. To use Quine's example (p. 272), the material 'There are wombats in Tasmania' can be translated into the formal '"Wombat" is true of some creatures in Tasmania.' We are no longer talking about wombats but about the truth-conditions of a certain sentence in the English language.

35 Ibid., p. 271. To move into a formal mode we would have to say: '"That's a Buick" is true of some cars.'

36 Of course, 'this' and 'that' may well seem to be the most general terms of all, applicable to everything.

37 *Tractatus Logico-Philosophicus*, trans. D.F. Pears and B.F. McGuinness (London: Routledge and Kegan Paul, 1961), 2.18

38 Ibid., 2.225.

39 Ibid., 4.022.

40 Ibid., 6.41.

41 Ibid., 6.42.

42 Ibid., 3.031.

43 Ibid, 6.13

44 Ibid., 6.54. See also, James Contant, 'A Prolegomena to the Reading of the Later Wittgenstein,' in Ludwig Nagl and Chantel Mouffe, eds., *The Legacy of Wittgenstein: Pragmatism or Deconstruction?* (Frankfort: Peter Lang, 2001), p. 97.

45 Ibid., s. 7.

46 See *Philosophical Investigations*, part I, s. 7. See also, 'The Blue Book,' in *The Blue and Brown Books* (New York: Harper Books, 1965), p. 17.

47 Cora Diamond suggests that Wittgenstein's 'criticism of the *Tractatus* may be viewed as a criticism of the *laying down of philosophical requirements.*' That, she adds, is the 'characteristic activity of the metaphysical spirit [and] may be contrasted with looking at the use, looking at what we do.' *The Realistic Spirit* (Cambridge, Mass.: MIT Press, 1991), pp. 20–1.

48 *Tractatus*, 5.61.

49 Ludwig Wittgenstein, *Philosophical Grammar*, ed. Rush Rhees and trans. Anthony Kenny (Los Angeles: University of California Press, 1978), part I, s. 72.

50 Ibid. part I, s. 23. 'Grammar describes the use of words in language. So it has somewhat the same relation to the language as the description of a game, the rules of a game, have to the game.'

51 *Philosophical Investigations*, part I, s. 23.

52 *Philosophical Grammar*, part I, s. 11.

53 See ibid., part I, ss. 14–15.

54 *Philosophical Investigations*, part I, s. 116.

55 Ibid., part I, s. 33.

56 Ibid., part I, s. 203.

57 See Cavell's example in *Claim of Reason*, pp. 169–80.

58 In other words, 'dog' is closer to a natural unit than 'beauty,' although my son's use of it shows how precarious that notion is. As for conceptual words such as 'beauty,' Wittgenstein writes in 'The Blue Book' (p. 25): 'We are unable to circumscribe clearly the concepts we use: not because we don't know their real definition but because there is no "real" definition to them.' With 'dog' we feel that there is something close to a 'real' definition.

59 'The Blue Book,' p. 27.

60 Gilbert Ryle, *The Concept of Mind* (London: Hutchinson, 1949), esp. pp. 15–24.

61 *Zettel*, ed. G.E.M. Anscombe and G.H. von Wright, trans. Anscombe (Los Angeles: University of California Press, 1970), no. 192.

62 They are 'empirical' because they are open to experience and to the kind of doubt experience brings – and therefore to proof or disproof. They thus raise epistemological issues.

63 See Thomas Morawetz, *Wittgenstein and Knowledge: The Importance of 'On Certainty'* (Amherst.: University of Massachusetts Press, 1978), ch. 2.

64 See T.S. Kuhn, *The Copernican Revolution* (Cambridge: Harvard University Press, 1957).

65 See *On Certainty*, nos. 35–42.

66 *Philosophical Investigations*, part II, p. 197.

67 *Zettel*, no. 261. See also, no. 256.

68 See Brian McGuinness, 'Freud and Wittgenstein,' in Brian McGuinness, ed., *Wittgenstein and His Times* (Chicago: University of Chicago Press, 1982), pp. 32–3.

69 Jacques Bouveresse, *Wittgenstein Reads Freud*, trans. Carol Cosman, (Princeton: Princeton University Press, 1995), p. 13.

70 Ludwig Wittgenstein, *Lectures and Conversations*, ed. Cyril Barret (Berkeley: University of California Press, n.d.), pp. 51–2.

71 See Alan Janik, 'Wittgenstein's Critical Hermeneutics: From Physics to Aesthetics,' in Nagl and Mouffe, *Legacy of Wittgenstein*, p. 71. See also, Wittgentein's *Zettel*, no. 382: 'In philosophizing we may not *terminate* a disease of thought. It must run its natural course and *slow* cure is all important.'

72 Schlick considered this choice in 'The Future of Philosophy' (reprinted in *The Linguistic Turn*) in the early 1930s. He opts for 'clarity,' convinced that this 'view of the nature of philosophy will be generally adopted in the future' (pp. 52–3). Not quite.

73 Northrop Frye, *Words with Power* (Markham, Ont.: Viking Press, 1990), p. 10.

74 At *Phaedo* 96–99d, Socrates recounts his turn away from 'nature philosophy.'

75 See Ian Hacking, *The Emergence of Probability* (Cambridge: Cambridge University Press, 1975) and *The Taming of Chance* (Cambridge: Cambridge University Press, 1990).

76 I intend no disrespect to literature; I am simply parodying how each side looks at the other.

77 Northrop Frye, *The Great Code: The Bible and Literature* (Toronto: Academic Press, 1982), p. 59.

78 *Metaphysics as a Guide to Morals* (London: Chatto and Windus, 1992), p. 212.

79 Iris Murdoch, 'The Sovereignty of Good over Other Concepts,' in *Existentialists and Mystics: Writings on Philosophy and Literature* (Harmondsworth: Peguin, 1999) p. 363.

80 At 38a of *Apology*.

81 Again, I am echoing Martha Nussbaum, *The Therapy of Desire* (Princeton: Princeton University Press, 1994).

Appendix 2

1 *The Twilight of the Idols* in *The Twilight of the Idols and the Anti-Christ*, trans. R.J. Hollinger (Harmondsworth: Penguin, 1968), 'The Problem of Socrates,' s. 5 (p. 31). Nietzsche refers to Socrates as 'a buffoon who got himself taken seriously.'

2 Ibid., s. 7 (p. 32).

3 Friedrich Nietzsche, 'On Ethics,' in *The Portable Nietzsche*, ed. and trans. Walter Kaufmann (Harmondsworth: Penguin, 1976), p. 31.

4 'On Truth and Lies in an Extra-Moral Sense,' in ibid., pp. 46–7.

5 *The Birth of Tragedy*, p. 160.

6 'On Truth and Lies,' p. 47.

7 See Alexander Nehamas's comments on Nietzsche's idea of 'instinct' in *The Art of Living* (Berkeley: University of California Press, 1998), p. 140.

8 Friedrich Nietzsche, *Beyond Good and Evil*, trans. R.J. Hollingdale (Harmondsworth: Penguin, 1973), s. 260.

9 I am not suggesting that Nietzsche's individual is in every respect self-created: that would be impossible. Insofar as she fashions herself she does so from the material available, which includes her historical and social context. See *Beyond Good and Evil*, s. 43.

10 *Art of Living*, p. 179. See also, Michel Foucault, *The Care of the Self*, trans. Robert Hurley (New York: Random House, 1986).

11 Iris Murdoch, 'The Sublime and the Beautiful Revisited,' in *Existentialists and Mystics Writings on Philosophy and Literature* (Harmondsworth: Penguin, 1999), p. 268. See also Sartre's consideration of one's relation to the 'other' in *Being and Nothingness*, part 3, ch. 1, esp. p. 302: 'The other is the indispensable mediator between myself and me. I am ashamed of myself *as I appear* to the other.' Also, p. 304: 'Thus shame is shame *of oneself before the other.*'

12 See Emmanuel Levinas, *Totality and Infinity*, trans. Alphonso Lingis (Pittsburgh: Duquesne University Press, 1969). For a succinct statement of the relation to the 'Other,' see Raoul Mortley, ed., *French Philosophers in Conversation* (New York: Routledge, 1991), pp. 16–17.

13 Simone de Beauvoir, *The Second Sex*, trans. H.M. Parshley (New York: Knopf, 1968), ch. IX.

14 A man, Beauvoir writes, projects upon a woman, 'what he desires and what he fears, what he loves and what he hates. And if it is so difficult to say anything specific about her, that is because man seeks the whole of himself in her and because she is All. She is All, that is, on the plane of the inessential; she is all the Other. And as the other, she is other than herself, other than what is expected of her. Being all, she is never quite *this* which she should be' (ibid., pp. 197–8).

Glossary of Names

An asterisk indicates a corresponding entry in one of the glossaries.

Adorno, Theodore (1903–60)   German philosopher and sociologist much influenced by Marx* and Hegel.* Founding member of the Frankfurt School in 1923. Forced to leave Germany for the United States in 1938. Works include *Negative Dialectics* and (with Max Horkheimer) *Dialectic of Enlightenment*.

Aeschylus (525–ca. 456 BCE)   Oldest of the three great tragic playwrights (with Sophocles and Euripides) of Classical Greece. Only seven of his more than seventy plays survive, including the intact trilogy, *Oresteia*.

Ambrose, Alice (1906–2001)   English logician* and analytic philosopher.* Studied under Wittgenstein* and G.E. Moore* at Cambridge.

Anaximander (ca. 550 BCE)   The middle (between Thales* and Anaximenes) of the three great Milesian* nature philosophers. Originator of the concept of the *apeiron*.*

Annas, Julia   Regents Professor of Philosophy at the University of Arizona. Clear, concise writer on many areas of ancient philosophy.

Anselm of Bec and Canterbury (St) (1033–1109)   Benedictine monk, born in Italy, became Archbishop of Canterbury in 1093. Platonist* in outlook. Famous for his 'ontological proof'* for the existence of God.

Aquinas, St Thomas (1224/5–74)   Dominican friar, born in Aquino, Italy, taught in Rome, Naples, and Paris. Often considered the greatest of medieval philosophers, he accommodated Aristotle* to Christianity and vice versa. Among his voluminous writings are *Summa Theologicae* and *Summa Contra Gentiles* (a summary of theology and a summary of the errors of the infidels).

Arendt, Hannah (1906–75)   Political philosopher, born in Germany, studied under Heidegger; fled Nazis for the United States in 1941. Works include *The Human Condition, Between Past and Future*, and *Eichmann in Jerusalem*.

Aristotle (384–322 BCE)   Born in Stagira in northern Greece; came to Athens to study at Plato's Academy, where he spent twenty years. Founded the Lyceum* (although his followers were known as 'peripatetics') in 335 BCE. In the Middle Ages, often referred to simply as 'The Philosopher.'

Austin, John Langshaw (1911–60)   Oxford linguistic philosopher and central figure of oxford ordinary language philosophy.* Works include *Philosophical Papers* and *How to Do Things with Words*.

Ayer, A.J. (1910–89)   English philosopher, first at University College London and then Oxford. A central figure of logical positivism,* which in 1936 he detailed in *Language, Truth and Logic*. Later work focused on epistemological issues. Works include *Language, Truth and Logic, The Foundations of Empirical Knowledge*, and *The Problem of Knowledge*. His two-volume autobiography is a wonderful read.

Barnes, Jonathan (b. 1942)   Professor of philosophy at the University of Geneva. Has written extensively on ancient philosophy, including scepticism.*

Barthes, Roland (1915–80)   French social and literary critic. Closely associated with structuralism* and semiotic theory.

Bentham, Jeremy (1748–1832)   English utilitarian.* Associated with the catchphrase 'the greatest happiness of the greatest number.' Author of the hedonic calculus.* Wrote widely on economics and politics. Entered Oxford at age twelve.

Berkeley, George (1685–1753)   Bishop of Cloyne. Irish idealist* philosopher. Famous for the catchphrase *esse est percipi*, 'to be is to be perceived.' Began from an empiricist* position and still managed to do away with the physical world.

Bolton, Martha Brandt   Professor of philosophy at Rutgers University in New Jersey. Writes on early modern philosophy.

Bouveresse, Jacques (b. 1940)   French philosopher at the University of Paris; since 1995 has held a chair at the Collège de France.

Brandom, Robert (b. 1950)   Distinguished Service Professor at the University of Pittsburgh. Principal concerns are philosophy of mind,* language, and logic.* Works include *Making It Explicit* and *Articulating Reasons* (which makes *Making It Explicit*, explicit).

Broughton, Janet (b. 1948)   Professor of Philosophy at the University of California, Berkeley.

Brown, Peter (b. 1935)   Pre-eminent historian of late antiquity. Wonderful writer.

Buridan, John (ca. 1295/1300–1356/60)   University of Paris nominalist* philosopher, logician,* and commentator on Aristotle.*

Burnyeat, Myles (b. 1939)   Professor of philosophy at Oxford University. Has written widely on scepticism* and Hellenistic philosophy.

Carnap, Rudolph (1891–1970)   German philosopher and leading member of the Vienna Circle* of logical positivists.* Emigrated to the United States in 1935. Taught at the University of Chicago and the University of California, Los Angeles.

Cavell, Stanley (b. 1926)   American philosopher; emeritus professor at Harvard University. Has written on aesthetics, epistemology,* ethics,* literature, and popular culture. His major work *The Claim of Reason* (on Wittgenstein* and other matters) is demanding, but a well worth the effort. Other works include *Must We Mean What We Say?* and *A Pitch of Philosophy*.

Chalmers, David (b. 1966)   Regents Professor of Philosophy and director of the Centre for Consciousness Studies at the University of Arizona. Interests include the philosophy of mind,* metaphysics,* and artificial intelligence. See his *The Conscious Mind*.

Churchland, Paul (b. 1942)   Professor of philosophy at the University of California, San Diego. Important figure in philosophy of mind* and cognitive science, which he would move away from the everyday 'folk' psychology of belief and desire towards neuroscience.

Cicero, Marcus Tullius (106–43 BCE)   Roman philosopher, politician, and orator whose work shows the influence of the Sceptical Academy and stoicism.* Works include *Laws* and *On the Nature of the Gods*.

Colish, Marcia L.   Until her retirement, Frederick Artz Professor of History at Oberlin College. She writes about medieval intellectual history.

Comte, Auguste (1798–1857)   French positivist.* Divided the evolution of human society into three stages: the theological, the metaphysical,* and the positive. The last was to be a scientific stage in which knowledge was derived from empirical research. Often considered one of the progenitors of sociology. See his *Cours de Philosophie Positive*.

Critchley, Simon (b. 1960)   English philosopher. Professor at the graduate faculty, New School of Social Research, in New York. Writes about continental philosophy,* ethics,* literature, humour, and psychoanalysis. Works include *Ethics–Politics–Subjectivity* and *Very Little ... Almost Nothing*.

Davidson, Donald (1917–2003)   Prominent American philosopher of mind* and language, whose theories have been both controversial and influential. Published work consists entirely of articles (collected in four volumes).

De Beauvoir, Simone (1908–86)   French novelist and existentialist* philosopher, whose magisterial *The Second Sex* (1949) is the seminal work of twentieth-century feminism and one of the great books of the century.

Deleuze, Gilles (1925–95)   French philosopher at the University of Paris VII. Empiricist and 'anti-transcendental' thinker. Works include *Anti-Oedipus* (with Félix Guattari) and *Nietzsche and Philosophy*.

Derrida, Jacques (1930–2004)   Important and controversial philosopher. Born in Algeria, studied in Paris; divided his time between France and the Unites States. Progenitor of deconstruction.* Eclectic and notoriously difficult writer. Works include *Writing and Difference*, *Grammatology*, *The Post Card*, and *Spectres of Marx*.

Descartes, René (1596–1650)   The 'father of modern philosophy,' important scientist, and mathematician. Most influential philosophical books are the rather expansively titled *Meditations on First Philosophy in Which the Existence of God and the Real Distinction between the Soul and the Body of Man Are Demonstrated* and *The Discourse on the Method of Properly Conducting One's Reason and of Seeking the Truth in Sciences*.

Dewey, John (1859–1952)   American pragmatist,* philosopher, and professor at Columbia University. Influenced by Hegel's* historicism.* Espoused fallibilism – the position that no claim to knowledge is infallible. Viewed social progress as a process of reconsidering and revising ideas in the light of experience. Works include *Reconstruction in Philosophy* and *Experience and Nature*.

Diamond, Cora   William R. Kenan Professor of Philosophy at the University of Virginia. Has written on Wittgenstein,* Frege,* philosophy of language, and ethics.* See her *The Realistic Spirit*.

Diogenes Laertes (3rd century)   Author of *Lives and Opinions of Eminent Philosophers*, a source book for biographical detail, anecdote, and hearsay.

Dummett, Michael (b. 1925)   Until his retirement, Wykeham Professor of Logic at Oxford University. Analytic philosopher.* Best known for his exhaustive exegesis of Frege's* work, *Frege: Philosophy of Language*. Very influential figure in Oxford philosophy.

Eagleton, Terry (b. 1943)   Long at Oxford, now at Manchester University in England. Literary critic with materialist and Marxist* leanings. Clear writer.

Eco, Umberto (b. 1932)   Italian philosopher, novelist, essayist, and journalist. Currently, president of the Scuola Superiori di Studi Umanistici at the University of Bologna. Medievalist and semioticist. Works include *Semiotics and the Philosophy of Language, Kant* and the Platypus, Travels in Hyperreality,* and *The Name of the Rose.*

Epicurus (c. 341–270 BCE)   Athenian philosopher, influenced by atomism* and the founder of the Epicurean School, often referred to as The Garden. See Epicureanism in Glossary of Terms.

Evans, Gareth (1946–80)   Oxford philosopher of mind* and language. His *The Varieties of References* was edited by John McDowell* and published posthumously. Like McDowell, his work is a critical extension of Kant's* insistence that the mind grasps the world spontaneously.

Fodor, Jerry (b. 1935)   American philosopher of cognitive science and philosophy of mind.* Argues that there is a fit between the causal and the logical* structure of thought. Professor of philosophy and psychology and a member of the Centre for Cognitive Science at Rutgers University. See his *Concepts: Where Cognitive Science Went Wrong.*

Foucault, Michel (1926–84)   French intellectual historian and philosopher, held a chair at the Collège de France. Very influential in the structuralist* and post-structuralist* debates of the 1960s, 1970s, and 1980s. His thought went through a number of stages but a common thread was the analysis of power and the way it creates the subjects upon which it is exercised. Works include *Madness and Civilization, The Order of Things, The Will Truth,* and *The History of Sexuality.*

Frege, Gottlob (1848–1925)   German logician* and philosopher of language. His work had an enormous impact on Bertrand Russell* and analytic philosophy.* His distinction between the sense and reference of a sentence has been the source of much discussion and debate. English readers can consult Michael Dummett's *Frege: Philosophy of Language.*

Frye, Northrop (1912–91)   Canadian literary critic at the University of Toronto. Works include *Fearful Symmetry, The Anatomy of Criticism,* and *The Great Code.*

Gaukroger, Stephen (b. 1950)   Professor of the history of philosophy and the history of science at the University of Sydney in Australia. Focuses on early modern natural philosophy.

Habermas, Jürgen (b. 1929)   German philosopher, student of Adorno,* and part of the second generation of the Frankfurt School.* First works were heavily influenced by both Kant* and Marx.* Later writings have concerned communication theory and represent a turn from foundationalism* towards naturalism.* Often presented, not unreasonably, as an opponent of Foucault,* Derrida,* and post-modernism,* in general. Works include *The Philosophical Discourse of Modernity* and *On the Pragmatics of Communication*.

Hacking, Ian (b. 1936)   Canadian philosopher (now retired) at the University of Toronto and the Collège de France. Has written lucidly on language, probability, mathematics, logic,* and other topics. Works include. *Why Does Language Matter to Philosophy?* and *The Emergence of Probability*.

Hadot, Pierre (b. 1922)   French philosopher and historian of Ancient Greece, especially of the Hellenistic era.

Hamlyn, D.W. (b. 1924)   English philosopher (now retired) at the University of London. Main areas of interest are metaphysics,* epistemology,* and psychology.

Hawking, Stephen (b. 1942)   World's most famous cosmologist,* whose *A Brief History of Time* was an enormous bestseller.

Hegel, G.W.F. (1770–1831)   German idealist* philosopher. Historicized* thought as the process of the 'world spirit's' march towards absolute knowledge. Although teleological,* his work has influenced non-teological but historically minded philosophers such as Heidegger* and Dewey.* Works include *The Phenomenology of Spirit* and *The Philosophy of Right*.

Heidegger, Martin (1889–1976)   German philosopher. Among the most influential thinkers of the twentieth century. Early work is deeply historical, concerned with the process of *Dasein*,* or 'human being,' where 'being' is a gerund. His brief, but unexplained, association with Nazism cast a cloud over his later career. Has remained an extremely influential thinker whose thought is grounded in innovative, illuminating (and sometimes perverse) translations of ancient Greek terms.

Heraclitus (of Ephesus; early 5th century BCE)   Presocratic* philosopher, whose aphorisms earned him the nicknames, 'the riddler' and 'the obscure.' Sometimes known as the philosopher of flux, for his doctrine that everything is in a constant state of change, while beneath this flux lies the order of 'reason' in the universe.

Hobbes, Thomas (1588–1679)   English moral* and political philosopher. Working from a concept of the 'state of nature' (a mythic condition before organized society) and the dangers inherent in it, he developed a justification for absolutist government. A materialist, he saw humans as motivated by pain and pleasure and hence the passions, which reason served. Most famous work is *The Leviathan*.

Howells, Christina   Professor of medieval and modern languages at the University of Oxford. Has written on Derrida* and deconstruction.*

Hume, David (1711–76)   Scottish empiricist* and sceptical* philosopher. A towering intellect, whose work famously caused Kant* to pause for a decade after reading it (Kant then produced his three 'critiques'). Wrote widely on moral philosophy,* politics, psychology, and ethics.* Works include *An Inquiry Concerning Human Understanding* and *An Inquiry Concerning the Principles of Morals*.

Husserl, Edmund (1859–1938)   German philosopher associated with the development of phenomenology.* Influenced Heidegger,* Sartre,* Levinas,* and Derrida,* among others. Among his works are *Ideas: General Introduction to Pure Phenomenology* and *Cartesian Meditations*.

Jardine, Lisa   Professor of Renaissance Studies at Queen Mary College, University of London. She has written extensively on modern European intellectual history.

James, William (1842–1910)   American pragmatist* philosopher and psychologist whose attitude is often labelled 'radical empiricism.' A proponent of free will, he took a roughly naturalist approach to questions about knowledge and truth, famously asserting that 'truth happens to an idea.' Works include *The Principles of Psychology*, *Pragmatism*, and *The Meaning of Truth*.

Jowett, Benjamin (1817–93)   Translator of Plato and Master of Balliol College, Oxford, 1870–93.

Kant, Immanuel (1724–1804)   German philosopher and perhaps the last great Enlightenment thinker. His later works centre around the 'critiques' (of *Pure Reason, Practical Reason*, and *Judgement*). The first concerns the conditions of empirical knowledge, the second the conditions of morality, and the third of aesthetic knowledge. He developed a deontological ethics* based on his concept of the categorical imperative.*

Kemp Smith, Norman (1872–1958)   Philosophy professor at Edinburgh University. Known for his translation of Kant's* *Critique of Pure Reason* and his commentary on it.

Kenny, Anthony (b. 1931)   Oxford philosopher. Has written on philosophy of religion, philosophy of mind,* Wittgenstein,* and medieval philosophy.

Kierkegaard, Søren (1813–55)   Danish philosopher. Often described either as an existentialist* or a forerunner thereof. Famously wrote under different pseudonyms and in a variety of styles. Works include *Philosophical Fragments, The Concept of Irory with Constant Reference to Socrates,* and *Either/or*.

Krell, David Farrell   Professor of philosophy at DePaul University in Chicago. Writes about Greek philosophy and contemporary European philosophy and literature.

Kripke, Saul (b. 1940)   American philosopher; professor emeritus at Princeton University. Principal interests include metaphysics,* language, and logic.* His *Naming and Necessity* is a classic and *Wittgenstein* on Rules and Private Language* has been an object of much analysis and debate.

Kuhn, Thomas (1922–96) American philosopher and historian of science. His *The Structure of Scientific Revolutions* was an instant classic and remains a must-read. His concept of the 'paradigms' that constitute 'normal science' and the strains to which they are subject – ones that sometimes lead to scientific revolutions – are at the centre of the work.

Kuklick, Bruce   Nichols professor of American history at the University of Pennsylvania.

Lacan, Jacques (1901–81)   French psychoanalyst with a Heraclitian* style. Gave Freud a linguistic (or Saussurean*) reading. Influenced structuralist* and post-structuralist* thought.

Leibniz, Gottfried (1646–1716)   German rationalist* philosopher (with Newton, co-inventor of calculus), who enunciated the principle of sufficient reason.* His concept of simple substances called 'monads' – roughly, the unextended, and therefore immaterial, but dynamic elements of matter – lies at the foundation of his metaphysics.*

Levinas, Emmanuel (1906–95)   French citizen, born in Lithuania. His work was influenced by phenomenology, Heidegger,* and Jewish philosophy and has, in turn, influenced continental philosophy,* in general, and deconstruction,* in particular. Principal interest was ethics,* where one of his themes was the 'face to face' relation with the 'Other.' See his *The Totality of Infinity*.

Lévi-Strauss, Claude (b. 1908)   Belgian-born anthropologist who was a principal architect of structuralism,* a method of analysis that he applied to the study of cultures.* Among his works are *The Raw and the Cooked* and *The Savage Mind*.

Locke, John (1632–1704)   English empiricist.* Perhaps the greatest philosopher of his generation. The enormous influence of his political philosophy and psychology ran through the next century. Works include *Second Treatise of Government* and *An Essay Concerning Human Understanding*.

Lovejoy, Arthur (1873–1962)   American philosopher and historian of ideas. His *The Great Chain of Being* is a classic.

MacIntyre, Alasdair (b. 1929) Scottish-born moral philosopher* with

Aristotelian* tendencies; professor at the University of Notre Dame. Works include *A Short History of Ethics, After Virtue,* and *Three Rival Versions of Moral Enquiry.*

Marx, Karl (1818–83)   German political economist. 'Father' of the communist movements of the nineteenth and twentieth centuries. Famously stood Hegel's* idealism* on its head (or upright, depending on one's point of view), thereby developing the theory known as 'historical materialism,' in which one 'mode of production' (feudalism, capitalism, socialism) succeeds its predecessor as a result of class struggle.

McDowell, John (b. 1942)   Originally at Oxford, now at the University of Pittsburgh. His work on philosophy of mind* and language is rooted in Wittgenstein.* His *Mind and World,* a kind of correction or extension of Kant's* views on how the eponymous terms connect, has received much attention and comment.

McGinn, Colin (b. 1950)   English philosopher; now at Rutgers University in New Jersey. Has written both technical and popular works on philosophy of mind,* consciousness, philosophy of language, moral philosophy.*

Menn, Stephen   Holds doctorates in philosophy and mathematics; teaches at McGill University in Montreal. Interests are the history of philosophy and the history and philosophy of mathematics.

Mill, John Stuart (1806–73)   Bentham's* close associate. The greatest of the second generation of English utilitarians.* Adopted a more qualitative approach to pleasure than did Bentham. Wrote on logic,* politics, economics, and social issues. His *On Liberty* is one of the classic tracts of political philosophy.

Montesquieu (Baron de) (1689–1755); Charles Louis de Secondat. French political philosopher whose *Spirit of the Laws,* influenced by Locke's* philosophy, is one of the great texts of the Enlightenment.

Moore, G.E. (1873–1958)   Cambridge philosopher. Associated with 'common sense' or ordinary language philosophy.* One of his goals was to combat what he took to be the extraordinary claims of the idealists.* His 'The Refutation of Idealism' and 'A Defence of Common

Sense' are important papers in this regard. He also produced an influential work on ethics*: *Principia Ethica*.

Murdoch, Iris (1919–99)   Irish-born novelist and philosopher at Oxford University. Produced works on Plato,* Sartre,* and a variety of topics including ethics.*

Nagel, Thomas (b. 1937)   Fiorello La Guardia professor of law at New York University. Respected writer on ethics,* philosophy of mind,* and epistemology.* Defender of the stabilizing power of reason. Works include *The View from Nowhere, Other Minds,* and *The Last Word*.

Nehamas, Alexander (b. 1946)   Professor of philosophy and humanities at Princeton University. Has written with great lucidity on Socrates,* Kierkegaard,* and Nietzsche.*

Neurath, Otto (1882–1945)   Austrian philosopher. Member of the Vienna Circle.* Fled to England (Oxford) to avoid Nazism. His boat metaphor is a famous anti-foundationalist image.

Nietzsche, Friedrich (1844–1900)   German philologist, philosopher, and writer of iconoclastic works. Opposed the systematic philosophy of the Enlightenment and especially of Hegel,* including the idea that there is a transcendent meaning to life or history. His work has been an important source of anti-metaphysical thought, especially among continental* and existentialist* philosophers. His catchphrase, known to almost everyone, is 'God is dead!'

Norris, Christopher   Distinguished research professor of philosophy at Cardiff University. Played an important part in introducing Derrida* and deconstruction* to English-speaking audiences. Has written on aesthetics, metaphysics,* and philosophy of language.

Nussbaum, Martha (b. 1947)   American philosopher; Ernst Freund Distinguished Service professor of law and ethics at the University of Chicago. Has written with great lucidity on Greek philosophy, the relation between philosophy and literature, education, women's issues, and social policy. Works include *The Fragility of Goodness, Love's Knowledge,* and *Sex and Social Justice*.

Ockham, William (ca. 1288–ca. 1349)   English Franciscan monk. Nominalist,* who disputed the possibility of a proof for the existence of God. Famous for Ockham's Razor – entities are not to be multiplied unnecessarily – although it does not appear in his writings.

Parmenides (b. ca. 510 BCE)   Founder of the Eleatic School.* Much revered philosopher in the ancient world. Argued that change was logically impossible and that our experience is, therefore, illusory. Eponymous character in one of Plato's* dialogues.

Pavel, Thomas (b. 1941)   Professor of romance languages and literature at the University of Chicago.

Peacocke, Christopher (b. 1950)   Was Waynflete professor of Metaphysical Philosophy at Oxford, now professor of philosophy at New York University. Writes on philosophy of mind* and psychology. See his *The Realm of Reason.*

Peirce, Charles Sanders (1839–1914)   American philosopher, logician,* and originator of pragmatism* (which he later changed to 'pragmaticism'). One of his fundamental notions was that a true idea is one to which any competent authority or observer would assent.

Plato (ca. 427–ca. 347 BCE)   Athenian philosopher; founder of the Academy.* His philosophy, known as classical realism,* centred on the somewhat variable theory of Forms* or Ideas. Author of roughly (the exact number is in dispute) twenty-six dialogues, which are usually divided into early, middle, and late periods. In the first of these, Socrates* is the central character, and Plato is probably doing a fair bit of exposition of his teacher's ideas. In the middle period, Socrates remains the central figure but more of Plato's own ideas begin to emerge. In the late dialogues, Socrates is less prominent and even absent.

Popper, Karl (1902–94)   Austrian-born philosopher. Known for his work in philosophy of science and political philosophy. A logical positivist,* empiricist,* and scientific realist.* Asserted that the hallmark of a scientific theory is that it is falsifiable because, based on induction,* it can never be absolutely verifiable. Wrote a famous polemic against Plato,* Hegel* and Marx,* all of whom he considered enemies of an 'open society.' See his *Objective Knowledge* and *The Open Society and Its Enemies*. For an entertaining account of his difficult relationship with Wittgenstein,* see David Edmond's and John Eidinow's *Wittgenstein' Poker*.

Putnam, Hilary (b. 1926)   Emeritus professor at Harvard. Among the foremost American philosophers of his generation. Has written on the philosophy of science, epistemology,* metaphysics,* and ethics.* Has adjusted his views from a strict realism* to an anti-foundationalist 'naturalized realism.' Works include *Representation and Reality, Renewing Philosophy*, and *Reason, Truth and History*.

Pyrrho of Elis (ca. 365–ca. 275 BCE)   Originator of Pyrrhonistic scepticism,* one of the two main branches of scepticism in the ancient world. Recommended confining oneself to reporting on appearances and thereby suspending judgment about everything as the best way to achieve a calm life.

Quine, Willard van Orman (1908–2000)   Occupant of the Edgar Pierce chair for philosophy at Harvard University from 1956 to 2000. Major figure in twentieth-century analytic philosophy.* Well known for his critique of the 'two dogmas of empiricism'* and for his concept of the indeterminacy of translation. Originally influenced by logical positivism.* Wrote on philosophy of language, metaphysics,* and epistemology.* Works include *From a Logical Point of View* (which contains 'Two Dogmas of Empiricism'), *Word and Object*, and *Ontological Relativity and Other Essays*.

Rawls, John (1921–2002)   American social and political philosopher at Cornell University, the Massachusetts Institute of Technology, and Harvard University. Author of the monumental *A Theory of Justice*. A core idea is that we assess social arrangements by imagining a starting point in which everyone is equal and in which the future is shrouded by a 'veil of ignorance.' From such a position, he argued, we would have to adopt a stance of equal concern for everyone.

Ricœur, Paul (b. 1913)   French philosopher at the Sorbonne, the University of Paris, and the University of Chicago. Scholar of hermeneutics.* Has also written on ethics* and politics. Works include *The Symbolism of Evil, Interpretation Theory*, and *Oneself as Another*.

Rorty, Richard (b. 1931)   American pragmatist,* has taught at Princeton and the University of Virginia and is now at Stanford University. His *Philosophy and the Mirror of Nature* launched an attack on traditional representationist* epistemology.* Also a proponent of bringing down what he sees as artificial borders between disciplines. This springs from his view that there is no objective world for philosophers to explicate, discover, or otherwise get in touch with. Works include *Consequences of Pragmatism, Philosophical Papers,* and *Contingency, Irony and Solidarity.*

Rovane, Carol   Professor of philosophy at Columbia University. Has written on metaphysics,* moral philosophy,* and scepticism.*

Russell, Bertrand (1872–1970)   English philosopher, mathematician, social activist, and popular writer: Winner of the 1950 Nobel prize for literature. Contributed greatly to the development of logic* and analytic philosophy.* An empiricist,* whose approach was known as logical atomism.* Wrote widely on epistemology* and metaphysics.* An easy stylist, his *A History of Western Philosophy* is an immensely enjoyable read. Mentor to Wittgenstein* when the latter first arrived at Cambridge in 1912. Works include *Principia Mathematica* (with Alfred North Whitehead *), *Logic and Knowledge,* and *The Problems of Philosophy.*

Ryle, Gilbert (1900–76)   Oxford analytic philosopher* and practitioner of ordinary language philosophy.* Famous for his catchphrase 'the ghost in the machine' (in *The Concept of Mind*), which referred to what he considered the mistaken Cartesian view of the mind as a separate substance inhabiting the body.

Sartre, Jean-Paul (1905–80)   Perhaps the best-known existentialist* philosopher of the twentieth century. Also a novelist, playwright, and political activist. Influenced by the German phenomenologist Edmund Husserl* and by Heidegger.* His major exposition of existentialism is *Being and Nothingness.*

Saussure, Ferdinand de (1857–1913)   Swiss linguist, whose work is at the foundation of modern linguistics. Exerted a strong influence on structuralism,* post-structuralism,* and semiotic theory. In France, the writings of Lacan,* Foucault,* Derrida,* and Barthes* bear the mark of his influence. His principal work is *Course in General Linguistics.*

Schelling, F.W.J. (1775–1854)   German idealist* philosopher in the tradition of both Kant* and Hegel.* Influenced the development of Romanticism, especially in England.

Schlick, Moritz (1882–1936)   Austrian philosopher and member of the Vienna Circle.* Proponent of extreme logical rigour in philosophy. In his view, most hitherto existing philosophical systems were meaningless insofar as they could not be tested according to the verification principle.* Murdered by one of his students.

Schopenhauer, Arthur (1788–1860)   German philosopher; re-presented Kant's* *noumena** and *phenomena** as aspects of the self – which appears phenomenally as an assertion of 'will.' Influenced Nietzsche* and Wittgenstein.* See his *The World as Will and Representation*.

Scruton, Roger (b. 1944)   English philosopher, broadcaster, and entrepreneur, whose work ranges over aesthetics, politics, and the history of philosophy. His *Modern Philosophy* is an excellent source book.

Sellars, Wilfrid (1912–89)   American philosopher of mind* and metaphysics.* Opposed all forms of foundationalism,* most memorably through his rejection of the 'myth of the given.'* See his *Empiricism and the Philosophy of Mind*.

Sextus Empiricus (2nd century)   Physician and sceptical* philosopher whose *Outlines of Pyrrhonism* revived the ideas of Pyrrho of Elis.'* His *Against the Professors* attacked the pretensions of dogmatic* philosophers. The revival of interest in him in the sixteenth century played an important part in the development of empiricism* (named after him) and modern science.

Sidgwick, Henry (1838–1900)   Professor of moral philosophy* at Cambridge. Developed a utilitarian* theory of ethics.* See his *The Methods of Ethics*.

Skinner, Quentin (b. 1940)   Regius professor of modern history at Cambridge University. Specializes in the intellectual history of early modern Europe. See his *The Foundations of Modern Political Thought*.

Socrates (ca. 470–399 BCE)   Athenian philosopher. Wrote nothing, but was muse to almost all subsequent Greek and Roman philosophers. What we know of him comes mainly from Plato* and another contemporary, Xenophon.* Principal character in Aristophanes's *The Clouds*. Famous for his question and answer 'Socratic method,'* he seems to have restricted himself to testing the ideas of others, as opposed to developing a comprehensive philosophy of his own. Executed in 399 BCE.

Strawson, Peter (b. 1919)   Oxford analytic philosopher* (now emeritus). Important parts of his work have been concerned with an exegesis and critique of Kant.* See his *Individuals* and *The Bounds of Sense*. Also examined issues in metaphysics,* epistemology, and logic.*

Stroud, Barry (b. 1935)   Canadian-born professor of philosophy at the University of California, Berkeley. Has written on epistemology,* language, scepticism,* Hume,* and Wittgenstein.* Works include *The Significance of Philosophical Scepticism* and *The Quest for Reality*.

Taylor, Charles (b. 1931)   Canadian philosopher; taught at McGill and Oxford. Has written on a wide variety of topics including political philosophy, the nature of modernity, ethics,* and multiculturalism, as well as Plato* and Hegel.* Works include *Hegel* and *Sources of the Self*.

Thales (ca. 625–ca. 550 BCE)   Often described as the first philosopher. Eldest of the Milesian* triumvirate of nature philosophers. Essentially a cosmologist* and astronomer, he famously predicted a solar eclipse in 585 BCE.

Vlastos, Gregory (1907–91); Was a professor of philosophy at Princeton. Highly respected writer on ancient philosophy in general and Socrates* and Plato* in particular. See his *Socrates, Ironist and Moral Philosopher*.

Whitehead, Alfred North (1861–1947)   English philosopher and mathematician. Co-author (with Bertrand Russell*) of *Principia Mathematica*. Famous aphorism was that all of philosophy is a series of footnotes to Plato.*

Williams, Bernard (1929–2003)   English moral philosopher,* principally at Cambridge University. Resurrected a notion of ethics* as a concern with 'living well' as opposed to a narrower deontological* notion of doing one's duty. Wrote an important book on Descartes.* Works include *Moral Luck, Shame and Necessity,* and *Descartes: The Project of Pure Enquiry.*

Wittgenstein, Ludwig (1889–1951)   Austrian philosopher who spent much of his working life at Cambridge University (where he appeared on Russell's* doorstep in 1912). With Heidegger,* one of the two most influential philosophers of the first half of the twentieth century. His career is generally divided into early and later periods, the first referring to the years leading to the publication of the *Tractatus Logico-Philosophicus,* which appeared in German in 1921 and in English in 1922. After a seven-year hiatus, he returned to Cambridge and philosophy in 1929. Although he published nothing more during his lifetime, he left behind a voluminous manuscript literature, including the *Philosophical Investigations,* which was published in 1953. In one way or another, his work is concerned with the nature of language and the ways in which language can 'bewitch' us.

Wright, Crispin (b. 1942)   Wardlaw professor at the University of Edinburgh. Has written on language, metaphysics,* epistemology,* Wittgenstein,* and Frege.* Works include *Truth and Objectivity* and *Rails to Infinity.*

Xenophanes of Colophon (ca. 560–ca. 470 BCE)   Presocratic* philosopher and originator of epistemology* as a philosophical concern. Distinguished between opinion (what appears to be true) and knowledge (what *is* true).

Xenophon (454–ca. 357 BCE)   Athenian solider of fortune and friend of Socrates.* Like Plato,* wrote Socratic dialogues, including the *Memorabilia* and the *Apology.*

Zeno of Elea (mid-5th century BCE)   Eleatic philosopher.* Famous for his paradoxes,* which were intended to demonstrate the logical* absurdity of our concepts of space and time.

Zuckert, Catherine (b. 1942)   Professor of political science at the University of Notre Dame. See her *Postmodern Platos.*

Glossary of Key Terms

An asterisk indicates a corresponding entry in one of the glossaries.

Academy   One of the four Athenian schools of philosophy (along with the Lyceum,* Stoicism* and Epicureanism*). It was founded by Plato* sometime after 390 BCE. Aristotle* spent twenty years there.

Analytic philosophy   A designation referring principally to a British, American, Australian (and originally Austrian) approach. Rooted in the logic* and linguistic analysis of Russell* and subsequently Wittgenstein.*

Analytic-synthetic distinction   From Kant.* An analytic statement is one in which the predicate is included in the subject (e.g., 'Bachelors are unmarried'), while a synthetic statement is one in which it is not so included (e.g., 'My car is red'). Analytic statements are, essentially, definitional, whereas synthetic ones are based on experience. But see synthetic *a priori*.* Quine* famously attacked this distinction as one of the 'two dogmas of empiricism.'

Antinomy   A term for a contradiction or paradox.* Kant* famously set out four 'antinomies' about which he thought it impossible to decide: (1) The world is temporally and spatially finite or it is infinite. (2) There is or is not a simple substance. (3) There is or is not free will (i.e., there is a 'self'). (4) There is or is not a necessary being (God).

Anti-realism   See realism.*

A priori / *a posteriori*   Terms referring, respectively, to things that can be known independently of evidence (e.g., that bachelors are unmarried) and to things that can only be known on the basis on evidence (e.g., that my car is red). They can be paired off with analytic* and synthetic* statements, but see synthetic *a priori*.*

Argument   The process of stating what one takes to be true (the conclusion) supported by the reasons why one believes it to be true (the premises).

Atomic proposition   Any logically simple sentence that is true or false independently of any other sentence. It is astonishingly hard to give an example: 'That is green' perhaps approximates one.

Atomism   The philosophy of a group of fifth century BCE physicalist philosophers – notably Leucippus and Democritus – who argued that all existing things were composed of a single substance: atoms. The word derives from 'a-toma,' which means, indivisible.

Being   Another name for existence and, hence, the subject matter of ontology.* The term is closely associated with Heidegger,* who variously wrote about 'Being,' 'being,' and even 'bey-ing'; he argued that we have to think of being, especially in 'human being,' as a verb rather than a noun.

Categorical imperative   Kant's* fundamental moral law. It states that the maxims by which one acts should be capable of being universalized – that is, they should apply to all people at all times in all circumstances – as compared to hypothetical imperatives which are dependent on certain conditions holding.

Categorical logic   A deductive calculus first formulated by Aristotle.* Its basic elements are the subject and predicate 'terms' in a sentence. Universal* and existential* quantifiers are then applied to the subject. The universally quantified sentence, 'All humans are mortal' has, e.g., the form '∀S are P.'

Certainty, epistemic and moral   Epistemic certainty is absolute, encompassing cases where the possibility of error has been ruled out. Moral certainty refers to cases with a very high degree of probability but which stop short of absolute certainty. Generally, knowledge derived from experience is morally certain, whereas knowledge derived within formal systems such as deductive logic* or mathematics is epistemically certain.

Classical realism   The name for Plato's* metaphysics.* It accords reality to the Forms.* Classical realism is, thus, a version of idealism.*

Cogito   Refers to Descartes'* catchphrase in his *Discourse on Method: Cogito ergo sum*, 'I think therefore I am.'

Coherence theory of truth   The view that the truth of a statement depends upon its relation to a set of surrounding statements. If it coheres (or hangs together) with those statements, it is true. If it contradicts them, it is false. Statements are thus true or false by virtue of their relation to language, rather than their relation to the world (as in the correspondence theory*).

Consequentialism   A moral theory – utilitarianism,* for example – according to which the value of an action is judged by its results.

Continental philosophy   A catch-all designation for the European philosophy of the past half-century or so. It covers everything from existentialism* to structuralism* to post-structuralism* to post-modernism* to deconstruction.* Rooted in Hegel* and Nietzsche.*

Correspondence theory of truth   The view that the truth of a statement is determined by whether the fact or 'state of affairs' it describes exists. The statement 'My car is red' is true if I have a red car. Unlike the coherence theory,* the truth of a statement is a result of its relation to the world, which makes it more strongly realist.*

Cosmogony   A theory or account of the origins of the universe.

Cosmological proof   A proof for the existence of God that is based on assumptions about the nature of the world (unlike the ontological proof*). Aquinas* offered five such proofs, one being that nature is orderly (or rational) indicates the existence of a rational creator.

Cosmology   The study of the nature of the universe as a whole. Nowa-

days it also refers to what astrophysicists such as Stephen Hawking*
do.

Dasein Literally, 'being-there.' Heidegger's* term for human existence.

Deconstruction The philosophical tendency associated with Derrida.*
It is, essentially, a non-stop struggle with metaphysics,* the goal being
to demonstrate the impossibility of 'Origins' – i.e., a foundational (see
foundationalism*) or immutable meaning* in what is said or written.
Arguing that the metaphorical and metonymic nature of language leaves
it eternally open (or 'unclosable'), Derrida attempts to 'deconstruct' all
projects for discovering a truth or meaning that will stand still.

Deduction Along with induction,* one of the branches of logic.* A
formal system of reasoning in which the principal concern is validity.*
In deduction, one reasons from accepted truths (or rules) to conclusions
that are entailed by those truths.

Diachrony and **synchrony** The analysis, respectively, of language as
an evolving and as a static system.

Différance A pun on the French verbs 'to differ' and 'to defer.' Derrida*
coined the term to express the openness of language. Given this openness, meaning* can always be other or different than it appears to be
and any metaphysical* notion of Origin or closure is eternally deferred.
What we say or write always deconstructs itself into its 'others.'

Deontology A theory of ethics,* often associated with Kant.* It maintains that one's duty is to perform certain actions no matter what the
consequences may be.

Dogmatism A term coined by ancient sceptics* to describe non-
sceptical philosophers, who thought it possible to attain knowledge and
develop coherent philosophical systems.

Dissemination As coined by Derrida,* it refers to the 'fact' that a text
has multiple meanings* that cannot be controlled.

Dualism An ontological* position according to which the mental and the material – or mind and body – are each basic entities, neither being reducible to the other. Descartes'* philosophy was dualistic. See *monism* and *pluralism*.

Eleaticism   The doctrines of the Presocratic* Eleatic school, founded by Parmenides.* With his principal acolytes, Zeno of Elea* and Melissus, Parmenides argued that our conceptions of time and space and, hence, the world as it appears to us, are logically absurd and cannot be true; everything is a great 'Oneness.' Plato* was influenced by the Eleatics.

Eliminativism   This position holds that psychological discussions of the mind should be replaced by neurological discussions of the brain.

Emotivism   A theory of ethics.* It takes emotions to be the basis of actions, with reason being only a secondary control on them.

Empiricism   A philosophical doctrine. It is based on the premise that knowledge comes from experience. Locke* rejected innate ideas,* arguing that the mind was a *tabula rasa* at birth, but Kant* wrapped his empiricism in a layer of transcendental idealism.* Some versions – phenomenalism,* for example – take us very far from an ordinary conception of experience.

Epicureanism   The doctrines of the Epicureans. One of the four schools of Athens, it was founded by Epicurus* in 306 BCE. Influenced by atomism,* the Epicureans espoused hedonism* and physicalism* and rejected any possibility of an afterlife.

Epistemology   The theory of knowledge. Epistemology is concerned with the general conditions of knowledge – how it is possible, how it is achieved, and how it is tested. Epistemology is an ancient and central part of philosophy that, in Platonic terms, asks how we can justify the beliefs we have; how we can know that they are true.

Essence and accident   This distinction is as old as Aristotle.* An essence is a characteristic without which a given 'thing' would not be what it is. For the Greeks, reason was, e.g., essential to being human. An accident is a contingent characteristic in whose absence the 'thing' will still be what it is. A person could, for example lose his crankiness and still be human. So, I am essentially rational but only accidentally cranky.

Ethics   The branch of philosophy concerned with the development of the rules or standards by which we conduct our lives. It is very closely linked to moral philosophy,* which is, essentially, the study of concepts of right and wrong (or good and evil).

Evil Demon   Descartes* introduces the *malin génie* in the first meditation as a mischievous anti-God, who deceives us about everything, including our existence. If such a being is conceivable, scepticism* cannot be overcome. But Descartes quickly assures us, in the second meditation, that such a being is not conceivable because we cannot be deceived about our own existence.

Existential quantifier   An attribute applied to subjects in categorical logic* and variables in predicate logic: It means 'some,' which stands for 'at least one.' The symbol is ∃. In categorical logic, the existential negation is 'some are not.'

Existentialism   Although rooted in the philosophy of Kierkegaard* and Nietzsche,* the term was first applied to Sartre* and the Paris writers around him in the 1930s. Its catchphrase 'existence precedes essence' means that there are no universal standards for a human life: we are what we do, the sum of our actions. Hence, we are 'condemned to be free.'

Forms   Since Plato* never quite states his theory of Forms (or Ideas) the same way twice, it is hard to say exactly what he meant by it. Essentially, the Forms exist in a separate world as archetypes for the things in this world, which are imperfect copies of the Forms. What 'things' have Forms is open to debate: abstractions such as Justice or Truth or Beauty or Goodness certainly would, and many physical things (humans, for example) as well. But how far Plato extended the idea is hard to say. Aristotle* (see also, *third man argument*) rejected the separate existence of the Forms, and Plato himself subjected the idea to criticism in his *Parmenides*.

Foundationalism   The position that there is an indubitable foundation from which to derive epistemically certain* knowledge.

Frankfurt School   A movement of German philosophers and sociologists centred around the Institute for Social Research, which was established at Frankfurt University in 1923. The School gave rise to what is known as 'critical theory,' which was, very roughly, a kind of Hegelian-based Marxism. Theodore Adorno,* Max Horkheimer, and Herbert Marcuse were central figures of the School. In recent years, Jürgen Habermas* is perhaps the name most famously identified with it.

Hedonism   An ethical* theory. It holds that the goal of human behaviour ought to be pleasure. It is also the psychological theory that humans are primarily motivated by fear of pain and love of pleasure. Pleasure is often defined negatively as the absence of pain.

Hedonic calculus   Also known as the felicific calculus. It is Bentham's* formula for evaluating pleasure by assessing its intensity, certainty, and duration. As far as I know, no one has ever succeeded in putting numbers to the procedure.

Hermeneutics   Originally the art of interpreting biblical texts. It is now used in reference to all texts.

Hermetics   The authors to a body of texts dating from early in the first millennium. It was long falsely attributed to an Egyptian priest Hermes Trismegistus. Espouses a kind of occult Platonism,* mixing magic with reason.

Historicism   The term has a number of different meanings. Perhaps the most prevalent is the view of history as subject to laws that allow one to predict events.

Holism   The idea that the whole is greater than the sum of the parts and that those parts can be understood only in relation to the whole. The coherence theory of truth* is holist insofar as it makes the truth of a sentence dependent on a set of sentences (or a theory).

Idealism   A theory of metaphysics.* It either makes all of reality mental or it makes the 'external world' dependent on a conscious mind. Berkeley's* philosophy is an example of the first view, while Kant's* transcendental idealism* and Hegel's* idealism are examples of the second.

Identity and difference   The issue of how to say what something is without also saying what it is not. It raises the Parmenidean* question of whether we can talk about 'what is not.'

Induction   With deduction,* a branch of logic.* It proceeds from specific observations to general conclusions. If the evidence is properly gathered, then one can be morally* certain* that the conclusion is true.

Innate ideas   An idea that is present in the mind at birth and is known by intuition* to be true. Both Plato* and Descartes* believed that there were innate ideas, although only Descartes thought that they were readily available for introspection.

Intuition   Knowledge that is spontaneous or immediate, which is to say, non-inferential. One has it without going through a process of reasoning. Innate ideas* are known intuitively, as are temporal and spatial ones in Kant's* philosophy.

Knowledge by acquaintance and **description**   From Russell.* The former is knowledge of anything confronted directly, such as feelings or objects of experience. The latter are things we know indirectly, through ideas. Shakespeare is, e.g., known by description since he is not and never will be a being with whom we are directly acquainted. Theoretically, knowledge by description is reducible to, or depends on, acquaintance.

Language-game   A central concept in Wittgenstein's* later work. It holds that language, like a game, is both conventional and rule-governed. There are many language-games. What a word means* can be determined only if one knows the game within which it is being used. Philosophical problems – the 'bewitchment' of language – arise when philosophers are not sufficiently sensitive to the game that is in play.

Law of the excluded middle   A logical* law stating that once something, call it X, has been identified, everything in existence is either X or it is not-X. There is no third, or middle, option.

Law of identity   A logical law stating that everything is what it is. In an argument,* therefore, we must clearly define our terms and then stick to the definition. As Quine* said, 'no entity without identity.'

Law of non-contradiction   A logical law, dating from Aristotle,*
stating that for any defined entity, call it X, nothing can simultaneously
be X and not-X.

Logic   The study of laws of reasoning. It has long been considered to
be the foundation of philosophy. See *deduction* and *induction*.

Logical atomism   A term, coined by Russell,* to designate his version
of empiricism.* It also refers to Wittgenstein's* method in the *Tractatus*.
For Russell, a logical atom* was a little 'patch' of perception, for example, a bit of colour or a sense of shape. In the *Tractatus*, when
Wittgenstein referred to combining 'things' (or 'objects' depending on
the translation) to make 'states of affairs,' he may have had logical
atoms in mind. The idea is that our sense of the world is built up from
these minute, and entirely theoretical, atomistic experiences.

Logical constants   Terms that link sentences (or propositions*) in
sentential logic.* They are: conjunction (and/but), disjunction (either ...
or), the hypothetical or conditional (if ... then), and the biconditional (if
and only if).

Logical positivism   The version of empiricism* associated with the
Vienna Circle* and greatly influenced by Russell's* logical atomism.*
Enamoured of logic* and mathematics, the Circle's objective was to
bring the rigour of science to philosophy. The most famous idea connected with logical positivism is the verification principle.*

Lyceum   One of·the four great philosophy schools of Athens. It was
founded by Aristotle* in 335 BCE.

Meaning   A term too amorphous to summarize. The basic issue is:
how do words and sentences bear meaning? Is it through reference to
the world or by reference to other words and sentences? In other words,
is meaning referential, grammatical, or even, syntactical? Does it depend
on a correspondence* or a coherence* theory of truth or no theory at all?
Frege's* distinction between the 'sense' and 'reference' of a sentence is
important to theories of meaning, as is the work of Wittgenstein,* Austin,* and Davidson.* Quine* 'attacks' the whole idea. Deconstructionists*
have made no end of mischief with the concept of meaning.

Metaphysics   The historical foundation of western philosophy. The project of articulating the ultimate nature of reality. The thrust of most post-modernism* (going back to Nietzsche*), and, of late, more than a little of analytic philosophy,* has been anti-metaphysical.

Milesian philosophy   The 'nature philosophy' of the three Presocratic* philosophers from Miletus (on the Ionian coast): Thales,* Anaximander,* and Anaximenes. They saw the world as being composed of four elements – earth, fire, air and water – and beneath them, the *apeiron*.*

Modal logic   First surfaces in Aristotle's* *Prior Analytics*. It distributes statements into the necessary and the possible – what must be and what might be. To say, for example, 'necessarily, all humans are mortal' is to assert that in all possible worlds* mortality is a characteristic of humans.

Monism   Like dualism* and pluralism,* an ontological* position asserting that all existing things can be reduced either to mental or material properties, but not both. In the first case, we have idealism,* in the second materialism. Eliminativism* is a monist position.

Moral philosophy   Closely linked to ethics,* a branch of philosophy. Essentially, it is the study of the concepts of right and wrong (or good and evil).

Myth of the given   A term coined by Wilfrid Sellars.* It refers to the, in his view mistaken, belief that our perceptual capacities put us directly in touch with objects.

Naturalism   A term used here to designate the anti-foundationalist epistemology.* It holds that knowledge is the product of social and historical forces – of our embeddedness in worlds – and so will shift and change over time.

Naturalistic fallacy   From Hume.* It is the attempt to derive what ought to be from what is, i.e., of moving from this world to a transcendent one.

New sceptics   A term used here to designate those post-modern* and pragmatist* philosophers who turn their scepticism* on philosophy itself, asking whether (or in what way) philosophy can still be said to exist.

Nominalism   An ontological* position denying the existence of universals.* In this view, universals are simply convenient names for groups of objects.

Noumena *and* **phenomena**   Kant's* terms for, respectively, the world-in-itself and the world as it appears to experiencing beings such as us. In Kant's formulation, one can never get beyond *phenomena* to *noumena*, and indeed, the latter is essentially just a limit to the phenomenal world of 'things.'

Ontological proof   Like the cosmological proof,* a demonstration that God exists. Instead of arguing from the world to God, it analyses the concept of a perfect being, and contends that anyone who understands that idea will also understand that there is necessarily a being who corresponds to it. (In short, a perfect being necessarily exists or else it would not be perfect.) The proof stems from St Anselm of Canterbury* and was used by Descartes* in his *Meditations*.

Ontology   A branch of metaphysics* concerned with the fundamental *kinds* of things that exist. The three principal ontological* positions are monism,* dualism,* and pluralism.*

Ontotheology   From Heidegger.* A slightly pejorative term for the attempt to view the world from what Putnam* called a god's-eye view, that is, objectively and comprehensively.

Ordinary language philosophy   Associated with Moore* and Wittgenstein* at Cambridge and Austin* and Ryle* at Oxford. Its basic premise is that philosophers must take their bearings from the ways in which language is ordinarily used, as opposed to inventing technical meta-languages intended to correct ordinary usage. A variant of analytic philosophy.*

Paradox   It can mean anything that contradicts accepted opinion. More technically, it refers to statements or arguments* that are self-contradictory. Take the Liar's Paradox: 'I am lying.' If it is true it is false and if it is false it is true. The problem with such paradoxes is that they often have no referent – lying about what? – and so they may simply be meaning-less statements.

Phenomenalism   A variant of empiricism.* It deals with the problem of the veil of perception* by talking of appearances – perceptions, rather than a remote and seemingly inaccessible reality. Phenomenal-ists reject all consideration of such a reality.

Phenomenology   A philosophical method associated with Edmund Husserl.* The fundamental idea is that philosophical analysis begins with a close inspection of the contents of one's consciousness. All exter-nal data, including one's assumptions about what the world is like, are to be 'bracketed' out. When this is done, the pure intentionality of consciousness – the fact that it is always directed towards something – becomes apparent. This is the starting point for an analysis of the essential features of experience. Given the immediacy of one's con-sciousness, phenomenology is a form of intuition.*

Philosophy of mind   A branch of metaphysics* concerned with the nature of the mind or human consciousness. Dealing with such matters as the relation, or lack thereof, of the mind and brain, intentionality, self-consciousness, and artificial intelligence, it overlaps with psychol-ogy and neurology.

Physicalism   The ontological* position, sometimes called 'material-ism,' that only physical, or material, objects exist, although these objects may be, in some cases, phenomenalist* ones.

Pluralism   The ontological* position that there are many different kinds of entities, all of which are irreducible to other kinds.

Positivism   A philosophical position that has its origins in the work of Henri Saint-Simon and Comte.* It was intended as a scientific and non-metaphysical method of acquiring knowledge, essentially, through the collection of data and the development of laws suggested by the data.

Possible worlds   The idea that worlds other than the existing one are possible. This view connects with modal logic*: Is the world we inhabit a necessary world or a possible one? In sentential logic,* truth tables* set out possible worlds. If, for example, we take any two statements p and q, there are four possible worlds: one in which both statements are true, one in which p is true and q is false, one in which p is false and q is true, and one in which both are false. Necessarily, only one of these worlds can exist at any time, although the one that does exist probably does not exist necessarily.

Post-modernism   An approach that rejects all definitions and so is, by definition, undefinable. The French philosopher Jean-François Lyotard described it as 'that which in the modern invokes the unpresentable in presentation itself.' The reader can perhaps see the affinity with the rejection of 'Origin' in deconstruction. Post-modernists reject the idea of absolute authorities. We are all our own authorities and we set our own standards. What is art? What is philosophy? Who can say?

Post-structuralism   Dates from the 1970s. As the name suggests, a reaction to structuralism.* Foucault* is probably the most famous thinker associated with it, although whether he would have accepted the designation is another question. Basically, it is a Nietzschean* perspective which emphasizes the arbitrariness of the Saussurean* sign* and, hence, the mutability – as opposed to the stability – of language, or 'discourse.'

Pragmatism   Coined by Peirce.* It holds practical results, or 'what works,' as the touchstone for evaluating thought. Thus, William James's* statement, 'Truth happens to an idea.'

Presocratics   Greek Philosophers who pre-date Socrates.* Only fragments of their works survive.

Principle of sufficient reason   From Leibniz.* It states that there is a reason every state of affairs is as it is, for if there were not, that state of affairs could not exist because there would be no adequate reason for it to do so.

Proposition   A sentence that carries a truth-value.*

Pythagoreans   A Presocratic* school founded by Pythagoras. They believed that the secret to the universe lay in the harmonies of mathematics. Plato* is said to have visited the school in the 390s BCE and in some of his dialogues espouses their belief in metempsychosis – the doctrine that the *psyche** is immortal and is reincarnated.

Radical doubt   Also known as 'systematic' and 'hyperbolic' doubt. It is Descartes'* sceptical* beginning in search of a stable foundation for knowledge. The idea is to doubt everything that it is not intuitively, at bottom, impossible to doubt – your own existence, for example.

Rationalism   Often associated with Descartes.* It stands in opposition to empiricism* as an epistemology* premised on innate ideas,* or, in a more modern context, the position that there are *a priori** truths. It places great emphasis on the role of reason, as opposed to observation or experience, in the pursuit of knowledge.

Realism and anti-realism   Realism is the ontological* commitment to the existence of mind-independent entities, whatever they may be; anti-realism denies such existence. Plato* was, for example, a realist about the Forms.* There are, of course, varieties of realism, the principal ones being direct and indirect.

Reductionism   Ontologically, the position that reality consists of a very small number of basic entities. Atomism,* for example, reduced everything to a single basic (i.e., indivisible) substance.

Regulative idea   In Kant,* an idea (such as God) required by reason even though its truth* cannot be demonstrated.

Relativism   The belief that the meaning,* value, and even the truth* of ideas are relative to their social, cultural, and historical context. It entails a denial of universal standards. Plato* despised the Sophists* in part because of their relativism.

Representationalism   A form of indirect realism that asserts that ideas in the mind are copies of things in the external world. This was Descartes'* view and it provides a wedge for scepticism* because there is always the possibility that the idea does not accurately represent the 'thing.' Innate ideas* do not suffer from this 'defect' because they do not represent. Rorty's* *Philosophy and the Mirror of Nature* is an extended criticism of representationalism.

Rigid designator   A term introduced by Saul Kripke* to refer to expressions that pick out, or designate, the same thing in all possible (i.e., imaginable) worlds. 'Freud' *necessarily* refers to the same person in all possible worlds in which he could exist even though the defining expression 'the founder of psychoanalysis' does not necessarily apply to him (or to anyone) in all those worlds. It is metaphysically necessary that, in whatever circumstances he might exist, Freud is Freud, but not that he be the inventor of psychoanalysis. He might have become a lawyer, for example, and still have been Freud. But he could not have been someone else and still have been Freud: That would violate the law of non-contradition.* Hence, rigid designators identify their objects without recourse to a stream of contingent descriptive phrases. Exactly how they do so – how they fix a reference – is a matter of some debate.

Scepticism   The position that knowledge is unattainable or even that there is nothing to know. Ancient Sceptics considered the pursuit of knowledge a futile and unsettling affair; better simply to live according to the appearances – that is, do what seems reasonable.

Scholasticism   The philosophy and theology of the medieval universities: by the mid-thirteenth century it had become largely a form of Aristotelianism.

Semantics   The theory of signs.* In Saussurean* terms, the relation between signifiers* and signifieds.* It concerns how words refer and what they refer to. In philosophy, it is tied to the investigation of truth conditions, i.e., establishing when a sentence is true.

Sense-data   The data immediately given in experience.

Sentential logic   Logic* in which the basic unit is the sentence rather than subject and predicate terms. Sentences are linked by logical constants.* Sometimes called propositional* logic.

Sign   For Saussure,* it consists of two parts: a signifier* and a signified.* The arbitrariness of the relation – that the two parts can be separated and the sign dismantled – has had important ramifications for linguistic philosophy.

Social constructionism   A naturalistic* theory that makes knowledge dependent upon social practices, meaning that it is neither value-free nor objective.

Socratic method   Socrates'* question-and-answer method of investigating concepts. See *elenchos*,* in Glossary of Greek Terms.

Sophism   The ideas of the Sophists,* a loose group of professional teachers, roughly contemporary with Socrates.* Plato* objected to their claim that they could teach people to be wise and to their apparent relativism* and even scepticism.* He gave them a worse reputation – as the word 'sophistry' indicates – than they perhaps deserved.

Stoicism   The last of the four great Athenian schools. Founded by Zeno of Citium around 300 BCE. Stoics sought *ataraxia*,* or calmness, which was to be attained through control of the emotions. Developed sentential logic* and a sophisticated epistemology.*

Structuralism   Derived from the work of Claude Lévi-Strauss. Influential theory in the 1960s and 1970s. Its basic idea is that societies and cultures could be read like Saussurean* systems of signs.*

Substance   In its Aristotelian* variant, distinguished from an attribute (or characteristic) by being constantly present in a 'thing.' It is not, however, an essence but the underlying 'being' to which attributes can attach themselves. It is the 'thingness' of the thing.

Syllogism   First used by Aristotle.* It means something like 'reckoning together' or even 'adding up': a three-sentence deductive* argument* consisting of two premises and a conclusion.

Synthetic *a priori*   From Kant.* It seems oxymoronic insofar as synthetic statements are known *a posteriori* and analytic ones *a priori*. Synthetic *a priori* judgments are, therefore, ones in which the predicate is not included in the subject – that is, they are not merely definitions – but which we, nonetheless, know to be true *a priori*: for example, the shortest distance between two points (on a flat surface) is a straight line. These judgments allow one to know, with epistemic certainty,* particular ideas that pertain to the world of experience. They, thus, help to overcome scepticism.*

Tautology   A statement that is true in all possible worlds.* The simplest form would be 'p or not-p.' The law of the excluded middle* is the law of tautology.

Teleology   The doctrine of final causes. It asserts that there is a pre-existing plan for the world or parts thereof. To take an example from Aristotle,* the teleological end of an acorn is an oak tree.

Third man argument   Aristotle's* term for the argument* against the regressive nature of Forms* in Plato's* *Parmenides*. It runs as follows: If there is a Form (F) 'Man,' then we now have a new group comprised of all men (M) plus the Form 'Man' (since they share 'man-ness'), and there must be a Form for this – let's call it M'. We now have a class of all men and a second class of all men plus the Form 'Man.' Hence, m^1, m^2, m^3 ... $m^{(n)}$ are members of class M, while m^1, m^2, m^3 ... $m^{(n)}$ and M are members of class M'. Thus begins an infinite regress.

Three laws of reason   Law of excluded middle,* law of identity,* and law of non-contradiction.*

Transcendental idealism   Name for Kant's* philosophy, in particular his insistence that our grasp of the phenomenal world rests upon categories of reason that are independent of experience: that is, the intuitions* of time and space and the categories of judgment. See phenomenalism.*

Truth   Who knows? Is it a property of sentences, warranted assertability, a redundant claim that what one says is borne out by the facts (whatever they are!) or, as Rorty* would have it, a compliment we pay to an idea? There are many theories about truth. The coherence* and correspondence* versions have been outlined here, and I will only add that I recommend that readers look up (somewhere) Saul Tarski's 'Truth-condition T.'

Truth table   A table used in sentential logic.* It sets out the conditions under which two or more statements joined by logical constants* are true or false.

Truth-value   In bivalent logic,* a statement, or proposition,* has one of two values – true or false.

Übermensch   Often translated as 'superman.' Nietzsche's* name for the creative or 'higher' individual who can make her life without being dragged down by 'slave morality.'

Universal quantifier   Applied to subjects in categorical logic* and variables in predicate logic, it means 'all' and is symbolized by ∀. In categorical logic, the universal negation is 'no.'

Universals   General terms that exist independently of any particular object. If, e.g., 'red' (or redness) is a universal term, then it exists apart from specific red objects. (See *nominalism*.) Plato* argued that without universals one cannot account for what all objects of a certain type – say, all red objects – have in common, because what they have in common is redness.

Utilitarianism   Hedonistic social and political philosophy associated with Bentham* and Mill,* and through the former, the idea of 'the greatest happiness of the greatest number' as the goal of government.

Validity   A judgment on the form of a deductive* argument.* To be valid, the truth* of the conclusion must follow necessarily from the truth of the premises.

Veil of perception   Also referred to as the 'veil of appearances.' It concerns a problem that arises from the indirect realism* of representationalism.* If we only know objects in the external world through our perceptions and, therefore, our ideas of them, how can we ever be (epistemically) certain that we have an accurate grasp of them? How, in other words, can a representationalist overcome scepticism*? Different solutions have been proposed. Descartes* employed innate ideas,* which he claimed to apprehend directly. Berkeley* resorted to idealism*; and many empiricists* became phenomenalists.* A more contemporary view is that the 'problem' does not need to be solved; the representationalist picture of the world that gives rise to it simply needs to be abandoned.

Verification principle   In logical positivism,* the assertion that the meaning* of a sentence lies in the method of deciding whether it is true.

Vicious circle   Technically, it is when members of a set can be defined only by reference to the set as a whole – for example, a basketball player is a member of the set of people who play basketball. Somewhat differently, it is when the conclusion of an argument* is assumed in the premises – for example, Descartes* is accused of proving God exists on the basis of innate ideas, which are ideas we can trust because they come from God.

Vienna Circle   The group of Austrian philosophers, including Carnap,* Schlick,* and Neurath,* who developed logical positivism.* The Circle began as early as 1907 but flourished in the 1920s and 1930s, until the rise of Nazism dispersed its members.

Weirdness principle   Invented by the author, it states that if a question is 'weird' – for example, 'How do you know you have a headache?' – it is probably a non-question, i.e., one that lies outside whatever language-game* is in play.

'What's that?' test   Invented by the author, from the suggestion that some signifiers* may refer to 'natural objects,' while others do not. A natural object is one that any sentient being would pick out and, if doing so for the first time, would ask, 'What's that?' All languages will have words for such objects. A tree is a natural object but a copse or grove is not. It has some relation, perhaps, to Kripke's* 'rigid designators.'

Glossary of Greek Terms

An asterisk indicates a corresponding entry in one of the glossaries.

Agathon　See *Arête*.*

Aitias logismos　An explanatory account: what a philosopher was to provide.

Akrasia　Weakness of will.

Apeiron　From Anaximander.* It means 'unbounded' or 'limitless' and refers to the inchoate matter from which the elements emerged.

Aporia　Confusion or perplexity.

Arête　Usually translated as 'virtue,' but also as 'excellence' (i.e., possessing skill). Essentially, it refers to 'goodness.' Its adjective is *agathon*, which is translated as 'good.'

Ataraxia　'Calmness' or 'unruffledness.' The Stoics,* Epicureans,* and Sceptics* considered it the goal of a good life.

Demiurgos　For Plato,* it is the 'great craftsman' who made the cosmos. Not God, but (I suppose) God's architect.

Doxa　Opinion or belief. A state between ignorance and knowledge.

Eikasia　'Image.' It refers to the lowest stage of cognitive development, essentially the stage of the chained prisoners in the Allegory of the Cave.

Elenchos   'Close examination.' It is the core of Socrates'* method in which, through questioning, he closely examines and refutes the definitions set before him.

Hegemonikon   'The chief or leading part.' It is the name the Stoics* name gave to the rational aspect of the *psyche*,* which for them became virtually the whole of the human *psyche.*

Ousia   'Being' or 'substance.' Aristotle's* term for that which underlies and supports all attributes.

Physiologia   'Nature philosophers' – we night call them scientists or physicists. A companion term is *physikoi.* The Milesian* philosophers were the first to be called this.

Poiesis   'Making,' from the verb 'to make' or 'to do.' It is the root of our word 'poetry.'

Psyche   Generally translated as 'soul.' It gradually came to represent the principle of life and individuality. It was either the seat of reason and wholly rational (in Stoicism*), or it harboured reason along with other sub-rational elements (in Plato* and Aristotle*).

Techne   'Art' or 'craft.' Essentially, it refers to activities that are teachable.

Tuche   Luck, or what happens to a person, as opposed to what one does to oneself. Aristotle* incorporated it into his ethics* by making it a variable affecting one's capacity to live the good life.

Suggested Readings

Chapter 1 What Is Philosophy?

Greek Philosophy

Brunschwig, Jacques, and Lloyd, G.E.R., eds. *Greek Thought: A Guide to Classical Knowledge.* Cambridge, Mass.: Belknap Press, 2000. An excellent range of articles by well-known scholars.

Hadot, Pierre. *What Is Ancient Philosophy?* Trans. Michael Chase. Cambridge, Mass.: Belknap Press, 2002. A good presentation of philosophy as a 'therapy' or way of life.

Kirk, G.S., Raven, J.E. and Schofield, M. *The Presocratic Philosophers.* 2nd ed. Cambridge: Cambridge University Press, 1983. An excellent source book, with both Presocratic fragments and commentary.

Plato and Socrates

Here are four quite different, interesting, and scholarly books.

Brisson, Luc. *Plato the Myth Maker.* Garrard Naddaf, translator. Chicago: University of Chicago Press, 1998.

Murdoch, Iris. *The Fire and the Sun.* Oxford: Oxford University Press, 1977. On Plato's banishment of the artists in *Republic.* A wonderful little book.

Nehamas, Alexander. *Virtues of Authenticity: Essays on Plato and Socrates.* Princeton: Princeton University Press, 1999.

Vlastos, Gregory. *Socrates, Ironist and Moral Philosopher.* Ithaca, N.Y.: Cornell University Press, 1991.

Scepticism

Annas, Julia, and Barnes, Jonathan. *The Modes of Scepticism.* Cambridge: Cambridge University Press, 1985.

Burnyeat, Myles, ed. *The Skeptical Tradition*. Berkeley: University of California Press, 1983.

Stroud, Barry. *The Significance of Philosophical Scepticism*. Oxford: Clarendon Press, 1984. A very good book, although not aimed at neophytes.

Modern Philosophy

Descombes, Vincent. *Modern French Philosophy*. L. Scott-Fox and J.M. Harding, translators. Cambridge: Cambridge University Press, 1980. A quarter of a century old. Excellent and still useful.

Scruton, Roger. *Modern Philosophy: An Introduction and Survey*. London: Mandarin Paperbacks, 1996. A good source book for analytic philosophy.

Chapter 2 Metaphysics: The Search for the God's-Eye View

General

Loux, Michael J. *Metaphysics: A Contemporary Introduction*. 2nd ed. London: Routledge, 2001.

– *Metaphysics: Contemporary Readings*. London: Routledge, 2002.

These companion volumes will introduce readers to leading thinkers in the field over the past fifty years.

Putnam, Hilary. *The Threefold Cord: Mind, Body and World*. New York: Columbia University Press, 1999. An interesting book by an important philosopher.

Descartes

Broughton, Janet. *Descartes' Method of Doubt*. Princeton: Princeton University Press, 2002. A good scholarly, yet accessible, treatment of the topic.

Menn, Stephen. *Descartes and Augustine*. Cambridge: Cambridge University Press, 2002. An excellent and detailed analysis of Descartes' philosophy in a slightly different context.

Gaukroger, Stephen. *Descartes: An Intellectual Biography*. Oxford: Clarendon Press, 1995. Not always easy reading. Worth the effort, especially if one wants to understand the 'scientific' Descartes.

Idealism

Vesey, G.N.A., ed. *Idealism Past and Present*. Cambridge: Cambridge University Press, 1982. A good source book.

Sprigge, Timothy L.S. *The Vindication of Absolute Idealism*. Edinburgh: University of Edinburgh Press, 1983. Somebody had to do it.

Kant

Körner, S. *Kant*. Harmondsworth: Penguin, 1955. Still my favourite introduction to Kant.

Thomson, Garrett. *On Kant*. Belmont, Calif.: Wadsworth Publishing, 2000. In the 'short introduction' genre. Intelligent and accessible.

Chapter 3 Wittgenstein's Ladder: The Modern Reaction to Metaphysics

General

McDowell, John. *Mind and World*. Cambridge: Harvard University Press, 1994. Important book. Not suggested for beginners.

Nagel, Thomas. *The View from Nowhere*. Oxford: Oxford University Press, 1986. Intelligent and very readable.

Quine, W.V. *Ontological Relativity and Other Essays*. New York: Columbia University Press, 1969. Advanced reading. Contains some of Quine's important ideas.

Rorty, Richard. *Consequences of Pragmatism*. Minneapolis: University of Minnesota Press, 1982. Rorty has an easy style, which is helpful to those new to philosophy.

Derrida and Deconstruction

Howells, Christina. *Derrida*. Cambridge: Polity Press, 1998. Not always easy reading – some chapters are more accessible than others – but an intelligent introduction.

Norris, Christopher. *Deconstruction: Theory and Practice*. 3rd ed. London: Routledge, 2002. Excellent introduction to Derrida and deconstruction.

Heidegger

Heidegger, Martin. *Pathmarks*. Ed. William McNeill. Cambridge: Cambridge University Press, 1998. A good selection of Heidegger's writings, but do not expect an easy passage.

Here are two short works that will introduce the reader to a notoriously difficult thinker.

Inwood, Michael. *Heidegger: A Very Short Introduction*. Oxford: Oxford University Press, 1997.

Steiner, George. *Heidegger*. Glasgow: Fontana, 1978.

Nietzsche

Deleuze, Gilles. *Nietzsche and Philosophy*. Trans. Hugh Tomlinson. New York: Columbia University Press, 1983. Not basic, by any means, but an interesting work by a first-rank 'continental' philosopher.

Nehamas, Alexander. *Nietzsche: Life as Literature*. Cambridge: Harvard University Press, 1985.

Nietzsche, Friedrich. *The Portable Nietzsche*. Ed. and trans. Walter Kaufmann. Harmondsworth: Penguin, 1976. Dip in, read slowly, have patience.

Chapter 4 Epistemology: The Ghost in the Metaphysical Machine?

General

BonJour, Laurence. *Epistemology: Classic Problems and Contemporary Responses*. Lanham, Md.: Rowman and Littlefield, 2002. A clear treatment of many of the issues introduced here.

Wray, K. Brad, ed. *Knowledge and Inquiry: Readings in Epistemology*. Peterborough, Ont.: Broadview Press, 2002. A good selection of articles by leading philosophers, for the most part in the analytic tradition.

Epistemology in Ancient Philosophy

Everson, Stephen, ed. *Epistemology. Companions to Ancient Thought*, vol. 1. Cambridge: Cambridge University Press, 1990.

Empiricism

Atherton, Margaret, ed. *The Empiricists: Critical Essays on Locke, Berkeley and Hume*. Lanham, Md.: Rowman and Littlefield, 1999.

Modern Classics

Ayer, A.J. *Language, Truth and Logic*. London: Penguin, 1971. The English manifesto of logical positivism.

Dewey, John. *Reconstruction in Philosophy*. Enlarged ed. Boston: Beacon Press, 1957.

Kripke, Saul. *Naming and Necessity*. Cambridge: Harvard University Press, 1972.

Kuhn, T.S. *The Structure of Scientific Revolutions*. 3rd ed. Chicago: University of Chicago Press, 1996.

Quine, W.V. *From a Logical Point of View*. New York: Harper Torchbooks, 1963.

Rorty, Richard. *Philosophy and the Mirror of Nature*. Princeton: Princeton University Press, 1979.

Russell, Bertrand. *The Problems of Philosophy*. Oxford: Oxford University Press, 1967.

Sellars, Wilfrid. *Empiricism and the Philosophy of Mind*. Cambridge: Harvard University Press, 1997.

Rationalism

Peacocke, Christopher. *The Realm of Reason*. Oxford: Clarendon Press, 1994. Very difficult for undergraduates but a defence of rationalism by a respected contemporary philosopher.

Pereboom, Derk, ed. *The Rationalists: Essays on Descartes, Spinoza and Leibniz*. Lanham, Md.: Rowman and Littlefield, 1999.

Chapter 5 Logic and Its Place in the Universe

General

Bergmann, Merrie, Moor, James, and Nelson, Jack. *The Logic Book*. 4th ed. Boston: McGraw-Hill, 2004. An excellent text that will introduce readers to the concepts underlying this chapter.

Kelley, David. *The Art of Reasoning*. 2nd expanded ed. New York: W.W. Norton, 1994. A more basic introduction to logic: my favourite.

Related Works

Hacking, Ian. *The Emergence of Probability*. Cambridge: Cambridge University Press, 1975. A very interesting book on the origins of probability and inductive reasoning.

Nagel, Thomas. *The Last Word*. Oxford: Oxford University Press, 1997. An intelligent and spirited defence of logic and reason in philosophy.

Chapter 6 Ethics: The Good, the Bad and the Beautiful

Ethics in the Ancient World

Annas, Julia. *Platonic Ethics, Old and New*. Ithaca, N.Y.: Cornell University Press, 2000.

Nussbaum, Martha. *The Fragility of Goodness*. Cambridge: Cambridge University Press, 1986. Highly recommended.

Williams, Bernard. *Shame and Necessity*. Berkeley: University of California Press, 1993.

Ethics in the Modern Word

MacIntyre, Alasdair. *After Virtue*. 2nd ed. Notre Dame: University of Notre Dame Press, 1984.

Rawls, John. *Lectures on the History of Moral Philosophy*. Ed. Barbara Herman. Cambridge: Harvard University Press, 2000.

Taylor, Charles. *Sources of the Self*. Cambridge: Harvard University Press, 1989.

General

Critchley, Simon. *Ethics–Politics–Subjectivity*. London: Verso, 1999. A good introduction to ethics in French philosophy and especially in the work of Derrida and Levinas.

Murdoch, Iris. *The Sovereignty of Good*. London: Routledge and Kegan Paul, 1970.

Nehamas, Alexander. *The Art of Living*. Berkeley: University of California Press, 1998. A must-read.

Chapter 7 Philosophy and Language: The House of Being

Saussure

Culler, Jonathan. *Ferdinand de Saussure*. Ithaca, N.Y.: Cornell University Press, 1986. A very good short introduction to Saussure's thought.

Saussure, Ferdinand de. *Course in General Linguistics*. LaSalle, Ill.: Open Court, 1991. More accessible than one might think.

Wittgenstein (Introductory)

Hacker, P.M.S. *Wittgenstein*. London: Routledge, 1999. At fifty-nine pages, if you want a very short introduction by an expert, this is it.

Kenny, Anthony. *Wittgenstein*. Harmondsworth: Penguin, 1973. A solid, comprehensive, introduction.

Pears, David. *Wittgenstein*. London: Fontana, 1988. Longer than Hacker, but very good.

Wittgenstein (Advanced)

Cavell, Stanley. *The Claim of Reason*. New York: Oxford University Press, 1979. Difficult, to be sure, but a classic by a first-rank American philosopher.

Diamond, Cora. *The Realistic Spirit*. Cambridge, Mass.: MIT Press, 1991. Not aimed at undergraduates, but thoughtful and will reward patient reading.

McGuinness, Brian, ed. *Wittgenstein and His Times*. Oxford: Basil Blackwell, 1982. Interesting stuff here and accessible enough.

Nagl, Luwig, and Mouffe, Chantel. *The Legacy of Wittgenstein: Pragmatism or Deconstruction*. Frankfurt: Peter Lang, 2001.

Dictionaries

A good dictionary of philosophy is an extremely handy tool. I have suggested an on-line encyclopedia below, but here are a couple of titles of 'hard copies.'

Audi, Robert, ed. *The Cambridge Dictionary of Philosophy*. Cambridge: Cambridge University Press, 1999.

Honderich, Ted, ed. *The Oxford Companion to Philosophy*. Oxford: Oxford University Press, 1995. The one I have used here. It is thorough and informative, although not always beginner-friendly. (Sometimes that is a not a bad thing for beginners.)

Websites

Here are a very few useful Websites that should be around for a while.

David Chalmers' Homepage   http://jamaica.u.arizona.edu/~chalmers/ Mainly philosophy of mind, but a good resource and jokes thrown in.

The Epistemology Page   http://pantheon.yale.edu/~kd47/e-page.htm Run by Keith DeRose at Yale University. A valuable resource for epistemology and related issues, such as scepticism.

Ethics Update   http://ethics.sandiego.edu/ Has been around since 1994 – so a good track record.

Stanford Encyclopaedia of Philosophy   http://pluto.stanford.edu/ An excellent resource.

Index

'good', 189; and participationalist epistemology, 133; on Plato's forms, 260n45; on politics, 200; on problem of certainty, 98; on rhetoric, 157; on 'substance' (*ousia*), 37; on universals, 34–5; on virtue, 289n44
ataraxia (calmness), 39
atomic propositions, 219, 221, 223
Atomists, monism and physicalism of, 33–4, 50
Austin, J.L., 24, 143, 241, 263–4n27
Ayer, A.J., 7, 106–7; logical positivism of, 8, 106–7, 110; on nature of philosophy, 8–10

Bach, J.S., 79
Barnes, Jonathan, 255n3, 256n5
Barthes, Roland, 295n14
Baudrillard, Jean, xi
Beauvoir, Simone de, 78; on the 'other' in ethics, 254, 302n14
Beckett, Samuel, 82, 131
being. *See* Aristotle; Berkeley
Bentham, Jeremy, 253; on democracy, 201–2; and the hedonic calculus, 193–4; on rights, 189–90
Berkeley, George (Bishop), 33, 34, 44, 106, 115; on 'being', 37; critique of realism by, 32; and *esse est percipi*, 30, 115; on God, 30, 98, 263n13; on idealism, 30, 110; on phenomenalism, 30; *Three Dialogues*, 5; on universals, 35
Bolton, Martha Brandt, 257n9
Borges, Jorge Luis, 84–5
Bouveresse, Jacques, 239
Brandom, Robert, 143–4, 160, 204–5, 224
Broad, C.D., 262n12

Brown, Peter, 256n7
Buridan's ass, 27
Burnyeat, Myles, 6

Carnap, Rudolph, 92
categorical imperative. *See* Kant
Cavell, Stanley, 20, 163, 217, 270n3
certainty, 31, 51–2, 267n49; Aristotle and problem of, 98
Chalmers, David, 263n22
change, on impossibility of, 40–4, 216
Chilon of Sparta, 189
Christian church, 50
Churchill, Winston, 202
Churchland, Paul, 280n73
Cicero, 169
classical realism. *See* Plato; realism
cogito ergo sum (I think, therefore I am). *See* Descartes
coherence theory of truth (holism), 125–33
Colish, Marcia, 280n70
comedy, ethics as, 194
Comte, Auguste, 66–7, 91
constructionism, 36, 62, 263n26
continental philosophy, ix, x, 10; and ethics, 286n2; and Hegel, 163
Copernicus, 265n36; and heliocentrism, 43–4, 122, 237
correspondence theory of truth, 105, 107–8, 127, 132, 204; pragmatic version of, 128
cosmogony and cosmology, 39
cosmological proof, 56, 267n52
Critchley, Simon, 202, 258n27
critical philosophy, 256n3

Darwin, Charles, 298n27
Dasein. See Heidegger
Davidson, Donald, 131

and signified, 88–90, 208–13; as
natural unit, 208–10 ; as paradigmatic systems, 211–12; and
semantics, 225–6
Skinner, Quentin, 129
Slovo, Margaret, *A World Apart*,
184–5, 291n67
social constructionism. *See* constructionism
Socrates, 89, 132, 154, 172, 205, 215,
223, 251–2; ancestor of sceptics and
dogmatists, x, 12, 15; in *Apology*,
82; on *arête*, 176–9; claim to
ignorance, 12; death of, 3, 18, 196;
and Diotima, 71; in *Euthyphro*, 204–
5, 215; and expulsion of the poets
in *Republic*, 19; father of, 258n29; on
the 'good', 176–9; and knowledge,
12; as logician, 165–6; Nietzsche
on, 179; in *Phaedrus*, 83–4; Plato's
portrait of, xi, 12; and Pythagorean
philosophy, 18, 71, 77; as sage,
260n51; and sophists, 12–13; on
virtue, 174–6; on writing, 273n34;
Xenophan's, 258n31, 285n48
Socratic: definition, 140; method
(aporetic, *elenchos*), x, 12–14, 99,
134, 140, 196, 214, 274n11, 293n102;
paradox, 288n33
Sophists, 12–13, 157, 258–9n32
Sophronicus, father of Socrates,
258n29
Spencer, Herbert, 298n27
soul, 14, 18, 71, 103, 138–9, 180, 183,
275n16. *See also, psyche*
substance. *See* Aristotle
Stoics: and direct realism, 45; as
dogmatic school, 5; on ethics, 170;
and rhetoric, 157; and the soul as
hegimonikon, 275n16

Stoppard, Tom, *Rosencrantz and
Guildenstern Are Dead*, 82
Strawson, Peter, 226, 267n50
Stroud, Barry, 287n24
structuralism, 208, 213; 'substance'
(*ousia*) and, 36–7, 46; syllogism
and, 153–5
substance (*ousia*), 36–7, 46
supplement, idea of, 297n23
synchrony in language. *See* Saussure

tautology. *See* logic
Taylor, Charles, 123, 133, 166, 191,
194–5; the 'good' life, 290n47; on
modern epistemology, 93, 117; and
moral horizons, 191–2; and politics,
198
techne (skill, art), 173, 190
teleology, 78, 178, 181, 195, 206
Thales, 292n81
therapy, philosophy as, 14–15, 18, 46,
91, 117, 233, 240, 301n71
third man argument, 260n45
time, metaphors for, 149–50, 162–3
tragedy. *See* ethics
truth, 71, 77, 78, 81, 89, 91; coherence
theory of (holism), 125–33; correspondence theory of, 105, 107–8,
127, 128, 132, 204; Derrida's view
of, 85, 136; and intuition, 101–2;
James's pragmatic version of, 119,
127; knowledge of tautological, 145;
Kuhn on, 127; and logic, 86, 153;
as metaphor, 120–1; metaphysics
and, 80; necessary, 53; Nietzsche
on, 251–2; Plato on, 19–20; and
propositions, 225; Quine on,
226; and relativism, 130–3; Rorty
on, 20–1, 128–30; sceptic and
dogmatic views of, 19–20; and